Microaggression Theory

Microaggression Theory

Influence and Implications

Edited by

Gina C. Torino
David P. Rivera
Christina M. Capodilupo
Kevin L. Nadal
Derald Wing Sue

This edition first published 2019.
© 2019 John Wiley & Sons, Inc.

The right of Gina C. Torino, David P. Rivera, Christina M. Capodilupo, Kevin L. Nadal, and Derald Wing Sue to be identified as the authors of the editorial material in this work has been asserted in accordance with law.

Registered Office
John Wiley & Sons, Inc., 111 River Street, Hoboken, NJ 07030, USA

Editorial Office
111 River Street, Hoboken, NJ 07030, USA

For details of our global editorial offices, customer services, and more information about Wiley products visit us at www.wiley.com.

Wiley also publishes its books in a variety of electronic formats and by print-on-demand. Some content that appears in standard print versions of this book may not be available in other formats.

Library of Congress Cataloging-in-Publication Data

Names: Torino, Gina C., editor.
Title: Microaggression theory : influence and implications / edited by Gina C. Torino [and four others].
Description: Hoboken, NJ : John Wiley & Sons, Inc., 2019. | Includes bibliographical references and index. |
Identifiers: LCCN 2018022532 (print) | LCCN 2018024513 (ebook) | ISBN 9781119420071 (Adobe PDF) |
    ISBN 9781119420064 (ePub) | ISBN 9781119420040 (hardcover)
Subjects: LCSH: Microaggressions. | Prejudices. | Discrimination.
Classification: LCC BF575.P9 (ebook) | LCC BF575.P9 M53 2019 (print) | DDC 303.3/85–dc23
LC record available at https://lccn.loc.gov/2018022532

Cover image: © tomograf/iStockphoto; © blurAZ/iStockphoto
Cover design by Wiley

Set in 10/12pt WarnockPro by Aptara Inc., New Delhi, India

V10003834_081818

This book is dedicated to Dr. Chester Pierce (1927–2016) who forged the path of microaggressions research for generations to come.

Contents

Acknowledgments

This book would not be possible without the support of so many of our colleagues who have advanced Microaggression Theory in both academia and mainstream discourse. First, we thank all of our brilliant authors who have contributed such thought-provoking and well-conceptualized chapters to this set; we are appreciative of your critical and refreshing takes on how far microaggression research has come and which directions it can go in the future. Second, we thank our original research team (also known as Sue's Crew) for their work in conceptualizing or publishing our original *American Psychologist* journal article and preliminary studies. Special thank you to Jennifer Bucceri, Marta Esquilin, Aisha Holder, Peter Donnelly, Annie Lin, Angela Kim, Rachel Kim, Nicole Jackson, Suah Kim, and Chantea Williams. Further, we would also like to acknowledge our colleagues and student research assistants who continued to work with us on expanding on both qualitative and quantitative research on microaggressions. These include Lauren Appio, Rebecca Rangel Campon, Melissa Corpus, E.J.R. David, Kristin Davidoff, Melissa DiCarlo, Tanya Erazo, Chassitty Fiani, Lauren Fisher, Alexis Forbes, Gerry Goodson, Katie Griffin, Sahran Hamit, Krista Herbert, Marie-Anne Issa, Jayleen Leon, Silvia Mazzula, Marc Johnston-Guerrero, Vanessa Meterko, Amanda Sisselman-Borgia, Avy Skolnik, Kristin Smith, Julie Sriken, Gloria Wong, Stephanie Wong, and Yinglee Wong. Finally, we acknowledge our family and loved ones for always encouraging and supporting us—especially Kaleohano Mendoza-Nadal, Harry Schwefel, Paulina Wee Sue, and S. K. Wolff.

About the Editors

Christina M. Capodilupo, Ph.D., is Adjunct Associate Professor in the Department of Counseling and Clinical Psychology at Teachers College, Columbia University. Her areas of interest include the etiology of eating disorders and body image issues for Women of Color and everyday experiences of oppression and their impact on mental health. She has published multiple works that explore the connections between racism and sexism with body image and feelings of self-worth. Recently, she and a colleague have developed a scale that measures gender microaggressions for women.

Kevin L. Nadal, Ph.D., is a Professor of Psychology at the City University of New York. He is the former Executive Director of the Center for LGBTQ Studies, the past President of the Asian American Psychological Association, and the cofounder of the LGBTQ Scholars of Color Network. He has written over 100 publications and 8 books including *Microaggressions and Traumatic Stress*; *Filipino American Psychology*; and *That's So Gay! Microaggressions and the Lesbian, Gay, Bisexual, and Transgender Community*.

David P. Rivera, Ph.D., is an Associate Professor of Counselor Education at Queens College, City University of New York. His research focuses on cultural competency and issues impacting the marginalization and well-being of People of Color, oppressed sexual orientation and gender identity groups, and low-income/first-generation college students, with a focus on microaggressions. He holds leadership roles with the American Psychological Association, the National Multicultural Conference & Summit, The Steve Fund, the Council for Opportunity in Education, and CLAGS: The Center for LGBTQ Studies.

Gina C. Torino, Ph.D., is an Associate Professor of Psychology at SUNY Empire State College. Dr. Torino has authored numerous scholarly articles on racial, gender, and other microaggressions, processes of White racial identity development, and teaching strategies for the development of cultural competencies. Moreover, she is a diversity consultant, a microaggression training specialist, and a New York State licensed psychologist.

Derald Wing Sue, Ph.D., is Professor of Psychology and Education in the Department of Counseling and Clinical Psychology at Teachers College, Columbia University. He served as presidents of the Society for the Psychological Study of Ethnic Minority Issues, the Society of Counseling Psychology, and the Asian American Psychological Association. He is known for his work on racism and antiracism, microaggressions, and the psychology of racial dialogues.

About the Authors

Dr. Myron R. Anderson serves MSU Denver, as the Chief Diversity Officer, responsible for developing a strategic vision to resolve campus climate issues. Anderson's research focuses on the intersection of microaggressions and workplace bullying, and he copublished the article "Hierarchal Microaggressions in Higher Education" and presented his research on "How to Move Climate Survey Data to Institutional Policy" at the University of Oxford.

Nallely Arteaga is a Ph.D. student in the Graduate School of Education at the University of California, Riverside. Her work examines the racialized processes traditional comprehensive high schools participate in to remove Black and Latinx students into alternative schools. Ms. Arteaga is a former continuation high school teacher.

Caryn Block is a Professor of Psychology and Education in the Social-Organizational Psychology Program at Teachers College, Columbia University. Her work focuses on the effects of stereotypes on individual work experiences and organizational processes. She examines how women and People of Color navigate careers when they are in the demographic minority. She also works with organizations to identify diversity dynamics in systems that may unwittingly impede the advancement of women and People of Color.

Thema Bryant-Davis is a licensed psychologist, Professor of Psychology at Pepperdine University, and Director of the Culture and Trauma research lab. She is a past psychology representative to the United Nations and a past president of the Society for the Psychology of Women. She is author of the book *Thriving in the Wake of Trauma: A Multicultural Guide* and co-editor of the books, *Religion and Spirituality in Diverse Women's Lives* and *Womanist and Mujerista Psychologies*. The California Psychological Association honored Dr. Bryant-Davis as Distinguished Scholar of the Year.

Allison Cabana is a participatory researcher and doctoral candidate in the Critical Social Psychology program at the Graduate Center at the City University of New York. Her work has included *What's Your Issue?*—a national

Participatory Action Research project investigating LGBTQ+ and GNC Youth of Color's experiences with community and identity.

Rebecca R. Campón, Ph.D., is a counseling psychologist who specializes in the areas of multiculturalism, internalized racism, and women's health. She is an Assistant Professor in the Department of Professional Psychology and Family Therapy at Seton Hall University. Dr. Campón has extensive clinical experience working with underrepresented populations in various outreach settings across the country, including Boston, Denver, and New York City areas. Her work focuses on appropriated racial oppression, health, and mental health of underrepresented populations and women's health issues.

D Anthony Clark is Senior Lecturer in the Faculty of Leadership and Interdisciplinary Studies at Arizona State University. His research interests are in modern U.S. culture and law, the sociology of race and indigeneity, and racial justice. He has published 17 articles, 25 essays and reviews, and delivered over 40 presentations. He is past president of the mid-America American Studies Association.

Maria C. Crouch, M.S., is a doctoral candidate in the Clinical-Community Psychology program with a rural and Indigenous emphasis at the University of Alaska Anchorage. She is of Deg Hit'an Athabascan, Mexican, and Scandinavian heritage. Her clinical, research, and community passions are rooted diversity, intersectionality, and Alaska Native mental health.

E.J.R. David, Ph.D., is an Associate Professor of Psychology at the University of Alaska Anchorage where he also directs the Alaska Native Community Advancement in Psychology Program. Dr. David has produced four books, *Brown Skin, White Minds: Filipino-/American Postcolonial Psychology; Internalized Oppression: The Psychology of Marginalized Groups; The Psychology of Oppression;* and *We Have Not Stopped Trembling Yet.* He has received national honors and recognitions for his work, including Fellow Status by the AAPA for "Unusual and Outstanding Contributions to Asian American Psychology."

John F. Dovidio is the Carl Iver Hovland Professor of Psychology, as well as Dean of Academic Affairs of the Faculty of Arts and Sciences, at Yale University. His research interests are in stereotyping, prejudice, and discrimination. Much of his scholarship, in collaboration with Dr. Samuel L. Gaertner, has focused on "aversive racism," a subtle form of contemporary racism.

Joanna M. Drinane is a doctoral candidate at the University of Denver and a doctoral intern at the University of Maryland. Her research focuses on psychotherapy process and outcome specifically looking at cultural processes, therapist effects, and within therapist identity-based disparities.

Michelle Fine is a Distinguished Professor of Critical Psychology and Women/Gender Studies at the Graduate Center CUNY. Her new book *Just*

Research in Contentious Times: Widening the Methodological Imagination is available from Teachers College Press.

David Frost, Ph.D., is a Senior Lecturer in Social Psychology at University College London. His research interests sit at the intersections of close relationships, stress, stigma, and health. His work has been recognized by grants and awards from the National Institutes of Health, Society for the Psychological Study of Social Issues, and the New York Academy of Sciences.

Cecile A. Gadson, M.A., is a doctoral candidate in the Counseling Psychology Program at the University of Tennessee, Knoxville. Currently, she is working under the mentorship of Dr. Jioni Lewis. Her research interests are focused on the influence of the intersection of race and gender on the emotional, mental, and physical health of young Black women and girls.

Aisha M. B. Holder is a Staff Psychologist at Columbia University Counseling and Psychological Services. Prior to pursuing a career in counseling psychology, Dr. Holder was a Vice President at JPMorgan Chase working in various business groups in Human Resources. Dr. Holder has coauthored articles on racial microaggressions published in *American Psychologist; Professional Psychology; Research and Practice*; and *Qualitative Psychology* journals.

Jacqueline Hyman is a second-year doctoral student in Counseling Psychology at Indiana University, with specialization in Sport and Performance Psychology. Her research interests within Sport Psychology take an identity-based approach by examining the impact of race, masculinity, and sexual orientation on athletes' perceptions of self in sport and society, particularly in times of athletic transition (i.e., athletic advancement, athletic retirement).

Dr. James M. Jones is Trustees Distinguished Professor of Psychological and Brain Sciences and Africana Studies and Director of the Center for the Study of Diversity at the Universality of Delaware. His books on race and diversity include, *Prejudice and Racism* (1972, 1997), and *The Psychology of Diversity: Beyond Prejudice and Racism* (2014; with Jack Dovidio and Deborah Vietze).

Jennifer Young-Jin Kim is a doctoral candidate in the Social-Organizational Psychology Program at Teachers College, Columbia University. Her research is focused on diversity and inclusion topics such as the negative effects of workplace microaggressions and ways to reduce their occurrence. She also works with organizations to facilitate conversations and interventions aimed at addressing workplace microaggressions.

Rita Kohli is an Assistant Professor in the Education, Society, and Culture Program in the Graduate School of Education at the University of California, Riverside. A former public school teacher, she is the codirector of the Institute for Teachers of Color Committed to Racial Justice and serves on the editorial board for the international journal *Race, Ethnicity and Education*.

Jioni A. Lewis, Ph.D., is an Assistant Professor in the Department of Psychology at the University of Tennessee, Knoxville. Her research is focused on the influence of subtle forms of racism and sexism on the health of Women of Color. She developed the Gendered Racial Microaggressions Scale, which is a self-report measure to assess the intersection of gender and racial microaggressions.

Fantasy T. Lozada is an Assistant Professor in the Department of Psychology, Developmental Psychology Area at Virginia Commonwealth University. Her work focuses on the intersections between culture, race, and emotion in predicting ethnic minority youth's socioemotional development in the context of familial, school, and technological constructs.

Jennifer L. Martin is an Assistant Professor of Teacher Education at the University of Illinois at Springfield. She is the editor of Racial Battle Fatigue: Insights from the Front Lines of Social Justice Advocacy (Recipient of the 2016 AERA Division B's Outstanding Book Recognition Award), and coauthor of *Teaching for Educational Equity: Case Studies for Professional Development and Principal Preparation*, Volumes I and II. Her most recent edited volume is *Feminist Pedagogy, Practice, and Activism: Improving Lives for Girls and Women.*

Silvia L. Mazzula, Ph.D., is a counseling psychologist with extensive experience on issues of diversity, equity, and inclusion. Her work focuses on social and cultural determinants of stress and trauma, including discrimination and microaggressions, culturally responsive research and scholarship, and Latinx mental health. She is an Associate Professor of Psychology at John Jay College of Criminal Justice and a founder and the Executive Director of the Latina Researchers Network, the country's first multi-disciplinary network for Latina researchers, scholars, and allies.

Elexia R. McGovern is an Assistant Professor in the Teacher Education Department in the College of Education at the California State University, Dominguez Hills. Her work explores culturally responsive literacy practices of home-grown, activist Teachers of Color. She is a former public high school teacher.

Anahvia T. Moody, B.A., is a doctoral student in the Counseling Psychology program at the University of Tennessee, Knoxville, working under the mentorship of Dr. Jioni Lewis. Her research interests are broadly focused on the experiences of African American women and girls, including gendered racial socialization and trauma. Her clinical interests are focused on body image among young women.

Duoc Nguyen is a doctoral candidate in the Social-Organizational Psychology Program at Teachers College, Columbia University. His research focuses on the effects of microaggressions and racism in the workplace using both qualitative and quantitative methods. He also works with organizations to improve their workforce capacity by hiring more effective employees through the creation and use of selections tools.

Jesse Owen is an Associate Professor in the Counseling Psychology Department at the University of Denver. His research focuses on psychotherapy process and outcome, with a focus on multicultural processes and therapists' multicultural orientation.

Adam R. Pearson is an Associate Professor of Psychology at Pomona College. His research explores how intergroup biases shape interaction, perception, and nonverbal behavior. He is recipient of an APA Early Career Achievement Award, the Morton Deutsch Award from the International Society for Justice Research, and the Social Psychology Network's Action Teaching Award for innovative teaching.

Louis A. Penner is a Professor of Oncology at Wayne State University and the Karmanos Cancer Institute. His work focuses on social psychological aspects of physician–patient interactions, with a special emphasis on racial health care disparities. Much of this work concerns how race-related attitudes can affect what transpires during racially discordant medical interactions. He has authored or coauthored over 150 scholarly articles, book chapters, and books.

Erica J. Peppers, M.P.H., is a counseling psychology doctoral student at the University of Tennessee, Knoxville. Her research interests are focused on the physiological impact of minority stressors on mental health and health disparities. She has presented her work at national conferences including the Association of Black Psychologists, the National Multicultural Conference and Summit, and the Winter Roundtable Conference.

Jessica Petalio is a doctoral student in the Ph.D. program in Clinical-Community Psychology at the University of Alaska Anchorage (UAA) with a rural, Indigenous, and cultural emphasis. Her research primarily focuses on ethnic minority psychology, Filipina/o American psychology, and microaggressions. As a San Francisco Bay Area native, Jessica has been actively involved in various Filipina/o American organizations at San Francisco State University and continues to serve the Filipina/o American community in Anchorage.

Dr. Rosalie Rolón-Dow is Associate Professor of Education and Associate Director of the Center for the Study of Diversity at the University of Delaware. Her publications on race include, *Diaspora Studies in Education: Towards a Framework for Understanding the Experiences of Transnational Communities* (2014; edited with Jason Irizarry), and articles in *Race, Ethnicity and Education* (2011), and *Diaspora, Indigenous and Minority Education* (2010).

Naila A. Smith is an Assistant Professor in the Department of Psychology at Dickinson College. She earned her Ph.D. in Applied Developmental Psychology from Fordham University. She studies how social relationships and contexts (e.g., classrooms, online) influence academic and socioemotional development from childhood through emerging adulthood. She focuses primarily on these developmental processes in immigrant and racial-ethnic minority populations.

Lisa Spanierman is Professor and Faculty Head of Counseling and Counseling Psychology at Arizona State University. Her research focuses on multicultural competence, white racial attitudes, and racial microaggressions. She has published more than 60 articles and chapters and co-edited *Unveiling Whiteness in the 21st century: Global Manifestations, Transdisciplinary Interventions*. She is a Fellow of the American Psychological Association.

Dr. Jesse A. Steinfeldt is a Psychologist and Associate Professor of Counseling Psychology at Indiana University. His research and clinical work revolve around the intersection of Multicultural Psychology, Sport Psychology, and the Psychology of Men and Masculinities. Dr. Steinfeldt has a personal and professional interest in First Nations empowerment; he has written several scholarly articles, given numerous presentations, and provided official testimony both nationally and internationally on the issue of the psychological impact of Native-themed mascots, nicknames, and logos in sport.

M. Clint Steinfeldt is an educator and lifelong college and high school football coach. A tribally affiliated descendent of the Oneida Nation, he has written extensively in the scholarly literature on the issue of Native-themed mascots, nicknames, and logos in sport. He incorporates critical thinking principles into his teaching, providing future generations with skills to become critical consumers of societal narratives.

Ashley M. Stewart is a graduate student in Educational Psychology at the University of Southern California. She earned her master's in Applied Developmental Psychology from New York University. She studies how experiences with media and technology both online and in classroom settings impact learning and development. She primarily focuses on ethnic minority populations in urban settings.

Karen W. Tao is an Assistant Professor in Counseling Psychology at the University of Utah. Her research and clinical work are driven by an overarching goal to reduce inequity in the access and quality of education and mental health services. Karen is interested in examining how people negotiate conversations about culture and difference and studying why multicultural competence matters.

Maria E. Torre, Ph.D., is the Director of The Public Science Project and faculty member in Critical Psychology at The CUNY Graduate Center. She introduced "participatory contact zones" to critical collaborative research, and continues to be interested in how democratic methodologies, radical inclusion, and a praxis of solidarity can inform a justice based public science for the public good.

Brendesha M. Tynes is an Associate Professor of Education and Psychology and Director of the Center for Empowered Learning and Development with Technology at the University of Southern California. Her research the past 16 years has focused on the construction of race and gender in online settings, online racial discrimination, and the design of digital tools that empower Youth of Color.

Marlene G. Williams, M.A., is a doctoral candidate in the Counseling Psychology Program at the University of Tennessee, Knoxville. Broadly, her research is focused on exploring Black women's experiences of gendered racial microaggressions and exploring dimensions of gendered racial identity development for Black women.

Dr. Kathryn S. Young is an Associate Professor of Secondary Education at Metropolitan State University of Denver in Denver, Colorado, and serves as the Faculty Fellow with the Office of Inclusion and Diversity. Her research interests include Disability Studies in Education, Inclusive Education, Culturally Sustaining Pedagogy, Diversity in Higher Education, and Microaggressions in Education and the Workplace.

Part I

Microaggression Theory

1

Everything You Wanted to Know About Microaggressions but Didn't Get a Chance to Ask

Gina C. Torino, David P. Rivera, Christina M. Capodilupo, Kevin L. Nadal, and Derald Wing Sue

Many controversies, myths, and misunderstandings have arisen over the definition of microaggressions and microaggression theory. In order to shed light on the questions and issues surrounding the concept and theory, we provide readers with answers and clarifications that contributing authors discuss in their chapters. It is not our intention to provide an exhaustive list of questions raised in research, theory, and in the manifestation of microaggressions, but rather to provide a thumbnail sketch of basic definitions. We have divided questions into four domains: (a) defining microaggressions, (b) myths about the concept, (c) their harmful impact, and (d) interventions that potentially lower the detrimental consequences.

Defining Microaggressions

1. **What are microaggressions?**

   Answer: Simply stated, "microaggressions are derogatory slights or insults directed at a target person or persons who are members of an oppressed group." Microaggressions communicate bias and can be delivered implicitly or explicitly. An example of an implicitly delivered microaggression might be a White woman clutching her purse tightly when an African American man enters an elevator. An explicitly expressed microaggression can occur when a woman overhears a male colleague tell another male colleague that she is a "bitch" after she asserts herself in the workplace.

Microaggression Theory: Influence and Implications, First Edition. Edited by Gina C. Torino, David P. Rivera, Christina M. Capodilupo, Kevin L. Nadal, and Derald Wing Sue.
© 2019 John Wiley & Sons, Inc. Published 2019 by John Wiley & Sons, Inc.

2. How do microaggressions manifest? What forms do microaggressions take?

Answer: Three types of microaggressions have been identified in the literature and supported by empirical work: microassault, microinsult, and microinvalidation. The term *microassault* refers to a blatant verbal, nonverbal, or environmental attack intended to convey discriminatory and biased sentiments. This notion is related to overt racism, sexism, heterosexism, ableism, and religious discrimination in which individuals deliberately convey derogatory messages to target groups. Using epithets like *spic* or *faggot*, hiring only men for managerial positions, and requesting not to sit next to a Muslim on an airplane are examples. Unless we are talking about White supremacists, most perpetrators with conscious biases will engage in overt discrimination only under three conditions: (a) when some degree of anonymity can be ensured, (b) when they are in the presence of others who share or tolerate their biased beliefs and actions, or (c) when they lose control of their feelings and actions. Because microassaults are most similar to old-fashioned racism, no guessing game is likely to occur as to their intent: to hurt or injure the recipient. Both the perpetrator and the recipient are clear about what has transpired. For this reason, microassaults are in many respects easier to deal with than those that are unintentional and outside the perpetrator's level of awareness (microinsults and microinvalidations).

Microinsults are unintentional behaviors or verbal comments that convey rudeness or insensitivity or demean a person's racial heritage/identity, gender identity, religion, ability, or sexual orientation identity. Despite being outside the level of conscious awareness, these subtle snubs are characterized by an insulting hidden message. For example, when a person assumes the Black woman standing in an academic office is a secretary (and not a professor) the underlying message is that Black women belong in service roles and are not intellectually capable of holding an advanced degree. African Americans and Latinx individuals consistently report that intellectual inferiority and assumptions about being less qualified and capable are common communications they receive from Whites in their everyday experiences. *Microinvalidations* are verbal comments or behaviors that exclude, negate, or dismiss the psychological thoughts, feelings, or experiential reality of the target group. Like microinsults, they are unintentional and usually outside the perpetrator's awareness. A common microinvalidation is when individuals claim that they do not see religion or color but instead see only the human being. Common statements such as "there is only one race: the human race" negate the lived experiences of religious and ethnic minorities in the United States.

3. Are microaggressions always unintentional and unconscious?

Answer: They may be either. Microaggressions vary on a continuum from being intentional to unintentional. They are often reflections of a worldview of inclusion–exclusion, normality–abnormality, or superiority–inferiority. As such, they are often invisible to the perpetrator. Microaggressions may be expressed in the form of implicit bias where the individual is unaware of the biased communication, or via explicit bias where the person is well aware that they are engaging in discriminatory actions. The theory identifies three forms of microaggressions: microassaults, microinsults, and microinvalidations. Microassaults are most similar to "old-fashioned" racism where it is most often conscious and deliberately expressed. Calling a Person of Color a racial epithet, or preventing a son or daughter from dating or marrying outside of one's race are examples of conscious intentionality. Although microinsults and microinvalidations may be intentional, they are most likely unintentionally communicated by the majority of dominant group members. Mistaking a Black person for a service worker, for example, is a microaggression that mistakenly views African Americans as less competent or capable.

4. How are microaggressions different from the everyday incivilities that can occur to everyone regardless of sociocultural identity?

Answer: While people of all racial groups may experience everyday incivilities (e.g., when strangers bump into you without apologizing; someone takes the parking space you were waiting for; having a supervisor who is condescending or unfriendly), microaggressions are more stressful because of the possibility that a person's race, gender, sexual orientation, or other identity group contributed to the interaction. When individuals of historically marginalized groups (e.g., People of Color, women, and LGBTQ people) are aware of historical or systemic discrimination or have experienced microaggressions in the past, they may be more conscious of how their identity groups impact interpersonal dynamics. When a person of historically privileged group (e.g., White people, men, heterosexual, and cisgender people) is the enactor of the incivility, even innocuous situations may be viewed as microaggressions.

Conversely, some people (especially individuals of historically privileged groups) may not view incivilities as microaggressions and instead are able to externalize or interpret other potential causes or reasons for the interaction. For instance, when someone bumps into you or takes the parking space you were waiting for, it might be easy to quickly the label the person as "a jerk." Further, because some people may not experience such incivilities often, the impact of such instances may not be as powerful as how microaggressions that are experienced more frequently or intensely by people of historically marginalized groups.

5. **How are hate crimes and overt conscious expressions of bigotry related to microaggressions?**

Answer: Although they may share some similarities, hate crimes are not the same as microaggressions. Hate crimes are violence-based bias perpetrated against targets with the intent to cause harm (often physical) toward people from marginalized groups. They are criminal acts that are illegal and qualitatively and quantitatively different from microaggressions. Hate crimes are usually conducted by perpetrators identified as bigots, White supremacists, or racists. Violence, intimidation, and direct abuse such as physical assaults, lynchings, and destruction of property are examples. Although microaggressions may cause significant harm as well, and can be consciously delivered, they usually come from well-intentioned people who are most likely unaware of their bias. In fact, most people who commit microaggressions would publicly condemn hate crimes. Addressing hate crimes requires legal action, while an educational approach is more likely in microaggressions.

6. **How are microaggressions against LGBTQ individuals different/same as racial microaggressions?**

Answer: Some racial microaggressions are similar to heterosexist and transphobic microaggressions; for instance, both LGBTQ people and People of Color can experience situations like being excluded in workplace situations, receiving poor customer service, feeling tokenized or exoticized, or hearing biased jokes or slurs. However, there are some microaggressions that may target people based on their identities differently; for example, same-sex couples may encounter glares of disgust when they show public displays of affection, which heterosexual couples may not experience. Meanwhile, Black Americans may be presumed to be a criminal (e.g., they are followed around in a store or by a police officer), whereas a White LGBTQ person may not have this experience. Further, there are certain environments and situations where microaggressions may be encountered differently. Because some LGBTQ people can often "pass" (e.g., other people presume they are heterosexual or cisgender), they may avoid certain microaggressions; meanwhile, many People of Color may always be conscious of racial microaggressions because their race is something that cannot be hidden. On the contrary, some People of Color may cope better with microaggressions because their parents or families may have socialized them to be aware of race and racism; conversely, LGBTQ people are often the only LGBTQ people in their families and may even experience microaggressions in their own homes. Thus, while microaggressions may manifest differently, they still have harmful impacts on people who experience them.

7. **How do intersecting identities influence the experience of microaggressions?**

   Answer: Intersectionality refers to an individual facing multiple forms of discrimination and oppression based on overlapping marginalized identities. Much of the work on intersecting identities has been pioneered by African American female scholars in the fields of political science, sociology, law, and more recently psychology. While much of the work on microaggressions to date has explored the manifestation of this phenomenon in relation to singular identity categories (i.e., racial microaggressions and gender microaggressions), emerging work supports the idea that there are distinct categories and themes of microaggressions related specifically to intersectionality. For example, gendered racial microaggressions refer to experiences that communicate discriminatory messages about being female and African American or Asian American (or another racial/ethnic group). These experiences are unique to the intersection of this particular gender and racial group membership and as such cannot be classified as a gender microaggression or a racial microaggression alone. Please see Chapter 4 for a thorough review of this literature.

8. **Aren't some microaggressions really macroaggressions? If not, is there such a thing as a macroaggression?**

   Answer: Microaggressions and macroaggressions are not the same concepts. There is much confusion concerning the use of the term *macroaggression*. Some incorrectly use the term to describe the overt and intentionally harmful form of microaggressions, otherwise known as microassualts (#2 above). Chester Pierce is credited with creating the term *microaggression* and intended for the term *micro* to convey the everyday, commonplace nature of these interactions. In contrast, the term *macroaggression*, defined by education scholars Lindsay Pérez Huber and Daniel Solórzano, represents the systemic and institutionalized forms of bias and oppression that impact the lives of entire groups of people. This is most evident in laws and public policies that create systems of oppression and disparities in education, employment, healthcare, and the criminal justice system, to name a few.

9. **Can mascots, media, and offensive symbols like the confederate flag and Klan hood be expressions of microaggressions?**

   Answer: Yes, microaggressions can be delivered through mascots, media, and offensive symbols. For example, the confederate flag has become a symbol of racism in contemporary culture, thus displaying this flag on one's car, house, or building communicates that the person or organization endorses the tenets of racism. Additionally, mascots for sports teams (e.g., "Redskins") negatively objectify a group of people (First Nations People). Contemporary removal of statues of individuals that supported racist efforts reflects the acknowledgment of the harmful impact that these statues represent.

10. Is there such thing as online microaggressions?

Answer: The Internet provides a giant stage upon which one can espouse their political and personal views—all with a guaranteed cloak of anonymity, if they so choose. Therefore, online social media forums, chat groups, blogs, and so forth, are places where blatant forms of discrimination are rampant and evident. A wealth of misinformation on the Internet also contributes to stereotypes and biased views of various social identity groups. Researchers have coined terms such as *online racial discrimination, cyber racism,* and *online hate crimes* to describe the more overt forms of racism, sexism, homophobia, xenophobia, and the like that take place on the Internet. However, recent investigations support the notion that online material such as visual imagery, memes, and video game content can transmit derogatory, insulting, and invalidating messages about marginalized groups in subtle and covert ways. In addition to these nonverbal manifestations of microaggressions, chat groups and comment walls provide forums for individuals to express invalidating views and statements without an intention of discrimination or hate. For example, a social media post about the recent fatal shooting of an unarmed Black youth by a police officer provokes opinions and sentiments across the nation, all shared on various online platforms. Well-intentioned individuals can respond to these incidents with color-blind statements such as "We are all human beings sharing the same race, and I only wish this hadn't happened" which represent a microinvalidation of the lived racial experience of Black men in America. How one experiences, interprets, and is impacted by statements such as these or by nonverbal material online (as opposed to experiencing them in vivo) represents a new area of study. For more discussion of the manifestation of online microaggressions, please see Chapter 12.

Myths About Microaggressions

11. Aren't we priming children to be biased when we teach them about microaggressions?

Answer: Microaggressions and contemporary forms of bias are theorized to be insidious and commonly occurring in part because people in

American society are socialized from an early age to not discuss issues of difference and to espouse egalitarian ideologies. This creates a false social dynamic where people are quick to dismiss prejudicial beliefs as the main precipitant behind a microaggressive encounter. Further, when people are unaware of the microaggression framework and issues of privilege and oppression, they lack the language to describe and make sense of the microaggressions they encounter across the lifespan. Research indicates that the microaggression framework helps people, including children, make sense of microaggressive encounters and the related impacts. Chapter 17 (Kohli, Arteaga, & McGovern) articulates the dynamic of microaggressions for children and teenagers in K-12 education. These scholars provide strategies for addressing microaggressions in K-12 education and suggest that the first step is having the ability to identify the microaggressive experience, which requires knowledge of the microaggression framework. Additionally, having knowledge of the microaggression framework can help young people avoid internalizing microaggressive messages, which can moderate the negative impact microaggressions have on a number of well-being and life-success outcomes.

12. Aren't microaggressions harmless, trivial, and simply small slights? Why make such a big thing out of them?

Answer: Far from being benign and insignificant, microaggression research indicates they take a heavy psychological and physical toll on targets. They have been found to be different than the everyday incivilities that anyone can experience regardless of race, gender, and sexual orientation/identity. Experiencing an insult from a rude clerk that is nonrace based, for example, may bring about feelings of anger or agitation, but when the incident ends it is over. Racial microaggressions, however, have an impact that is both quantitatively and qualitatively different. For targets, microaggressions are continual, never-ending, and cumulative in nature. Marginalized group members experience them from the time they awake until they go to sleep. They experience them from the moment of birth until they die. As a result, People of Color are under constant race-related stress that requires constant vigilance and psychological arousal. It would be a monumental mistake to dismiss microaggressions as only "small slights" that have minimal harmful impact.

13. With all the talk about microaggressions, I'm afraid to say anything at all about race or differences? Doesn't microaggression theory stifle free speech?

Answer: Should people shy away from these conversations, for fear of offending someone? The reality is that any discussion of worldviews is likely to offend someone, and we do not all need to agree. We just need to be respectful of each other's lived experience and be flexible in our thinking. When someone is offended by a statement, belief, or action based on their identity, the most productive way to address this is through engaging discourse between the two groups. Microaggression opponents argue that Republican, Christian, and conservative ideas in particular have been shut down and stifled. They argue that social justice warriors (SJWs) are attacking these perspectives and punishing those who hold these views. In reality, these viewpoints tend to cause multiple groups to feel marginalized. For example, opposing abortion and gay marriage will alienate some women and men. If you hold these views, prepare to hear their effects on others. They cause others to feel angry, terrified, sad, and so forth. A healthy dialogue allows both perspectives to co-exist, no matter how difficult, tense, and heavy that conversation may be. The reality is that it is easier to stay silent or assign blame than it is to sit with the complexity of emotions that arise when microaggressions are named and processed by all parties.

14. **Dominant group members aren't the only ones with biases, stereotypes, and prejudices. People of Color, for example, do as well. Why are we always accusing Whites as the only group that commits microaggressions? Can't People of Color commit microaggressions against one another?**

Answer: It is true that people of all groups may have biases, stereotypes, and prejudices toward other people; in fact, studies on implicit biases support that people of all groups may have particular preferences toward different groups based on race, gender, skin color, size, and so forth. Because of these biases, people of any group may mistreat others based on their identities. However, we tend to concentrate on microaggressions committed by people of historically privileged groups (e.g., White people, men, and heterosexual people) because such interactions are reflective of power and systemic oppression. From a young age, children are socialized to believe that the experiences of historically privileged groups are normalized (i.e., American standards of beauty, cultural values, styles of communication are all based on White, male, heteronormative, and upper-class perspectives). Thus, when people of historically marginalized groups experience microaggressions, the incident may have a more negative impact because they are reminders of their lack of power and privilege. For example, when a White man makes demeaning comments about a Woman of Color, the interaction is a manifestation of the systemic racism and sexism that prevent Women of Color from succeeding. In fact, a Woman of Color who hears such a comment may feel retraumatized from the multiple amounts of times that she has been demeaned in the past due to her race and gender. Conversely, if a Woman of Color makes a demeaning comment about a White man and hurts his feelings, he is still part of a group that has the most systemic power in this country (e.g., White men make the most money, hold most government positions). He is likely to have experienced such instances in his life, so the comment may be viewed as an isolated event and may not have a lasting effect on his mental health.

Because of systemic oppression and stereotyped messages that people learn about different groups, People of Color can also commit microaggressions against each other. For instance, when an Asian American commits a criminality microaggression toward a Black American (e.g., follows a Black person in a store, holds her purse closer to her when a Black man enters an elevator), the microaggression may be retraumatizing due to the anti-Black racism that many Black people experience by Asian Americans. In some ways, the interaction may be even more hurtful because they presume that the Asian American should be more aware of racism (whereas they may expect such microaggressions from White Americans). Similarly, if an Asian American man encounters an emasculating microaggression from a Black or Latino man (e.g., someone says that Asian men are feminine or have small penises), he may feel retraumatized from past similar microaggressions. He may also feel more hurt because he presumes that another Man of Color would be more sensitive or aware of the harmful impact of stereotypes.

Impact of Microaggressions

15. **Can microaggressions affect problem solving and learning?**

Answer: Yes, microaggressions can negatively impact one's ability to concentrate, to solve problems, and to learn new material. Studies suggest that hostile racial climates perpetuated through microaggressions on college campuses disrupt students' ability to concentrate and to participate in class discussions. Such disruption inhibits students' ability to learn new material. Moreover, experiencing microaggressions in the classroom has been linked to feelings of invisibility, isolation, and self-doubt, all of which impair one's ability to focus on tasks and solve problems in the classroom.

16. **How do microaggressions affect work productivity?**

Answer: Workplace microaggressions affect work productivity in several ways. Types of microaggressions experienced in workplace settings include lack of representation of one's own group, invisibility, invalidation of one's individual experience, and exclusion from social events. Collectively, these types of microaggressions can lead to high rates of depression, isolation, and absenteeism in the workplace. Perceptions (often misperceptions) of worker attitudes and behavior by supervisors can lead to reprimanding and negative performance plan evaluations. These outcomes can detrimentally impact salary increases and promotion. Moreover, microaggressions can lead to turnover and dismissal.

17. Can microaggressions impact mental and physical well-being?

Answer: Yes, a decade of research has found that microaggressions have negative impacts on mental and physical health. In fact, numerous assessments and measures have been created to examine the microaggressions experienced by People of Color, women, and LGBTQ people. Results from those studies find that a higher cumulative amount of microaggressions negatively impacts symptoms related to depression, anxiety, and trauma; behavioral health issues like alcohol use and eating disorders; and psychological constructs such as self-esteem, worldview, and academic achievement. Recent, correlational studies have also found that microaggressions have negative health consequences—including pain, fatigue, physical functioning, and perceptions of general health.

18. How do microaggressions impact people with privileged identities, such as in White people?

Answer: Everyone in society is negatively impacted by the prejudicial ideologies that give life to systems of privilege and oppression, and that impact individual institutional functioning. Although the impact of microaggressions is qualitatively and quantitatively different for those in oppressed and privileged social locations, the costs to those with privileged identities are most often overlooked. However, it is necessary to consider and understand how those with more privileged identities are both positively and negatively impacted by microaggressions. In Chapter 9, Clark and Spanierman delineate the psychosocial costs of microaggressions to White people. These scholars suggest that people who benefit from a system of privilege and oppression have a skewed perception of social reality and are often unaware of the role they play in maintaining their privilege at the social and economic expense of the oppressed. The associated impacts include a wide range of cognitive, affective, behavioral, moral, and spiritual costs. For example, the false sense of social reality can lead to a denial of individual bias and an overreliance on an egalitarian worldview whereby the privileged extend cognitive effort to appear nonbiased. The emotional and behavioral costs can include fear fueled by stereotype that leads to avoiding interpersonal interaction with those from different racial and social identity groups. These costs can run very deep and influence moral development where the privileged develop a loss of humanity and respect for basic human rights in order to maintain the benefits associated with their privilege.

Intervention and Prevention

19. What can educational institutions do to address microaggressions on campus?

Answer: When universities and other educational institutions commit to understanding and addressing microaggressions at the systemic level, they are likely to engender real and enduring change on their campuses. Just as scholars have discussed the inherent flaws in a one-course approach to understanding diversity and multiculturalism in a curriculum, singular approaches toward addressing microaggressions (such as a single workshop on the topic for faculty, or a one day discussion in a classroom based on a checklist of experiences) will be superficial and potentially lead to a greater misunderstanding and division between groups. Therefore, providing multiple educative offerings across a variety of campus opportunities is paramount in an authentic effort to eradicate microaggressions.

Microaggressions can be described and understood academically and intellectually through discussions of subtle forms of discrimination and related theories, but there will also always be an emotional processing aspect to this work that does not always feel natural in classrooms and other spaces within academic institutions. Providing a range of educative offerings that allow for the exploration of microaggression experience on campus from both an intellectual and emotional point of view will strengthen community and build pathways to change. Therefore, workshop series, summits, continuous learning, and professional development opportunities that seek to expand awareness on how different groups of people experience the campus environment and university at-large will benefit the overall institutional climate. Moreover, offering these programs to all members of the campus community (from staff to students to professors and deans) is crucial. For a detailed exploration of systemic practices that reduce microaggressions on campus, please see Chapter 18.

20. What can I do to address and prevent microaggressions?

Answer: People can help to address and prevent microaggressions interpersonally, institutionally, and systemically. While this book will provide a comprehensive review of how to do so, previous scholars have identified both small and large ways to do so. As a smaller example, parents may engage in the process of racial socialization—or teaching their children about the realities of racism and systemic oppression in age-appropriate ways. When young people are socialized from a younger age to understand systems and injustices, they are more likely to be comfortable in talking about differences and are more likely to cope with discrimination. For People of Color, racial socialization influences one's ability to succeed academically. Thus, talking about issues related to race, gender, sexual orientation, ability, class, religion, and other identities may assist children in being more comfortable in recognizing systemic oppression, which may help them to address such issues when they are adults.

An example of a larger-scale way to address microaggressions is to advocate for systemic policies that educate constituents on microaggressions—which can potentially change cultures that are often biased, discriminatory, or noninclusive. For instance, leaders in educational institutions can introduce students to curriculum on microaggressions, group dynamics, and intercultural communication. Teachers can reevaluate how curriculum may be culturally biased and may advocate for changes accordingly. Students may also vocalize their disdain with any injustices they notice in their school policies or cultures. While you will find several other recommendations for how to address microaggressions throughout the book, we acknowledge that there are so many different cultural and historical dynamics that may prevent someone from being able to address microaggressions in any group or environment. However, we hope that readers will be able to find ways to consider and integrate these recommendations however possible.

21. Can an organization or a workplace do anything to prevent and address microaggressions?

Answer: Yes, they can. One of the best ways to prevent and address microaggressions in the workplace is through diversity training initiatives. It is recommended that these initiatives include training methods to enhance awareness of biases. For example, one way this can be accomplished is by implementing trainings that include the Implicit Association Test (IAT), a computer-based test that measures reaction times to pairings (e.g., images of White and Black individuals with the words good and bad). Reaction time to these pairings indicates the preferences or biases of the individual taking the test. Other interventions include dedicating resources to increasing workplace awareness of microaggressions and having regular discussions of the impact of microaggressions on management decisions and employee performance. Moreover, workplaces can mitigate the adverse effects of microaggressions through leadership and manager accountability, mentorship, and employee resource groups and recruitment of racially and culturally diverse staff members.

22. How can people cope or deal with microaggressions? What can White allies or bystanders do to stem the expression of microaggressions?

Answer: There are a number of coping strategies people can use to mitigate the negative consequences of exposure to microaggressions. First, knowledge of the microaggressions framework can be a source of liberation for people who experience microaggressions in their daily lives. For example, having a language to internally process microaggressive encounters can reduce the cognitive energy associated with making sense of the covert nature of microaggressions. Similarly, being knowledgeable of the microaggressions framework can allow people to more effectively engage with social support, a time-tested stress buffer. Over the past 10 years, society has witnessed a dramatic rise in attention to microaggressions. This includes people, especially young people, engaging in social activism around microaggression issues and advocating for institutional change. Actively working to increase awareness about microaggressions and work toward solutions to reduce their occurrence can serve as a coping strategy. Active engagement in anti-microaggression movements can be a source of empowerment and help people from internalizing the negative messages embedded in microaggressive encounters that lead to compromises in well-being. Similarly, White and privileged allies can work toward stemming the expression of microaggressions by understanding their bias and the ways that it manifests via microaggressions. They can advantageously use their privilege by educating about microaggressions to their peers and others who share their privileged identities. Privileged allies can also disrupt the microaggressive encounters they witness by validating the experience of the microaggressed.

2

Aversive Racism, Implicit Bias, and Microaggressions

John F. Dovidio, Adam R. Pearson, and Louis A. Penner

The Civil Rights Legislation of the 1960s not only defined many forms of discrimination as illegal but also made egalitarianism a more prominent and widely accepted principle governing intergroup relations in the United States (Pearson, Dovidio, & Gaertner, 2009). Although blatant biases against Black Americans and other traditionally devalued groups in U.S. society continue to exist, subtle forms of bias toward these groups also play a major role in shaping intergroup relations and contributing to the social disadvantage and persistent disparities (economically, socially, and in health) experienced by members of these groups. Moreover, because these biases may be deeply rooted in history and reinforced by current societal ideologies, White Americans, the traditionally socially dominant group in the United States, may express their bias without conscious intention or even awareness. Nevertheless, this subtle discrimination can have a profound impact on intergroup relations and ultimately reinforce the hierarchical nature of these relations in American society.

In this chapter, we consider the role of one form of contemporary bias, aversive racism, in the expression of racial microaggressions. Microaggressions are "everyday subtle and often automatic 'put-downs' and insults directed toward Black Americans" (Sue, 2010, p. 5). Here, we describe underlying psychological processes that may prompt behavioral manifestations of prejudice, including those that manifest within social interactions, such as microaggressions. Although the dynamics of aversive racism and microaggressions can relate to many socially devalued groups in the United States and internationally (Dovidio, Gaertner, & Pearson, 2017), to illustrate how these concepts relate to one another we focus on racial bias among White Americans.

Specifically, we explain the origin and dynamics of aversive racism, discussing the role of implicit racial bias in both subtle and blatant forms of discrimination. We then show how aversive racism among White Americans can affect the ways they communicate with Black Americans in interracial interactions and

Microaggression Theory: Influence and Implications, First Edition. Edited by Gina C. Torino, David P. Rivera, Christina M. Capodilupo, Kevin L. Nadal, and Derald Wing Sue.
© 2019 John Wiley & Sons, Inc. Published 2019 by John Wiley & Sons, Inc.

identify how these processes, in turn, can produce racial misunderstandings and divergent perspectives. Next, we illustrate how biases in both verbal and nonverbal behavior in social interactions can contribute to societal disparities, using research in the context of healthcare as a case example. We conclude by considering the implications of research on aversive racism and implicit bias for developing interventions designed to combat subtle forms of discriminatory behavior, including microaggressions, and identify key challenges and productive avenues for future research.

Aversive Racism and Implicit Bias

The profound changes in law and values initiated, in part, by the Civil Rights Legislation do not mean that Whites are necessarily becoming less racially biased. Instead, for many White Americans who endorse egalitarian values, the nature of their racial bias has evolved to a more subtle, but still pernicious, form of racial bias—aversive racism (Dovidio et al., 2017; Gaertner & Dovidio, 1986).

In contrast to traditional forms of racial bias, aversive racism operates often unconsciously in subtle, indirect, and rationalizable ways. At a conscious (or explicit) level, aversive racists may sympathize with victims of past injustice, support principles of racial equality, and genuinely regard themselves as non-prejudiced. However, at the same time, they possess nonconscious negative feelings and beliefs about Blacks rooted in basic psychological processes (e.g., social categorization) that manifest at an implicit level (Dovidio et al., 2017; Gaertner & Dovidio, 1986). The combination of conscious, explicit egalitarian attitudes coupled with nonconscious, implicit racial bias characterizes aversive racism.

Implicit biases, which are most commonly measured using response-latency tasks such as the Implicit Association Test (IAT; Greenwald, Poehlman, Uhlmann, & Banaji, 2009), are automatically activated responses that can occur without conscious awareness. Although most White Americans eschew racist attitudes explicitly, a substantial percentage of them (estimated from 44% to 70%; Nosek, Hawkins, & Frazier, 2011; Pew Research Center, 2015) show evidence of implicit negative attitudes toward Black Americans. Implicit attitudes result from repeated exposure to positive or negative information about a group, either through socialization or direct experience and can be relatively resistant to change in response to new information. Because they can reflect cultural associations, unlike explicit biases, implicit racial biases often do not vary substantially as a function of sociodemographic characteristics (e.g., education or socioeconomic status) or an individual's profession. Moreover, because the two types of bias differ in a person's awareness and ability to control them, explicit and implicit racial biases are typically weakly correlated and both independently predict discriminatory behavior (Greenwald et al., 2009).

Aversive Racism, Implicit Bias, and Interracial Interaction

Explicit and implicit attitudes shape the ways White Americans interact with Black Americans in different but consequential ways. Because aversive racists have egalitarian explicit attitudes and can readily recognize and thus inhibit blatant forms of discrimination, they may avoid overt displays of bias in interpersonal exchanges with Black Americans. However, because many aversive racists are unaware of their implicit biases, these biases can affect subtle behaviors that they are less aware of, are less able to control, or that they do not recognize as discriminatory. These behaviors can include nonverbal signals (e.g., physical distancing) as well as verbal comments that may not be recognized as racist by well-intentioned Whites but may be experienced as demeaning by Blacks (i.e., microaggressions; Sue, 2010).

Different orientations of Whites toward Black relative to White interaction partners are particularly reflected in Whites' subtle communicative behaviors. In general, Whites interact differently with Black compared to White partners in social encounters in ways that may be both positive and negative. In some cases, Whites may appear more anxious or avoidant and less friendly nonverbally, and may show less behavioral synchrony in their interactions with a Black relative to a White partner (for a review, see Toosi, Babbitt, Ambady, & Sommers, 2011). In other cases, to the extent Whites are concerned about appearing prejudiced, they may show *greater* verbal or nonverbal friendliness in interactions with Blacks, which may be perceived as compensating for prejudice in ways that can engender threat among minorities (Mendes & Koslov, 2013).

Although both aversive racism and microaggression approaches focus primarily on subtle forms of bias, there are several key distinctions. As Sue (2010) observed, "Racial microaggressions are most similar to aversive racism in that they generally occur below the level of awareness of well-intentioned people" (p. 9). However, researchers investigating aversive racism and those studying microaggressions have typically emphasized different levels of analysis. Whereas research on aversive racism has studied underlying *psychological* mechanisms, such as conflicting conscious and nonconscious attitudes and the processes and conditions under which these attitudes predict discrimination toward Blacks, research on microaggressions has focused primarily on different *behavioral* manifestations of racial biases and their societal consequences. As summarized by Sue (2010), "researchers of microaggressions focus primarily on describing the dynamic interplay between perpetrator and recipient, classifying everyday manifestations, deconstructing hidden messages, and exploring internal (psychological) and external (disparities in education, employment, and health care) consequences" (p. 9). However, recent work on implicit bias, aversive racism, and nonverbal and verbal communication bridges these different research traditions.

For example, research on aversive racism and communication has found that explicit and implicit racial biases predict different types of behaviors toward Blacks. For example, Dovidio et al. (1997) showed that whereas Whites' explicit prejudice predicted more overt forms of bias shown in their self-reported evaluations of Blacks, Whites' implicit bias predicted negative nonverbal behaviors reflecting discomfort (rate of blinking) and dislike (gaze aversion). Similarly, McConnell and Leibold (2001) reported that White Americans' implicit racial bias, but not their explicit racial attitudes, predicted how much Whites talked and the frequency with which they made speech errors and speech hesitations in interactions with Black Americans. These socially distant and potentially dismissive behaviors, which may be perceived by Blacks as slights or invalidations in social exchanges, represent common forms of microaggressions (Sue, 2010).

The different effects of explicit and implicit biases can also fuel divergent perspectives and experiences of Whites and Blacks in interracial interactions. Dovidio, Kawakami, and Gaertner (2002) demonstrated that whereas White Americans' explicit (self-reported) racial attitudes predicted their relatively controllable verbal expressions in their interactions with Black partners, Whites' implicit attitudes predicted negative nonverbal behaviors. Moreover, Whites' explicit attitudes and positive verbal behaviors predicted their assessments of how friendly they appeared during exchanges with a Black partner. Black interaction partners, in contrast, weighed Whites' nonverbal behavior more heavily than verbal behavior in their impressions of their partner and the interaction. Consequently, Whites and Blacks had differing assessments of the same interaction, and Blacks' awareness of conflicting positive verbal and negative nonverbal behavior undermined how trustworthy they saw the White partner. Thus, research on microaggressions and aversive racism converge in examining how biases are expressed, perceived, and interpreted in social exchanges.

Although the subtle verbal expressions and nonverbal behaviors driven by aversive racists' implicit racial bias may be expressed without their awareness, these behaviors continue to have a significant negative impact on the economic, physical, and mental well-being of Black Americans and to be perceived by Blacks as racial discrimination. Indeed, a recent meta-analysis on effects of subtle (including implicit bias and microaggressions) and overt (i.e., blatant) forms of racial and gender discrimination on psychological and physical health and workplace performance found relationships similar in magnitude (Jones, Peddie, Gilrane, King, & Gray, 2016). Next, we illustrate these effects in the context of healthcare interactions.

Health and Healthcare Interactions

Across the lifespan, Blacks experience poorer health than Whites in the United States (as well as in Europe and Australia; see Dovidio, Penner, Calabrese, &

Pearl, 2017). In the United States, for example, deaths due to heart diseases are 22% higher among Blacks than Whites, and the mortality rate due to cancer among Blacks is about 13% higher than it is for Whites (National Center for Health Statistics, 2016). Importantly, differences in death rates typically exceed differences in incidence rates. For example, in 2015, the Black–White difference in the incidence of breast cancer was quite small; it was 3% higher for Black women than for White women. In the same year, deaths due to breast cancer were 40% higher among Black than White women (National Center for Health Statistics, 2016).

Although a variety of different factors (e.g., access to healthcare and differential exposure to environmental toxins) likely play a role in racial disparities in health, there is mounting evidence that racial bias among healthcare providers may also be involved. For example, Black patients are less likely to be prescribed pain medications and, when given medication, are administered lower quantities, compared to Whites, even for life-threatening and terminal conditions (e.g., metastatic cancer; see Hoffman, Trawalter, Axt, & Oliver, 2016). Moreover, an analysis of over one million clinical visits for children diagnosed with respiratory infections found that, even after controlling for relevant medical and socioeconomic variables, Black children were significantly less likely than White children to receive antibiotics from their physicians (Gerber et al., 2013).

In general, physicians in the United States tend to display relatively low levels of explicit (self-reported) racial prejudice and report conscious efforts to not discriminate against Black patients, often asserting that Black patients receive even higher-quality care than White patients in their practice (Sabin, Rivara, & Greenwald, 2008). As with the general population, however, physicians may harbor negative implicit attitudes about Blacks. For example, in a sample of approximately 2,500 U.S. physicians, Sabin, Nosek, Greenwald, and Rivara (2009) found evidence of negative implicit racial biases against Blacks among White, Hispanic/Latino, and Asian physicians. By contrast, Black physicians, on average, displayed low or no implicit racial bias. Students in U.S. medical schools show similarly strong levels of implicit racial bias when they begin medical training and display comparable levels when they complete medical school (van Ryn et al., 2015). Thus, physicians can also conform to the profile of an aversive racist—nonprejudiced explicitly but racially biased implicitly.

Given that the vast majority of physicians in the United States are not Black, subtle bias in patient–physician interactions can disproportionately impact the quality of care that Blacks receive, relative to Whites. Patient-centered care, in which the doctor–patient interaction is characterized by trust and mutual respect, predicts greater patient satisfaction and, in turn, greater adherence by patients to treatments and better health outcomes (Stewart et al., 2003). Relative to medical interactions between a doctor and a patient of the same race, racially discordant medical interactions are shorter in length and involve less positive affect and are less patient-centered (for reviews, see Penner, Phelan, Earnshaw, Albrecht, & Dovidio, 2017; Shen et al., 2017). In particular, White physicians spend significantly less time answering questions, providing health education, planning treatment, and building a relationship with Black relative to White patients, and also make less effort to involve Black patients in medical decision-making.

Consistent with work on aversive racism, whereas White physicians' explicit racial bias is typically a weak predictor of the quality of patient care (Penner & Dovidio, 2016), implicit racial bias systematically predicts lower-quality medical interactions with Black patients (Hall et al., 2015; Maina, Belton, Ginzberg, Singh, & Johnson, 2017). Moreover, consistent with research on microaggressions, physicians' implicit racial bias typically affects their behavior in subtle ways that may nevertheless be recognized and perceived as disrespectful by Black patients. Indeed, Cooper et al. (2012; see also Blair et al., 2013) found that Black patients rated more implicitly biased physicians as expressing less positive affect and providing lower-quality care compared to those with lower levels of implicit bias. Also, Hagiwara and colleagues have found that physicians higher in implicit bias talked more and used more anxiety-related words when interacting with Black patients (Hagiwara et al., 2013; Hagiwara, Slatcher, Eggly, & Penner 2017). Both kinds of behaviors might reasonably be seen as microaggressions by the Black patients.

A sample of oncologists who appeared nonprejudiced on a self-report measure showed similar effects (Penner et al., 2016). Oncologists higher in implicit racial bias had shorter interactions, and patients and observers rated these oncologists' communication as less patient-centered and supportive. The oncologists' higher implicit bias was also associated with patients showing less trust of their physician, having less confidence in recommended treatments, and perceiving treatments as more difficult to adhere to and complete successfully. Ratings of independent coders corroborate these perceptions: In medical interactions with Black patients, healthcare providers higher in implicit racial bias speak faster, are less patient-centered, and spend less time with the patients (Cooper et al., 2012).

Although Black patients generally perceive doctors higher in implicit racial bias less favorably, this effect may be particularly pronounced when doctors are low in explicit prejudice—the aversive racist profile. Specifically, Penner et al. (2010) found that Black patients who interacted with aversive racist physicians were less satisfied with the interaction and felt less close to their physicians than Black patients who interacted with other physicians, including physicians who were high on both implicit and explicit bias. These effects may be due, in part, to a lack of awareness of personal bias among implicitly biased physicians who indicate low levels of bias on self-report measures. Indeed, doctors low in explicit bias reported that they involved Black patients more in the medical decision-making process during the visit than did those high in explicit bias.

Hagiwara, Dovidio, Eggly, and Penner (2016) further compared how physicians who fit the unique profile of an aversive racist (low in explicit racial bias and high on implicit bias) responded to different types of patients. On average, these physicians did not differ from the other physicians in the affect they displayed toward Black patients; however, their responses did differ as a function of whether their patients' previously reported experiences with everyday discrimination. When these physicians interacted with patients who reported more personal experiences with discrimination, they exhibited lower levels of positive affect and higher levels of negative affect during the interaction, relative to their interactions with patients who reported low levels of past discrimination. If the cause was simply that the high discrimination patients were more difficult, these effects should have been observed across all physicians' reactions. Rather, only the aversive racist physicians responded in this manner to the high discrimination patients, suggesting that aversive racism among White physicians' can impact the quality of patient care that Blacks receive, and particularly those with a history of experiencing discrimination.

Together, these findings suggest that subtle bias, expressed in verbal and nonverbal slights consistent with microaggressions, can contribute to racial disparities in healthcare. Behavioral manifestations of bias can lead to miscommunication, divergent perspectives, and, ultimately, mistrust in both informal (e.g., casual conversations) and formal settings (e.g., medical interactions). Although these biases may be expressed unintentionally and go unrecognized as slights by Whites, they can nonetheless shape interactions in consequential ways that disadvantage Blacks and been seen by Blacks as bias. For example, Black patients who experience these slights in their medical encounters are less satisfied with their medical care and, because of the mistrust aroused by these behaviors, are less likely to adhere to guidance offered by White doctors. Therefore, subtle bias can pose a substantial barrier to realizing quality medical care.

Research on aversive racism and implicit bias, including within medical contexts, dovetails with several tenets of work on microaggressions. In explaining the dynamics of microaggressions, Sue (2010) observed that "socialization and cultural conditioning imbue within people unconscious and biased attitudes and beliefs that ... make their appearance in unintentional biased behaviors" (p. 48). Sue (2010) further noted, "While most of us are willing to acknowledge the harmful impact of overt racism ... racial microaggressions are usually considered banal or small offenses.... Trivializing and minimizing racial microaggressions by some Whites often appear to be a defensive reaction to being blamed and guilty" (p. 51). Aversive racists may not only fail to recognize subtle ways they discriminate against Black, but when confronted by the possibility that their behavior is racially motivated, they may seek nonracial explanations for their behavior to preserve a nonprejudiced self-image (Dovidio et al., 2017).

The work that we have reviewed in this chapter helps bridge research on implicit bias and aversive racism with studies of microaggressions by illuminating how subtle forms of bias shape communication and impressions in interracial interactions. These connections help to integrate work on microaggressions with the sizable empirical literatures on racial prejudice and discrimination, as recommended by Lilienfeld (2017), bringing insight and theory from research on social cognition, communication, and intergroup relations. However, future work might reduce the gap further between studies of aversive racism that have traditionally focused on the causes of subtle bias, and research on behavioral manifestations of bias characterized by microaggressions. In the next section, we consider theoretical and practical benefits of further integrating these two areas of research.

Aversive Racism, Implicit Bias, and Microaggressions: Integration

Work on aversive racism and interracial communication has identified some specific behaviors (e.g., lack of visual contact; Dovidio et al., 1997) that can fuel mistrust in social exchanges, but this research could benefit from further consideration of microaggressions in these effects. Microaggression research offers a useful taxonomy for understanding behavioral manifestations of prejudice within everyday social exchanges. Adopting the complementary perspectives of aversive racism and microaggressions can guide research and intervention to more formally identify and address the types of verbal and nonverbal slights that are most commonly expressed by aversive racists, and most consistently experienced by Blacks as offensive.

For example, in a recent study (Voigt et al., 2017), untrained participants rated the level of (dis)respect communicated by police officers to Black and White community members based on statements transcribed from information captured with police body cameras during police stops. Blacks have a particularly strong motivation to be respected by Whites in their interracial encounters (Bergsieker, Shelton, & Richeson, 2010; Shelton & Richeson, 2015). The participants' ratings showed that police officers expressed greater disrespect when they were interacting with Black than a White community member. Furthermore, linguistic analyses by Voigt et al. (2017) of police statements during police-community member interactions indicated that verbal disrespect toward Blacks was most strongly associated with addressing the community member with informal (e.g., "dude" or "bud") rather than formal titles (e.g., "sir," or "Ms."), greater speech disfluencies (e.g., "w-well"), and greater use of negative words. Greater respect for Whites compared to Blacks was communicated through reassuring statements (e.g., "don't worry"), use of positive words, and mentions of safety (e.g., "drive safely now"). Understanding the specific patterns of behaviors that contribute to mistrust among Blacks can help to inform interventions designed to bolster trust between law enforcement and the communities they serve.

Similarly, research on racial microaggressions could benefit from insights from aversive racism. The particular way a microaggression toward a Black person is expressed likely differs between aversive racists and explicitly racist Whites. Explicitly racist Whites may tend to use more directly demeaning terms (e.g., informal titles, such as "buddy"). By contrast, the microaggressions expressed by aversive racists may manifest more nonverbally, or in some cases, may be in the form of overcorrecting for bias through exaggerated verbal or nonverbal *positivity* (e.g., Mendes & Koslov, 2013), which may be perceived as condescending by Blacks.

Work on aversive racism, and on implicit racial bias generally, has identified underlying processes that correspond to subtle behaviors that adversely affect the dynamics of interracial interactions. Nevertheless, evidence for *causal* relationships between implicit bias and discriminatory behavior (e.g., whether changes in implicit bias produce changes in behavior) remains mixed, leaving open the question of what types of interventions may be most effective for reducing microaggressions and other behavioral manifestations of prejudice (see Forscher & Devine, 2017).

In their meta-analysis of over 400 studies, Forscher et al. (2017) found that implicit bias is malleable, but that changing implicit bias does not necessarily lead to changes in explicit bias or behavior. However, they revealed little evidence that *changes* in implicit bias mediate changes in explicit prejudice or discriminatory behavior. Thus, Forscher et al. (2017) proposed that interventions that focus on improving structural features that cause biases on both behavioral and cognitive tasks (e.g., enhancing opportunities for intergroup contact) or provide people with strategies to resist biasing influences in the environment may be more effective than those that target implicit biases alone (see Devine, Forscher, Austin, & Cox, 2012; see also Penner, Blair, Albrecht, & Dovidio, 2014).

Future Directions in Research on Subtle Bias and Microaggressions

Increasing knowledge about whether (and perhaps when) microaggressions are expressed intentionally or unintentionally has important implications for understanding the different perspectives that Whites and Blacks have about race relations. As Lilienfeld (2017) explained, because it implies a form of aggression, the term *microaggression* may suggest to broad audiences an intentional negative act, thus obscuring the substantial role that unconscious bias may play in shaping these behaviors. Moreover, if confronted and described as a microaggression, a White person who is an aversive racist may be quick to deny the action or its negative impact because it is inconsistent with a non-prejudiced self-image. To the extent that such accusations elicit defensiveness or emphasize external (vs. internal) reasons to control prejudice (i.e., to avoid social sanctions rather than affirm one's egalitarian values), they may be counterproductive and *increase* rather than reduce explicit and implicit bias, at least temporarily (see Legault, Gutsell, & Inzlicht, 2011). Longer term, such experiences may increase Whites' likelihood of adopting a colorblind ideology to help protect themselves from being accused of being racist, which can reduce intergroup trust by signaling to Blacks that their unique perspectives are not valued (Apfelbaum, Sommers, & Norton, 2008).

These types of responses can be damaging to race relations not only for developing interpersonal relationships but also for addressing hostility and resentment between Whites and Blacks more broadly. Blacks, who tend to show heightened sensitivity to subtle and nonverbal cues of prejudice (Richeson & Shelton, 2005; see also Shelton & Richeson, 2015), may readily detect microaggressions and perceive them as discriminatory. Moreover, because of their frequent experience of discrimination in daily life (Pew Research Center, 2016), Blacks may interpret these slights as intentional and thus as evidence of blatant racism. Moreover, the denial of these actions or their harm may be seen as a further attempt to invalidate the experience of the target. Nevertheless, communicating the discriminatory and harmful nature of microaggressions, which Whites may tend to dismiss as racial bias because of the often ambiguous nature of such expressions, may paradoxically strengthen and reinforce growing perceptions of anti-White bias among some U.S. Whites (Norton & Sommers, 2011). Thus, understanding the communication aspects of microaggressions from the perspectives of both Whites and Blacks, as well the social psychological impact of microaggression terminology in everyday exchanges, is a critical avenue for future scholarship.

Future research might also further investigate factors that can escalate miscommunication around microaggressions into race-based tension and conflict, as well as identify ways to effectively enhance mutual recognition and understanding of the harm of microaggressions. Both approaches can help increase the effectiveness of interventions designed to limit expressions of microaggressions and reduce their adverse interracial consequences. For instance, viewing interracial encounters as learning or "growth" opportunities can significantly improve intergroup relations generally (Migacheva & Tropp, 2013), which may also be an effective approach for building mutual understanding around microaggressions and their impact.

One of our basic premises is that aversive racists, because they harbor implicit biases, will be likely to discriminate against Blacks and members of other traditionally devalued groups when norms permit such expressions or obscure the recognition of the action as unfair, harmful treatment. Overtly discriminatory rhetoric, such as comments articulated during the most recent U.S. presidential campaign devaluing historically stigmatized and marginalized groups, may thus give license to some White Americans to engage in more direct forms of discrimination. Some of these actions may be extreme. For example, such comments may play a role in the 66% increase in hate crimes against Muslims in the United States from 2014 to 2015 (Ansari, 2016), with a notable increase occurring after presidential candidate Trump's speech announcing a proposed ban on Muslim immigrants (Levin, 2017). Although awareness of a greater prevalence of blatant forms of bias might make aversive racists' egalitarian values more salient and thus inhibit their own expression of bias, it is also possible that, because their bias is unconsciously motivated and unintentional, it may facilitate their display of subtle biases. A political climate in which blatant bias is increasingly common might not only relax normative constraints against bias but also make subtle forms of bias, by contrast, appear less harmful or discriminatory, which may desensitize aversive racists to their own potential for bias. To address this issue further, research might investigate the extent to which exposure to blatant expressions of bias may reduce Whites' perceptions that more subtle forms of discrimination, such as microaggressions, constitute bias, or disinhibit them (consciously or unconsciously) from engaging in such behaviors.

Additional research might also productively explore the positive and negative psychological and physiological consequences of the use of microaggression terminology in everyday exchanges. The growing popularity of microaggression language in public discourse suggests its utility for characterizing the lived experiences of Blacks and members of other stigmatized groups. For these individuals, the use of microaggression language may reduce uncertainty in interpreting ambiguous behaviors that can be stress-inducing. Attributions to discrimination can shift explanations for causes of rejection from internal to external reasons, which can bolster self-esteem and buffer stress responses, reflected in increased anger and physiological reactivity indicative of a challenge rather than threat response (Mendes, Major, McCoy, & Blascovich, 2008). Nevertheless, perceived discrimination and physiological responses associated with anger are also related to increased risk of cardiovascular disease and hypertension. Thus, the long-term psychological and health consequences of these attributions remain an important avenue of inquiry.

Conclusion

In conclusion, we believe that the shared assumptions and converging evidence of research on aversive racism and on microaggressions are mutually informative, theoretically and practically. Moreover, the somewhat different emphases of these two scholarly perspectives—attention to intrapsychic dynamics of the perpetrators of subtle bias in the study of aversive racism and the different behavioral manifestations of these processes in research on microaggressions— provide complementary insights into interracial interactions and race relations more generally.

Research on aversive racism, which we illustrated in terms of relations between White and Black Americans but which also applies to relations with other historically stigmatized groups, illuminates how unintentional slights, which may be communicated nonverbally as well as verbally, may be expressed toward Blacks by well-intentioned Whites. Moreover, because these expressions are rooted in unconscious processes, Whites may engage in these behaviors without intention or awareness and may be motivated to deny evidence of the race-based nature of their actions. Because of the unconscious influences underlying these processes, discriminatory behavior can occur even in highly structured settings, such as in physician–patient interactions. Although the bias may be subtle, the consequences are significant, as illustrated in this chapter. Future research, practice, and policy can thus benefit from understanding more fully the relationship between aversive racism and microaggressions and pursuing new insights guided by the similarities and differences in these approaches.

References

Ansari, A. (2016, November 15). *FBI: Hate crimes spike, most sharply against Muslims—CNN*. Retrieved from http://www.cnn.com/2016/11/14/us/fbi-hate-crime-report-muslims/index.html.

Apfelbaum, E. P., Sommers, S. R., & Norton, M. I. (2008). Seeing race and seeming racist? Evaluating strategic colorblindness in social interaction. *Journal of Personality and Social Psychology, 95*, 918–932.

Bergsieker, H. B., Shelton, J. N., & Richeson, J. A. (2010). To be liked versus respected: Divergent goals in interracial interactions. *Journal of Personality and Social Psychology, 99*, 248–264.

Blair, I. V., Steiner, J. F., Fairclough, D. L., Hanratty, R., Price, D. W., Hirsh, H. K., ... Havranek, E. P. (2013). Clinicians' implicit ethnic/racial bias and perceptions of care among Black and Latino patients. *Annals of Family Medicine, 11*, 43–52.

Cooper, L. A., Roter, D. L., Carson, K. A., Beach, M. C., Sabin, J. A., Greenwald, A. G., & Inui, T. S. (2012). The associations of clinicians' implicit attitudes about race with medical visit communication and patient ratings of interpersonal care. *American Journal of Public Health, 102*, 979–987.

Devine, P. G., Forscher, P. S., Austin, A. J., & Cox, W. T. L. (2012). Long-term reduction in implicit race bias: A prejudice habit-breaking intervention. *Journal of Experimental Social Psychology, 48*, 1267–1278.

Dovidio, J. F., Gaertner, S. L., & Pearson, A. R. (2017). Aversive racism and contemporary bias. In F. K. Barlow & C. G. Sibley (Eds.), *The Cambridge handbook of the psychology of prejudice* (pp. 267–294). Cambridge, United Kingdom: Cambridge University Press.

Dovidio, J. F., Kawakami, K., & Gaertner, S. L. (2002). Implicit and explicit prejudice and interracial interaction. *Journal of Personality and Social Psychology, 82,* 62–68.

Dovidio, J. F., Kawakami, K., Johnson, C., Johnson, B., & Howard, A. (1997). On the nature of prejudice: Automatic and controlled processes. *Journal of Experimental Social Psychology, 33,* 510–540.

Dovidio, J. F., Penner, L. A., Calabrese, S. K., & Pearl, R. L. (2017). Physical health disparities and stigma: Race, sexual orientation, and body weight. In B. Major, J. F. Dovidio, & B. G. Link (Eds.), *The Oxford Handbook of Stigma and Health* (pp. 267–294). New York, NY: Oxford University Press.

Forscher, P. S., & Devine, P. G. (2017). *Knowledge-based interventions are more likely to reduce legal disparities than are implicit bias interventions.* Retrieved from https://osf.io/preprints/psyarxiv/8cgg5.

Forscher, P. S., Lai, C., Axt, J., Ebersole, C. R., Herman, M., Nosek, B. A., & Devine, P. G. (2017). *A meta-analysis of change in implicit bias.* Unpublished manuscript, Department of Psychology, University of Wisconsin, MD.

Gaertner, S. L., & Dovidio, J. F. (1986). The aversive form of racism. In J. F. Dovidio & S. L. Gaertner (Eds.), *Prejudice, discrimination, and racism* (pp. 61–89). Orlando, FL: Academic Press.

Gerber, J. S., Prasad, P. A., Localio, R., Fiks, A. G., Grundmeier, R. W., Bell, L. M., … Zaoutis, T. E. (2013). Racial differences in antibiotic prescribing by primary care pediatricians. *Pediatrics, 131,* 677–684.

Greenwald, A. G., Poehlman, T. A., Uhlmann, E. L., & Banaji, M. R. (2009). Understanding and using the Implicit Association Test: III. Meta-analysis of predictive validity. *Journal of Personality and Social Psychology, 97,* 17–41.

Hagiwara, N., Dovidio, J. F., Eggly, S., & Penner, L. A. (2016). The effects of racial attitudes on affect and engagement in racially discordant medical interactions between non-Black physicians and Black patients. *Group Processes and Intergroup Relations, 19,* 509–527.

Hagiwara, N., Penner, L. A., Gonzalez, R., Eggly, S., Dovidio, J. F., Gaertner, S. L., … Albrecht, T. L. (2013). Racial attitudes, physician–patient talk time ratio, and adherence in racially discordant medical interactions. *Social Science & Medicine, 87,* 123–131.

Hagiwara, N., Slatcher, R. B., Eggly, S., & Penner, L. A. (2017). Physician racial bias and word use during racially discordant medical interactions. *Health Communication, 32,* 401–408.

Hall, W. J., Chapman, M. V., Lee, K. M., Merino, Y. M., Thomas, T. W., Payne, B. K., … Coyne-Beasley, T. (2015). Implicit racial/ethnic bias among health care professionals and its influence on health care outcomes: A systematic review. *American Journal of Public Health, 105,* e60–e76.

Hoffman, K. M., Trawalter, S., Axt, J. R., & Oliver, M. N. (2016). Racial bias in pain assessment and treatment recommendations, and false beliefs about biological differences between Blacks and Whites. *Proceedings of the National Academy of Sciences, 113,* 4296–4301.

Jones, K. P., Peddie, C. I., Gilrane, V. L., King, E. P., & Gray, A. L. (2016). Not so subtle: A meta-analytic investigation of the correlates of subtle and overt discrimination. *Journal of Management, 42,* 1588–1613.

Legault, L., Gutsell, J. N., & Inzlicht, M. (2011). Ironic effects of antiprejudice messages: How motivational interventions can reduce (but also increase) prejudice. *Psychological Science, 22,* 1472–1477.

Levin, B. H. (2017, June 29). *United States Department of Justice Hate Crime Summit: Hate crimes rise in major American localities in 2016.* Retrieved from https://csbs.csusb.edu/sites/csusb_csbs/files/Levin%20DOJ%20Summit%202.pdf.

Lilienfeld, S. O. (2017). Microaggressions: Strong claims, inadequate evidence. *Perspectives on Psychological Science, 12,* 138–169.

Maina, I. W., Belton, T. D., Ginzberg, S., Singh, A., & Johnson, T. J. (2017). A decade of studying implicit racial/ethnic bias in healthcare providers using the implicit association test. *Social Science and Medicine.* doi:10.1016/j.socscimed.2017.05.009.

McConnell, A. R., & Leibold, J. M. (2001). Relations among the Implicit Association Test, discriminatory behavior, and explicit measures of racial attitudes. *Journal of Experimental Social Psychology, 37,* 435–442.

Mendes, W. B., & Koslov, K. (2013). Brittle smiles: Positive biases toward stigmatized and outgroup targets. *Journal of Experimental Psychology: General, 142,* 923–933.

Mendes, W. B., Major, B., McCoy, S., & Blascovich, J. (2008). How attributional ambiguity shapes physiological and emotional responses to social rejection and acceptance. *Journal of Personality and Social Psychology, 94,* 278–291.

Migacheva, K., & Tropp, L. R. (2013). Learning orientation as a predictor of positive intergroup contact. *Group Processes & Intergroup Relations, 16,* 426–444.

National Center for Health Statistics. (2016). *Health, United States, 2015: With special feature on racial and ethnic health disparities.* Hyattsville, MD: National Center for Health Statistics.

Norton, M. I., & Sommers, S. R. (2011). Whites see racism as a zero-sum game that they are now losing. *Perspectives on Psychological Science, 6,* 215–218.

Nosek, B. A., Hawkins, C. B., & Frazier, R. S. (2011). Implicit social cognition: From measures to mechanisms. *Trends in Cognitive Sciences, 15,* 152–159.

Pearson, A. R., Dovidio, J. F., & Gaertner, S. L. (2009). The nature of contemporary prejudice: Insights from aversive racism. *Social and Personality Psychology Compass, 3*, 314–338.

Penner, L. A., Blair, I. V., Albrecht, T. L., & Dovidio, J. F. (2014). Reducing racial health care disparities: A social psychological analysis. *Policy Insights from the Behavioral and Brain Sciences, 1*, 204–212.

Penner, L. A., & Dovidio, J. F. (2016). Colorblindness and Black–White health disparities. In H. Neville, M. Gallardo, & D. Sue (Eds.), *What does it mean to be color-blind? Manifestation, dynamics, and impact* (pp. 275–293). Washington, DC: American Psychological Association.

Penner, L. A., Dovidio, J. F., Gonzalez, R., Albrecht, T. L., Chapman, R., Foster, T., … Eggly, S. (2016). The effects of oncologist implicit racial bias in racially discordant oncology interactions. *Journal of Clinical Oncology, 24*, 2874–2880.

Penner, L. A., Dovidio, J. F., West, T. W., Gaertner, S. L., Albrecht, T. L., Dailey, R. K., & Markova, T. (2010). Aversive racism and medical interactions with Black patients: A field study. *Journal of Experimental Social Psychology, 46*, 436–440.

Penner, L. A., Phelan, S. M., Earnshaw, V., Albrecht, T. L., & Dovidio, J. F. (2017). Patient stigma, medical interactions, and healthcare disparities: A selective review. In B. Major, J. F. Dovidio, & B. G. Link (Eds.), *The Oxford handbook of stigma and health* (pp. 183–202). New York, NY: Oxford University Press.

Pew Research Center. (2015). *Exploring racial bias among biracial and single-race adults: The IAT.* Retrieved from http://www.pewsocialtrends.org/2015/08/19/exploring-racial-bias-among-biracial-and-single-race-adults-the-iat.

Pew Research Center. (2016). *On views of race and inequality, Blacks and Whites are worlds apart.* Retrieved from http://www.pewsocialtrends.org/2016/06/27/on-views-of-race-and-inequality-blacks-and-whites-are-worlds-apart/.

Richeson, J. A., & Shelton, J. N. (2005). Thin slices of racial bias. *Journal of Nonverbal Behavior, 29*, 75–86.

Sabin, J. A., Nosek, B. A., Greenwald, A. G., & Rivara, F. P. (2009). Physicians' implicit and explicit attitudes about race by MD race, ethnicity, and gender. *Journal of Healthcare for the Poor and Underserved, 20*, 896–913.

Sabin, J. A., Rivara, F. P., & Greenwald, A. G. (2008). Physician implicit attitudes and stereotypes about race and quality of medical care. *Medical Care, 46*, 678–685.

Shelton, J. N., & Richeson, J. A. (2015). Interacting across racial lines. In M. Mikulincer, P. R. Shaver, J. F. Dovidio, J. A. Simpson, M. Mikulincer, & P. R. Shaver (Eds.), *Group Processes: Vol. 2. APA handbook of personality and social psychology* (pp. 395–422). Washington, DC: American Psychological Association.

Shen, M. J., Peterson, E. B., Costas-Muñiz, R., Hernandez, M. H., Jewell, S. T., Matsoukas, K., & Bylund, C. L. (2017). The effects of race and racial concordance on patient-physician communication: A systematic review of the literature. *Journal of Racial and Ethnic Health Disparities.* doi:10.1007/s40615-017-0350-4.

Stewart, M., Brown, J. B., Weston, W. W., McWhinney, I. R., McWilliam, C. L., & Freeman, T. R. (2003). *Patient-centered medicine: Transforming the clinical method* (2nd ed.). Abingdon, United Kingdom: Radcliffe Medical Press Ltd.

Sue, D. W. (2010). *Microaggressions in everyday life: Race, gender, and sexual orientation.* New York, NY: Wiley.

Toosi, N. R., Babbitt, L. G., Ambady, N., & Sommers, S. R. (2011). Dyadic interracial interactions: A meta-analysis. *Psychological Bulletin, 138,* 1–27.

van Ryn, M., Hardeman, R., Phelan, S., Burgess, D. J., Dovidio, J. F., Herrin, J., … Przedworski, J. (2015). Medical school experiences associated with change in implicit racial bias among 3547 students: A medical student CHANGES study report. *Journal of General Internal Medicine, 30,* 1748–1756.

Voigt, R., Camp, N. P., Prabhakaran, V., Hamilton, W. L., Hetey, R. C., Griffiths, C. M., … Eberhardt, J. L. (2017). Language from police body camera footage shows racial disparities in officer respect. *Proceedings of the National Academy of Sciences, 114,* 6521–6526.

3

Multidimensional Models of Microaggressions and Microaffirmations

James M. Jones and Rosalie Rolón-Dow

Introduction

> The chief vehicle for pro-racist behaviors are **microaggressions**. These are subtle, stunning, often automatic, and nonverbal exchanges which are "put downs" of blacks by offenders. The offensive mechanisms used against blacks often are innocuous. The cumulative weight of their never-ending burden is the major ingredient in black-white interactions. This accounts for a near inevitable perceptual clash between blacks and whites in regard to how a matter is described as well as the emotional charge involved.
>
> (Pierce, Carew, Pierce-Gonzalez, & Wills, 1978, p. 65)

Harvard psychiatrist Chester Pierce, widely acknowledged as the original author of the microaggressions idea, saw it as an occurrence that surfaced in the everyday interactions of Blacks and Whites. It reflected the subtle ways in which Whites gained, maintained, or expressed their superiority over Blacks. For Pierce, these occurrences were subtle, automatic, and aversive. Over the past nearly half century, the concept of microaggressions has evolved theoretically, empirically, and practically and, yes, politically. Microaggression work has expanded from an account of Black–White strained interactions, to a paradigm for interactions across multiple boundaries of social distinctions, all marked by status differences.

We approach this topic from two perspectives: multidimensionality of racism (MMR) (Jones, 1972, 1997) and critical race theory (CRT) (Bell, 1987, 1993; Delgado, 1995; Delgado & Stefancic, 2017). The MMR (Jones, 1972) is articulated by a scaffolding of influences that affect the lives of Black people—culture, institutions, and individuals. Microaggressions, generally discussed in

Microaggression Theory: Influence and Implications, First Edition. Edited by Gina C. Torino, David P. Rivera, Christina M. Capodilupo, Kevin L. Nadal, and Derald Wing Sue.

the context of interpersonal and intergroup interactions, are associated with individual behavior. However, individual beliefs, attitudes, and behaviors are significantly influenced by the institutions in which they are embedded and the culture that guides the values, practices, and expressions of racial beliefs. Culture defines the meaning of race, situations implement those meaning in its philosophy and practices, and individuals act on them with or without awareness.

Critical race theory (Bell, 1987, 1993; Delgado, 1995; Delgado & Stefancic, 2017) evolved in the 1980s as a radical critique of the role played by legal processes in the failure of the civil rights movement of the 1950–1960s to achieve the social justice and expansion of opportunity it heralded. CRT proposes that white supremacy and racial power are maintained over time, and argues for the need to transform the relationship between law and racial power, thereby achieving racial emancipation and anti-subordination. The basic tenets of CRT conjoin with the MMR to provide a broad context for understanding the origin and manifestations of microaggressions. We argue that to fully understand microaggressions, you must place them in this multidimensional/CRT framework.

We first discuss the MMR and the role of CRT in it. Although what we present is relevant to many socially devalued groups in our society, for purposes of illustration, we focus on the example of Black Americans in relation to White Americans. We examine the idea of *counterstories*—narratives of the experiences of marginalized and "othered" persons, in the context of a racial justice standard. We discuss why counterstories are important and what we can learn from them. We briefly review relevant constructs of microaggressions and how these are understood in the context of a multidimensional CRT framework. We also introduce a more robust conceptualization of microaffirmations, as a way to account for resistance and agency in the face of racism. Finally, drawing on examples from a storytelling project—*Tell It Like It Is*—currently under way at the University of Delaware, we use the counterstories approach to illustrate and better understand experiences of microaggressions and microaffirmations. Using a multidimensional CRT framework to analyze the stories, we illustrate the insidious ways that racism is felt and lived through everyday acts; we also show ways that resistance to racism and efforts toward racial justice is also undertaken in the course of everyday life.

Multidimensional Perspectives on Racism

Multidimensional Model of Racism (MMR)

MMR argues that racism is normalized in U.S. culture, institutions, and individual psyches. The multidimensional model of racism is depicted schematically

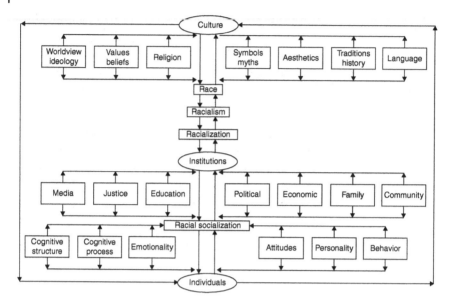

Figure 3.1 Multidimensional Model of Racism.

in Figure 3.1. The model proposes that racism is a product of beliefs that supported the slave trade and rationalized the exploitation, oppression, and dehumanization that accompanied it. These views were instantiated in all aspects of the culture and gave meaning to racism through the cultural products and practices of religion, worldview, emergent traditions, language, symbols, and mythology. A view of race emerged which, over time, informed the formation of institutions whose functions and practices sustained these meanings. Every institution of the United States reflected these racist beliefs and honed them in their everyday practices. Individuals became socialized and acculturated to these beliefs, and their ubiquity and cultural depth penetrated individual psyches. Thus, racism continues to permeate every dimension of life in the United States, and whether consciously practiced, or unconsciously manifested, the perversion of race results in the tentacles of racism, wrapped around U.S. society and psyches.

It is important to note that the MMR model is both hierarchically and temporally dynamic. That is, the dynamics of racism penetrate across societal dimensions from culture to individuals, but also, evolve and influence life over the history of the country. Historical narratives provide meanings that create and sustain stereotypes of human groups.

Metastasized racism spreads throughout society and infiltrates thoughts, emotions, and behavior both in overt and covert ways. Overt manifestations of racism are obvious—slavery, Jim Crow, Immigration acts, Chinese Exclusion Laws, Trail of Tears dislocation of Native Americans, lynchings, white riots, and so forth (see Jones, Dovidio, & Vietze, 2014). Beginning in 1790 with the principle that one must be White of European descent to be a citizen of the United States, all "others" were cast as lesser in varying degrees. The meanings of race were embodied in institutional actions such as the three-fifths compromise that apportioned Black slaves between humanity and property. *Race* became a way to stratify human groups (Smedley, 1993). The rationalization and embodiment of this idea evolved through *racialism*—beliefs that organize perceptions around racial categories and give rise to ideas and values associated with them—and *racialization*—transformation of racialism beliefs into active instruments of categorization and judgment. Once the race categories are created, racialism processes assign them values, and racialization projects activate those values. This triumvirate of concepts and mechanisms results in a deep-seated belief and value system that perpetuates the fundamental notions of white supremacy, and "otherness."

Critical Race Theory (CRT)

Critical race theory, rooted in legal scholarship, provides another approach to racism. CRT seeks to explain why efforts to achieve racial justice may be thwarted by the legal approaches based on normative universal legal principles and their application. Five major tenets of CRT help explain the persistent racial inequality in America:

Normalcy of racism. Because racism is an ingrained feature of our landscape, it looks ordinary and natural to people in the culture;

Racist cultural mythology. Racism is sustained by myths and pre-suppositions and received wisdom that make up common culture and render Blacks and others "one-down" from the beginning;

Interest convergence. White elites will tolerate or encourage racial advances for Blacks and other racial groups only (and especially) when they also promote White self-interest;

Call to context. The emerging facts of one's life render general legal doctrines or laws incapable of stipulating the manner in which racial justice can be achieved. These judgments about fairness are highly sensitive to these contexts, which are understood not so much by legal argument but by counterstories that emerge from individual experiences; and

Challenges to dominant ideology. Critique of individual rights, not group rights, challenge the efficacy of a colorblind ideology, normative standards for equal opportunity, and meritocracy. CRT theorists argue that these claims obscure power and privilege of dominant groups, and rationalize continued social inequality as normal—*system justification*! (Jost and Banaji, 1994).

Psychological CRT

Psychological CRT describes basic psychological processes that produce and sustain racial biases, which, in turn, explain the persistence of racial inequalities. Five major themes describe the racial attitudes and judgments and their affective and behavioral consequences that produce and perpetuate racial inequality.

Spontaneous and persistent influence of race. Race is *spontaneously* derived from social information and continues to affect the course and meaning of encounters and experiences. Normalization of everyday beliefs and stereotypes about race leads to unconscious processes that often influence behavior below awareness. Explicitly articulated good intentions can mask underlying ambivalence or be undermined by implicit processes about how one's behavior will be interpreted. Thus, understanding each other across racial boundaries becomes more important than ever.

Divergent racial experiences require more complex approaches and policies. Fairness is not a natural consequence of abstract principles or logical judgments but is derived from the meanings that vary by our collective and individual social histories (hence the importance of counterstories). Racial policies often have asymmetrical effects on different racial groups.

Racialized policies may have divergent racial effects. Racial groups diverge with respect to calculations of costs and benefits of racial policies—colorblind policies are evaluated negatively and multicultural/diversity approaches more favorably by majorities and minorities, respectively. Race is both less and more than it seems. Perceptions of outgroup homogeneity supports the social significance of race, yet psychological and behavioral facts attest to significant heterogeneity within racial groups.

Growing primacy of racial identity. Racial and other social identities are increasingly important. First, racial identity may serve a *self-protective* role. The greater perceived outgroup rejection, the stronger the likelihood of greater racial identity. Many measures of racial identity describe this linkage between in-group preference and outgroup rejection (e.g., Vandiver et al., 2002). Further, for Blacks, increasing levels of academic disidentification are associated with higher self-esteem and fewer White friends (Steele, 1997). Second, because of increasing *salience* of racial identity, strategies for reducing intergroup conflict can no longer focus exclusively on Whites, but must consider the interpersonal dynamics of cross-racial interactions.

Critical race theory and its psychological counterpart both require a *multidimensional approach*. Each racial/ethnic group has a different place in American society that originated under different circumstances and has been maintained by different mechanisms of bias and conflict. Institutions have been shaped by the desire to maintain a socioeconomic order of control and self-interest. Individuals at times aid and abet that system and at times are victims of it. Differences reflect both divergent cultural origins and emergent cultural differences spawned by adaptation and coping in the United States.

Microaggressions reflect, generally, individuals' more subtle "learnings" about the systems of dominance and power and often result in behaviors that appear to be normal and largely innocent of any malicious intent. The multidimensionality approach allows us to connect different levels of influence on psychological phenomena and social interaction. The simple question "Where are you from?" can be fraught with meaning at multiple levels with innocent, insensitive, and at times sinister effect. In later sections, we deconstruct some of this complexity through the experiences of individuals whose stories exemplify processes by which microaggressions are revealed and experienced.

Resilience and resistance. Individuals are not merely victims in the face of racism. Rather, they resist and enact behaviors to promote ideologies that support racial justice. Racial microaffirmations, which will be discussed shortly, also center the experiences of People of Color, arguing that to promote racial justice we must understand how People of Color develop a sense of belonging and how they are affirmed, included, and helped to succeed. If we address both individual acts and cultural elements of institutions through microaffirmations, this will benefit all people.

Counterstories of Microaggressions and Microaffirmations

While a MMR and CRT lead to understandings of race as an ingrained feature in the fabric of institutional life, it is still often difficult to grasp how racism is manifested and resisted in the course of everyday life. Majoritarian stories and perspectives, which are largely told by dominant groups, downplay the significance of race and racism in current social arrangements, perpetuate cultural understandings of a fair and meritocratic society, and naturalize conditions in which certain racial groups are at the top and others are at the bottom (Delgado, 1989; Delgado & Stefancic, 1993). Counter-storytelling emerges as a central part of a critical race methodology; it values the experiential knowledge of People of Color as a way to reveal the themes underlying CRT (Bernal, 2002; Delgado & Stefancic, 2017; Solórzano & Yosso, 2002). Counter-storytelling offers a way to show, analyze, and learn about race and racism and their intersections with other salient social categories.

Counterstories provide distinctive knowledge of those who experience the most dire consequences of racialization and current racial arrangements or as Bell (1993) describes, by the "faces at the bottom of the well." Unlike dominant groups whose reality is reflected in generalizations and interpretations made from scholarship, marginalized groups need the particularity and call to context that counterstories provide (Delgado, 1993). Counterstories focus on how racism is manifested and resisted in the course of everyday life and are told from the perspective of those racial others who have historically been omitted or misrepresented (Bernal, 2002). These alternative narratives of present social arrangements provide color-conscious understandings that disrupt notions of colorblindness, race neutrality, and linear racial progress (Solórzano & Yosso, 2002).

The CRT literature is replete with various forms of counterstories that illustrate CRT themes including family histories, narratives, biographies, autobiographies, composite stories, parables, and chronicles (Bell, 1993; Delgado, 1989). In our counter-storytelling project, we focus on collecting narratives that illuminate how race, racism, and racial justice work is manifested in the lives of undergraduate students at a predominantly white institution (PWI). As such, the project's focus is on stories of microaggressions and microaffirmations because these concepts demand attention to racial acts, conversations, and experiences that occur in the course of everyday lives.

Microaggressions are thoroughly described throughout this book. Our point is simply to situate microaggressions in a complex understanding of racism. In that complexity, understanding the occurrence of microaggressions requires multilevel analysis and situating the analysis in institutional and societal contexts. In this accounting, the entire enterprise is embedded in an historical narrative that produces divergent meanings and manners of response. Everyone within society is socialized within the context of culture and institutions that have racism woven into their fabric. Individuals are repositories for all of these functions and expressions of race—microaggressions are manifestations of this edifice in the ways we interact with each other.

Microaggressions are one way that People of Color are racialized—their race is made the most salient thing about them. Racializing individuals is part of a pattern of racism with long historical roots. Microaggressions are related to racism in two ways: First, microaggressive behavior creates and perpetuates a hierarchy of status and social significance. As Pierce et al. (1978) propose these subtle "put-downs" maintain a pro-racist hierarchy. In this regard, they are instruments of racism that sustain, in part, a racist status quo. Microaggressions can also be a consequence of racism—a manifestation of the infiltration of racism in our culture, institutions, and psyche. Through racialization acts, meanings (and stereotypes and misrepresentations) of race and of particular racial groups are constructed in ways that perpetuate racism. The prevalence of microaggression experiences in an institution indicates the presence or even prevalence of racism in that institution. Like the canary in the coalmine (Guinier & Torres, 2002), they tell us that the context is toxic, that all are at risk, and that vigilance is essential action is required. The toxic culture engenders a toxic psyche and between them produce behaviors and experiences of racism. As cultural psychologists put it "culture and psyche make each other up!" (Shweder & Sullivan, 1993).

Microaffirmations are less detailed in the literature on everyday experiences related to marginalized social identities. Rowe (2008) defines microaffirmations as "apparently small acts, which are often ephemeral and hard-to-see, events that are public and private, often unconscious but very effective, which occur wherever people wish to help others to succeed" (p. 46). Building on this definition, we advance the concept of racial microaffirmations. Racial microaffirmations occur through verbal and nonverbal acts experienced by minoritized racial groups in ways that account for their racialized reality or resist the impact of racism.

Microaffirmations, whether enacted consciously or unconsciously, have positive impacts on the lives of People of Color by promoting their success, by affirming, recognizing, validating, or protecting their identities, social positionality, and experiences. Just as there are different types of microaggressions (Pérez Huber & Solórzano, 2015), there are different ways that microaffirmations are enacted and experienced including verbally (in both speaking and written form), kinesically (through body language), or visually (through images). Microaffirming experiences disrupt racialized institutional arrangements, cultural practices, or policies that are corrosive to minoritized individuals or they may proactively seek to create new cultural norms or policies that promote racial equity and justice. In this way, microaffirmations display or nurture hope, agency, and resistance in the face of systemic racism. Locating microaffirmations in a multidimensional/CRT framework provides a rationale for focusing on the experiences of People of Color because to promote resistance to racism and move toward racial justice, we must understand what facilitates the success, affirmation, validation, and inclusion of racially minoritized individuals despite the presence of racism within institutions.

The *Tell It Like It Is* Project

In this section, we provide two examples of counterstories from the *Tell It Like It Is* storytelling project at the University of Delaware. In this project, we use qualitative narrative interviewing to document microaggressions and microaffirmations that students experience or witness on UD's campus related to race and other socially significant categories (e.g., student generational status, international status, and disability status). Through the storytelling project, we are creating an archive of stories that illuminates the ways diverse individuals perceive and navigate their place and role in the campus community and the ways that campus climate perspectives are shaped in and through the students' experiences. These counterstories of race microaggressions and microaffirmations show how structural level racism understood through the multidimensional/CRT framework is manifested and resisted in the course of everyday lives.

We first invite you to listen to a story told by Shawna, an African American female student who is part of an Honors program at the university, as she describes a conversation she overheard while studying in the residence hall lounge where students were gathered.

"Do I belong here?"

Hearing some people's conversations would kind of be hurtful. [One time] I was just studying in the lounge and there was probably around seven or eight White men and women talking in the lounge. They weren't floor mates, but they were from the honors program. I remember them having a discussion about the FAFSA [financial aid] forms. They were talking about minorities and getting financial aid, and how the only reason we're able to afford it is because we get handouts. They were talking about it, and I kind of looked up from my books to listen, and they were just saying, "Yes, you have to be piss-poor or a minority to get any money. You basically have to be dead broke."

I was just [thinking], I've applied to a lot of scholarships and that's the reason I was able to come to UD, but it's not because it was just handed to me. I was just thinking to myself, I don't consider myself piss-poor and even though I am a minority, I don't look at that as a negative thing, and I don't look at us getting a handout. I work for what I get, so it was frustrating to hear them describe it as a handout. It was frustrating for me to hear that because the reason why I am able to go to UD is because I get financial aid because my dad would just never be able to afford this on his own.

I don't think they even acknowledged the fact that I was there. I think that was probably even a little more frustrating just because I'm sitting right there. I don't think they really cared that I was there, and I think they were just having their own conversation, they were going to talk about whatever they wanted to talk about no matter who was in the room.

Because they were making these accusations, I felt like I was always put in a place [that I needed to] defend myself or defend the reason why I was here at UD. I think it made me question even more than why I'm at UD, [it made me question] why am I in the honors program? Do I belong here? It makes you feel like… Did I earn my spot to be here or did they need to fill a diversity quota and get me here?

I think [in my Residence Hall] there was a lot of freshmen who were coming from hometowns where [their hometown] was all they knew; maybe they hadn't really met any Black people before or had any Black friends and then they were all coming together. They're moving away from home. They don't want to be uncomfortable, so they find people who think like them, who act like them. That made me uncomfortable just living around that, around people who just weren't open minded to learning about anything else. When I came to college,

> I was forced to be uncomfortable and learn about different types of people just because that was who was around me. I think for them that wasn't their reality. They kind of got to stay in their bubble of being comfortable and being around people who were just like them.

In this experience, that lasts just a few minutes, we witness a microaggression that has both verbal and kinesic (nonverbal communications through gestures and movements) dimensions (Pérez Huber & Solórzano, 2015). Shawna is offended by the conversation as the students express simplistic assumptions about the financial package minoritized and low-income students receive. The incident also has a kinesic dimension as Shawna is rendered invisible by the students' lack of awareness or consideration of her physical presence in the room. An understanding of this microaggression through the multidimensional/CRT model of racism focuses on the racialisms (beliefs, ideas, and values about racial categories) evident in the incident and it considers the judgments that follow based on those racialisms.

In this example, racialisms are activated to perpetrate principles of "whiteness as property"—the right of Whites to exclude others from the privileges inherent in a White identity (Harris, 1993). In the past, this was done through laws and policies that prohibited People of Color from attending universities such as the University of Delaware—which was desegregated by court order in 1951. In the present, "whiteness as property" is partially carried out through cultural mindsets that construct some groups of students worthy of the benefits and privileges inherent in belonging to the university; while others, described in this story as "piss-poor" and "minority," are still rendered as outsiders who receive access to the benefits and privileges of the university only through an undeserved handout.

Furthermore, the impact of historically racist admission policies is not considered by the perpetrators of this microaggression in their judgments about the proper qualifications for financial aid. Instead, they develop a code for financial aid that rests on the assumption that financial aid is an ill-gotten gain received by less-qualified students who cannot compete on the same level as those "legitimate" students. "We," meaning White and middle-class, students are here because of a presumptive meritocratic admissions policy—one that is fair and equitable.

Given that minoritized groups are no longer barred from entering the university doors, it is difficult for many individuals to notice the covert ways that racism is perpetuated and manifested in everyday life. In telling her story, however, Shawna is very explicit about how this incident challenges her sense of belonging at the university. The students in the lounge promote a mindset that perpetuates race and class-based boundaries to belonging in the Honors community; their perspective is at odds with Shawna's experiences and mindset. In this incident, her voice and perspective are not considered—the White students in the lounge act as if they understand the reality of minoritized or poor students who receive financial aid. She explains that the remarks feel accusatory and lead her to feel that she has to defend and explain herself. Yet, these students do not seek out that explanation from her or from students like her. They act as if *their* understanding of reality *is* reality!

Shawna also challenges narratives of diversity, equity, and inclusive excellence promoted by many institutions of higher education, including the University of Delaware, as laudable and central components of their mission and work with students. While universities may be quicker to respond to overt racist incidents that continue to happen across campuses, subtle microaggressive experiences can easily undermine the confidence that minoritized students have in their university's capacity to live up to these goals. Yet, Shawna's story illustrates how this everyday, unnoticed incident in her residence hall takes a psychological toll, allowing self-doubt to creep in about whether she belongs at the university.

As a result of the incident, she begins to speculate about how the university policies work, wondering—"was the university just trying to fill a diversity quota?" She feels uncomfortable knowing that this is the mindset of some of the students in her residence hall as she observes their unfamiliarity and lack of experience with Black people. The wedge between her and these students is deepened through this microaggression, and opportunities for creating a new reality of learning, engagement, and productive dialogue across different life experiences is diminished.

The multidimensional/CRT framework reveals how microaggressions function to normalize racism, rendering it invisible to many. Shawna's presence at the university and her active participation as a successful student in many dimensions of university life embodies the core meaning of inclusive excellence. A seemingly small, brief encounter with fellow students reflects a larger orbit of cultural beliefs, institutional policies and practices, and psychological effects that implicate the multidimensional nature of race and racism. As we have noted, microaggressions can be a manifestation or a consequence of racism. Regardless of its origin, addressing the effects of students' experience of microaggressions is crucial to a richer understanding of what is required to create equitable and inclusive environments that promote the success of minoritized students.

The multidimensional/CRT model of racism also includes attention to the ways that struggle, resistance, and proactive efforts toward creating more racially just institutions are part of both individual and collective racial realities. Experiences that document microaffirmations provide a way to understand those efforts at addressing racism. In this second story from the *Tell It Like It Is* project, Joyce, an African American student, explains an experience that led her to feel affirmed at the university.

"Affirms Your Blackness"
I'm working on a project for a Living and Learning Community for African American students. Yes, we have the Center for Black Culture, but you can't sleep there. You don't get to go home to that. It is a home away from home, but they close at five. Creating a space on campus where students can have that community 24/7 is really important. [We're] not saying it would be mandatory and just because you're Black you have to live there, but giving the Students of Color that option [would be] really instrumental. Meeting with different people on campus to see if we can get this up and running has been extremely helpful. We actually competed in a competition to see who would get money and grants. We didn't win, but people still had interest. They were like, "How can we help you?" Having those people come together and realizing that there are disparities regarding race around this campus really affirmed my being, [it] affirmed my reason for being here. Having that affirmed that there is a need and they're willing to help was really crucial. I've had support from Doctor Jennings who is in the administrative side of the university. She supports us. Her realizing that there is something to be said about race on this campus and that there is a need for this really affirmed my identity as a Black student. I felt supported. I even felt loved. I was like, "Okay, she sees this as a need and she sees that we need to do this." I felt like they loved who I was as a Black woman, and they were willing to do whatever they could to help me feel that comfort and that community that I needed on a 24/7 basis. I live at home with a Black family, so my blackness was always affirmed. Living in a residence hall with majority White students, my blackness isn't always affirmed. I can't always talk to other students about issues that I'm facing because they don't understand. The idea of feeling loved was like loving your blackness, Doctor Jennings was talking about that. She was talking about being in spaces that affirm your blackness, like looking on the wall and seeing something that reflects you, seeing a piece of African art or coming into a room or a home where there's a bunch of black and brown faces, seeing that is loving your blackness.

Microaffirmations can come in the form of validating acts or words that recognize the ways race impacts lived experiences. Joyce details several ways that she was validated as she worked to establish a residential community that considers the benefits that African American students can gain from living with each other. First, she mentions that she felt affirmed when other individuals on campus recognized that race is significant in shaping students' experiences; in this case, in the realm of how students experience their living situations on residence halls. More specifically, she mentions that having an administrator recognize and respond to the specific housing needs of minoritized students helped her feel supported and loved as a Black woman.

Microaffirmations are manifestations of efforts to acknowledge, address, or combat the normalized racism at the institutional and psychological level. As outlined in the multidimensional/CRT model of racism, an analysis of racial microaffirmations considers how affirming everyday experiences acknowledge or disrupt institutional policies, cultural practices, or ideologies that sustain racism. Alternatively, more proactive microaffirmations may establish a different norm of alternative ideologies guided by racial justice and by the lived experience of People of Color.

In this story, Joyce and Dr. Jennings acknowledge that the racial demographics of the university residence halls have differential impact on the experience of Black as compared to White students. For Black students, the predominantly White residence halls create a context where they repeatedly experience solo status. The underrepresentation of Students of Color at the university sustain a norm for residence halls as spaces that more easily and unconsciously represent, affirm, and validate the identities of White students. Joyce, however, expresses the added burden that Black students need to overcome in order to experience the residence halls as a place of familiar belonging.

As outlined by Sue et al. (2007), microaggressions can be environmental in nature through the exclusion of visual artifacts that represent a particular racial group. Joyce questions how Black students can love their blackness and feel at home in the absence of affirming environmental cues in the residence halls (her reference to African art) or given the minimal presence of other black and brown faces.

As a focus on the psychological elements of CRT suggests, divergent racial experiences require complex approaches and policies. Joyce suggests that an alternative living community for Black students acknowledges that racial identities shape how students experience the residence halls. Joyce seeks to create a residence hall community that will serve as a counterspace for her and other students who share similar experiences because of their racial identities. Counterspaces can help students address the psychological impacts of being part of a PWI by cultivating a sense of home, bolstering a sense of belonging (Yosso, Smith, Ceja, & Solórzano, 2009), and fostering a positive racial climate (Solórzano, Ceja, & Yosso, 2000) for minoritized students. Dr. Jennings' support serves as an affirmation because it lends institutional power and support to the need for these counterspaces. These counterspaces are not separatists attempts on the part of minoritized students, but are ways that students can love their Black identities and create a place of belonging. The institutional support offered by Dr. Jennings is critical to nurturing in Joyce, the hope that attention will be paid to her racialized reality as a Black woman. This element of hope in microaffirming experiences is crucial in multidimensional/CRT perspectives on race because it illustrates concrete ways that individuals and communities do not simply surrender to pervasive, normalized racism. Rather, they continue to resist and engage in the struggle for social justice and a better life.

Conclusions and Implications

The multidimensional model of race and CRT illustrates the pervasive ways that racism manifests itself in everyday life experiences—often through institutional practices and policies. Counterstories that center the lived experiences of minoritized individuals help us understand racism when they achieve any of the following: (a) they illuminate the ways racialisms and cultural mythologies are expressed; (b) they show how individuals are racialized; (c) they illustrate the harmful impacts of dominant ideologies; or (d) they point to institutional processes and policies that do not account for racialized realities. Furthermore, as we have shown, counterstories also help reveal the ways that racism is resisted and that efforts toward racial justice are always present in the face of racism.

Listening to counterstories of microaggressions and microaffirmations is important for individuals across racial groups. These stories help us understand what microaggressions and microaffirmations are, how they are perpetrated, and how they impact the target and can hopefully lead to efforts to minimize microaggressions and maximize microaffirmations. For the target of microaggressions, there may be benefits in constructing a narrative about the microaggressions they experience (Pennebaker, 2000) and for developing strategies for responding to and interrupting microaggressions. The experiential knowledge captured through storytelling is readily available, but it needs to be captured and utilized to better understand and address the problems of race in our country. In this chapter, we only highlight two stories and the lessons they teach; we believe there is additional insight and cumulative learning potential in listening to multiple stories.

We are not suggesting that a focus on microaffirmations is an easy solution to racism nor that microaffirmations are parallel to experiences of microaggressions in frequency, magnitude, or impact. Pittinsky (2016) offers a helpful suggestion when he writes that "Understanding the full range of microbehaviors— both positive and negative—gives us a way to take them more seriously, realize their worth, and harness their strength" (p. 80). Our chapter illustrates that looking at microaggression and microaffirmation counterstories can lead to a broader understanding of the ways racism is perpetuated through daily encounters as well as the ways it is resisted. By including this fuller range of everyday behaviors, we can more fully grasp the nuances of everyday forms of racism as well as the practices we can engage in to create cultural and institutional norms that embody racial justice principles and ideologies.

References

Bell, D. (1987). *And we are not saved: The elusive quest for racial justice.* New York, NY: Basic Books.

Bell, D. (1993). *Faces at the bottom of the well: The permanence of racism.* New York, NY: Basic Books.

Bernal, D. D. (2002). Critical race theory, Latino critical theory, and critical raced-gendered epistemologies: Recognizing students of color as holders and creators of knowledge. *Qualitative Inquiry, 8*(1), 105–126.

Delgado, R. (1989). Storytelling for oppositionists and others: A plea for narrative. *Michigan Law Review, 87*(8), 2411–2441.

Delgado, R. (1993). On telling stories in school: A reply to Farber and Sherry. *Vanderbilt Law Review, 46,* 665–676.

Delgado, R. (1995). *Critical race theory: The cutting edge.* Philadelphia, PA: Temple University Press.

Delgado, R., & Stefancic, J. (1993). Critical race theory: An annotated bibliography. *Virginia Law Review,* 461–516.

Delgado, R., & Stefancic, J. (2017). *Critical race theory: An introduction.* New York, NY: NYU Press.

Guinier, L., & Torres, G. (2002). *The Miner's Canary: Enlisting race, resisting power, transforming democracy.* Cambridge, MA: Harvard University Press.

Harris, C. I. (1993). Whiteness as property. *Harvard Law Review,* 1707–1791.

Jones, J. M. (1972; 1997). *Prejudice and racism* (2nd ed.). New York, NY: McGraw-Hill.

Jones, J. M., Dovidio, J. F., & Vietze, D. L. (2014). *The psychology of diversity: Beyond prejudice and racism.* New York, NY: Wiley-Blackwell.

Jost, J. T., & Banaji, M. R. (1994). The role of stereotyping in system-justification and the production of false consciousness. *British Journal of Social Psychology, 33*(1), 1–27.

Pennebaker, J. W. (2000). Telling stories: The health benefits of narrative. *Literature and Medicine, 19*(1), 3–18.

Pérez Huber, L., & Solórzano, D. (2015, November). *Racial microaggressions: What they are, what they are not and why they matter.* (Latino Policy and Issues Brief No. 30). Retrieved from http://www.chicano.ucla.edu/files/PB30.pdf.

Pierce, C. M., Carew, J. W., Pierce-Gonzalez, D., & Wills, D. (1978). An experiment in racism: TV commercials. In C. Pierce (Ed.), *Television and education* (pp. 62–68). Beverly Hills, CA: Sage Publications.

Pittinsky, T. L. (2016). Backtalk: Why overlook microaffirmations? *Phi Delta Kappan, 98*(2), 80–80.

Rowe, M. (2008). Micro-affirmations and micro-inequities. *Journal of the International Ombudsman Association, 1*(1), 45–48.

Shweder, R. A., & Sullivan, M. A. (1993). Cultural psychology: Who needs it? *Annual Review of Psychology, 44,* 497–523.

Smedley, A. (1993). *Race in North America: Origin and evolution of a worldview.* Boulder, CO: Westview Press.

Solórzano, D., Ceja, M., & Yosso, T. (2000). Critical race theory, racial microaggressions, and campus racial climate: The experiences of African American college students. *Journal of Negro Education,* 60–73.

Solórzano, D. G., & Yosso, T. J. (2002). Critical race methodology: Counter-storytelling as an analytical framework for education research. *Qualitative Inquiry, 8*(1), 23–44.

Steele, C. M. (1997). A threat in the air: How stereotypes shape intellectual identity and performance. *American Psychologist, 52*(6), 613.

Sue, D. W., Capodilupo, C. M., Torino, G. C., Bucceri, J. M., Holder, A., Nadal, K. L., & Esquilin, M. (2007). Racial microaggressions in everyday life: Implications for clinical practice. *American Psychologist, 62*(4), 271.

Vandiver, B. J., Cross, W. E., Worrell, F. C., & Fhagen-Smith, P. E. (2002). Validating the cross racial identity scale. *Journal of Counseling Psychology, 49*(1), 71–85.

Yosso, T., Smith, W., Ceja, M., & Solórzano, D. (2009). Critical race theory, racial microaggressions, and campus racial climate for Latina/o undergraduates. *Harvard Educational Review, 79*(4), 659–691.

4

Intersectionality Theory and Microaggressions: Implications for Research, Teaching, and Practice

Jioni A. Lewis, Marlene G. Williams, Anahvia T. Moody, Erica J. Peppers, and Cecile A. Gadson

The concept of intersectionality, which considers the ways that simultaneous membership in multiple social identity categories is linked to interlocking systems of oppression, power, and privilege, has gained increased attention inside and outside of academia in the last several years (Bowleg & Bauer, 2016). Contemporary social justice movements have embraced intersectional politics in the fight for equality and coalition building (Hancock, 2016). For example, the cofounders of the hashtag-turned-racial justice movement, #BlackLivesMatter, are three Black women who explicitly highlight the intersections of racism, sexism, classism, heterosexism, transphobia, and xenophobia in their fight for equity, justice, and liberation (Garza, 2016). At the same time, the concept of microaggressions has also traveled outside of the academy and landed squarely in the crosshairs of current political debates about freedom of speech, with many conservative politicians and journalists (e.g., Lukianoff & Haidt, 2015) arguing that educating individuals about microaggressions is nothing more than political correctness run amok. Given the recent popularity of the terms *intersectionality* and *microaggressions*, it is imperative that researchers and psychologists gain a deeper understanding of the meaning of these academic concepts. As such, it is important to outline the history of intersectionality theory and intersectional scholarship in the field of psychology. In addition, it is important to delineate how intersectionality theory can be applied to microaggressions research to expand our knowledge about these subtle forms of oppression and their impact on the psychological well-being of marginalized groups.

In this chapter, we will briefly review research on microaggressions with special attention to intersections of race, gender, sexual orientation, social class, and religion. Given the importance of making the "invisible visible" in the study

Microaggression Theory: Influence and Implications, First Edition. Edited by Gina C. Torino, David P. Rivera, Christina M. Capodilupo, Kevin L. Nadal, and Derald Wing Sue.

of microaggressions (e.g., Sue, 2011), we focus our review on research that highlights the impact of intersectional microaggressions on the health of historically marginalized groups. We highlight directions for future microaggression research that centers an intersectional analysis in the psychological study of people with intersecting identities. We also provide recommendations for educators to engage in intersectional pedagogy. This chapter ends with recommendations for practitioners to better understand intersectional microaggressions to become more culturally competent in their clinical work.

Herstory of Intersectionality Theory

Although intersectionality has been a recent concept in the field of psychology, it is grounded in the *herstory* of Black feminism, which dates back to the mid-nineteenth century when women, such as Sojourner Truth, an abolitionist and women's rights activist, highlighted the marginalization of Black women in the suffrage movement. She gave a speech at the 1851 Ohio Women's Rights Convention highlighting the ways that White women tried to exclude Black women from getting the right to vote. Throughout the twentieth century, there were numerous Women of Color scholars, writers, and activists that articulated the unique marginalization of Women of Color at the intersection of race and gender oppression (Hancock, 2016; May, 2015). In 1977, the Combahee River Collective, a group of Black feminists, articulated the struggles of Black women in the contemporary feminist movement by stating, "We ... find it difficult to separate race from class from sex oppression because in our lives they are most often experienced simultaneously" (Combahee River Collective, 1995, p. 234). Thus, Black feminist theory and research paved the way for research on intersectionality (Cole, 2009; Collins, 2000).

In 1989, critical legal scholar Kimberlé Williams Crenshaw introduced the concept of intersectionality in her critique of antidiscrimination law, which often excluded Black women at the intersection of racial and gender discrimination. Crenshaw argued that Black women could experience discrimination that could resemble racism experienced by Black men, sexism experienced by White women, or the combined effects of race and gender oppression (i.e., double jeopardy). However, Crenshaw (1989) argued that Black women often "experience discrimination as Black women—not the sum of race or sex discrimination, but as Black women" (p. 149). Thus, this framework critiques a single-axis analysis of discrimination and pushes a more nuanced exploration of intersecting forms of oppression. In 1990, sociologist Patricia Hill Collins wrote her seminal book, *Black Feminist Thought*, which details the ways that African American women's oppression is rooted in a matrix of domination, which refers to the ways that forms of oppression are organized by power to produce and sustain inequality. Thus, both Crenshaw and Collins similarly articulated the importance of centering marginalized people, namely, Women of Color, in the study of the intersection of racial and gender oppression (Hancock, 2016; May, 2015).

Intersectional Approaches in Psychology

Although early articulations of intersectionality have been focused on systems-level processes given its interdisciplinary history in legal studies, critical race studies, women's studies, and sociology, scholars in the field of psychology have applied intersectionality to individual-level variables, such as exploring the impact of interlocking forms of discrimination on the health and well-being of marginalized individuals (Cole, 2009). There is some debate in the field of psychology about the best way to explore intersecting identities and forms of oppression. Psychology researchers have utilized various approaches to study discrimination including single-axis (e.g., single identity analysis, such as race only or gender only), comparative (e.g., comparing Black women to Black men or comparing White women to Black women), additive (e.g., measuring racism and sexism separately and then adding them together), interactional/multiplicative (e.g., measuring racism and sexism separately and then creating a statistical interaction term), and intersectional (measuring the unique intersection of the simultaneous experience of racism and sexism; Cole, 2009; Lewis & Grzanka, 2016; Shields, 2008; Thomas, Witherspoon, & Speight, 2008).

Intersectionality scholars (Bowleg & Bauer, 2016; Crenshaw, 1989) argue that the simultaneous experience of both racism and sexism is greater than the sum of its parts, which refers to the unique experience of the simultaneous effects of multiple forms of oppression. Some scholars (Cho, Crenshaw, & McCall, 2013; Collins & Bilge, 2016) also argue that an intersectional lens necessitates an intersectional analytic disposition. We agree with intersectional scholars who argue that an intersectional approach encompasses an intersectional analytic disposition that explores multiple forms of oppression simultaneously (e.g., Bowleg, 2008; Bowleg & Bauer, 2016). Drawing on Dill and Kohlman (2012) as well as Lewis and Grzanka (2016), we argue that these approaches can be ordered on a continuum from weak to strong intersectionality, with the comparative approach representing a weaker form of intersectionality (e.g., the inclusion of multiple social identities as categories) to the intersectional approach representing a stronger form of intersectionality (e.g., analyzing interlocking forms of oppression, inequality, and power). In the next section, we briefly review the literature on intersectional microaggressions. Given the paucity of research on intersectional microaggressions and the large body of research on racial microaggressions, we focus our review on the ways that racial microaggressions intersect with gender, sexual orientation, class, and religious microaggressions. Given the lack of any intersectional microaggression studies related to disability status, we were unable to include intersections with disability in this selected review.

Intersections of Race and Gender Microaggressions

One construct grounded in intersectionality theory is *gendered racism*, which describes Black women's unique experience of discrimination based on the intersection of racism and sexism (Essed, 1991). Much of the current research on gendered racism focuses on overt experiences of the intersection of racial and gender discrimination. However, recently there has been a burgeoning area of empirical research on the intersection of racial and gender microaggressions. Lewis, Mendenhall, Harwood, and Huntt (2016) coined the term *gendered racial microaggressions* to refer to "subtle everyday behavioral, verbal, and environmental expressions of oppression based on the intersection of one's race and gender" (p. 51). Lewis et al. (2016) created a taxonomy of gendered racial microaggressions based on a qualitative study with Black college women. Their findings highlighted six gendered racial microaggression themes which included *Expectation of a Jezebel* (e.g., being exoticized, sexualized, and objectified by men), *Expectation of the Angry Black Woman* (e.g., being perceived as the stereotype of an "angry Black woman"), *Struggle for Respect* (e.g., messages that question one's intelligence and challenge leadership), *Invisibility* (e.g., being marginalized, invisible, or silenced in professional settings), *Assumptions of Communication Styles* (e.g., preconceived notions about Black women's communication styles), and *Assumptions of Aesthetics* (e.g., messages about Black women's physical appearance, including body type, hairstyles, and facial features) (Lewis et al., 2016).

Building on the previous qualitative work on gendered racial microaggressions, Lewis and Neville (2015) developed the Gendered Racial Microaggressions Scale (GRMS), which is a self-report measure to assess the frequency and stress appraisal of intersecting racial and gender microaggressions experienced by Black women. In a diverse sample of adult Black women, Lewis and Neville (2015) developed a multidimensional scale with four subscales: *Assumptions of Beauty and Sexual Objectification* (i.e., stereotypes and assumptions about Black women's beauty, attractiveness, standards of beauty, hairstyles, facial features, and body size), *Silenced and Marginalized* (i.e., experiences of being marginalized and silenced in academic and professional settings), *Strong Black Woman Stereotype* (i.e., being perceived to be "too" strong, independent, or assertive), and *Angry Black Woman Stereotype* (i.e., verbal comments or nonverbal behaviors that communicate the stereotype of being an angry Black woman). In addition, Lewis and Neville (2015) found that these intersectional racial and gender microaggressions were significantly related to psychological distress.

Although a majority of the intersectional research on racial and gender microaggressions has focused on African American women, there has been some empirical research that has highlighted specific racial microaggressions that are gendered based on other racial and ethnic groups. For example, in a qualitative study with Asian American individuals, Sue, Bucceri, Lin, Nadal, and Torino (2007) found that women reported experiencing racial microaggressions specific to their gender, such as exoticization, which included perceiving Asian women as exotic, subservient, and sexually available to service men. In a qualitative study with Filipino American individuals, women reported microaggressions that communicated sexual objectification, while men reported microaggressions that included de-sexualization and de-masculinization (Nadal, Escobar, Prado, David, & Haynes, 2012). In another study, Latina women were more likely to experience school and workplace racial microaggressions compared to Latino men (Nadal, Mazzula, Rivera, & Fuji-Doe, 2014). Although these studies highlight the ways that racial microaggressions can differentially impact the experiences of women and men of color, more research is needed to explore gendered racial microaggressions experienced by Asian, Latinx, and Native American individuals.

Intersections of Race and Sexual Orientation Microaggressions

Within the psychology literature, there is a large body of research on the negative impact of homophobia and heterosexist discrimination for lesbian, gay, bisexual, transgender, queer (LGBTQ) people. Research shows that experiencing heterosexist discrimination has been associated with a host of negative outcomes, such as decreased self-esteem, internalized homophobia, and increased risk of future victimization (Fineran, 2002; Moradi et al., 2010; Pilkington & D'Augelli, 1995; Robinson & Rubin, 2016). There is also a body of work that highlights the unique experiences of racism and heterosexism for LGBT People of Color (e.g., DeBlaere et al., 2014; Szymanski & Sung, 2010). For example, Szymanski and Sung (2010) used an additive approach to explore the relations between racism and heterosexism on psychological distress for Asian American LGBTQ individuals. They found that heterosexism in Communities of Color, internalized heterosexism, race-related dating and relationship problems in the LGBT community, and the level of disclosure of one's sexual orientation were significant predictors of psychological distress among Asian American LGBTQ individuals. Although these findings add to our understanding of the separate effects of racism and heterosexism, this approach does not explore the intersectional effects of multiple forms of oppression.

A critical contribution to the literature on the subtle discriminatory experiences of LGBT People of Color and multiple minority stress is the LGBT

People of Color Microaggressions Scale (Balsam, Molina, Beadnell, Simoni, & Walters, 2011). This scale was developed using a three-phase mixed methods study design. First, Balsam et al. (2011) conducted a series of focus groups and in-depth interviews with a total of 112 LGBT People of Color to identify themes and develop items for the scale. Several themes emerged including, racism in the LGBT community, heterosexism in racial/ethnic minority communities, problems with relationships and dating, concerns about immigration status, and rejection by other LGBT People of Color. Then, the authors chose to develop scale items based on microaggressions uniquely experienced by LGBT People of Color and also found in the existing literature, which resulted in three subscales: *Heterosexism in Racial/Ethnic Minority Communities* (e.g., "feeling unwelcome at groups or events in your racial/ethnic community"), *Racism in Dating and Close Relationships* (e.g., "being rejected by potential or sexual partners because of your race/ethnicity"), and *Racism in LGBT Communities* (e.g., "feeling misunderstood by White LGBT people"; Balsam et al., 2011, p. 169). Balsam et al. (2011) validated their measure and found the three-factor structure had the best model fit. The scale was also significantly related to psychological distress, such that greater experiences of microaggressions were positively related to greater psychological distress. In addition, they found that men reported experiencing greater microaggressions than women, lesbians and gay men reported experiencing greater microaggressions than bisexual men and women, and Asian Americans reported greater microaggressions than African American and Latinx individuals. Although this scale addresses a gap in the literature on the microaggression experiences of LGBTQ People of Color, more research is needed to explore the within-group variability within this multiple marginalized population.

Intersections of Race and Social Class Microaggressions

Historically, systemic racism has been linked to classism in that both are systems of oppression that have served to uphold a social hierarchy, with more power and access to resources concentrated at the top by predominantly White wealthy individuals (Smith, Mao, & Deshpande, 2016). There is a dearth of empirical research on the intersections of racism and classism. Classism is defined as the "practices, attitudes, assumptions, behaviors, and policies through which social institutions function to perpetuate the deprivation and low status of poor people" (Smith & Mao, 2012, p. 526). Smith and Redington (2010) have conducted research on classist microaggressions, which can intersect with racial microaggressions, such as making comments like "that's ghetto." In addition, Black women often experience intersecting race, gender, and class microaggressions, such as the stereotype of the "welfare queen" (Collins, 2000). Racial and class microaggressions are similar in that they are both based on stereotypes and biases that equate People of Color and lower socioeconomic status individuals with inferiority pertaining to an individuals' intelligence, education, and success (Sue et al., 2008).

Although there is currently a dearth of empirical research focused explicitly on intersectional race and class microaggressions, there is some research on racial microaggressions that provides evidence for the influence of the intersections of class on these subtle forms of oppression. For example, in a study of the racial microaggression experiences of Filipino individuals, Nadal, Escobar, et al. (2012) found that participants reported assumptions that they had lower paying jobs, such as line cooks or delivery boys. In another study, Mexican-origin adolescents reported being called derogatory names, which referred to negative perceptions of work ethic and social class specific to their race (Balagna, Young, & Smith, 2013). Black middle-class youth have also reported being assumed to be less intelligent and poor by their peers and educators (Allen, 2012). Research has demonstrated that racial microaggressions that communicate assumptions of inferiority are associated with greater psychological distress (Nadal, Griffin, Wong, Hamit, & Rasmus, 2014) and classist microaggressions reportedly contribute to feelings of exclusion (Smith et al., 2016). Absent from the current microaggression literature is an explicit focus on the intersection of racism and classism, which greatly influences the mental and physical health of People of Color, women, and poor people. By focusing more on this intersection, microaggression researchers can gain a deeper understanding of how social class and race intersect as systems of oppression that influence marginalized populations in their daily lives.

Intersections of Race and Religious Microaggressions

Research on religious discrimination is a budding area of research that has only been explored within the past decade (Husain & Howard, 2017). Existing literature has explored prejudice toward Muslim (Islamophobia) and Jewish individuals (anti-Semitism) (Nadal, 2008). Nadal, Issa, Griffin, Hamit, and Lyons (2010) developed a taxonomy of religious microaggressions, which provided the groundwork for validation and further empirical work across multiple marginalized religious groups. However, the initial exploration of religious microaggressions began with research on Islamophobia in Muslim American groups (Nadal, Griffin, et al., 2012). Nadal et al. (2010) recognized that while there are several types of religious microaggressions, it is difficult to differentiate discriminatory behavior as attributable to religious prejudice, racial prejudice, or ethnic prejudice. In addition, Husain and Howard (2017) conducted a study that focused on religious microaggressions experienced by Muslim Americans and reported that the loss of religious integrity may be more detrimental than conformity to racial standards considering the centrality of religion in the lives of Muslim Americans (Husain & Howard, 2017). The cumulative effects of religious microaggressions and the long-term effect of distancing oneself from one's racial or ethnic group are not well documented in the literature (Husain & Howard, 2017). While the impact of racial microaggressions has been associated with feelings of powerlessness, decreased sense of belongingness, forced compliance, loss of integrity, and pressure to represent one's group, qualitative research to date has not yet explored the intersections between religious and racial microaggressions (Husain & Howard, 2017). Future research on intersectional microaggressions experienced by religious and racial/ethnic minorities is needed to better understand the unique impact of these microaggressions on religious and racial/ ethnic marginalized groups.

Summary

Taken together, research indicates that multiple marginalized individuals experience various types of microaggressions based on the intersections of their identity groups. A majority of the empirical research on intersectional microaggressions has focused on the intersections of racial and gender microaggressions, or gendered racial microaggressions, experienced by African American women (Lewis et al., 2016; Lewis & Neville, 2015). Some research also highlights the unique types of microaggressions experienced by Asian, Latinx, and Native American women; however, more research is needed to further explore how these intersectional microaggressions uniquely impact women and men of color. There has also been some research on the intersection of race and sexual orientation microaggressions for LGBTQ People of Color (Balsam et al., 2011; DeBlaere et al., 2014). However, little is known about the unique experiences of specific LGBTQ racial/ethnic groups, such as the experiences of Latina bisexual women or the experiences of Asian gay men. There is also a paucity of research on intersections between race and class, religion, or disability microaggressions. More research is needed to explore intersectional microaggressions related to disability status. For example, it is important to explore intersections between disability, race, and class microaggressions given the lack of any empirical work in this area. It is imperative to explore these multiple marginalized groups and their intersectional microaggression experiences to better understand their impact on mental health and well-being. In the next section, we will provide recommendations for future microaggression research that centers on an intersectional analysis in the psychological study of people with intersecting identities. In addition, we provide recommendations for educators to engage in intersectional pedagogy and for practitioners to better understand intersectional microaggressions in their clinical work.

Recommendations for Research, Teaching, and Clinical Practice

Intersectional Microaggressions and Future Research

The key to implementing intersectionality into any research study is to have an understanding that intersectionality is more than just a focus on intersecting identities, but it is a focus on interlocking systems of oppression (Bowleg, 2008; Cole, 2009; Lewis & Grzanka, 2016). Thus, applying intersectionality theory to microaggression research necessitates a deeper understanding of microaggressions that moves beyond a focus on intersecting identities and toward a focus on subtle forms of interlocking oppression and structural inequality. Applying intersectionality theory to microaggression research will help to move beyond assessing microaggressions of singular identities and will allow researchers to capture the complexities and intersectional nature of microaggressions based on multiple marginalized identities. This involves using an intersectional analytic disposition at each step of the research process (Bowleg, 2008; Cho et al., 2013). The following section will focus on best practices for how to apply intersectionality theory throughout the research process from forming intersectional research questions to frame the study and guide the methods to data analysis and interpreting findings within a sociohistorical context of intersecting oppression, privilege, and power.

The first step in the research process is to develop the research question. Intersectional scholars (e.g., Bowleg, 2008; Lewis & Grzanka, 2016; Shields, 2008) highlight the importance of framing research questions in an intersectional way in order to fully capture interlocking identities and experiences of oppression. In many qualitative and quantitative microaggression research studies, research questions tend to focus on singular identities and do not take into account multiple identities that can impact experiences of microaggressions (Nadal et al., 2015). For example, if a researcher were interested in exploring the microaggression experiences of Asian gay men, it would be important to avoid asking additive research questions about participants' experiences of microaggressions based on their separate racial/ethnic, sexual orientation, and gender identities. Instead, the researcher should be intentional in constructing an intersectional research question that captures their experiences at the intersection of all three identities as an Asian gay man. In addition, it would also be important to explore the ways that racism, heterosexism, and traditional notions of masculinity shape individuals' experiences of microaggressions in their everyday life.

It is also important to consider choosing the specific type of research design that will be best to answer the research question. A majority of intersectionality studies have tended to use qualitative research methods because these research designs tend to allow researchers to ask complex questions that consider experiences within a sociocultural context (Bowleg, 2008). Recently, there has been an increase in quantitative intersectionality research, and most intersectionality scholars are in agreement that multiple research methods are important to utilize to better explore interlocking systems of oppression, power, and privilege (Cole, 2009; Else-Quest & Hyde, 2016). Thus, incorporating mixed methodology by using both qualitative and quantitative methods can be fruitful in the study of intersectional microaggressions. For example, the GRMS (Lewis & Neville, 2015) was initially based on qualitative focus groups with Black women to develop the survey items. These items were developed based on the phenomenological experiences of the participants and captured the intersection of racial and gender microaggressions. A majority of microaggression measures focus on one aspect of identity and form of oppression, namely, race and racism. However, it is necessary for intersectional microaggression measures to be created to accurately measure multiple forms of oppression. Thus, we encourage the development of more intersectional measures to capture experiences at the intersection of multiple identities.

In regards to data analysis and interpretation, an intersectional approach requires researchers to consider ways to analyze data that moves beyond single-axis, comparative, and additive approaches. In addition, an intersectional approach will require microaggression researchers to use knowledge they have about the sample's social location to inform their interpretation of the data (Bowleg, 2008). Doing so will allow the researcher to situate the findings within a sociohistorical context of the microaggressions and multiple identities being explored. This also requires researchers to move beyond the raw data and to consider the contextual meaning of the results. For example, someone conducting a study on the microaggression experiences of Latina bisexual women will need to consider the unique history of racism, sexism, and heterosexism that Latina bisexual women experience in the United States in their data analysis and interpretation. This will allow the researcher to gain a deeper understanding of *how* these marginalized identities intersect and influence their experiences of microaggressions based on race, gender, and sexual orientation.

Microaggression studies that apply intersectionality theory have yielded results that support the notion that microaggressions are often experienced at the intersection of multiple identities. For example, Nadal et al. (2015) conducted a study to re-analyze existing qualitative microaggression studies to explore intersectional microaggressions. They found that participants of color in their sample reported microaggressions that they experienced based on multiple identities, not just their race. For example, when asked about gender microaggressions, Muslim women described experiencing microaggressions based on the intersection of their race, gender, and religion. Muslim women reported experiencing negative comments from others about wearing traditional Muslim clothing such as the hijab (Nadal et al., 2015). Thus, an intersectional approach should apply intersectionality to one's data analysis and interpretation. Future intersectional microaggression research studies could take further steps to acknowledge the complexity of the ways that multiple marginalized identities influence experiences of microaggressions. For example, a study exploring microaggressions that Muslim LGBT women experience would ask research questions that are inclusive of individuals' intersecting identities by asking questions such as "What types of microaggressions do Muslim LGBT women experience?" rather than asking "What types of microaggressions do individuals experience based on being Muslim and LGBT and women?" Then, the researcher would analyze and interpret the data within the sociohistorical context that is associated with these intersecting marginalized identities. This study could discuss the ways in which a Muslim LGBT woman's religious beliefs, sexual orientation, and gender intersect by discussing the unique history of gender norms, cultural values, and the relation between religious beliefs and sexuality, and how these constructs influence their experiences.

Intersectional Microaggressions and Teaching

Intersectional pedagogy includes an analysis of privileged and oppressed identities that create systemic inequalities, analyzes power dynamics, involves educator and student personal reflection of intersecting identities, and promotes social action and community engagement (Case & Rios, 2016, Grzanka, 2016). Although the term *intersectional pedagogy* is relatively new, an awareness of multiple and intersecting identities and an analysis of systems of power, privilege, and oppression is grounded in multicultural, critical liberatory, and feminist pedagogy (Enns, Sinacore, Ancis, & Phillips, 2004). Specifically, these approaches share a similar goal grounded in Friere's (1970) work, which includes helping students to develop critical consciousness through shared power, participatory dialogue, and self-reflection and praxis. An intersectionality approach encourages educators to use a critical lens when discussing microaggressions and to become more aware of intersectional microaggressions in the classroom (Grant & Zwier, 2011). It is important for educators to increase their awareness about the intersectional microaggressions associated with their student's intersecting marginalized identities (Grant & Zwier, 2011). Educators should also critically reflect on their own intersecting identities and past experiences or engagement in microaggressions. This knowledge and awareness will help educators build a culturally responsive curriculum that incorporates intersecting identities and challenges stereotypes and is sensitive to the intersectional microaggressions that marginalized individuals experience (Grant & Zwier, 2011).

This can be practiced in the classroom by interweaving discussions about power and privilege into regular classroom activities (Jones & Wijeyesinghe, 2011) or through various critical analysis assignments that require students to critically examine intersecting identities and oppressions (Case & Lewis, 2012; Case & Rios, 2016). Doing so will allow the educator to cultivate critical consciousness (Jones & Wijeyesinghe, 2011). For example, if an educator wants to discuss the disproportionate rates of White people in higher education they may choose to situate this discussion within a sociohistorical context of White supremacy and exclusionary educational laws and practices, which has limited access to higher education for People of Color in the United States. In addition, the educator could also highlight how this limited access to resources could also get communicated through environmental and interpersonal racist and classist microaggressions on college campuses. The educator would need to be knowledgeable of the racist and classist microaggressions that People of Color and working-class people experience in order to discuss them in ways that do not perpetuate biases, but encourage students to critically challenge biases. An intersectional approach to teaching will allow educators to create a pedagogy that is relatable and culturally responsive to students' intersecting marginalized identities.

Intersectional Microaggressions in Therapy

There is a growing body of research on microaggressions in therapy (Constantine, 2007; Owen, Tao, Imel, Wampold, & Rodolfa, 2014). However, the majority of this research has focused on singular identities and experiences with microaggressions in therapy. For example, research has found that many of the existing racial microaggressions experienced by People of Color in their everyday life can also occur in therapeutic settings (Constantine, 2007). Thus, therapists can perpetrate intersectional microaggressions in the therapy room, working with marginalized clients and this negatively impacts the therapeutic alliance. For example, Mazzula and Nadal (2015) highlighted a case vignette of microaggressions in therapy between a 40-year-old recently divorced African American woman client and a 28-year-old White American doctoral psychology intern. During one therapy session, the therapist committed a gendered racial microaggression against her client when she expressed surprise that her client was married to her partner who she had a child with. Mazzula and Nadal (2015) highlight that the therapist's surprise at the length of her African American female client's relationship with her ex-husband was influenced by stereotypes of African American families (e.g., single-mother households) and beliefs surrounding African American female sexuality (e.g., "Jezebel" stereotype of Black female promiscuity) (Collins, 2000).

Research on microaggressions experienced by marginalized clients in therapy shows that these microaggressions have a negative impact on the therapeutic alliance (Gómez, 2015; Mazzula & Nadal, 2015; Owen et al., 2014). Research indicates that clients are often aware of microaggressions perpetrated by therapists, which negatively impacts perceptions of their therapists' cultural competence, which in turn, is related to a reduced likelihood that clients will continue in therapy (Constantine, 2007). In the case vignette, the 40-year-old African American female client did not return to therapy after confronting her therapist's dismissiveness of the role of racism in her life (Mazzula & Nadal, 2015). This incident created a rupture in the therapeutic relationship and the client no longer felt safe to talk to her therapist. This can be a common occurrence when microaggressions emerge in therapy. It is important for mental health professionals to develop skills to be able to provide corrective emotional experiences for multiple marginalized clients in therapy rather than perpetuate client's experiences of trauma related to past discrimination.

Conclusion

In this chapter, we highlighted intersectionality theory and ways to apply an intersectional analysis to research on microaggressions. We hope that the provided recommendations for research, teaching, and clinical practice are helpful as psychologists seek to apply intersectionality theory to experiences of microaggressions. This is one way to more accurately make the invisible visible and understand the complex nature of the subtle and insidious forms of oppression that occur in everyday life.

References

Allen, Q. (2012). Photographs and stories: Ethics, benefits and dilemmas of using participant photography with Black middle-class male youth. *Qualitative Research, 12*(4), 443–458. doi:10.1177/1468794111433088.

Balagna, R. M., Young, E. L., & Smith, T. B. (2013). School experiences of early adolescent Latinos/as at-risk for emotional and behavioral disorders. *School Psychology Quarterly, 28*(2), 101. doi:10.1037/spq0000018.

Balsam, K. F., Molina, Y., Beadnell, B., Simoni, J., & Walters, K. (2011). Measuring multiple minority stress: The LGBT people of color microaggressions scale. *Cultural Diversity and Ethnic Minority Psychology, 17*(2), 163–174. doi:10.1037/a0023244.

Bowleg, L. (2008). When Black+ lesbian+ woman≠ Black lesbian woman: The methodological challenges of qualitative and quantitative intersectionality research. *Sex Roles, 59*(5–6), 312–325. doi:10.1007/s11199-008-9400-z.

Bowleg, L., & Bauer, G. (2016). Invited reflection: Quantifying intersectionality. *Psychology of Women Quarterly, 40*(3), 337–341. doi:10.1177/0361684316654282.

Case, K. A., & Lewis, M. K. (2012). Teaching intersectional LGBT psychology: Reflections from historically Black and Hispanic-serving universities. *Psychology & Sexuality, 3*(3), 260–276. doi:10.1080/19419899.2012.700030.

Case, K. A., & Rios, D. (2016). Infusing intersectionality: Complicating the psychology of women course. In K. Case (Ed.), *Intersectional pedagogy: Complicating identity and social justice* (pp. 82–109). New York, NY: Routledge.

Cho, S., Crenshaw, K. W., & McCall, L. (2013). Toward a field of intersectionality studies: Theory, applications, and praxis. *Signs: Journal of Women in Culture and Society, 38*(4), 785–810. doi:10.1086/669608.

Cole, E. R. (2009). Intersectionality and research in psychology. *American Psychologist, 64*(3), 170–180. doi:10.1037/a0014564.

Collins, P. H. (2000). *Black feminist thought: Knowledge, power and the politics of empowerment.* New York, NY: Routledge.

Collins, P. H., & Bilge, S. (2016). *Intersectionality.* Cambridge, UK: Polity Press.

Combahee River Collective (1995). Combahee river collective statement. In B. Guy-Sheftall (Ed.), *Words of fire: An anthology of African American feminist thought* (pp. 232–240). New York, NY: New Press (Original work published 1977).

Constantine, M. G. (2007). Racial microaggressions against African American clients in cross-racial counseling relationships. *Journal of Counseling Psychology, 54*(1), 1–16. doi:10.1037/0022-0167.54.1.1.

Crenshaw, K. (1989). Demarginalizing the intersection of race and sex: A Black feminist critique of antidiscrimination doctrines, feminist theory, and antiracist politics. *University of Chicago Legal Forum, 8*, 139–167.

DeBlaere, C., Brewster, M. E., Bertsch, K. N., DeCarlo, A. L., Kegel, K. A., & Presseau, C. D. (2014). The protective power of collective action for sexual minority women of color: An investigation of multiple discrimination experiences and psychological distress. *Psychology of Women Quarterly, 38*(1), 20–32. doi:10.1177/0361684313493252.

Dill, B. T., & Kohlman, M. H. (2012). Intersectionality: A transformative paradigm in feminist theory and social justice. In S. N. Hesse-Biber (Ed.), *Handbook of feminist research: Theory and praxis* (Vol. 2, pp. 154–174).

Else-Quest, N. M., & Hyde, J. S. (2016). Intersectionality in quantitative psychological research: II. Methods and techniques. *Psychology of Women Quarterly, 40*(3), 319–336. doi:10.1177/0361684316647953.

Enns, C. Z., Sinacore, A. L., Ancis, J. R., & Phillips, J. (2004). Toward integrating feminist and multicultural pedagogies. *Journal of Multicultural Counseling and Development, 32*, 414–427.

Essed, P. (1991). *Understanding everyday racism: An interdisciplinary theory.* Newbury Park, CA: Sage.

Fineran, S. (2002). Sexual harassment between same-sex peers: Intersection of mental health, homophobia, and sexual violence in schools. *Social Work, 47*(1), 65–74. doi:10.1093/sw/47.1.65.

Friere, P. (1970/2007). *Pedagogy of the oppressed.* New York, NY: Continuum International.

Garza, A. (2016). A herstory of the #blacklivesmatter movement. *The Feminist Wire, 2014*. Retrieved from: https://news.northseattle.edu/sites/news .northseattle.edu/files/blacklivesmatter_Herstory.pdf.

Gómez, J. M. (2015). Microaggressions and the enduring mental health disparity: Black Americans at risk for institutional betrayal. *Journal of Black Psychology, 41*(2), 121–143.

Grant, C. A., & Zwier, E. (2011). Intersectionality and student outcomes: Sharpening the struggle against racism, sexism, classism, ableism, heterosexism, nationalism, and linguistic, religious, and geographical discrimination in teaching and learning. *Multicultural Perspectives, 13*(4), 181–188. doi:10.1080/ 15210960.2011.616813.

Grzanka, P. R. (2016). Undoing the psychology of gender: Intersectional feminism and social science pedagogy. In K. Case (Ed.), *Intersectional pedagogy: A model for complicating identity and social justice* (pp. 61–79). New York, NY: Routledge.

Hancock, A. M. (2016). *Intersectionality: An intellectual history*. New York, NY: Oxford University Press.

Husain, A., & Howard, S. (2017). Religious microaggressions: A case study of Muslim Americans. *Journal of Ethnic & Cultural Diversity in Social Work: Innovation in Theory, Research & Practice, 26*(1–2), 139–152. doi:10.1080/ 15313204.2016.1269710.

Jones, S. R., & Wijeyesinghe, C. L. (2011). The promises and challenges of teaching from an intersectional perspective: Core components and applied strategies. *New Directions for Teaching and Learning, 2011*(125), 11–20. doi:10.1002/ tl.429.

Lewis, J. A., & Grzanka, P. R. (2016). Applying intersectionality theory to research on perceived racism. In A. N. Alvarez, C. T. H. Liang, & H. A. Neville (Eds.), *The cost of racism for people of color: Contextualizing experiences of discrimination* (pp. 31–54). Washington, DC: American Psychological Association.

Lewis, J. A., Mendenhall, R., Harwood, S. A., & Huntt, M. B. (2016). "Ain't I a woman?": Perceived gendered racial microaggressions experienced by Black women. *The Counseling Psychologist, 44*(5), 758–780. doi:10.1177/ 0011000016641193.

Lewis, J. A., & Neville, H. A. (2015). Construction and initial validation of the gendered racial microaggressions scale for Black women. *Journal of Counseling Psychology, 62*(2), 289–302. doi:10.1037/cou0000062.

Lukianoff, G., & Haidt, J. (2015). The coddling of the American mind. *The Atlantic, 316*(2), 42–52.

May, V. M. (2015). *Pursuing intersectionality, unsettling dominant imaginaries*. New York, NY: Routledge.

Mazzula, S. L., & Nadal, K. L. (2015). Racial microaggressions, whiteness, and feminist therapy. *Women & Therapy, 38*(3–4), 308–326. doi:10.1080/02703149 .2015.1059214.

Moradi, B., Wiseman, M. C., DeBlaere, C., Goodman, M. B., Sarkees, A., Brewster, M. E., & Huang, Y. P. (2010). LGB of color and white individuals' perceptions of heterosexist stigma, internalized homophobia, and outness: Comparisons of levels and links. *The Counseling Psychologist, 38*(3), 397–424. doi:10.1177/0011000009335263.

Nadal, K. L. (2008). Preventing racial, ethnic, gender, sexual minority, disability, and religious microaggressions: Recommendations for promoting positive mental health. *Prevention in Counseling Psychology: Theory, Research, Practice and Training, 2*(1), 22–27.

Nadal, K. L., Davidoff, K. C., Davis, L. S., Wong, Y., Marshall, D., & McKenzie, V. (2015). A qualitative approach to intersectional microaggressions: Understanding influences of race, ethnicity, gender, sexuality, and religion. *Qualitative Psychology, 2*(2), 147. doi:10.1037/qup0000026.

Nadal, K. L., Escobar, K. M., Prado, G. T., David, E. J. R., & Haynes, K. (2012). Racial microaggressions and the Filipino American experience: Recommendations for counseling and development. *Journal of Multicultural Counseling and Development, 40*(3), 156–173. doi:10.1002/j.2161-1912.2012 .00015.x.

Nadal, K. L., Griffin, K. E., Hamit, S., Leon, J., Tobio, M., & Rivera, D. P. (2012). Subtle and overt forms of Islamophobia: Microaggressions toward Muslim Americans. *Journal of Muslim Mental Health, 6*(2), 15–37. doi:10.3998/jmmh.10381607.0006.203.

Nadal, K. L., Griffin, K. E., Wong, Y., Hamit, S., & Rasmus, M. (2014). The impact of racial microaggressions on mental health: Counseling implications for clients of color. *Journal of Counseling & Development, 92*(1), 57–66. doi:10.1002/j.1556-6676.2014.00130.x.

Nadal, K. L., Issa, M., Griffin, K. E., Hamit, S., & Lyons, O. B. (2010). Religious microaggressions in the United States: Mental health implications for religious minority groups. In D. W. Sue (Ed.), *Microaggressions and marginality: Manifestation, dynamics, and impact* (pp. 287–310). Hoboken, NJ: Wiley.

Nadal, K. L., Mazzula, S. L., Rivera, D. P., & Fuji-Doe, W. (2014). Microaggressions and Latina/o Americans: An analysis of nativity, gender, and ethnicity. *Journal of Latina/o Psychology, 2*, 67–78. doi:10.1037/lat0000013.

Owen, J., Tao, K. W., Imel, Z. E., Wampold, B. E., & Rodolfa, E. (2014). Addressing racial and ethnic microaggressions in therapy. *Professional Psychology: Research and Practice, 45*(4), 283–290. doi:10.1037/a0037420.

Pilkington, N. W., & D'Augelli, A. R. (1995). Victimization of lesbian, gay, and bisexual youth in community settings. *Journal of Community Psychology, 23*(1), 34–56. doi:10.1002/1520-6629(199501)23:1<34::AID-JCOP2290230105> 3.0.CO;2-N.

Robinson, J. L., & Rubin, L. J. (2016). Homonegative microaggressions and posttraumatic stress symptoms. *Journal of Gay & Lesbian Mental Health, 20*(1), 57–69. doi:10.1080/19359705.2015.1066729.

Shields, S. A. (2008). Gender: An intersectionality perspective. *Sex Roles, 59*(5–6), 301–311.

Smith, L., & Mao, S. (2012). Social class and psychology. In N. A. Fouad, J. A. Carter, & L. M. Subich (Eds.), *APA handbook of counseling psychology, Theories, research, and methods* (Vol. 1, pp. 523–540). Washington, DC: American Psychological Association.

Smith, L., Mao, S., & Deshpande, A. (2016). "Talking across worlds": Classist microaggressions and higher education. *Journal of Poverty, 20*(2), 127–151. doi:10.1080/10875549.2015.1094764.

Smith, L., & Redington, R. (2010). Class dismissed: Making the case for the study of classist microaggressions. In D. W. Sue (Ed.), *Microaggressions and marginalized groups in society: Race, gender, sexual orientation, class and religious manifestations* (pp. 269–285). New York, NY: Wiley.

Sue, D. W. (2011). The challenge of White dialectics: Making the "invisible" visible. *The Counseling Psychologist, 39*(3), 415–422. doi:10.1177/0011000010390702.

Sue, D. W., Bucceri, J., Lin, A. I., Nadal, K. L., & Torino, G. C. (2007). Racial microaggressions and the Asian American experience. *Cultural Diversity and Ethnic Minority Psychology, 13*(1), 72–81. doi:10.1037/1099-9809.13.1.72.

Sue, D. W., Nadal, K. L., Capodilupo, C. M., Lin, A. I., Torino, G. C., & Rivera, D. P. (2008). Racial microaggressions against Black Americans: Implications for counseling. *Journal of Counseling & Development, 86*(3), 330–338. doi:10.1002/ J.1556-6678.2008.tb00517.x.

Szymanski, D. M., & Sung, M. R. (2010). Minority stress and psychological distress among Asian American sexual minority persons. *The Counseling Psychologist, 38*(6), 848–872. doi:10.1177/0011000010366167.

Thomas, A. J., Witherspoon, K. M., & Speight, S. L. (2008). Gendered racism, psychological distress, and coping styles of African American women. *Cultural Diversity and Ethnic Minority Psychology, 14*(4), 307. doi:10.1037/1099-9809 .14.4.307.

Part II

Detrimental Impact of Microaggressions

5

Microaggressions: Clinical Impact and Psychological Harm

Jesse Owen, Karen W. Tao, and Joanna M. Drinane

It started as a great day for Lily, a 43-year-old Japanese American mother of two. She had just finished an energizing workout and was looking forward to her second therapy session with Dr. Saito. It had been such a relief to find an Asian American psychologist in a mid-size city where she and her family had just moved. There was little racial–ethnic diversity, and she had already felt some discomfort in being one of the visible minorities at her new company of 50 employees. There was one other Asian American woman, Kaifen, a 52-year-old Chinese American woman who had already been with the organization for 15 years. Today, Lily wanted to talk to Dr. Saito about two interactions she had with coworkers. The first involved, Mark, an African American colleague who walked up to her in the lunchroom and said, "Hey, Kaifen. How's it going?" She was bewildered at how Mark had mistaken her for her coworker, one with whom he had worked with for years. The second incident involved a White colleague who in the bathroom said, "You know, I'm always so amazed at how Asian women age so well. Your skin is flawless. What's your secret?" After a short check-in with Dr. Saito, she described both incidents, hoping for some suggestions on how to handle the situations and for a bit of moral support. She was baffled by the situation and even more so by how Dr. Saito responded. Dr. Saito said, "I wonder if there were other reasons Mark may have mistaken you for Kaifen. Any thoughts?" A few moments later, the doctor went on to say, "Sounds your coworker, the woman, may be finding a way to connect with you and she was unsure of how to start a conversation."

This example provides a glimpse into the complexity of microaggressions and highlights the challenge of not only understanding but also exploring the psychological and interpersonal impact associated with microaggression-related experiences. For Lily, both coworker interactions were experienced as insulting and providing even more evidence for what Iris Kuo writes, "People look at us without really seeing us. Instead, they simply see our race" (Kuo, 2016).

Microaggression Theory: Influence and Implications, First Edition. Edited by Gina C. Torino, David P. Rivera, Christina M. Capodilupo, Kevin L. Nadal, and Derald Wing Sue.
© 2019 John Wiley & Sons, Inc. Published 2019 by John Wiley & Sons, Inc.

For Lily, these encounters in the workplace were confusing and painful, and she (Lily) was subsequently wounded by her encounter with Dr. Saito, an Asian American woman, whom she hoped would commiserate with her experience. Instead, her therapist added insult to injury by indirectly criticizing her for being "too sensitive" and then burdening her by implying that she should reconsider the intentions of her colleagues.

Dr. Saito's comments, albeit insulting to Lily, demonstrate a common dilemma. In this case, we observe a "clash of racial realities," in that two Asian American women interpret similar cross-racial interactions differently (Sue et al., 2007, p. 277). It is plausible the therapist's comments are fueled by countertransference (e.g., unconscious reaction to her own past racist encounters) or racial identity schema (e.g., contact; Helms, 1995). Regardless, this situation highlights how activating racially charged interactions can be and the ripple effect of harm microaggressions can cause. In this chapter, we will examine the various dimensions of microaggression theory and research, while also presenting findings related to the clinical impact and psychological harm associated with these pernicious cultural ruptures.

As noted in previous chapters, microaggressions represent a shift in the conceptualization of the expression of bias in that rather than being overt and open, they are covert and subtle in nature and can be couched in casual conversation (Sue, 2010; Sue et al., 2007). Sue et al. (2007) outlined three forms of racial microaggressions: (a) microinsults (e.g., stating a racial/ethnic minority (R-EM) individual is a credit to their race or pathologizing cultural values/beliefs, such as how R-EMs' communicate), (b) microinvalidations (e.g., colorblind attitudes, such as not seeing race or assuming R-EMs are being too sensitive to racial–ethnic comments), and (c) microassaults (e.g., use of the blatant racism but not in the presence of anyone from that race) (Pierce, Carew, Pierce-Gonzalez, & Willis, 1978; Sue et al., 2007). Although there are related concepts (e.g., subtle racism and benevolent sexism), we will focus our review on the construct of microaggressions with particular attention to studies conducted between 2007 and 2017.

Psychological Harm of Microaggressions: A Review of the Research

The empirical study of microaggressions has typically utilized three approaches: (a) correlational designs where individuals complete self-report measures of perceived microaggressions, and their scores are correlated with psychological functioning measures, (b) experimental studies wherein individuals are randomized to microaggression conditions or controls, or (c) qualitative studies where in-depth interviews or focus groups are utilized to capture rich narratives from individuals who have experienced microaggressions. Experimental designs are able to rule out many of the third-variable confounds that correlational and qualitative designs cannot; however, all designs have merit. Most importantly, all of these studies point to the same conclusion: *Microaggressions are negatively associated with various aspects of psychological health, and they can complicate and impair interpersonal relationships.*

We first conducted a review of published studies since 2007 that explicitly assessed microaggressions occurring outside of therapy and their relationship to mental health outcomes. For this initial review, we only included quantitative studies that reported bivariate correlations between microaggressions and mental health outcomes in order to provide an overall analysis. We screened over 200 articles that met our original search terms, which resulted in 21 studies (see Table 5.1). Although we attempted to be comprehensive in our approach, we did not intend this review to be as comprehensive as one that would occur

Table 5.1 Summary of Microaggression Studies Associated with Mental Health.

References	r	Sample size (n)
Anderson et al. (2015)	−0.30	163
Balsam, Molina, Beadnell, Simoni, and Walters (2011)	−0.18	297
Bowleg et al. (2016)	−0.23	578
Burrow and Hill (2012)	−0.24	214
Hu and Taylor (2016)	−0.28	449
Huynh (2012)	−0.25	360
Kaufman, Baams, and Dubas (2017)	−0.41	267
Kim (2016)	−0.24	144
Kim, Kendall, and Cheon (2016)	−0.25	156
Lewis and Neville (2015)	−0.25	259
Mercer et al. (2011)	−0.30	385
Nadal, Griffin, Wong, et al. (2014)	−0.14	225
Nadal, Wong, Griffin, et al. (2014)	−0.12	506
O'Keefe, Wingate, Cole, Hollingsworth, and Tucker (2015)	−0.21	405
Robinson and Rubin (2016)	−0.64	170
Smith, Hung, and Franklin (2011)	−0.32	661
Sohi and Singh (2015)	−0.24	214
Torres, Driscoll, and Burrow (2010)	−0.35	174
Torres and Taknint (2015)	−0.34	113
Woodford, Paceley, Kulick, and Hong (2015)	−0.27	417
Overall random effect	−0.293	6,276

Note: We recoded all variables to be within the directionality in order to conduct the overall weighted random effect.

when preparing a traditional meta-analysis (e.g., we did not include unpublished data, dissertations, or code for moderators).

Collectively, the studies included over 6,000 participants from diverse backgrounds (e.g., sexual minorities, R-EMs). The results revealed that microaggressions are associated with various aspects of psychological functioning, including depressive symptoms, self-esteem, anger, positive and negative effect, substance use, overall psychological distress, rumination, stress, and overall psychological well-being (e.g., Blume, Lovato, Thyken, & Denny, 2012; Mercer, Zeigler-Hill, Wallace, & Hayes, 2011; Nadal, Griffin, Wong, Hamit, & Rasmus, 2014; Nadal, Wong, Griffin, Davidoff, & Sriken, 2014; Nadal, Wong, Sriken, Griffin, & Fuji-Doe, 2014; Nadal et al., 2015; Pieterse, Todd, Neville, & Carter, 2012; Schoulte, Schultz, & Altmaier, 2011; Wang, Leu, & Shoda, 2011). For illustration, we report the correlations and sample size per study in Table 5.1 (if there was more than one mental health variable, we averaged the correlations). The correlations were recoded to account for the directionality of the effects. We computed the overall random effect based on meta-analytic principles (Hedges & Olkin, 1984). In brief, random effect models allow for generalization to the larger population of studies as compared to just generalizing to the studies included in the analysis. The overall random effect resulted in a weighted $r = -0.293$ (95% confidence intervals ranged from -0.23 to -0.34[1]). In other words, individuals' ratings of microaggressions accounted for 8.6% of the variance in their mental health functioning.

It is important to situate this effect into broader perspective. The association between microaggressions and mental health outcomes is similar to or larger than the association between other foundational psychological factors and mental/physical health, including (a) the association between ethnic identity and mental health functioning ($r = 0.22$; Smith & Silva, 2011), (b) the placebo effect in medicine ($r = 0.14$; Hróbjartsson & Gøtzsche, 2013; Wampold, Minami, Tierney, Baskin, & Bhati, 2005), (c) the effectiveness of brief CBT for depression ($r = 0.20$), (d) the association between social support and mental health functioning ($r = 0.27$; Prati & Pietrantoni, 2010), (e) the association between exercise and depression and anxiety ($r = 0.24, 0.19$, respectively; Rebar et al., 2015), (f) the association between lower SES and depression ($r = 0.16$; Lorant et al., 2003), (g) the association between positive marital quality and physical and mental health (r range from 0.07 to 0.33; Proulx, Helms, & Buehler, 2007; Robles, Slatcher, Trombello, & McGinn, 2014). While this list is not exhaustive, these studies demonstrate a robust association between microaggressions and mental health as well as a consistency of findings with other commonly recognized psychological concepts.

It is important to note that recent critics of the microaggression research have challenged the validity of conclusions based heavily on correlational analyses

---

[1] To note there was significant variability between studies ($Q = 103$, $p < .01$).

and therefore have challenged the notion that the field must tackle this head on (Haidt, 2017; Lilienfeld, 2017). It is not out of question to consider directionality by posing an alternative research question: Are individuals who are more psychologically distressed more likely to perceive and be negatively impacted by microaggressions? For instance, are individuals who have experienced greater life stressors predisposed to view each interaction through a lens of injustice? Corresponding interpretations have in fact been widely asserted and have culminated in the coinage of "victimhood culture" by sociologists who claim U.S. culture is in the state of transition from dignity culture to one of victimhood (Campbell & Manning, 2014). They assert that this culturally supported ideology is observed by the rise of people who

> are intolerant of insults, even if unintentional, and react by bringing them to the attention of authorities or to the public at large … victimization [is] a way of attracting sympathy, so rather than emphasize either their strength or inner worth, the aggrieved emphasize their oppression and social marginalization.
>
> (Campbell & Manning, p. 716)

Although this ideology is divorced from the reality of decades of inequities, injustices, and systemically sanctioned forms of discrimination, these sentiments raise larger questions about the readiness of society to address this specific form of oppression.

Additionally, this perspective highlights the interpersonal and societal nature of microaggressions, albeit from a deficit victim blaming lens. Fortunately, researchers have employed different research designs to view these concerns through an empirical lens. For example, Tran and Lee (2014) implemented an experimental methodology in an effort to better understand the impact of a specific type of racial microaggression. In this study, researchers examined the reaction of Asian American participants to receiving comments, which were seemingly complimentary in nature and simultaneously imbued with a negative stereotype. Sixty-eight participants were assigned to one of three conditions in which they interacted with White confederates whose final statements varied in their degree of racial loading. In the control condition, a confederate said, "Nice talking to you." The low racial loading condition confederate said, "Nice talking to you. You speak English well." The high racial loading confederate said, "Nice talking to you. You speak English well for an Asian." Researchers found significant differences on a range of interpersonal variables (e.g., enjoyed the conversation, feeling accepted) between the high racial loading condition and the control condition; however, there were no significant differences between the low racial loading and control conditions. The authors describe how the experience of a microaggression of this nature can be "interpersonally damaging" and can cause interactions to be viewed less favorably.

The use of qualitative methodology has also added to the literature by capturing more of the subtleties of identity-based microaggressions. Qualitative studies allow for a more in-depth analysis of individuals whose identities are marginalized and are not adequately represented in the literature. For example, a qualitative study by Nadal, Davidoff, Davis, and Wong (2014) considered the emotional, behavioral, and cognitive reactions to microaggressions among nine trans gender participants. Building upon a directed content analysis (DCA) that identified the 12 types of microaggressions targeting trans or gender-nonconforming individuals, this study used DCA to measure people's reactions to these denigrating experiences. The researchers uncovered emotional reactions including anger, betrayal, distress, hopelessness and exhaustion, and invalidation. Further, some of the cognitive reactions included rationalization, experiencing the situation as a double bind, and a need for vigilance and self-preservation. In the behavioral realm, reactions included confrontation, be it direct or indirect, and passive coping (via diffusing, deflecting, or appeasing the perpetrator of the microaggression). This use of qualitative methodology gave voice to this group of clients and revealed the destructive psychological and physical effects of trans and gender-related bias.

The scope of many microaggression studies, including those that are qualitative in nature, is often limited to one specific identity (e.g., impact of racial microaggressions). Building upon this foundation, researchers have also begun to qualitatively examine intersectional microaggressions (Nadal et al. 2015). Nadal et al. (2015) analyzed data from six previous studies each of which involved the collection of data in an identity-specific focus group format. The total sample included 80 participants of diverse identities (65% female, 24% male, 8% transgender male-to-female, and 4% transgender female-to-male). Forty percent of participants identified as lesbian, gay, or bisexual, and 77.5% identified as R-EMs. This study used a combination of approaches from Qualitative Secondary Analysis and Consensual Qualitative Research to uncover intersectional domains under which microaggressions occur. The study yielded the following eight themes: (a) the exoticization of People of Color, (b) gender-based stereotypes for lesbians and gay men, (c) disapproval of LGBT identity by racial, ethnic, and religious groups, (d) assumption of inferior status of Women of Color, (e) invisibility and desexualization of Asian men, (f) assumptions of inferiority or criminality of Men of Color, (g) gender-based stereotypes of Muslim men and women, and (h) Women of Color as spokespersons. This methodological approach revealed that microaggressions are experienced in complex ways. Individuals with multiple marginalized identities are often confronted with indignities in numerous contexts and are oppressed by the very reference groups to which they belong.

Observing Microaggressions: Was That Racist?

As noted in our initial scenario, Lily and her therapist, Dr. Saito, held explicitly different interpretations of the workplace interactions Lily experienced.

Despite both women identifying as Asian American, this situation emphasizes the haziness surrounding a microaggressive interaction by various stakeholders—recipient, committer, bystander, and ally. Microaggressions are transactional in nature wherein perspectives on intention and subsequent impact vary depending upon the individuals involved and their cultural context. As such, the study of microaggressions presents

> a complex scientific challenge because it deals with both explicit and implicit bias; explores the lived realities of marginalized groups in our society; frames microaggressive dynamics as an interaction between perpetrator, target, and the external environment; pushes powerful emotional buttons in the actors; and is difficult to separate from the sociopolitical dimensions of oppression, power, and privilege.
>
> (Sue, 2017, p. 171)

Indeed, one of the common dilemmas for the study of microaggressions is that the experiences are often characterized by vague or tacitly veiled comments, and they are delivered by individuals who may or may not be close to the recipient (Sue et al., 2007). The ambiguity of a statement or behavior, the context in which a microaggression is delivered, as well as the individuals involved in the interaction can produce a wide range of reactions (e.g., denial and anger). However, one of the most common initial reactions to a microaggression is confusion (Sue, 2010). This "deer-in-headlights" moment often requires some amount of time for individuals to process or identify what occurred. If the interaction is subsequently defined as a microaggression, two questions frequently emerge, including: Why am I offended? or Why was this same statement inoffensive when _____ said it to me last week? Accordingly, the measurement of these individual and contextual response differences requires new methods to tap into the ambiguity surrounding microaggressions. Equally, or perhaps most, critical is a focus on how to accurately assess and ultimately address impact of microaggressions. For example, an individual's acute reaction to a microaggression may be confusion and worry, whereas a cumulative or chronic outcome may be internalization and subsequent anxiety and depression. Moreover, we must also consider the relational aspects of microaggression interactions.

This complexity was recently illuminated in a recent study, which examined the perceptions of observers to a simulated interaction between a student and a professor. Tao, Owen, and Drinane (2017) examined the responses of observers who were randomly assigned to one of four video-recorded scenarios involving a Black female student and a White female professor (both actors) speaking with each other at the end of a class. A scenario included (a) no microaggression, (b) an extremely ambiguous microaggression, (c) a somewhat ambiguous microaggression, or (d) an overt microaggression. Observers ($N = 261$) were asked to indicate their positive and negative emotional valences toward the professor and the student as well as to rate the actors' level of likability and cultural biasedness. The mean age of the sample was 25. One hundred and fifteen participants were in their first year of college, 79 in their second year, 15 in their third year, 35 in their fourth year, and 17 did not indicate their grade-level. Forty-nine percent of the sample was from a R-EM group and 51% identified as White. Results indicated a significant difference between the overt microaggression condition and the other three scenarios on participants' negative and positive emotions and attributions toward the professor (i.e., higher cultural biasedness and lower positive valence). However, there were no differences between the no microaggression, very ambiguous, and ambiguous conditions. Interestingly, there were no significant differences between R-EM and White participants' ratings.

These findings highlight the intricacies inherent in many racial–ethnic microaggression situations. For example, it seems activating negative responses to a microaggression (perhaps a proxy for action in a real situation) is difficult unless all of the cues (e.g., racially microaggressive statements or behaviors) are unequivocally clear as demonstrated in the overt microaggression condition. Thus, contextual ambiguity is a likely psychological obstacle to individuals' ability to respond. A more hopeful result, however, was that both White and R-EM participants did not differ in their perceptions of the cross-race interactions in the four scenarios. This result encourages the ongoing examination of how attunement to instances of racial discrimination develops, particularly for those individuals who are not directly involved in an interaction. How do we begin envisioning a paradigm in which "otherwise silent and passive observers" are empowered to become more active and vocal in countering the harmful psychological impact of racism (Ishiyama, 2006)? Clearly, more research is needed to better understand the nuances of the perception and impact of microaggressions for those exposed to them.

Up to this point and aside from our case example, we have focused mainly on microaggressions outside of the therapeutic context. Unfortunately, as was seen in the case of Lily, microaggressions that can occur in everyday life can also enter the therapy room. In this next section, we highlight what is known about microaggressions in therapy, and we end with a perspective for therapists to consider while navigating the complexities of cultural ruptures.

Clinical Impacts of Microaggressions

Ideally, the therapy environment is a "safe place," free of microaggressions. Despite their best intentions, all individuals (trained therapists, included) are fallible and susceptible to implicit biases. Approximately 43–81% of clients report experiencing at least one microaggression in therapy, and these reports do not vary by the clients' racial/ethnic status or the race-ethnicity identity of therapist (DeBlaere et al., under review; Hook et al., 2016; Owen, Imel, Adelson, & Rodolfa, 2012; Owen et al., 2015). Further, Hook et al. (2016) examined microaggressions in a sample of 2,212 R-EM clients and found that the most commonly experienced microaggressions involved therapists' avoidance of or minimization of cultural issues, as well as therapists' subtle expression of cultural stereotypes. Unfortunately, these findings convey just how common microaggressions are in the therapy and their impact on the process and outcome of psychotherapy.

The experience of microaggressions in therapy has been associated with negative therapeutic processes, such as ruptures in the therapeutic alliance. Relatedly, clients who experience microaggressions in therapy report less benefit from therapy. There are seven known studies that took place in university counseling as well as community-based settings that examined clients' experiences of racial–ethnic microaggressions in relation to psychotherapy processes and/or outcomes (Constantine, 2007; Davis et al., 2016; DeBlaere et al., under review; Hook et al., 2016; Morton, 2011; Owen et al., 2011, 2015). In addition to race-focused studies, there are two known studies that examined gender microaggressions against women (DeBlaere et al., under review; Owen, Tao, & Rodolfa, 2010), and one study about microaggressions against LGBQ clients in therapy (Shelton & Delgado-Romero, 2011). We provide an overall random effect for the association between microaggressions and process variables, and then one for microaggressions and therapy outcome variables. The process variables, or factors that guide treatment, were primarily the working alliance and cultural humility. The working alliance is commonly defined as an agreement on the goals for treatment, the methods to reach those goals, and the relational bond between the client and therapist (Horvath, Del Re, Flückiger, & Symonds, 2011). Cultural humility reflects an other-oriented stance, which is marked by openness, curiosity, lack of arrogance, and genuine desire to understand clients' cultural identities (Hook, Davis, Owen, Worthington, & Utsey, 2013). The measures of therapy outcomes typically included measures of psychological well-being or clients estimate of their overall improvement in therapy across a range of domains (e.g., interpersonal, work, and social).

As seen in Table 5.2, there was a negative association between microaggressions and therapeutic processes (weighted random effect, $r = -0.45$) and with therapy outcomes (weighted random effect, $r = -0.24$). These associations are similar to those in other psychotherapy research. For instance, in a meta-analysis, Nienhuis et al. (2016) found positive associations between genuineness, empathy, and alliance ($r = 0.59$, 0.50, respectively), which are comparable to the association between microaggressions and process factors. Additionally, the microaggression–therapy outcome association is consistent with other empirically supported relational factors, such as the alliance–outcome association ($r = 0.28$; Horvath et al., 2011) and empathy–outcome

Table 5.2 Summary of Microaggression Studies in Psychotherapy.

References	r Process	r Outcome	Sample size (n)
Constantine (2007)			
Alliance	−0.40	–	40
Satisfaction	–	−0.66	
Davis et al. (2016)			
Alliance	−0.36	–	128
Cultural humility	−0.25	–	
Improvement		−0.32	
DeBlaere et al. (under review)			
Alliance (RE)	−0.32	–	212
Alliance (women)	−0.29	–	
Cultural humility (RE)	−0.53	–	
Cultural humility (women)	−0.52	–	
Psychological well-being (RE)	–	−0.12	
Psychological (women)	–	−0.23	
Morton (2011)			
Alliance	−0.39		35
Owen et al. (2010)			
Alliance	−0.33	–	121
Psychological well-being	–	−0.22	
Owen et al. (2011)			
Alliance	−0.29	–	232
Psychological well-being	–	−0.18	
Owen et al. (2014)			
Alliance	−0.28	–	120
Psychological well-being	–	−0.27	
Hook et al. (2016)			
Cultural humility	−0.49	–	2,212
Overall random effect	−0.45	−0.24	3,100/853

association ($r = 0.31$; Elliott, Bohart, Watson, & Greenberg, 2011). Moreover, the microaggression–therapy outcome association is larger than other psychotherapy processes, including therapist competence ($r = 0.07$) and adherence to treatment manuals ($r = 0.02$) (Webb, DeRubeis, & Barber, 2010). Accordingly, microaggressions have a comparable impact on the clinical process as other well-known psychotherapy processes.

Conceptually, microaggressions represent a special subset of clinical ruptures that can erode clients' trust in their therapists and their belief in therapy as an emotionally safe endeavor (Constantine, 2007; Owen et al., 2012). That is, microaggressions weaken the therapeutic relationship and thus attenuate clinical outcomes. Fortunately, research has also been able to demonstrate the buffering effect of the working alliance. For example, establishing a strong foundational alliance or relational base can enable clients and therapists to better navigate the experience of microaggressions (Owen et al., 2012).

To maintain a strong alliance, therapists need also to be able to recognize and react when microaggressions occur. For example, in a sample of 120 R-EM clients, 53% of clients reported experiencing at least one racial–ethnic microaggression over the course of therapy (Owen et al., 2015). Of those clients who experienced a racial–ethnic microaggression, 76% reported it was not addressed. Of the 24% of clients reporting the microaggression was addressed, all but one noted the microaggression was resolved. Additionally, clients who experienced a microaggression not addressed by their therapist reported weaker working alliance compared to clients with whom no microaggression occurred and to clients with whom microaggressions were discussed and resolved (Owen et al., 2015). Clearly, it is vital for therapists to address microaggressions in order to protect against shift in the therapeutic relationship.

Needless to say, it is necessary to identify microaggressions before they can be addressed. Are *therapists* even able to detect them? In an observer study (Owen et al., 2018) practicing therapists ($N = 78$) were randomly assigned to one of two video vignettes in which a counselor (actor) commits either (a) three racial–ethnic microaggressions or (b) no microaggressions within a counseling session. Participants rated the counselor in the video on their sensitivity as well as on three dimensions of their multicultural orientation (MCO) (i.e., cultural humility, comfort, and opportunities). Researchers also examined the extent to which therapists were able to accurately identify the three microaggressions in the first condition. Results revealed participants rated the "therapist" in the microaggression condition as significantly less sensitive, less culturally comfortable, less culturally humble, and less attuned to cultural opportunities when compared to the "therapist" in the neutral condition. In reviewing the number of participants who detected a microaggression, 38–52% accurately identified one of the three microaggressions. Less than one-quarter (i.e., 22%) of participants recognized all three.

This study illuminates a vital process in addressing the psychological harm caused by microaggressions—the importance for individuals to be able to identify when one has occurred. Central to the training and ongoing professional development of multiculturally oriented therapists is enhancing their level of awareness of how, when, and with whom cultural ruptures might arise. Although increased intentionality may lead to the prevention of microaggressions (despite their occurrence being inevitable), the long-term focus of the field should emphasize the ability to notice when they happen and how to acknowledge them. Studies on microaggressions occurring in therapy (e.g., Hook et al., 2016; Owen, Tao, Imel, Wampold, & Rodolfa, 2014) provide evidence that they are not clinical or psychological deal-breakers. In fact, the importance of addressing them is as advantageous to clinical outcomes as never having committed them at all (Owen et al., 2014). Accordingly, it is vital for researchers and counselor trainers to identify factors leading to therapists' detection ability and better understand processes that promote or disengage therapists from processing microaggressions with their clients.

The empirical studies we described above stress the importance in training and honing therapeutic acumen to be able to (a) identify when a microaggression has occurred, (b) address and examine the effects of a microaggression soon after it has occurred, and (c) leverage a strong working alliance to successfully repair a microaggressive rupture. In the next section, we describe a framework for assisting therapists at all levels to address these common and pernicious interactions.

A New Way Forward: Therapists' Multicultural Orientation

Psychotherapy is an opportune context to address the impact of microaggressions—either as they emerge within the therapeutic relationship or as they are brought in as a topic of discussion by the client. Many therapists, however, are often at a loss for how to engage in conversations about microaggressions, as detailed earlier with our initial scenario, or they do not recognize when that arise. The MCO framework provides a useful heuristic and can be leveraged to meaningfully confront microaggressions. The MCO framework includes three pillars to help therapists' guide their way of being with clients (Owen, 2013).

The first pillar is *cultural humility*, which reflects the intrapersonal and interpersonal aspects foundational to the MCO framework. Culturally humble therapists balance two key aspects: (a) a keen awareness of their own cultural values and (b) the ability to stay present with others, while conveying respect, lack of superiority, and curiosity about the clients' cultural experiences (Davis, Worthington, & Hook, 2010; Hook et al., 2013). In multiple studies, clients' perceptions of their therapists' cultural humility has been positively related to therapy outcomes and negatively associated with microaggressions (Hook et al., 2013, 2016; Owen et al., 2014, 2016). That is, therapists who were rated as exhibiting more cultural humility were also less likely to commit microaggressions. Cultural humility and its associated characteristics, curiosity and openness, can be emphasized during therapeutic discussions about microaggressions so they can be more validating and exploratory in nature.

The second pillar of the MCO framework, *cultural opportunities*, describes the therapeutic markers wherein the clients' cultural beliefs, values, or other aspects of the client's cultural identity can be explored (Owen et al., 2016;

Owen, 2013). These in-session moments are frequent as clients often share their cultural values or when therapists initiate conversations that infuse cultural identities and values into the process of healing. Simply, cultural opportunities should be considered as natural unfolding processes over the course of therapy, rather than a set of guidelines to which all therapists must adhere. Empirically, Owen et al. (2016) found that clients reported better therapy outcomes when they felt their therapists were properly attending to their cultural values and identities. In the example of Lily, her sharing in session is an explicit cultural opportunity that the therapist missed. Recognizing and attending to this marker may have led to enhanced depth of connection and mutual understanding between the client and the therapist.

The third pillar of the MCO framework is *cultural comfort*. Cultural comfort is the therapist's emotional state while discussing culturally relevant conversations with clients. The hallmarks of cultural comfort include feeling at ease, open, calm, and relaxed. Although these conversations can be anxiety-provoking, it is key for therapists to be able to conjure up courage for and with their client. At the same time, cultural discomfort can be helpful for therapists to engage in reflexivity in order to confront potential assumptions and to seek consultation and supervision to properly address their reactions. Empirically, Owen et al. (2015) found therapists' cultural comfort partially accounted for racial/ethnic therapy outcome disparities within their caseloads. Processing the discomfort associated with recognizing one's potential for microaggressions and one's association with a majority group is relevant and should be done in order to prevent the avoidance that leads to these cultural ruptures going unaddressed. Accordingly, these three components of the MCO framework have initial empirical support and can be a useful way of conceptualizing and strategizing around interventions dedicated to addressing microaggressions in therapy.

Summary

Throughout this chapter we have highlighted three major aspects within the microaggression literature. Specifically, there are multiple ways in which researchers have attempted to understand its manifestation and its impact in daily interactions as well as in clinical settings. First, we found that microaggressions were associated with decreased functioning, accounting for 8.6% of the variance in psychology functioning. This figure parallels other common predictors of psychological functioning, such as social support. This evidence across over 20 studies supports the need for further examination of microaggression as a psychological construct. Second, within a therapy context, clients who experience microaggressions also report worse connection with their therapist as well as worse therapy outcomes. Our overview of the current body of research provides strong evidence for practitioners, policymakers, and investigators to consider microaggressions as more than just random occurrences that affect a select few, but instead to prioritize the proliferation of this topic as a significant public health issue. Given this evidence, it is time for the psychological community and the public to develop strategies for how to promote awareness and to facilitate the active confrontation of microaggressions. Ultimately, mental health professionals are particularly well positioned to increase awareness of and to confront the damaging relational, social, and individual impacts of microaggressions.

References

Anderson, R. E., Hussasin, S. B., Wilson, M. N., Shaw, D. S., Dishion, T. J., & Williams, J. L. (2015). Pathways to pain: Racial discrimination and relations between parental functioning and child psychosocial well-being. *Journal of Black Psychology, 41*(6), 491–512.

Balsam, K. F., Molina, Y., Beadnell, B., Simoni, J., & Walters, K. (2011). Measuring multiple minority stress: The LGBT People of Color Microaggressions Scale. *Cultural Diversity and Ethnic Minority Psychology, 17*(2), 163.

Blume, A. W., Lovato, L. V., Thyken, B. N., & Denny, N. (2012). The relationship of microaggressions with alcohol use and anxiety among ethnic minority students in a historically White institution. *Cultural Diversity and Ethnic Minority Psychology, 18*, 45.

Bowleg, L., English, D., del Rio-Gonzalez, A. M., Burkholder, G. J., Teti, M., & Tschann, J. M. (2016). Measuring the pros and cons of what it means to be a Black man: Development and validation of the Black Men's Experiences Scale (BMES). *Psychology of Men & Masculinity, 17*(2), 177.

Burrow, A. L., & Hill, P. L. (2012). Flying the unfriendly skies? The role of forgiveness and race in the experience of racial microaggressions. *The Journal of Social Psychology, 152*(5), 639–653.

Campbell, B., & Manning, J. (2014). Microaggression and moral cultures. *Comparative Sociology, 13*, 692–726.

Constantine, M. G. (2007). Racial microaggressions against African American clients in cross racial counseling relationships. *Journal of Counseling Psychology, 54*(1), 1–17.

Crawford, E. P. (2013). Stigma, racial microaggressions, and acculturation strategies as predictors of likelihood to seek counseling among Black college students. *Dissertation Abstracts International, 73*.

Davis, D. E., DeBlaere, C., Brubaker, K., Owen, J., Jordan, T. I., Hook, J. N., & Van Tongeren, D. R. (2016). Microaggressions and perceptions of cultural humility in counseling. *Journal of Counseling & Development, 94*(4), 483–493. doi:10.1002/jcad.12107.

Davis, D. E., Worthington Jr., E. L., & Hook, J. N. (2010). Humility: Review of measurement strategies and conceptualization as personality judgment. *The Journal of Positive Psychology*, 5(4), 243–252.

DeBlaere, C., Zelaya, D. G., Bowie, J., Chadwick, C. N., Davis, D. E., Hook, J. N. & Owen, J. (under review). *Multiple microaggressions and racial/ethnic minority women in counseling: A meditational model.*

Elliott, R., Bohart, A. C., Watson, J. C., & Greenberg, L. S. (2011). Empathy. *Psychotherapy*, 48(1), 43.

Haidt, J. (2017). The unwisest idea on campus: Commentary on Lilienfeld (2017). *Perspectives on Psychological Science*, 12(1), 176–177.

Hedges, L. V., & Olkin, I. (1984). Nonparametric estimators of effect size in meta-analysis. *Psychological Bulletin*, 96(3), 573–580.

Helms, J. E. (1995). An update of the Helm's White and POC racial identity models. In J. G. Ponterotto, J. M. Casas, L. A. Suzuki, & C. M. Alexander (Eds.), *Handbook of multicultural counseling* (pp. 181–198). Thousand Oaks, CA: Sage Publications.

Hook, J. N., Davis, D. E., Owen, J., Worthington Jr., E. L., & Utsey, S. O. (2013). Cultural humility: Measuring openness to culturally diverse clients. *Journal of Counseling Psychology*, 60(3), 353.

Hook, J. N., Farrell, J. E., Davis, D. E., DeBlaere, C., Van Tongeren, D. R., & Utsey, S. O. (2016). Cultural humility and racial microaggressions in counseling. *Journal of Counseling Psychology*, 63(3), 269–277.

Horvath, A. O., Del Re, A. C., Flückiger, C., & Symonds, D. (2011). Alliance in individual psychotherapy. *Psychotherapy*, 48(1), 9.

Hróbjartsson, A., & Gøtzsche, P. C. (2013). Is the placebo powerless? An analysis of clinical trials comparing placebo with no treatment. In F. G. Miller, L. Colloca, R. A. Crouch, & T. J. Kaptchuk (Eds.), *The placebo: A reader* (pp. 36–44). Baltimore, MD: Johns Hopkins University Press.

Hu, E., & Taylor, M. J. (2016). The relationship among ethnicity-related experiences, minority mental health, and ethnic awareness in social interactions. *Journal of Ethnic & Cultural Diversity in Social Work*, 25(3), 193–207.

Huynh, V. W. (2012). Ethnic microaggressions and the depressive and somatic symptoms of Latino and Asian American adolescents. *Journal of Youth and Adolescence*, 41, 831–846.

Ishiyama, F. I. (2006). *Anti-discrimination response training leader's manual (117 pages)*. Framingham, MA: Microtraining.

Kaufman, T. M. L., Baams, L., & Dubas, J. S. (2017). Microaggressions and depression symptoms in sexual minority youth: The roles of rumination and social support. *Psychology of Sexual Orientation and Gender Diversity*. doi:10.1037/sgd0000219.

Kim, P. Y. (2016). Religious support mediates the racial microaggressions mental health relation among Christian ethnic minority students. *Psychology of Religion and Spirituality*. doi:10.1037/re10000076.

Kim, P. Y., Kendall, D. L., & Cheon, H. S. (2016). Racial microaggressions, cultural mistrust, and mental health outcomes among Asian American College Students. *American Journal of Orthopsychiatry, 87*(6), 663.

Kuo, I. (2016, February 12). *Why do my co-workers keep confusing me with other people? Because I'm Asian.* Retrieved from: https://www.washingtonpost.com.

Lewis, J. A., & Neville, H. A. (2015). Construction and initial validation of the Gendered Racial Microaggressions Scale for Black Women. *Journal of Counseling Psychology, 62*(2), 289.

Lilienfeld, S. O. (2017). Microaggressions: Strong claims, inadequate evidence. *Perspectives on Psychological Science, 12*(1), 138–169.

Lorant, V., Deliège, D., Eaton, W., Robert, A., Philippot, P., & Ansseau, M. (2003). Socioeconomic inequalities in depression: A meta-analysis. *American Journal of Epidemiology, 157*(2), 98–112.

Mercer, S. H., Zeigler-Hill, V., Wallace, M., & Hayes, D. M. (2011). Development and initial validation of the inventory of Microaggressions Against Black Individuals. *Journal of Counseling Psychology, 58*, 457–469.

Morton, E. (2011). The incidence of racial microaggressions in the cross-racial counseling dyad. *Dissertation Abstracts International, 72*, 6416.

Nadal, K. L., Davidoff, K. C., Davis, L. S., & Wong, Y. (2014). Emotional, behavioral, and cognitive reactions to microaggressions: Transgender perspectives. *Psychology of Sexual Orientation and Gender Diversity, 1*(1), 72.

Nadal, K. L., Davidoff, K. C., Davis, L. S., Wong, Y., Marshall, D., & McKenzie, V. (2015). Intersectional identities and microaggressions: Influences of race, ethnicity, gender, sexuality, and religion. *Qualitative Psychology, 2*(2), 147–163.

Nadal, K. L., Griffin, K. E., Wong, Y., Hamit, S., & Rasmus, M. (2014). The impact of racial microaggressions on mental health: Counseling implications for clients of color. *Journal of Counseling and Development, 92*, 57–66.

Nadal, K. L., Wong, Y., Griffin, K. E., Davidoff, K., & Sriken, J. (2014). The adverse impact of racial microaggressions on college students' self-esteem. *Journal of College Student Development, 55*(4), 462–474.

Nadal, K. L., Wong, Y., Sriken, J., Griffin, K., & Fuji-Doe, W. (2014). Racial microaggressions and Asian Americans: An exploratory study on within-group differences and mental health. *Asian American Journal of Psychology, 6*(2), 136–144.

Nienhuis, J. B., Owen, J., Valentine, J. C., Black, S. W., Halford, T. C., Parazak, S. E., … Hilsenroth, M. (2016). Therapeutic alliance, empathy, and genuineness in individual adult psychotherapy: A meta-analytic review. *Psychotherapy Research*, 1–13.

O'Keefe, V. M., Wingate, L. R., Cole, A. B., Hollingsworth, D. W., & Tucker, R. P. (2015). Seemingly harmless racial communications are not so harmless: Racial microaggressions lead to suicidal ideation by way of depression symptoms. *Suicide and Life-Threatening Behavior, 45*(5), 567–576.

Owen, J. (2013). Early career perspectives on psychotherapy research and practice: Psychotherapist effects, multicultural orientation, and couple interventions. *Psychotherapy, 50*(4), 496.

Owen, J., Drinane, J., Tao, K., Adelson, J., Hook, J., Davis, D., & Foo Kune, N. (2015). Racial/ethnic disparities in client unilateral termination: The role of therapists' cultural comfort. *Psychotherapy Research, 27*(1), 102–111.

Owen, J., Imel, A., Adelson, J., & Rodolfa, E. (2012). "No show": Therapist racial/ethnic disparities in client unilateral termination. *Journal of Counseling Psychology, 59*, 314–320.

Owen, J., Imel, Z., Tao, K., Wampold, B., Smith, A., & Rodolfa, E. (2011). Cultural ruptures: Working alliance as a mediator between clients' perceptions of microaggressions and therapy outcomes. *Counselling and Psychotherapy Research, 11*, 204–212.

Owen, J., Tao, K., Drinane, J., DasGupta, D., Zhang, D., & Adelson, J. (2018). An experimental test of microaggression detection in psychotherapy: Therapist multicultural orientation. *Professional Psychology: Research and Practice, 49*(1), 9.

Owen, J., Tao, K. W., Drinane, J. M., Hook, J., Davis, D. E., & Kune, N. F. (2016). Client perceptions of therapists' multicultural orientation: Cultural (missed) opportunities and cultural humility. *Professional Psychology: Research and Practice, 47*(1), 30.

Owen, J., Tao, K. W., Imel, Z. E., Wampold, B. E., & Rodolfa, E. (2014). Addressing racial and ethnic microaggressions in therapy. *Professional Psychology: Research and Practice, 45*(4), 283–290.

Owen, J., Tao, K., & Rodolfa, E. (2010). Microaggressions against women in short-term psychotherapy: Initial evidence. *The Counseling Psychologist, 38*, 923–946.

Pierce, C., Carew, J., Pierce-Gonzalez, D., & Willis, D. (1978). An experiment in racism: TV commercials. In C. Pierce (Ed.), *Television and education* (pp. 62–88). Beverly Hills, CA: Sage.

Pieterse, A. L., Todd, N. R., Neville, H. A., & Carter, R. T. (2012). Perceived racism and mental health among Black American adults: A meta-analytic review. *Journal of Counseling Psychology, 59*(1), 1–9.

Prati, G., & Pietrantoni, L. (2010). An application of the social support deterioration deterrence model to rescue workers. *Journal of Community Psychology, 38*(7), 901–917.

Proulx, C. M., Helms, H. M., & Buehler, C. (2007). Marital quality and personal well-being: A meta-analysis. *Journal of Marriage and Family, 69*(3), 576–593.

Rebar, A. L., Stanton, R., Geard, D., Short, C., Duncan, M. J., & Vandelanotte, C. (2015). A meta-meta-analysis of the effect of physical activity on depression and anxiety in non clinical adult populations. *Health Psychology Review, 9*(3), 366–378.

Robinson, J. L., & Rubin, L. J. (2016). Homonegative microaggressions and posttraumatic stress symptoms. *Journal of Gay & Lesbian Mental Health, 20*(1), 57–69.

Robles, T. F., Slatcher, R. B., Trombello, J. M., & McGinn, M. M. (2014). Marital quality and health: A meta-analytic review. *Psychological Bulletin, 140*(1), 140.

Schoulte, J., Schultz, J., & Altmaier, E. (2011). Forgiveness in response to cultural microaggressions. *Counselling Psychology Quarterly, 24*(4), 291–300. doi:10.1080/09515070.2011.634266.

Shelton, K., & Delgado-Romero, E. A. (2011). Sexual orientation microaggressions: the experience of lesbian, gay, bisexual, and queer clients in psychotherapy. *Journal of Counseling Psychology, 58*(2), 210–221.

Smith, T. B., & Silva, L. (2011). Ethnic identity and personal well-being of people of color: A meta-analysis. *Counseling Psychology, 58*(1), 42–60. doi:10.1037/a0021528.

Smith, W. A., Hung, M., & Franklin, J. D. (2011). Racial battle fatigue and the miseducation of black men: Racial microaggressions, societal problems, and environmental stress. *The Journal of Negro Education, 80*(1), 63–82.

Sohi, K. K., & Singh, P. (2015). Collective action in response to microaggressions: Implications for social well-being. *Race and Social Problems, 7*, 269–280.

Sue, D. W. (2010). *Microaggressions in everyday life: Race, gender, and sexual orientation.* Hoboken, NJ: Wiley.

Sue, D. W. (2017). Microaggressions and "evidence" empirical or experiential reality? *Perspectives on Psychological Science, 12*(1), 170–172.

Sue, D. W., Capodilupo, C. M., Torino, G. C., Bucceri, J. M., Holder, A., Nadal, K. L., & Esquilin, M. (2007). Racial microaggressions in everyday life: Implications for clinical practice. *American Psychologist, 62*(4), 271.

Tao, K. W., Owen, J., & Drinane, J. M. (2017). Was that racist? An experimental study of microaggression ambiguity and emotional reactions for racial–ethnic minority and white individuals. *Race and Social Problems.* doi:10.1007/s12552-017-9210-4.

Torres, L., Driscoll, M. W., & Burrow, A. L. (2010). Racial microaggressions and psychological functioning among highly achieving African Americans: A mixed methods approach. *Journal of Social and Clinical Psychology, 29*(10), 1074–1099. doi:10.1521/jscp.2010.29.10.1074.

Torres, L., & Taknint, J. T. (2015). Ethnic microaggressions, traumatic stress symptoms, and Latino depression: A moderated mediational model. *Journal of Counseling Psychology, 62*(3), 393–401.

Tran, A. T., & Lee, R. M. (2014). You speak English well! Asian Americans' reactions to an exceptionalizing stereotype. *Journal of Counseling Psychology, 61*(3), 484–490. doi:10.1037/cou0000034.

Wampold, B. E., Minami, T., Tierney, S. C., Baskin, T. W., & Bhati, K. S. (2005). The placebo is powerful: Estimating placebo effects in medicine and psychotherapy from randomized clinical trials. *Journal of Clinical Psychology, 61*(7), 835–854. doi:10.1002/jclp.20129.

Wang, J., Leu, J., & Shoda, Y. (2011). When the seemingly innocuous "stings": Racial microaggressions and their emotional consequences. *Personality and Social Psychology Bulletin, 37*, 1666–1678.

Webb, C. A., DeRubeis, R. J., & Barber, J. P. (2010). Therapist adherence/competence and treatment outcome: A meta-analytic review. *Journal of Consulting and Clinical Psychology, 78*(2), 200.

Woodford, M. R., Paceley, M. S., Kulick, A., & Hong, J. S. (2015). The LGBQ social climate matters: Policies, protests, and placards and psychological well-being among LGBQ emerging adults. *Journal of Gay & Lesbian Social Services, 27*(1), 116–141.

6

Microaggressions: Considering the Framework of Psychological Trauma

Thema Bryant-Davis

> *We wear the mask that grins and lies*
> *It hides our checks and shades our eyes …*
>   Paul Laurence Dunbar

Systemically oppressed, marginalized, and targeted individuals often wear masks for survival and self-preservation. These masks, which can appear super strong, stoic, unbothered, humorous, driven, hard, or blank, do not reveal the reality of emotional wounds that covert maltreatment can create. Understanding and addressing the potentially traumatizing impact of accumulated microaggressions is a critical role for mental health professionals. Microaggressions occur within a context of historical traumas that underscore the potentially traumatizing impact of these acts. Historical traumas are the severe traumas enacted against cultural groups with intergenerational consequences, including war, enslavement, relocation, and genocide (Levin, 2009). These traumas may result in long-term psychological distress as a result of the violation, disenfranchisement, and dehumanization (Brave Heart, Chase, Elkins, & Altschul, 2011; Leary, 2005).

Defining Microaggressions

Microaggressions are intentional or unintentional brief acts of subtle or covert bias and discrimination aimed at persons from targeted groups, which may trigger memories of past individual or collective acts of oppression (Helms, Nicolas, & Green, 2012; Sue, 2010). These acts are insults that deny the experience, worth, and/or humanity of the marginalized group member (Sue et al.,

Microaggression Theory: Influence and Implications, First Edition. Edited by Gina C. Torino, David P. Rivera, Christina M. Capodilupo, Kevin L. Nadal, and Derald Wing Sue.
© 2019 John Wiley & Sons, Inc. Published 2019 by John Wiley & Sons, Inc.

2007). Social pressures have resulted in socializing individuals that overt acts of discrimination are not acceptable, but the decrease in these acts have resulted in more subversive acts of bias; the subtler acts while less recognized by majority group members can be quite distressing to target group members (Constantine, 2007; Sue et al., 2008).

Microaggressions have three classifications: microassaults that are overt acts of discrimination such as stereotypical comments or jokes; microinsults that are verbal or behavioral messages that convey a bias such as following a racial minority in a store, acknowledging a White student waiting in the school office and ignoring an African American student, or speaking in a patronizing tone to a person using a wheelchair; and microinvalidations which are verbal communications that deny, refute, or minimize a marginalized persons experiences such as telling a woman that a situation is being too sensitive for identifying sexism or telling an African American they are incorrect in their labeling of an experience as racism (Curry, 2010; Nadal, 2018; Sue, 2010).

Initially, the research in this area focused on the experience and impact of microaggressions against African Americans; however, later scholarship developed which explored the experiences of diverse ethnic minorities (Pierce, Carew, Pierce-Gonzalez, & Willis, 1978; Sue & Constantine, 2007). The research with African Americans found that racial microaggressions could result in diminished sense of self-worth, anger, self-blame, confusion, frustration, and depression (Sue et al., 2008). The categories of microaggressions against ethnic minorities include the myth of meritocracy (the assumption that ethnic minorities are impoverished because they do not work hard), assumption of criminality, ascription of second-class citizen status, ascription of lower or higher intelligence, assumption of pathological cultural values, and denial of racism (Sue et al., 2007). Nadal (2011) created the 45-item Racial and Ethnic Microaggressions Scale that includes six subscales, namely Second-Class Citizen and Assumptions of Criminality, Assumptions of Interiority, Workplace and School Microaggressions, Exoticization and Assumptions of Similarity, and Environmental Microaggressions. Currently, there is research that includes the experience of microaggressions against members of various marginalized groups including women and sexual minorities (Robinson & Rubin, 2016). The most common gender microaggression reported in a qualitative study was sexual objectification, which can foster psychological distress (Capodilupo et al., 2010). Microaggressions against sexual minorities [e.g., lesbian, gay, bisexual, transgender, and queer (LGBTQ) people] include heterosexist language, assumption of abnormality, oversexualization, assumed sinfulness, denial of heterosexism, homophobia, and endorsement of heteronormative culture (Nadal et al., 2011; Platt & Lenzen, 2013). One study found that LGBTQ participants who reported a higher number of homonegative microaggressions also reported a high level of posttraumatic stress disorder (PTSD) symptoms (Robinson & Rubin, 2016).

Microaggression Trauma

Traumatic events are extreme stressors that disrupt one's psychological well-being as well as one's life functioning (Foa, Keane, Friedman, & Cohen, 2008). Researchers exploring the potential trauma of microaggressions have looked beyond traditional notions of physical, single-event trauma to acknowledge emotional trauma (Bryant-Davis & Ocampo, 2006). They have examined microaggressions as causing emotional pain or threat of emotional pain and threatening one's life integrity or quality of life (housing and employment discrimination) (Bryant-Davis & Ocampo, 2005). Many microassaults such as being followed around a store based on an assumption of criminality or being stopped by the police due to racial or religious profiling may not appear to rise to the level of an extreme stressor. However, extreme stress may be triggered as a result of the cumulative nature of the event, for example, repeatedly and consistently being stopped at airport security or always having women of other races grab their purses or jump out of elevators when you enter.

Critique of the Trauma Lens for Understanding Racist Incidents

The developing of the trauma framework for exploring racist incidents has not been without critique. The primary criticism centers on concerns regarding the pathologizing of People of Color (i.e., non-White people), the level of severity of the incidents, and dismissal and denial of the prevalence and impact of racism. The first concern that is often raised by People of Color is that a trauma lens unfairly focuses on people who experience discrimination as the ones having a problem, that of being traumatized instead of placing the pathology on perpetrators. People of Color, understandably, are concerned with the tendency of psychologists to present them as dysfunctional, unhealthy, at-risk, and problematic, while ignoring their strengths and skills.

In response to this, it should be noted that while much of trauma literature focuses on the experience of the victims, there is also a body of work that attends to the pathology of the perpetrators. Additionally, PTSD is one of the rare diagnoses that points to a cause external to the person who causes trauma. In other words, being victimized is not inherently dysfunctional; however, an overwhelming experience may result in an array of negative symptoms. Being mindful of this critique, however, it is important for researchers to examine not only the consequences of racially motivated behaviors (e.g., police brutality, perpetrators of hate violence), but also the psychological antecedents and the historical biases of the perpetrators (e.g., police violence).

The second critique often comes from those who have experienced, or work with persons who have experienced, more traditionally recognized forms of trauma. Such clinicians and researchers note that being called a derogatory name or being followed by security in a store because one is assumed to be a criminal does not compare to the devastation of sexual assault, war, child abuse, or intimate partner abuse. While this critique is understandable, there are three responses to support the use of the trauma lens regarding severity (Bryant-Davis & Ocampo, 2005). The first is the need to be cautious about creating hierarchies of pain as some trauma survivors often feel dismissed if, for example, the molestation they experienced did not include penetration or the intimate partner abuse they experienced was psychological and not physical. The second response is that looking at a microaggression in isolation will not support the notion of trauma, but when one considers the cumulative effect of these incidents over time they have the potential of being traumatizing. Finally, when one focuses on police brutality in particular, the incidents are actually acts of physical aggression, and they are perpetrated by very powerful people. Physical assaults including those perpetrated by police officers against ethnic minorities fit the criteria for a traumatic event.

An additional critique of the trauma framework being applied to racist incidence can be summarized as the argument of the racism-deniers, those persons who believe racism is no longer an issue and that any incidents of racism are minimal and often falsely reported or exaggerations by overly sensitive people. Persons who propose this argument often engage in the traditional victim-blaming that is often seen in other forms of interpersonal trauma. Victim-blaming is based in the social psychology concept of the belief in a just world (Niemi, 2018). People who believe in a meritocracy or just world conclude that good things happen to good people and if something bad happened to you then you must have caused it. Clinicians in this category may also avoid discussing racism and acts of discrimination in session, dismissing them as irrelevant to the client's well-being (Levin, 2006). In cases of police brutality, persons in support of this argument would respond by saying that the so-called victim is really a "thug" and a "criminal" who would not have been hurt if he/she followed the law, or that there are other extenuating circumstances that influenced the situation. Racism deniers who blame the victim believe all acts of aggression against racial and ethnic minorities are caused by criminal behavior and are therefore justifiable and not traumatic.

A final critique is the need to discuss these issues with caution as empirical studies lag behind theoretical developments. While children of various racial and ethnic backgrounds are vulnerable to psychological distress in the aftermath of trauma, there needs to be continued research to establish the ways in which racially and ethnically motivated traumas play a unique role in effecting development (Sigal & Weinfeld, 1989). One primary challenge to addressing this critique is that membership in a culturally targeted group increases one's risk to direct trauma so the historical trauma and direct trauma often coexist.

While there is a growing body of research that examines racist incidents from a traumatology lens, the studies within this framework that have focused on police brutality are minimal. Much of the scholarship is theoretical with need

for further investigative study. Additionally, much of the research on police brutality have ignored intersectional issues such as the potentially traumatizing
consequences for Women of Color, LGBTQ Persons of Color, People of Color
of diverse socioeconomic status (SES) backgrounds, and ethnic minorities with
disabilities. Additionally, as with the traditional trauma field, much more attention has been given to the negative effects and coping process of victims than on
the antecedents and intervention development for perpetrators and potential
perpetrators.

Psychoanalytic theory proposes that there are two ways of understanding
trauma—shock trauma and strain trauma. Psychologists should examine both
of these from the perspective of their meaning for the individual and not an
external determination of whether the event qualifies as traumatic (Fleischer,
2017). While shock trauma is an acute, horrific, overwhelming event, strain
trauma is a low-level sustained trauma that over time creates negative psychological consequences (Akhtar, 2009). Along with the cumulative factor, there is
the memory-eliciting factor. Being stopped by the police may trigger extreme
stress as a result of the invoking of memories of prior times the individual has
been racially or religiously profiled or invoking memories of cases known to the
individual of persons from their same racial or religious background who have
been beaten, killed, or unjustly detained by police officers. The convergence
of historical trauma with contemporary trauma in the form of microaggressions is explored in the lives of American Indians. Evans-Campbell (2008) notes
that microaggressions are traumas that undermine American Indians' individual and collective identities as they interact with historical large-scale, physical
traumas enacted upon American Indian communities.

The cumulative impact of microaggressions and the negative memories
elicited by microaggressions has shown to have the potential to result in posttrauma symptoms, namely intrusive thoughts, avoidance, and hypervigilance
(Carter, 2007; Carter, Forsyth, Mazzula, & Williams, 2005). Microaggressions
may also produce posttrauma symptoms such as hopelessness, shame, anger,
fear, or PTSD depending on a number of variables such as number of prior
microaggressions, nature of past event memory elicited by the current event,
level of threat, and length of exposure (Helms et al., 2012). Additional trauma-
related symptoms may include dissociation and self-harm (Erchull, Liss, &
Lichiello, 2013). Microaggressions can also have an additive trauma effect as
was observed with Asian veterans who experienced racism and had higher rates
of PTSD; the experiences of racial harassment by other U.S. military persons
and having to kill persons who looked like them increased the traumatic nature
of their combat exposure (Loo et al., 2001). While PTSD symptoms such as
nightmares have been observed in survivors of microaggression trauma, Whitbeck, Adams, Hoyt, and Chen (2004) argue that PTSD does not capture the
full impact of the trauma because of its focus on the individual, contemporary experience to the neglect of the historical, collective (family, community,

and societal) effect. One-fifth of American Indian elders, for example, reported that they think about the historical traumas, such as the theft of their land, at least once a day (Evans-Campbell, 2008). American Indians report experiences of distress at the crossroads of historical trauma with contemporary, commonplace microaggressions such as being asked if they are a real Indian, being told they do not look Indian, witnessing the appropriation of their sacred rituals and objects, and employers asking them to cut their hair (Walters, 2003). Targeted group members such as American Indians, African Americans, Latinos, women, religious minorities, and sexual minorities have experienced institutionalized, additive traumas that become multiplicative when we consider intersectional identities in which one may be a member of multiple targeted groups (Bryant-Davis & Ocampo, 2005; Evans-Campbell, 2008; Lewis & Neville, 2015; Nadal, 2018; Nadal et al., 2015; Sue et al., 2007).

Researchers who examined the trauma of microaggressions have used an array of terms including insidious trauma, cultural trauma, racist incident trauma, racism, ethnoviolence, intergenerational trauma, and societal trauma, among others (Bryant-Davis & Ocampo, 2005; Carter, 2007; Helms et al., 2012; Root, 1992). Interpersonal traumatic events are usually beyond the target's control, hostile, sudden, unexpected, and stress-inducing. Acts of discrimination may fit these criteria with the added component of connecting to prior microaggressions, hate crimes, or historical acts such as genocide, slavery, internment, medical experimentation, mass deportation, and mass incarceration.

Psychologists have theorized the traumatic impact of these acts to extend beyond PTSD and to include such outcomes as difficulty concentrating, difficulty remembering, distrust, somatic complaints, confusion, shame, guilt, anger, and self-blame (Bryant-Davis & Ocampo, 2005; Carlson, 1997). Bryant-Davis and Ocampo (2005), as well as Carter (2007), proposed models of racist-incident-based trauma, which explores the negative mental health consequences of discrimination that targets marginalized groups with the aims of disempowerment and dehumanization through psychological, social, and financial access denial. Race-based traumatic stress can be defined as follows: (a) psychological wounds that are motivated by the ideology of superiority, hate, and/or fear of a person or group of people as a result of their race; (b) a racially driven stressor that surpasses the target's normative coping resource; (c) a racially motivated, interpersonal severe stressor that causes bodily harm or threatens one's life integrity including safety and survival resources such as housing or employment; or (d) a severe interpersonal or institutional stressor motivated by racism that evokes from the target a sense of fear, dread, helplessness, or horror (Bryant-Davis & Ocampo, 2005; Carter, 2007; Loo et al., 2001).

Bryant-Davis and Ocampo (2005) proposed that racist incident-based trauma may result in shock, fear, anger, shame, self-blame, distrust, confusion, numbness, and symptoms of PTSD. Survivors may respond with avoidance or proactive, life-enhancing solutions (Carter, 2007). As opposed to veterans who attempt to heal from PTSD after exiting the battlefield, survivors of microaggressions often continue to face daily verbal, behavioral, and environmental indignities and insults (Sue et al., 2007).

In a study examining ethnic microaggressions against Latinos, the microaggressions predicted posttrauma symptoms, namely avoidance, re-experiencing, and hyper-arousal; these trauma symptoms then predicted depression. The researchers go beyond the documentation of trauma symptoms to the groundbreaking investigation of moderators and mediators (Torres & Taknint, 2015). Additionally, ethnic identity and self-efficacy mediated the relationship between ethnic microaggressions and posttrauma symptoms such that those with low ethnic identity and those with low self-efficacy endorsed higher trauma symptoms (Torres & Taknint, 2015). The gender microaggression of sexual objectification can be seen as a hostile invalidation, which has consequences often related to trauma such as self-objectification and self-harm (Erchull et al., 2013). Essentially, trauma symptoms resulting from experiences of microaggressions may contribute to poor mental health outcomes.

Trauma from microaggressions can also manifest uniquely based on intersections of identity such as gender and race (Vasquez, 1994). Additionally, Muslims and Sikhs may experience trauma-inducing microaggressions based on the intersection of their race, religion, and country of origin (Abu-Ras & Suarez, 2009; Ahluwalia, 2011). Whether sexualized street harassment or profiling at airports, aggressors may respond differently based on the intersectional identity of the target.

Contemporary Relevance of Microaggression Trauma

After the presidential election of 2016, there has been a rise in hate crimes and discrimination toward women, racial minorities, immigrants, sexual minorities, and religious minorities (Southern Poverty Law Center, 2017). Whether sexism in the presidential campaign, hostility toward Black Lives Matter protestors or undocumented immigrants, or verbal harassment of Muslims after the election, these microaggressions have elicited distress in both the primary targets and those who experience it vicariously through family and friends or the media (Nadal, 2018). While there are multiple potentially traumatizing microaggressions that have been noted in media and scholarly outlets alike, it is important to also acknowledge the mobilization that has occurred to counter these traumas. There have been multiple large-scale, awareness-raising marches led by multiple groups including women, immigrants, and scientists. Moreover, there has been much engagement around justice and oppression issues in social media and political participation, as well as more theoretical and empirical psychological literature on the trauma of oppression. A growing number of psychology theorists, researchers, educators, organizational leaders, and clinicians have been active in examining the dynamics, effects, and possible responses to microaggression trauma.

Clinical Implications

Along with researching the motivation and effects of microaggressions, investigators have examined the protective factors and coping strategies. Two factors that have buffered the impact of microaggressions are advocacy and allies (Ahluwalia, 2011). Another factor, which may psychologically protect microaggression trauma survivors, is culturally congruent counseling (Bryant-Davis & Ocampo, 2005). Conversely, insensitive counseling can result in a secondary trauma that invalidates or even blames the victim. In the aftermath of subtle discrimination that is often combined with the denial of the aggressor, the survivor may feel drained, confused, angry, and in need of a trusted person who can validate their experiences (Fleischer, 2017). Acknowledgment and training on assessing and treating microaggression traumas is critical as therapists who do not identify, assess, interpret, or appropriately treat these psychological injuries are likely to misdiagnosis, pathologize, or minimize a major source of distress (Bryant-Davis & Ocampo, 2005; Nadal, 2018).

Treatment should begin with a thorough assessment, which includes obtaining a full trauma history including microaggression trauma. Tools such as the Race-Based Traumatic Stress Symptoms Scale can be used to determine if the microaggression was painful and unexpected and the resulting symptoms of distress if any that the client is experiencing (Carter & Saint-Barket, 2015). These measures can be readministered over time to see the impact of any of the therapeutic interventions. Below are three approaches to treating survivors of microaggression trauma, one based on ego psychology, one based on a spiritual–cultural framework, and one based on a cultural trauma-focused approached (Fleischer, 2017; Bryant-Davis & Ocampo, 2005).

Fleischer (2017) proposes an ego psychology approach to treating survivors of microaggression trauma due to the acknowledgment of internal and external factors and the use of a bio-psycho-social–spiritual framework. He stresses the importance of reality testing and observing ego, as well as determining if the perspective of one's community is balanced. Fleischer (2017) argues that an inability to see microaggressions where they exist as well as a tendency to see them where they do not exist can both be very dangerous and harmful. Fleischer (2017) contends that certain persons, particularly those with thought disorder or trauma histories, have difficulty accurately perceiving reality. In his model, the counselor should affirm the client's experience but with a supportive tone also ask questions to determine if the person is certain a microaggression has occurred and to determine if the persons they trust are able to provide balanced feedback about the possibility that the event may not have been a microaggression. A case study is provided of an African American male student who according to the author was misperceiving microaggressions. It is disturbing that an article on macroaggressions only includes one case study that focuses on an African American whose perceived microaggressions were not real. While reality testing and observing ego are important psychological factors, it is concerning that the author presents them as the cornerstone for how to care for someone who presents with microaggression trauma. Trauma-focused therapists should never start from a place of disbelief and investigating the accuracy of a client's presenting problem as the foundation of trauma treatment. Certainly, there is room for reality testing and observing ego in treatment, but the care of a trauma survivor has additional critical components.

A second approach developed by Curry (2010) focuses on adopting principles from pastoral counseling that may be integrated with other evidence-based forms of psychotherapy such as cognitive-behavioral therapy (CBT). Curry notes that African Americans, in particular, endorse high rates of religiosity and have found religion and spirituality helpful protective factors in preserving their emotional well-being. Curry (2010) argues that Eurocentric approaches to counseling such as CBT set the therapy goals for the client instead of empowering them to set goals for themselves. (In light of this critique, it is noteworthy that the practice standard of CBT therapy is the adoption of a goal-setting process that is collaborative effort and centers the client's needs and aspirations.) The spiritual themes that therapists working with spiritually oriented survivors of microaggressions include existential meaning making, moral development, affirmation of racial, ethnic, and spiritual values and identity, coping, life adjustment, and forgiveness. Strategies that are recommended include use of spiritually themed music, spiritually focused bibliotherapy, spiritual proverbs and poems, storytelling, narrative therapy, and possibly church attendance for those who are interested (Curry, 2010). This framework of seeing microaggression trauma as having spiritual consequences and needing a holistic psychosocial–spiritual response is noteworthy and culturally congruent for religious and spiritually oriented clients, but Curry (2010) neglects one important component. An important part of African American faith tradition is protest. From resistance to slavery to the civil rights movement, African American faith leaders were at the forefront of the resistance to oppression. However, for the first time in African American history, faith communities are not undergirding the current anti-oppression movement, the Black Lives Matter Movement. In essence, one of the primary contemporary critiques of the Black Church and Christian religion is the shift away from collective mobilization to individual prosperity. Unfortunately, Curry's (2010) model highlights forgiveness and adjustment on the part of the survivor without any challenge to, or resistance to, oppression. While spiritually integrated psychotherapy is likely a culturally congruent approach to adopt with many marginalized community members, it is important that the aim broaden beyond forgiveness and coping to liberation and empowerment.

Bryant-Davis and Ocampo (2005) proposed earlier recommendations for trauma-focused treatment with survivors of racist-incident microaggressions, which can be applied to other microaggressions as well. The model accounts for internal and external factors and adopts a ethnopolitical perspective that starts from an acknowledgment of oppression as opposed to starting from a place of reality testing (Comas-Díaz, 2000). The counselor actively embraces an anti-oppression stance based in the awareness that oppression is unhealthy for both the survivor and the aggressor (Bryant-Davis & Ocampo, 2006). Theme exploration and resolution are recommended whether the client meets the criteria for PTSD or not as other researchers have noted the survivor's distress may manifest in a number of diverse ways. The recommended themes are acknowledgment that the microaggression has occurred, which requires shattering self-blame; disclosure and sharing with trusted sources of social support; taking active steps to preserve their safety and self-care; grieve and mourn the losses; shame, self-blame, and internalized oppression; healthy versus unhealthy expressions of anger; effective coping strategies; and resistance strategies such as activism and advocacy. Similarly, and more recently, Comas-Díaz (2016) proposes a model for the treatment of racial trauma that includes assessment, processing of traumatic events, promotion of psychological decolonization, and finally engagement in social action. Comas-Díaz (2016) adds the integral component of psychological decolonization, which empowers the client to move from internal healing to external engagement. Nadal, Griffin, Wong, Hamit, and Rasmus (2014) add to the idea of activism or social action by describing survivors of microaggression trauma as having to confront three questions: did the microaggression occur; should the client respond; and how should they respond. Nadal et al. (2014) notes that responding and not responding can have challenging effects that may be helpful to explore with the counselor as the client makes the decision that is best for them.

The need to explore trauma-focused themes for treatment of microaggression traumas is quite evident. The following provide some presenting problems for three clients who over the course of treatment disclosed experiencing microaggressions traumas. Consider ways you would introduce and explore the recommended themes in the care of these survivors:

1. Sekou is a 36-year-old Christian, heterosexual West African immigrant who comes from a financially successful family of business owners who have always worked for themselves. Sekou came to therapy to heal from a dating relationship that ended poorly. Sekou has experienced microaggressions at work by his White supervisor and coworkers. These experiences have been very distressing as he has never experienced them before. Sekou shares that when he shared his distress with some African Americans at the job, they

explained that these insults and invalidations were just a part of life in the United States. Sekou presents as confused, sad, and shocked as he tries to figure out what his options are professionally, socially, and emotionally.

2. Mata is a 28-year-old, heterosexual, low-income, Indian American, single, Muslim woman who presents after a surge of hate crimes against Muslim women in her community following the 2016 presidential election. She reports about women having verbal insults yelled at them by passing cars, men pulling on their hijab, and several women who were kidnapped by groups of White men, raped, and then dropped back off onto the street. Mata reports living in constant fear and grief about what has happened to members of her community and the fear that any microaggression could grow into a full-scale assault. She also explores the socioreligious pressure to not complain but to forgive and remain silent.

3. Maria is a 32-year-old, Catholic, heterosexual, single, middle-income Latina. She was molested as a toddler and raped during college. She presents with social anxiety and has a lot of fear related to gender microaggressions, specifically men making sexual comments to her, making sexual gestures toward her, and looking at her "like she is a piece of meat." While she would like to get married one day, she fears it will not happen because she has begun to wear clothes that are too big, no make-up, and not do her hair in an attempt to stop the microaggressions.

Each of these clients has experienced microaggression traumas that have occurred many times. These incidents were shocking and painful, resulting in psychological distress that lasted well beyond the moment of the act. Themes of acknowledgment, disclosure, mourning, shame, anger, safety and self-care, coping, and eventually resistance of various forms were explored (Bryant-Davis, 2007). As Comas-Díaz (2000) noted, a decolonized psychology was needed for the clients to feel empowered to resist these varied acts of oppression through voice, community, and agency. As a therapist, I adopt an anti-oppression stance that centers culturally congruent approaches to trauma-focused treatment.

Policy

Given the plethora of research articles that psychologists have published on the deleterious effects of microaggressions, a strong case stands for policies that support the redress of these potentially traumatizing actions. Education and training of future psychologists need to incorporate information on microaggression trauma in their curriculum. Professors can cover the material in a number of courses including but not limited to trauma psychology, multicultural psychology, social psychology, and psychology of women. Additionally, mental health service agencies need policies on assessment of microaggression trauma and continuing education on the topic as well. Any evaluation of counselors should include the client's experience of the therapist response to any disclosures of discrimination or bias. Finally, researchers need to begin routinely to include in their publications, policy implications beyond the therapeutic office. Microaggression trauma research has implications for school policies, organizational policies, criminal justice policies, and healthcare policies, among others.

Future Directions

Researchers and clinicians need to continue to expand the view of microaggression trauma to reach beyond PTSD. While those symptoms are present for some, there are additional symptoms of distress that therapists may overlook by narrowly focusing on PTSD. Case studies and qualitative research can create space for more exploration in the ways microaggression trauma effects individuals and communities. Intersectional experiences of microaggression trauma also need continued acknowledgment and investigation. The unique ways in which one's multiple identities are responded to in society and the culturally contextualized ways in which one makes meaning and responds to the traumas have intracultural variation that should be recognized. While the traditional trauma literature has a full body of research on posttraumatic growth and thriving, there is a need for the investigation of these concepts for survivors of microaggression trauma. What does growth in the face of ongoing oppression look like and how can mental health professionals foster and protect that growth? Finally, researchers need to determine the contributing factors that motivate perpetrators of microaggression traumas and effective ways to prevent them.

Conclusion

Microaggressions can rise to the level of a psychological trauma based on either the cumulative effect of multiple acts over time or single events that trigger memories of prior personal or collective traumatic acts of oppression. The effects of microaggression trauma can be severe including such symptoms as anger, avoidance, anxiety, hypervigilance, intrusive thoughts, emotional dysregulation, decreased self-esteem, depression, fear, confusion, and distrust. Microaggressions occur across diverse cultural groups and can vary based on intersectional identity markers such as gender, nativity, race, religion, and sexual orientation. While there have been a few practitioners who have made recommendations for interventions to address microaggression trauma, the author rejects the centering of reality testing or forgiveness without resistance, agency, or empowerment. Practitioners should promote supportive belief, an anti-oppression stance, exploration of traumatic material and related psychological themes, cultivation of liberation, and engagement in social justice response of the client's choosing through the potential use of the client's voice, artistry, power, spirituality, and community resources (Bryant-Davis & Ocampo, 2006; Comas-Díaz, 2000, 2016). By creating a safe space where survivors of microaggression trauma can unmask, psychologists can facilitate healing and empowerment.

References

Abu-Ras, W. M., & Suarez, Z. E. (2009). Muslim men and women's perception of discrimination, hate crimes, and PTSD symptoms post 9/11. *Traumatology, 15*(3), 48–63. doi:10.1177/1534765609342281.

Ahluwalia, M. (2011). Holding my breath: The experience of being Sikh after 9/11. *Traumatology, 17*(3), 41–46.

Akhtar, S. (2009). *Comprehensive dictionary of psychoanalysis.* London, United Kingdom: Karnac.

Brave Heart, M. Y. H., Chase, J., Elkins, J., & Altschul, D. B. (2011). Historical trauma among indigenous peoples of the Americas: Concepts, research, and clinical considerations. *Journal of Psychoactive Drugs, 43*(4), 282–290.

Bryant-Davis, T. (2007). Healing requires recognition: The case for race-based traumatic stress. *The Counseling Psychologist, 35*(1), 135–143. doi:10.1177/0011000006295152.

Bryant-Davis, T., & Ocampo, C. (2005). The trauma of racism: Implications for counseling, research, and education. *The Counseling Psychologist, 33*(4), 574–578.

Bryant-Davis, T., & Ocampo, C. (2006). A therapeutic approach to the treatment of racist-incident-based trauma. *Journal of Emotional Abuse, 6*(4), 1–22. doi:10.1300/J135v06n04_01.

Carlson, E. B. (1997). *Trauma assessments: A clinician's guide.* New York, NY: Guilford.

Capodilupo, C. M., Nadal, K. L., Corman, L., Hamit, S., Lyons, O., & Weinberg, A. (2010). The manifestation of gender microaggressions. In D. W. Sue (Ed.), *Microaggressions and marginality: Manifestation, dynamics, and impact* (pp. 193–216). New York, NY: Wiley.

Carter, R. T. (2007). Racism and psychological and emotional injury: Recognizing and assessing race-based traumatic stress. *Counseling Psychologist, 35,* 13–105.

Carter, R. T., Forsyth, J. M., Mazzula, S. L., & Williams, B. (2005). Racial discrimination and race-based traumatic stress: An exploratory investigation. In

R. T. Carter (Ed.), *Handbook of racial–cultural psychology and counseling: Training and practice* (Vol. 2, pp. 447–476). Hoboken, NJ: Wiley.

Carter, R. T., & Saint-Barket, S. M. (2015). Assessment of the impact of racial discrimination and racism: How to use the race-based traumatic stress symptom scale in practice. *Traumatology, 21*(1), 32–39. doi:10.1037/trm0000018.

Comas-Díaz, L. (2000). An ethnopolitical approach to working with people of color. *American Psychologist, 55*(11), 1319–1325. doi:10.1037/0003-066X.55 .11.1319.

Comas-Díaz, L. (2016). Racial trauma recovery: A race-informed therapeutic approach to racial wounds. In A. N. Alvarez, C. H. Liang, H. A. Neville, A. N. Alvarez, C. H. Liang, & H. A. Neville (Eds.), *The cost of racism for people of color: Contextualizing experiences of discrimination* (pp. 249–272). Washington, DC: American Psychological Association. doi:10.1037/14852-012.

Constantine, M. G. (2007). Racial microaggressions against African American clients in a cross racial counseling relationship. *Journal of Counseling Psychology, 54*, 1–16.

Curry, J. R. (2010). Addressing the spiritual needs of African American students: Implications for school counselors. *Journal of Negro Education, 79*(3), 405–415.

Erchull, M. J., Liss, M., & Lichiello, S. (2013). Extending the negative consequences of media internalization and self-objectification to dissociation and self-harm. *Sex Roles, 69*(11–12), 583–593.

Evans-Campbell, T. (2008). Historical trauma in American Indian/native Alaska communities. *Journal of Interpersonal Violence, 23*(3), 316–338.

Fleischer, L. M. (2017). Ego psychological contributions to understanding microaggressions in clinical social work practice. *Psychoanalytic Social Work, 24*(1), 1–17. doi:10.1080/15228878.2016.1226905.

Foa, E. B., Keane, T. M., Friedman, M. J., & Cohen, J. A. (Eds.) (2008). *Effective treatments for PTSD: Practice guidelines from the International Society for Traumatic Stress Studies.* New York, NY: Guilford Press.

Helms, J. E., Nicolas, G., & Green, C. E. (2012). Racism and ethnoviolence as trauma: Enhancing professional and research training. *Traumatology, 18*(1), 65–74.

Leary, J. G. (2005). *Post traumatic slave syndrome: America's legacy of enduring injury and healing.* Milwaukee, OR: Uptone Press.

Levin, A. (2006). Battling depression among Blacks means confronting racism's legacy. *Psychiatric News, 41*(24), 4–17.

Levin, A. (2009). How much does historical trauma add to Indians' health problems? *Psychiatric News, 44*(16), 9–11.

Lewis, J. A., & Neville, H. A. (2015). Construction and initial validation of the gendered racial microaggressions scale for Black women. *Journal of Counseling Psychology, 62*, 289–302.

Loo, C. M., Fairbank, J. A., Scurfield, R. M., Ruch, L. O., King, D. W., Adams, L. J., & Chemtob, C. M. (2001). Measuring exposure to racism: Development and validation of a Race-Related Stressor Scale (RRSS) for Asian American Vietnam veterans. *Psychological Assessment, 13*, 503–520.

Nadal, K. L. (2011). The Racial and Ethnic Microaggressions Scale (REMS): Construction, reliability, and validity. *Journal of Counseling Psychology, 58*, 470–480.

Nadal, K. (2018). *Microaggressions and traumatic stress: Theory, research, and clinical treatment.* Washington, DC: American Psychological Association.

Nadal, K. L., Davidoff, K. C., Davis, L. S., Wong, Y., Marshall, D., & McKenzie, V. (2015). A qualitative approach to intersectional microaggressions: Understanding influences of race, ethnicity, gender, sexuality, and religion. *Qualitative Psychology, 2*, 147–163. doi:10.1037/qup0000026.

Nadal, K. L., Griffin, K. E., Wong, Y., Hamit, S., & Rasmus, M. (2014). The impact of racial microaggressions on mental health: Counseling implications for clients of color. *Journal of Counseling & Development, 92*, 57–66. doi:10.1002/j.1556-6676.2014.00130.x.

Nadal, K. L., Issa, M., Leon, J., Meterko, V., Wideman, M., & Wong, Y. (2011). Sexual orientation microaggressions: "Death by a thousand cuts" for lesbian, gay, and bisexual youth. *Journal of LGBT Youth, 8*, 1–26.

Niemi, L. (2018). Victim blaming. In K. L. Nadal (Ed.), *The Sage encyclopedia of psychology and gender.* Thousand Oaks, CA: Sage.

Pierce, C., Carew, J., Pierce-Gonzalez, D., & Willis, D. (1978). An experiment in racism: TV commercials. In C. Pierce (Ed.), *Television and education* (pp. 62–88). Beverly Hills, CA: Sage.

Platt, L. F., & Lenzen, A. L. (2013). Sexual orientation microaggressions and the experience of sexual minorities. *Journal of Homosexuality, 60*, 1011–1034.

Robinson, J. L., & Rubin, L. J. (2016). Homonegative microaggressions and posttraumatic stress symptoms. *Journal of Gay & Lesbian Mental Health, 20*, 57–69. doi:10.1080/19359705.2015.1066729.

Root, M. P. (1992). Reconstructing the impact of trauma on personality. In L. S. Brown & M. Ballou (Eds.), *Personality and psychopathology: Feminist reappraisals* (pp. 229–265). New York, NY: Guilford Press.

Sigal, J. J., & Weinfeld, M. (1989). *Trauma and rebirth: Intergenerational effects of the Holocaust.* New York, NY, England: Praeger Publishers.

Southern Poverty Law Center. (2017). *Update: 1,094 Bias-Related Incidents in the Month following the Election.* Retrieved from https://www.splcenter.org/hatewatch/2016/12/16/update-1094-bias-related-incidents-month-following-election.

Sue, D. W. (2010). *Microaggressions in everyday life: Race, gender, and sexual orientation.* Hoboken, NJ: Wiley.

Sue, D. W., Capodilupo, C. M., Torino, G. C., Bucceri, J. M., Holder, A. M. B., Nadal, K. L., & Esquilin, M. (2007). Racial microaggressions in everyday life:

Implications for clinical practice. *American Psychologist, 62*, 271–286. doi:10.1037/0003-066X.62.4.271.

Sue, D. W., & Constantine, M. G. (2007). Racial microaggressions as instigators of difficult dialogues on race: Implications for student affairs educators and students. *College Student Affairs Journal, 26*, 136–143.

Sue, D. W., Nadal, K. L., Capodilupo, C. M., Lin, A. I., Torino, G. C., & Rivera, D. P. (2008). Racial microaggressions against Black Americans: Implications for counseling. *Journal of Counseling & Development, 86*, 259–260.

Torres, L., & Taknint, J. T. (2015). Ethnic microaggressions, traumatic stress symptoms, and Latino depression: A moderated mediational model. *Journal of Counseling Psychology, 62*, 393–401. doi:10.1037/cou0000077.

Vasquez, M. J. T. (1994). Latinas. In L. Comas-Díaz & B. Greene (Eds.), *Women of color: Integrating ethnic and gender identities in psychotherapy* (pp. 114–138). New York, NY: Guilford Press.

Walters, K. (2003). *Microaggressions in urban American Indian populations.* Presentation to the Centers for Disease Control, Atlanta, GA.

Whitbeck, L., Adams, G., Hoyt, D., & Chen, X. (2004). Conceptualizing and measuring historical trauma among American Indian people. *American Journal of Community Psychology, 33*, 119–130.

7

Factors Contributing to Microaggressions, Racial Battle Fatigue, Stereotype Threat, and Imposter Phenomenon for Nonhegemonic Students: Implications for Urban Education

Jennifer L. Martin

This chapter will review the phenomena of microaggressions, racial battle fatigue (RBF), stereotype threat, and imposter phenomenon, all of which can be caused by a lack of knowledge, sensitivity, empathy, and respect for identity characteristics/social identities deviating from the dominant norm such as race, class, gender, sexuality, language, citizenship status, disability status, religious affiliation, and so forth. These phenomena often play out in schools—often negatively impacting academic success. Culturally responsive teachers value and respect the identities of all of their students and work to dismantle systems of oppression that cause them harm: situational and institutional (Frattura & Capper, 2007). Some teachers, ill-prepared to work with students different from them, do real harm to many of their students by perpetrating microaggressions, which can lead to the related phenomena of racial (and other forms of) battle fatigue, stereotype threat, and imposter phenomenon—causing a reduction in academic success for nonhegemonic students.

Introduction and Review of Key Terms

Microaggressions are subtle slights, intentional or not, including statements, actions, minimizations, and invalidations, serving to trivialize one's gendered, racialized, or other identity-based experiences by those who do not share those same experiences, thus denying their significance (Nadal, 2010; Sue, 2017; Sue, Capodilupo, & Holder, 2008; Sue, Capodilupo, Nadal, & Torino, 2008). According to Smith, Allen, and Danley (2007): "The impact of racial microaggressions

Microaggression Theory: Influence and Implications, First Edition. Edited by Gina C. Torino, David P. Rivera, Christina M. Capodilupo, Kevin L. Nadal, and Derald Wing Sue.
© 2019 John Wiley & Sons, Inc. Published 2019 by John Wiley & Sons, Inc.

on individual Black targets become communicable as the psychological and emotional pain of the incidents is passed on to family, friends, and the larger social group and across generations" (p. 554). Racialized microaggressions can cause psychological stress, physiological stress, and behavioral stress (Franklin, Smith, & Hung, 2014). Within educational settings, microaggressions can include "(a) nonverbal forms, (b) false assumptions based on stereotypes, (c) overt racial remarks, and (d) low teacher expectations" (Franklin et al., 2014, p. 308). Ong, Burrow, Fuller-Rowell, Ja, and Sue (2013) found that the "hidden nature" of microaggressions often make them "invisible" to perpetrators (p. 197).

Sue, Bucceri, Nadal, and Torino (2007) classified microaggressions into three areas: microassaults, microinsults, and microinvalidations. Microassaults are explicit identity-based derogations, verbal or nonverbal, intended to harm the target, such as racial epithets. Microinsults convey insensitivity toward one's heritage or identity; for example, microinsults can include the "model minority" myth experienced by many Asian Americans, indicating that they experience little racism, despite evidence to the contrary (Ong et al., 2013). Microinvalidations involve the denial of one's experiences with racism (and other -isms), thus effectively dismissing or invalidating them (Sue, Capodilupo, Nadal, et al., 2008). These denials are usually perpetrated by members of the dominant culture, or hegemonic persons. According to Sue (2017), "People of Color, for example, often have their lived racial realities about bias and discrimination met with disbelief by our society. They are often told that they are oversensitive, paranoid, and misreading the actions of others" (p. 171).

Sue, Capodilupo, and Holder (2008) found that Black students in particular face microaggressive behaviors by White teachers that "... negate their contributions, communicate low expectations, and exclude their participation in school activities" (p. 330). These experiences increase self-doubt, low self-esteem, and various psychological and physiological health issues. Additionally, individuals experiencing microaggressive behavior also face the added stress of deciding how to deal with the microaggressive conduct, and either directly or peripherally, with the perpetrator. The way in which the target responds may confirm stereotypes that the perpetrator holds about the target's identity group, which places the target in a double bind (Sue, Capodilupo, & Holder, 2008). For example, if a Black woman challenges a microaggressive comment, she may be deemed to be overreacting, labeled as aggressive, and stereotyped as an "angry Black woman." This causes additional stress for the target.

White and otherwise hegemonic people may feel guilty about issues of race, and/or their associated level of privilege, to distance themselves from issues of racism and other -isms by ignoring or denying the existence of microaggressions to protect their self-image of being good people, and dismiss the implication that they in fact benefit from the oppressions of others (Sue, Capodilupo,

Nadal, et al., 2008). The term *gaslighting* is used to describe the psychological phenomenon of manipulating someone to question their own sanity (Sarkis, 2017). Gaslighting is commonly used against targets of microaggressions so that perpetrators can gain power and control. Experiencing microaggressions, explicit racism, denials of these experiences, and gaslighting can eventually lead to RBF.

RBF (and other forms of battle fatigue) involves the cumulative impact of experiencing daily microaggressions and other forms of societal racism (and other -isms), which causes a negative impact on the health and well-being of nonhegemonic populations (Franklin et al., 2014; Smith, Mustaffa, Jones, Curry, & Allen, 2016; Smith, Hung, & Franklin, 2011; Smith et al., 2007). RBF is used to describe three major stress responses, physiological, psychological, and behavioral, and involves the energy expended on coping with and fighting racism (and other -isms), which is exacted on racially marginalized and stigmatized groups, such as dealing with daily microaggressions (Smith, 2008). It is important for teachers to address inequities in the school, classroom, and curriculum; otherwise, only "majoritarian" discourses will be perpetuated, and students possessing counternarratives may be marginalized. As Chaisson (2004) states, "Subverting discourses on race functions to perpetuate the racial system that advantages Whites for being white and oppresses racial minorities" (p. 346). Initially, the dismantling and problematizing of White privilege can cause anger and defensiveness in majority populations, which speaks to the necessity of such an undertaking, especially in predominantly White schools (Chaisson, 2004). Counternarratives are an important aspect of this conversation. Counternarratives problematize and/or cast doubt on the validity of hegemonic discourse or "accepted wisdom" perpetuated by the majority that also can communicate racial (and other) stereotypes and represent the telling of lesser-known tales and also critiquing commonly told ones (Solórzano & Yosso, 2001). Without them, only hegemonic, Eurocentric, "majoritarian" discourses will prevail (DeCuir & Dixson, 2004).

RDF imposes a cumulative effect, where "... race, gender, and other factors intersect to create specific, unique conditions of disadvantage (or privilege) for some compared to others" (Smith et al., 2007, p. 553). The disadvantages that RBF can cause include headaches, high blood pressure, digestive problems, stress, fatigue, sleep problems, loss of confidence, anger, fear, procrastination, neglecting responsibilities, resentment, hopelessness, and helplessness, and so forth (Franklin et al., 2014; Smith et al., 2007, 2016). These problems can lead to the related problems of lower grades, dropping out, and drug abuse for college students. RBF is both physically and emotionally debilitating (Franklin et al., 2014).

Dealing with racism and RBF can negatively impact Students of Color attending college. Latina/o students and Students of Color in general experience more racial hostility on college campuses and racial stressors than their White peers, causing them to question their academic self-concepts, hope for the future, and feelings of belonging (Franklin et al., 2014). According to Smith et al. (2016), Black males attending Predominantly White Institutions (PWIs) often experience "hypervisibility" and "hypersurveillance," stemming from anti-Black stereotyping, which can then lead to RBF.

African American college students, particularly males, have the added weight of defying stereotypes about their intellect (Smith et al., 2007). African American males are pressured to excel in spite of racially biased course content and racially insensitive professors, inducing stereotype threat (Steele & Aronson, 1995). All of these factors can influence retention and graduation.

Stereotype threat is the fear of confirming a negative stereotype held about one's group by others not possessing the same identity (Steele & Aronson, 1995). Activating negative stereotypes can hinder testing performance for children and adults (Aronson, 2004). Low teacher expectations as well as perceived discrimination can lead to stereotype threat, and thus lower performance on tests (Thames et al., 2013). This heightened fear to "represent" for one's racial/ethnic/gender (or other) group may result in higher stress and lower academic performance. Steele (2010) pinpoints the identity categories that are often rife for stereotype threat: age, sexual orientation, race, gender, ethnicity, political affiliation, mental illness, disability, and so forth. Steele (2010) further illuminates the danger of stereotype threat, "We know what 'people think.' We know that anything we do that fits the stereotype could be taken as confirming it" (p. 5). Thus, the vicious circle is perpetuated. If teachers are unaware of their implicit biases, and of the phenomenon of stereotype threat, they are likely to perpetuate it. Aronson (2004) found that repeated exposure to stereotype threat can cause a "disidentification" in students, thereby causing students to no longer feel an affinity for a field of study to which they once identified. When students feel that they are not viewed as part of the group ("belonging uncertainty"), their sense of belonging and achievement can be undermined (Walton, 2007).

Imposter phenomenon (or imposter syndrome) is a psychological phenomenon where nonhegemonic individuals question their competence in their current role: student, teacher, leader, and so forth, because they may be the only person representing their race, gender, or other minoritized identity, and thus feel "phony" in comparison to those around them (Dancy, 2017). Imposter phenomenon also involves one's attribution of success to external factors, such as chance or luck, feeling as though one does not deserve success, and downplaying one's successes (Dancy, 2017). According to Ewing, Richardson, James-Myers, and Russell (1996), academic self-concepts combined with racial identity perspectives can contribute to imposter feelings. Students who find themselves within a supportive learning community can assuage the impact of imposter phenomenon, which presupposes a counternarrative of the oppressive ideas of one's minoritized group.

Clance and Imes (1978) first used the term *imposter syndrome* to identify feel-ings of fraudulence in working women; however, since then, scholars have since expanded the concept of imposter phenomena to various identity categories where individuals attribute their success to external factors, despite evidence to the contrary (Caselman, Self, & Self, 2006). However, phenomenon is still expe-rienced more commonly by people of historically marginalized groups, such as People of Color, immigrants, and people of lower socioeconomic statuses (Dancy, 2017). Nonhegemonic people, particularly those working or studying within hegemonic environments, are often taught that they must "work twice as hard to be half as good" (Weir, 2017, p. 24).

According to Ahlfeld (2010), there are factors that can ameliorate imposter phenomenon, including resiliency and resourcefulness, facilitating supportive relationships, finding significant work, and viewing one's work as significant; these coping mechanisms can serve to dismantle "feeling like a fraud." Addi-tional compensatory strategies include cultivating and maintaining relation-ships with mentors and focusing upon one's strengths/areas of expertise (Weir, 2017).

Teachers are at risk of creating RBF, stereotype threat, and imposter phe-nomenon within their students if they do not actively cultivate cultural compe-tence and culturally responsive teaching practices, and continually reflect upon the impact they have on students. Stereotyped ideas about good teaching are ubiquitous, and teachers can easily fall into the trap of teaching in the ways in which they have been taught, which do not necessarily include cultural com-petence or culturally responsive practices. It may be that teachers lacking in a critical intersectional analysis come to resemble their own institutions, and thus perpetuate, rather than challenge, the status quo; this can have disastrous implications for nonhegemonic students.

Students in the Classroom

In a variety of school settings (K-12–postsecondary), many nonhegemonic stu-dents feel "isolation and alienation": that they have to leave certain aspects of their identities at the school door in order to be successful (Carter Andrews, 2012, p. 1). According to Carter Andrews, "These feelings often result from structural features within the school (e.g., tracking, lack of culturally diverse curriculum, biased teacher attitudes and beliefs, negative stereotypical beliefs held by White peers, and discriminatory policies) that represent forms of insti-tutional racism" (p. 5). Warikoo, Sinclair, Fei, and Jacoby-Senghor (2016) found that teachers do in fact treat students differently based upon their race, yet many teacher educators continue to endorse the notion of colorblindness, and the associated myth that if we just treat everyone the same, that everything will work out fine.

The civil rights of Students of Color within all schools is not only a cause for concern for critical pedagogues and social justice educators but it should also be for all teachers and teacher educators: a disproportionate number of Students of Color are referred for special education services, and disciplined more frequently and unfairly. White middle-class children are thus the "unmarked norm" against which the developmental progress of other children is measured (O'Connor & Fernandez, 2006). Further, both O'Connor and Fernandez (2006) and Blanchett (2006) argue that the underachievement of Students of Color is exacerbated by their disproportionality in underfunded schools with unqualified or uncertified teachers lacking experience. The desire to "give back" without the requisite knowledge and mindset to view Students of Color from asset perspectives has done its damage. The data clearly demonstrate this, yet we continue to educate underprepared teachers to work in urban schools with historically marginalized student populations.

There are many common words and phrases leveled against Students of Color (Morris, 2016). For example, loud, disrespectful, aggressive, urban, ghetto, thug, not college material, does not care about school/future (this includes student and family), and incapable of learning. These words and phrases serve to perpetuate low expectations for marginalized student populations, can be delivered directly to students as macro/microaggressions, and can lead to spirit murder, stereotype threat, RBF, and negative self-fulfilling prophecies. Spirit murder is common in schools because of inadequate teacher training, cultural mismatch, and deficit thinking. The notion of "spirit murdering" conceptualized by Williams (1991), and later explicated by Love (2017), is "... 'the personal, psychological, and spiritual injuries to People of Color through the fixed, yet fluid and moldable, structures of racism, privilege, and power'" (p. 199). I argue that spirit murdering can occur with any individual who problematizes, troubles, or questions the status quo, particularly if that individual possesses a nonhegemonic status, that is, women, and members of the LGBTQ+ community, as well as People of Color and Indigenous populations; in short, those possessing little to no power may be subjected to spirit murder, especially if they question institutional or systemic practices that do not serve to support them.

According to Warikoo et al. (2016), teachers treat students differently based on race, and this differential treatment contributes to disparities in achievement based on race, "Explicit attitudes are beliefs and evaluations about people and things that individuals knowingly endorse and have complete discretion over whether they disclose" (p. 508). If left unaddressed, over time, implicit biases lead to deeply rooted and debilitating cycles of inequities within schools (Jones et al., 2012). Many teachers have lower expectations both behaviorally and academically for students different from them, which leads to classroom macro and microaggressions (Kohli & Solórzano, 2012), stereotype threat, and RBF.

Relatedly, when students learn these messages, they may internalize oppressive feelings about themselves, which may then affect how they perform academically (Dancy, 2017). Further, they may develop impostor phenomenon, which affects their self-confidence and productivity, even when they have the intellect and skills to achieve (Dancy, 2017). Pipeline schools, many of which are urban charter schools, play a key role in the school-to-prison-pipeline (Alexander, 2010), and focus primarily on compliance—about sitting down and staying quiet—preparing students more for prison than for democratic possibilities (Morris, 2016). In many of these spaces, silence is the expectation for many students, particularly if they are Black and Brown, read *urban*. Such schools are and should be considered Apartheid schools. The concept of the "White savior" is rife within Apartheid schools where the students are perceived to be in need of "saving" by the innocent and righteous White teacher (Matias, 2016). According to Matias and DiAngelo (2013),

> … while the system of White supremacy has shaped Western political thought for hundreds of years, it is never named nor identified as a system at all. In this way, White supremacy is rendered invisible while other political systems are identified and studied. Much of its power is drawn from its invisibility. (p. 5)

If White majority pre-service teacher candidates are not asked to confront issues of race throughout their education, they will be hard-pressed to do so as professionals. Explicitly negative attitudes about race, now hidden within the philosophy of colorblindness, do not negate their persistence. Warikoo et al. (2016) argue that explicit racism has decreased in our current milieu, but implicit negative associations exist, which result in more subtle forms of racism.

If specific conversations about race are not broached within teacher education programs, racist practices of sorting of nonhegemonic students will continue, contributing to the mis-education of Students of Color, and by extension, of White students who receive the implicit message that they are superior. When students are "spirit murdered," they may experience what Kohl (1994) describes as "not-learning," or, "Deciding to actively not-learn something involves closing off part of oneself and limiting one's experience. It can require actively refusing to pay attention, acting dumb, scrambling one's thoughts, and overriding curiosity" (p. 4). Additionally, as Erickson (1987) states, "Learning what is deliberately taught can be seen as a form of political assent. Not learning can be seen as a form of political resistance" (p. 344).

In a ground-breaking study, Goff et al. (2014) argue that Black and Brown children are perceived as older and thus, more responsible for their actions than their White counterparts. These misperceptions (based on implicit bias) have grave consequences for nonhegemonic students and contribute to their dehumanization and criminalization. Goff et al. found that teachers do not perceive

Black and Brown students as possessing the "essence of innocence," as do their White peers. Morris (2016) argues that African American girls specifically are viewed negatively in much more insidious and subversive ways, with the discipline of and control of appearance, often done in informal ways, but with the end result being the punishment of Black girl aesthetics, such as natural hair, dreadlocks, or braids, being deemed as "disruptive." According to Morris,

> The politicization (and vilification) of thick, curly, and kinky hair is an old one. Characterizations of kinky hair as unmanageable, wild, and ultimately "bad hair" are all signals (spoken and unspoken) that Black girls are inferior and unkempt when left in their natural state. (p. 92)

In addition to aesthetics, African American girls are also often disciplined for their "attitudes": as Morris indicates (2016), "'Willful defiance' is a widely used, subjective, and arbitrary category for student misbehavior that can include everything from a student having a verbal altercation with a teacher to refusing to remove a hat in school or complete an assignment" (p. 70). In sum, the issue of the containment of the Black girl within schools is a specific crime perpetrated on Black girls, which must be immediately rectified through our teacher education programs.

According to Smith et al. (2011), "Depending on the social environment, the level of rigidity, and its obstinate racial control, Blacks will experience more or less intense racial microaggressions" (p. 67). And, "… racism and racial microaggressions operate as psycho-pollutants in the social environment and add to the overall race-related stress for Black men, Black women, and other racially marginalized groups" (p. 67). I would argue that the White teachers in this space have little understanding of these phenomenon, but only view their students from the perspective of cultural deprivation. Furthermore, this school operates from a perpetual state of institutionalized racism, defined by Ture and Hamilton (1992) as relying on

> … the active and pervasive operation of anti-Black attitudes and practices. A sense of superior group position prevails: Whites are "better" than Blacks; therefore, Blacks should be subordinated to Whites. This is a racist attitude and it permeates the society, on both the individual and institutional level, covertly and overtly. (p. 5)

Students possessing intersectional identities, and/or LGBTQ+ status, living with a disability, and students with mental health issues may also feel excluded and subjected to microaggressions in school because they deviate from the dominant norm: White, male heterosexual, able-bodied, and so forth (Nadal, Whitman, Davis, Erazo, & Davidson, 2016). This sense of intersectional exclusion can lead to feelings of impostorship (Dancy, 2017). LGBTQ+ students, for example, may experience various microaggressions attacking their sexual and gender identities including, but not limited to, heterosexist and homophobic language, disapproval of LGBTQ+ identities, denials of homo/transphobia, perceptions that LGBTQ+ individuals are pathological, stereotypes and/or fetishism of LGBTQ+ individuals, and so forth (Nadal et al., 2016). In fact, 85% of LGBTQ+ students report experiencing verbal harassment, making this population of students the most vulnerable to school-based harassment (Kosciw, Greytak, Palmer, & Boesen, 2013).

Students possessing intersectional identities in schools can also be subjected to microaggressive conduct devaluing their multiple minority statuses, thus exacerbating the amount of minority stress they experience (Nadal et al., 2016). Students possessing intersectional identities may also be subjected to microaggressions by members of one of their own shared minority groups because their other intersectional identities deviate from the expectations of their shared racial group, for example, and/or they may be subjected to microaggressive comment for one identity that perpetrators perceive as in direct conflict with their other intersecting identities—leaving the target in a no-win situation.

Haberman (1991) terms a "pedagogy of poverty"—likely in urban schools and Communities of Color—based on rote memorization, drill and kill strategies, banking concept of education, teacher-centered, highly rigid and structured, and rife with low expectations. This pedagogy is the direct inverse of what Ladson-Billings (1994) deems "culturally relevant teaching," or "... teaching about questioning (and preparing students to question) the structural inequality, the racism, and the injustice that exist in society" (p. 18). According to Smith et al. (2011), People of Color "continue to be viewed as outsiders and treated in stereotypic and racist ways" (p. 64). They speak of Black males in particular having to

> spend mental energy considering whether they are genuinely accepted or just being tolerated ... discerning the difference between individually supportive Whites and destructive actions by Whites as a collective ... [and] confront additional and unique race-based stress identifying when, where, and how to resist oppression, versus when, where, and how to accommodate to it. (pp. 65–66)

According to Harris Combs (2016), "The master narrative of colorblindness does not serve the interests of People of Color, and it serves to silence and reject their epistemologies" (p. 160).

Teaching and Teacher Education

Just as our K-12 education system has been whitewashed (Sandoval, Ratcliff, Buenavista, & Martin, 2016), so too have our teacher education programs.

Nieto (2010) argues that teacher education programs, "notorious for their homogeneity" screen out Candidates of Color stating:

> Because of their cultural uniformity, and unless there are conscious strategies to the contrary, preservice programs often serve as a mechanism for reproducing negative and racist attitudes and beliefs that later get translated into teaching approaches that continue to create inequitable education. (pp. 61–62)

Thus, teacher candidates, untrained and unprepared to question the status quo, are unprepared to teach their Students of Color in an emancipatory way, for full democratic participation and possibility (Loewen, 2010). Instead, teacher education programs prepare teacher candidates to teach Students of Color only for assimilation to the status quo, which necessitates deculturalization (Spring, 2013), including the destruction of native and home languages, and cultures.

The whitewashing of teacher education not only involves the chosen curriculum as master narrative and the candidates who are recruited and admitted into teacher education programs (read White), but also candidate expectations for Students of Color that are cultivated within said programs; this act of whitewashing results in a perpetual nonquestioning of these ideological uncritical and harmful practices. According to Nieto (2010):

> For…White students, the teachers thought of success as academic excellence, whereas for their African American students, especially those perceived to be discipline problems, success was defined as "feeling good about school, adjusting to rules and expectations, having positive interactions with adults, and attaining a sense of belonging." (pp. 117–118)

Likewise, Loewen (2010) found with regularity that practicing teachers expected White students to succeed and Black students to fail regardless of social class.

Despite the above-noted issues within teacher education, there are critical pedagogues working to dismantle institutional structures that are harmful to scholars possessing nonhegemonic statuses as well as institutional structures within K-12 schools operating from deficit mindsets, and thereby harming, that is, spirit murdering, the students who attend them. According to Paris (2012), "Deficit approaches … [view] … the languages, literacies, and cultural ways of being of many students and communities of color as deficiencies to be overcome in learning the demanded and legitimized dominant language, literacy, and cultural ways of schooling" (p. 93). In sum, there are uncritical and apolitical aspects of the field of education: teachers who attempt to indoctrinate their students to assimilate into traditional American culture, understanding little else, disciplining, and punishing those students who do not abide, while not seeing any of their actions as political, problematic, or controversial. Within the field of teacher education, scholars must not only critique but also dismantle the deficit approaches that serve to undermine nonhegemonic students.

As Britzman (2003) argues, "The problem of conformity in teacher education stems in part from its emphasis on training" (p. 46). As a field, we are not collectively focused on knowledge creation per se, or on critical analysis of schools and institutions and the culturally irresponsive individual and systemic practices that occur within, but rather on the practitioner aspects of the field, for example, writing proper lesson plans and objectives, following state and national standards, and practicing classroom management. If we want our teachers to do better for our nonhegemonic students, then we too must be better. The unexamined problem of Whiteness has much to do with this lack of examination. According to Matias (2016):

> Whiteness then sets the prevailing context for which US teacher education exists and operates. The context of white-teacher-as-savior is aligned with the teachers' psychosocial experiences with race and whiteness despite their lack of diverse racial and socioeconomic upbringing. Many of my teacher candidates have explained that their desire to become an urban-focused teacher hinges on their privilege of whiteness, and thus feel the "need to give back." Yet nearly all cannot articulate why: what makes them feel compelled or guilty enough to give back? What racialized processes have they undergone that leads them to believe they are apt to teach urban students of color? And, most importantly, how will this impact urban students of color? (p. 231)

There are many problems with this unexamined "White savior" complex. Why do these students, still in the process of completing their teacher education programs, think they have anything to "give back" yet? Do White teacher candidates in their early 20s, with little to no knowledge of urban Communities of Color, view these urban Students of Color and their families from such a deficit perspective that they believe they can contribute anything? Do they say such things about suburban schools? Would they even begin to know how to critique the harmful institutional practices that exist in many urban schools—where students have lower expectations placed upon them because of racial prejudice, implicit bias, and zip code? Most teacher education programs do not prepare White students to engage in such critical conversations.

The notion of caring is prominent within teacher education and K-12 teaching, but it is a concept that is not critically examined or theorized, and often lacks the quality of *authentic caring* for historically marginalized students because it lacks the component of action and an underlying un-examination of racial bias. As teacher educators, we must become comfortable with this discomfort, to challenge our pre-service teachers (most of whom are White) to examine their racial and cultural biases. Matias and Zembylas (2014) delve into the concept of caring as a mask to hide White racial animus, stating that

> declarations of caring and empathy are often empty or inauthentic, because they fail to be accompanied by action ... such expressions of caring fail to recognize how they are embedded in modalities of racism and social inequality that are perpetuated by assuming that declarations of caring are enough to alleviate the other's suffering (pp. 321–322).

Racial pity and disgust on the part of White teacher candidates and White teachers are directly connected to low academic expectations and deficit thinking about Students of Color, their families, and their communities, which, in turn, can cause stereotype threat and internalized racial stereotypes.

Case Study: An Invitation to Speak at an Urban Charter School

As a former K-12 teacher and now a teacher educator, I was recently invited to an urban charter school to provide a guest lecture for a class of fifth-graders. I was informed that at this charter school, all curriculum had been suspended so that teachers could focus on "character education." *Abrasive, aggressive, disrespectful,* and *loud* were some of the words the teacher used to describe his students prior to my visit.

I was invited to give a lesson on "character education" to these students, but I was not going to do that. I was informed that these children "did not know how to behave," and that the teachers were attempting to inspire the students to be "good people." My initial reaction was shock and anger. I suspected that it was the teachers who needed education, and not the students. I planned a lesson for what I thought would be appropriate for a fifth-grade classroom, including viewing Dr. Bettina Love's TED on *Hip Hop, Grit and Academic Success*, some discussion of culturally responsive schools, a writing prompt, and ending with a creative expression exercise on student culture. I suspected that I would not have any behavior problems. I was right.

After introducing myself to these students, all African American, and one international student of Middle Eastern descent, I asked students what they thought I wanted them to do while watching the movie. They answered, "Be quiet!" I responded, "Yes, but that was not what I was thinking. What else?" They answered, "Stay in our seats!" I stated, "Okay, but also not what I was thinking." They responded a few more times with behavioral expectations, but finally they stated, "Take notes!" I said, "Yes, exactly. Please write down anything important that you hear in the film." As I walked around during the film, I noticed a very small boy struggling to write with a marker. I asked him, "Would you like a pencil to write with?" He responded, "Yes, I would love a pencil." I then asked the teacher for a pencil. He replied, "We don't give them pencils. All they do is break them and throw them on the floor." I went to my purse and found a pen to give the student. He did not attempt to break it, or throw it on the floor.

After the film, I asked the students what Dr Love argued was the most important thing about any school. They all answered, "Love!" They were correct, but, unfortunately, this was not what they were experiencing within their own school. I then asked the students to write one sentence discussing the most important aspect of the film in their estimation. The true highlight of this exercise was when one boy discussed spirit murder, as does Love in her TED Talk. He said something like, "Sometimes schools can spirit murder their students when they do not value the students' cultures." It was that deep. I am sure the teacher heard this comment, but I am not sure he was listening.

The students attending this urban charter school were being prepared for a future of compliance. There was no art or music offered. Their school was situated in a deserted former strip mall. The students' playground was the concrete parking lot; their only equipment at recess was a lone basketball hoop, a few jump ropes, and one broken hula hoop. On my way out of the classroom, I noticed a list of rules written on the whiteboard, most of which I broke without even realizing it:

1. Getting out of seat
2. Talking (noise)
3. Saying rude things to each other—shut up, gay, bald, and so forth
4. Disrespect to adults—back talk, smack lips, and roll eyes
5. Yelling!
6. Leaving room without permission
7. Dancing in or out of seat
8. Leaning/tipping chair or desk backwards, forwards, sideways
9. No sharing food

The first principle of the hidden curriculum of this school is that the students are not worthy or capable of learning content because they needed to learn first "how to behave." The culture within the White teaching staff did not see any contradiction between their expectations for these children, and what they would expect and demand for their own—but they saw themselves as "nice" and "good" people, so the problems within the school could not have anything to do with them. These students were experiencing racial microaggressions from their teachers in the form of low expectations and stereotypes, which have serious impact not only on learning but also on the mental health of students (Nadal, Griffin, Wong, Hamit, & Rasmus, 2014). The suspension of a formal curriculum in place of behavior and character education is an extreme form of violence perpetrated upon these students. The second principle of the hidden curriculum of this school was that these students did not act in ways that they were supposed to act, according to White middle-class values.

At the end of my visit that day, I toured the school. I visited a K-first grade classroom, and stood at the door. The door was open, and tiny children approached me, interested in who I was. "I like your earrings," was a comment that I remember. These children were curious and alert, but I was taken aback by the White teacher in the room, the only White presence, yelling at the children to "sit still," and "stay in your chairs"; she shouted that she would call their parents and that they were "on red." I could not fathom how this White woman could yell at these children. I again witnessed racialized microaggressions in the classroom. These teachers' low expectations for students will only lead to negative academic consequences for these students.

These students were not viewed as children and rather were viewed as "little criminals," who were in need of discipline as opposed to education. I witnessed dehumanization, criminalization, and an attempt at control. I hypothesize that these students experience a silent form of RBF because of their treatment in the school including frustration, hopeless, and anger, which can result in real health challenges and behavioral responses. Upon taking my leave of this urban charter school, I implored my host to not fight the battle of the pencil, but to provide students what they need to learn. I attempted to make the connection between culturally responsive curriculum and students' success, but I am not sure if they were equipped to hear me. I am not sure that my noted devastation at the realities of this Apartheid school was taken into consideration.

Conclusion

Although public schools are the best hope we have to educate the most students of all identities, teachers and teacher educators can and must do better. If my case study is any indication of what can occur in schools when *people are watching*, microaggressions perpetrated upon students, which can lead to the associated phenomenon of stereotype threat and RBF, what happens when no one is watching? We must do better. We must do better in recruiting Teachers of Color. We must do better to create culturally responsive curriculums both in higher education and in K-12 schools, that is, curriculums that are not whitewashed: devoid of the history of claims of racial superiority by Whites, and the dismantling of Indigenous and cultural languages and histories of various peoples living inside and outside of the contiguous United States.

Previous research has suggested that not only are disciplinary techniques negatively associated with educational outcomes, but also they are inequitably levied toward Students of Color (Lewis, Butler, Bonner, & Joubert, 2010; Monroe, 2005; Perry & Morris, 2014; Skiba, Michael, Nardo, & Peterson, 2002). Is the problem that most teachers are White, and unaccustomed to working with populations different from them? Is it that they are operating from stereotyped notions of their students and thus deficit thinking? Can White teachers be prepared to work in culturally diverse settings? According to Milner (2006, 2008), for teachers to be prepared to work in diverse settings, they must be well versed in the following areas: cultural and racial awareness, critical reflection, and the merging of theory and practice. They must also be committed to defying the notion that lack of student success, particularly in urban schools, is the fault of students, their parents, their home cultures, and their communities. To this end, we must advocate for teacher education programs that challenge and confront the dominant social order (Bolotin Joseph, Luster Bravmann, Windschitl, Mikel, & Stewart Green, 2000). Although this work is difficult and White students may tend to resist it (Martin, 2015a, 2015b; Milner, 2013), we have no other choice.

Teacher educators must advocate for asset perspectives when viewing all students in their respective communities: tapping into students' prior cultural knowledge when teaching new knowledge can help to establish dynamic mental models that network to the learners' existing schema, adding meaning to the new knowledge for the learner (Griner & Stewart, 2012; Moll, Amanti, Neff, & González, 1992). As teacher educators, we must provide our future educators with mindsets, dispositions, and practices aimed at closing opportunity gaps for all students, but for Students of Color in particular.

References

Ahlfeld, A. J. (2010). The imposter phenomenon revisited: The intersection of race, gender, and professional status for women of color. *Dissertation Abstracts International, 70*(9-B), 5803.

Alexander, M. (2010). *The new Jim Crow: Mass incarceration in the age of colorblindness.* New York, NY: The New Press.

Aronson, J. (2004, November). The threat of stereotype. *Educational Leadership, 62*, 14–19.

Blanchett, W. J. (2006). Disproportionate representation of African American students in special education: Acknowledging the role of white privilege and racism. *Educational Researcher, 35*(6), 24–28.

Bolotin Joseph, P., Luster Bravmann, S., Windschitl, M. A., Mikel, E. R., & Stewart Green, N. (2000). *Cultures of Curriculum.* Mahwah, NJ: Lawrence Erlbaum Associates.

Britzman, D. P. (2003). *Practice makes practice: A critical study of learning to teach.* New York, NY: State University of New York Press.

Carter Andrews, D. J. (2012). Black achievers' experiences with racial spotlighting and ignoring in a predominantly White high school. *Teachers College Record, 114*, 1–46.

Caselman, T. D., Self, P. A., & Self, A. L. (2006). Adolescent attributes contributing to the imposter phenomenon. *Journal of Adolescence, 29*, 395–405.

Chaisson, R. L. (2004, October). A crack in the door: Critical race theory in practice at a predominantly white institution. *Teaching Sociology, 32*, 345–357.

Clance, P. R., & Imes, S. A. (1978). The imposter phenomenon in high achieving women: Dynamics and therapeutic intervention. *Psychotherapy: Theory, Research and Practice, 15*, 241–247.

Dancy, T. E. (2017). Imposter syndrome. In K. Nadal (Ed.), *The SAGE encyclopedia of psychology and gender* (pp. 21–23). Los Angeles, CA: SAGE.

DeCuir, J. T., & Dixson, A. D. (2004). "So when it comes out, they aren't that surprised that it is there": Using critical race theory as a tool of analysis of race and racism in education. *Educational Researcher, 33*, 26–31.

Erickson, F. (1987). Transformation and school success: The politics and culture of educational achievement. *Anthropology and Education Quarterly, 18*, 335–356.

Ewing, K. M., Richardson, T. Q., James-Myers, L., & Russell, R. K. (1996). The relationship between racial identity attitudes, worldview, and African American graduate students' experiences of the imposter syndrome. *Journal of Black Psychology, 22*, 53–66.

Franklin, J. D., Smith, W. A., & Hung, M. (2014). Racial battle fatigue for Latina/o students: A quantitative perspectives. *Journal of Hispanic Higher Education, 13*, 303–322.

Frattura, E. M., & Capper, C. A. (2007). *Leading for social justice: Transforming schools for all learners.* Thousand Oaks, CA: Corwin Press.

Goff, P. A., Jackson, M. C., Leone, D., Lewis, B. A., Culotta, C. M., & DiTomasso, N. A. (2014). The essence of innocence: Consequences of dehumanizing Black children. *Journal of Personality and Social Psychology, 106*(4), 526–545.

Griner, A. C., & Stewart, M. L. (2012). Addressing the achievement gap and disproportionality through the use of culturally responsive teaching practices. *Urban Education, 48*, 585–621.

Haberman, M. (1991). The pedagogy of poverty versus good teaching. *Phi Delta Kappan, 73*, 290–294.

Harris Combs, B. (2016). Presumed biased: The challenge and rewards of teaching "post-racial" students to see racism. In D. M. Sandoval, A. J. Ratcliff, T. L. Buenavista, & J. R. Martin (Eds.), *"White" washing American education: The new culture wars in ethnic studies, Higher Education* (Vol. 2, pp. 149–164). Santa Barbara, CA: Praeger.

Jones, J. M., Cochran, S. D., Fine, M., Gaertner, S., Mendoza-Denton, R., Shih, M., & Sue, D. W. (2012). *Dual pathways to a better America: Preventing discrimination and promoting diversity.* Washington, DC: American Psychological Association, Presidential Task Force on Preventing Discrimination and Promoting Diversity.

Kohl, H. (1994). *"I won't learn from you" and other thoughts on creative maladjustment.* New York, NY: The New Press.

Kohli, R., & Solórzano, D. G. (2012). Teachers, please learn our names! Racial microaggressions and the K-12 classroom. *Race, Ethnicity & Education, 15,* 441–462.

Kosciw, J. G., Greytak, E. A., Palmer, N. A., & Boesen, M. J. (2013). *The 2013 national school climate survey: The experiences of lesbian, gay, bisexual and transgender youth in our nation's schools.* New York, NY: GLSEN.

Ladson-Billings, G. (1994). *The dreamkeepers: Successful teachers of African American children.* San Francisco, CA: Jossey-Bass.

Lewis, C. W., Butler, B. R., Bonner III F. A., & Joubert, M. (2010). African American male discipline patterns and school district responses resulting impact on academic achievement: Implications for urban educators and policy makers. *Journal of African American Males in Education, 1*(1), 7–25.

Loewen, J. W. (2010). *Teaching what really happened: How to avoid the tyranny of textbooks and get students excited about doing history.* New York, NY: Teachers College Press.

Love, B. L. (2017). Difficult knowledge: When a black feminist educator was too afraid to #sayhername. *English Education, 49,* 197–208.

Martin, J. L. (Ed.) (2015a). *Racial battle fatigue: Insights from the front lines of social justice advocacy.* Santa Barbara, CA: Praeger.

Martin, J. L. (2015b). Self-study of social justice teaching on the tenure track: A pedagogy of vulnerability. In J. L. Martin (Ed.), *Racial battle fatigue: Insights from the front lines of social justice advocacy* (pp. 3–28). Santa Barbara, CA: Praeger.

Matias, C. E. (2016). White skin, black friend: A Fanonian application to theorize racial fetish in teacher education. *Educational Philosophy and Theory, 48,* 221–236.

Matias, C. E., & DiAngelo, R. (2013, Summer–Fall). Beyond the face of race: Emo-cognitive explorations of White neurosis and racial cray–cray. *Educational Foundations,* 3–20.

Matias, C. E., & Zembylas, M. (2014). "When saying you care is not really caring": Emotions of disgust, Whiteness ideology, and teacher education. *Critical Studies in Education, 55,* 319–337.

Milner, H. R. (2006). Preservice teachers' learning about cultural and racial diversity: Implications for urban education. *Urban Education, 41,* 343–375.

Milner, H. R. (2008). Disrupting deficit notions of difference: Counter-narratives of teachers and community in urban education. *Teaching and Teacher Education, 24,* 1573–1598.

Milner, H. R. (2013). *Start where you are, but don't stay there: Understanding diversity, opportunity gaps, and teaching in today's classrooms.* Cambridge, MA: Harvard.

Moll, L. C., Amanti, D., Neff, D., & González, N. (1992). Funds of knowledge for teaching. *Theory into Practice, 31,* 132–141.

Monroe, C. R. (2005). Why are "bad boys" always black? Causes of disproportionality in school discipline and recommendations for change. *The*

Clearing House: A Journal of Educational Strategies, Issues and Ideas, 79, 45–50.

Morris, M. W. (2016). *Pushout: The criminalization of black girls in schools.* New York, NY: The New Press.

Nadal, K. L. (2010). Gender microaggressions: Implications for mental health. In M. A. Paludi (Ed.), *Feminism and women's rights worldwide, Mental and Physical Health* (Vol. 2, pp. 155–175). Santa Barbara, CA: Praeger.

Nadal, K. L., Griffin, K. E., Wong, Y., Hamit, S., & Rasmus, M. (2014). The impact of racial microaggressions on mental health: Counseling implications for clients of color. *Journal of Counseling & Development, 92,* 57–66.

Nadal, K. L., Whitman, C. N., Davis, L. S., Erazo, T., & Davidson, K. C. (2016). Microaggressions toward lesbian, gay, bisexual, transgender, queer, and genderqueer people: A review of the literature. *Journal of Sex Research, 53,* 488–508.

Nieto, S. (2010). *The light in their eyes: Creating multicultural learning communities.* New York, NY: Teachers College Press.

O'Connor, C., & Fernandez, S. D. (2006). Race, class, and disproportionality: Reevaluating the relationship between poverty and special education placement. *Educational Researcher, 35*(6), 6–11.

Ong, A. D., Burrow, A. L., Fuller-Rowell, T. E., Ja, N. M., & Sue, D. W. (2013). Racial microaggressions and daily well-being among Asian Americans. *Journal of Counseling Psychology, 60,* 188–199.

Paris, D. (2012). Culturally sustaining pedagogy: A needed change in stance, terminology, and practice. *Educational Researcher, 41,* 93–97.

Perry, B. L., & Morris, E. W. (2014). Suspending progress collateral consequences of exclusionary punishment in public schools. *American Sociological Review, 79,* 1067–1087.

Sandoval, D. M., Ratcliff, A. J., Buenavista, T. L., & Martin, J. R. (Eds.) (2016). *"White" washing American education: The new culture wars in ethnic studies, Higher Education* (Vol. 2, pp. 149–164). Santa Barbara, CA: Praeger.

Sarkis, S. (2017). 11 Signs of gaslighting in a relationship. *Psychology Today.* Retrieved from https://www.psychologytoday.com/blog/here-there-and-everywhere/201701/11-signs-gaslighting-in-relationship.

Skiba, R. J., Michael, R. S., Nardo, A. C., & Peterson, R. L. (2002). The color of discipline: Sources of racial and gender disproportionality in school punishment. *The Urban Review, 34,* 317–342.

Smith, W. A. (2008). Higher education: Racial battle fatigue. In R. T. Schaefer (Ed.), *Encyclopedia of race, ethnicity, and society* (pp. 615–618). Thousand Oaks, CA: Sage Publications.

Smith, W. A., Allen, W. R., & Danley, L. L. (2007). "Assume the position ... you fit the description" Psychological experiences and racial battle fatigue among African American male college students. *American Behavioral Scientist, 51,* 551–578.

Smith, W. A., Hung, M., & Franklin, J. D. (2011). Racial battle fatigue and the Misseducation of Black men: Racial microaggressions, societal problems, and environmental stress. *Journal of Negro Education, 80,* 63–82.

Smith, W. A., Mustaffa, J. B., Jones, C. M., Curry, T. J., & Allen, W. R. (2016). "You make me wanna holler and throw up both my hands!" Campus culture, Black misandric microaggressions, and racial battle fatigue. *International Journal of Qualitative Studies in Education, 29,* 1189–1209.

Solórzano, D. G., & Yosso, T. J. (2001). Critical race and latcrit theory and method: Counterstorytelling: Chicana and Chicano graduate school experiences. *Qualitative Studies in Education, 14,* 471–495.

Spring, J. (2013). *Deculturalization and the struggle for equality: A brief history of the education of dominated cultures in the United States* (7th ed.). New York, NY: McGraw-Hill.

Steele, C. M. (2010). *Whistling Vivaldi: How stereotypes affect us and what we can do.* W.W. Norton & Company.

Steele, C. M., & Aronson, J. (1995). Stereotype threat and the intellectual test performance of African Americans. *Journal of Personality and Social Psychology, 69,* 797–811.

Sue, D. W. (2017). Microaggressions and "evidence": Empirical or experiential reality? *Perspectives on Psychological Science, 12,* 170–172.

Sue, D. W., Bucceri, J., Lin, A. I., Nadal, K. L., & Torino, G. C. (2007). Racial microaggressions and the Asian American experience. *Cultural Diversity & Ethnic Minority Psychology, 13,* 72–81.

Sue, D. W., Capodilupo, C. M., & Holder, A. M. B. (2008). Racial microaggressions in the life experience of Black Americans. *Professional Psychology: Research and Practice, 39,* 329–336.

Sue, D. W., Capodilupo, C. M., Nadal, K. L., & Torino, G. C. (2008). Racial microaggressions and the power to define reality. *American Psychologist,* 277–279.

Thames, A. D., Hinkin, C. H., Byrd, D. A., Bilder, R. M., Duff, K. J., Mindt, M. R., … Streiff, V. (2013). Effects of stereotype threat, perceived discrimination, and examiner race on neuropsychological performance: Simple as Black and White? *Journal of the International Neuropsychological Society, 19,* 583–593.

Ture, K., & Hamilton, C. V. (1992). *Black power: The politics of liberation.* New York, NY: Vintage.

Walton, G. M. (2007). A question of belonging: Race, social fit, and achievement. *Journal of Personality and Social Psychology, 92,* 82–96.

Warikoo, N., Sinclair, S., Fei, J., & Jacoby-Senghor, D. (2016). Examining racial bias in education: A new approach. *Educational Researcher, 45,* 508–514.

Weir, K. (2017). *Feel like a fraud?* American Psychological Association. Retrieved from http://www.apa.org/gradpsych/2013/11/fraud.aspx.

Williams, P. (1991). *The alchemy of race and rights: Diary of a law professor.* Cambridge, MA: Harvard University Press.

8

Microaggressions and Internalized Oppression: Intrapersonal, Interpersonal, and Institutional Impacts of "Internalized Microaggressions"

E.J.R. David, Jessica Petalio, and Maria C. Crouch

Mark, a 12-year-old Filipino American boy, came home from school one day to share some exciting news with Gemma, his 17-year-old "Ate" or older sister: He has a crush—his first one—on a girl who just recently transferred to his school! After a few minutes of Mark exhilaratingly telling his sister the many things he likes about his crush—such as her smile, her laugh, and how she is an awesome athlete—Ate Gemma gave Mark some well-intentioned advice. She said, "This is awesome! Well, now you need to be 'pogi' [good-looking or handsome] so you can get her attention and like you back. You need to stop playing outside too much so you're not exposed to the sun as much. You can't get any darker. For now, go to the bathroom and look into the medicine cabinet, get the 'Eskinol' [a skin-lightening face wash]. You need to start whitening your face!" Heeding his older sister's advice, Mark ran to the bathroom to begin what would become a many years-long skin-whitening habit. He had come to believe that a lighter skin-tone is more attractive and desirable than darker skin.

In this brief story, one that is likely familiar to many Filipinos and other People of Color (see David, 2013, 2014), we see a type of microaggression that is often not recognized, as most examples, discussions, and literature on microaggressions tend to involve microaggressions *between* groups (and not so much the microaggressions that happen *within* groups). For instance, when Gemma communicated to her younger brother Mark that his brown skin is not as attractive and that he would be more attractive if he had lighter skin, she commits what can be referred to as within-group microaggressions. We hypothesize

Microaggression Theory: Influence and Implications, First Edition. Edited by Gina C. Torino, David P. Rivera, Christina M. Capodilupo, Kevin L. Nadal, and Derald Wing Sue.
© 2019 John Wiley & Sons, Inc. Published 2019 by John Wiley & Sons, Inc.

that within-group microaggressions result from internalized oppression—or through a process in which the disparaging attitudinal (interpersonal) and structural (institutional) messages that permeate the environment seep into an oppressed individual who, in turn, begins to think, feel, and behave in biased ways toward themselves and their own group (David, 2013, 2014). When people commit within-group microaggressions against others of their own group (e.g., a lesbian who mocks another lesbian for "being too butch"; a woman who tells another woman that sexism does not exist), such incidents may be reflective of the perpetrator's internalized oppression and may be just as (or perhaps even more) derogatory and insulting as microaggressions that are perpetrated by people of other groups.

Further, we argue that when people struggle with internalized oppression, they may often commit microaggressions toward themselves. For instance, in the story above, Mark behaved in a microaggressive manner toward himself—when he began to use skin-whitening products to rid himself of his brown skin. This type of *intrapersonal* microaggression—or one that is committed toward one's own self—can manifest with different identity groups too (e.g., a Person of Color who undergoes plastic surgery to alter any physical features that they deem "too ethnic"; a bisexual man who voluntarily enters an "Ex-Gay" group in an attempt to change his sexual orientation). As most published works on microaggressions tend to be about *interpersonal* or *systemic* microaggressions, intrapersonal microaggressions are also less explored in the literature. Just like with within-group microaggressions, intrapersonal microaggressions are also where we begin to see the connections between microaggressions and internalized oppression, as well as the insidious detrimental impact of microaggressions that can literally and metaphorically destroy people psychologically, physically, or both.

To this end, this chapter will discuss *internalized microaggressions*—or the subtle, often unintentional discrimination that manifests as a result of one's biases toward her/his/their own group—as well as how internalized microaggressions operate and affect people on the intrapersonal, interpersonal, and institutional levels. We begin with a brief summary of the microaggressions construct, followed by an overview of oppression and internalized oppression. Then, we present a conceptual framework for the manifestations and psychological implications of internalized microaggressions—demonstrating a need for increased research and service attention on this insidiously destructive phenomenon.

Microaggressions

Sue et al. (2007) developed a conceptualization of nonblatant forms of oppression they termed microaggressions—"brief and commonplace daily verbal, behavioral, and environmental indignities, whether intentional or unintentional, that communicate hostile, derogatory or negative racial slights and insults to the target person or group" because of their social group (p. 273). Although microaggressions were first mentioned by Piece and colleagues back in 1978 (Pierce, Carew, Pierce-Gonzalez, & Willis, 1978), it was not until after Sue and colleagues revived the term and further developed the construct in 2007 that microaggressions became widely known and systematically researched. Indeed, since Sue and colleagues' seminal article, the academic and popular literature on microaggressions has rapidly grown. For instance, a search on *PsycINFO*—the largest database of psychology-related literature in the world—shows only four results on "microaggression" between 1900 and 2007 (i.e., Constantine & Sue, 2007; Pierce et al., 1978; Solórzano, Ceja, & Yosso, 2000; Sue et al., 2007). However, from 2008 onwards *PsycINFO* provided 209 hits for "microaggression" (as of May 20, 2017), seemingly attesting to the salience and significance of the microaggression construct for many people—especially people who are members of historically marginalized social groups.

In addition to developing an integrated framework for understanding subtle forms of oppression, another significant contribution of Sue et al.'s (2007) pivotal paper is the delineation of three types of microaggressions: (a) microassaults, (b) microinsults, and (c) microinvalidations. First, microassaults are explicit and conscious exchanges that are often intended to hurt target groups but are often dismissed as being innocuous, harmless, or unrelated to bias. These behaviors can include name-calling, bullying, avoidant behavior, or purposeful discriminatory actions based on social group membership (e.g., using derogatory epithets, making demeaning jokes, or explicitly not inviting someone to an event based on their social group membership). Second, microinsults are characterized by subtle snubs and slights, frequently unknown or unconscious to the perpetrator, but that clearly convey a hidden insulting message to the recipient (e.g., repeatedly failing to ask a woman to be the lead on a project, giving a Person of Color poor service at a restaurant, expressing disgust to certain foods that another culture considers to be a delicacy). Third, microinvalidations are characterized by communications that exclude, negate, or nullify the thoughts, feelings, or experiential reality of a person and their social group (e.g., proclaiming a colorblind ideology, telling an LGBTQ Person of Color that racism, heterosexism, and transphobia do not exist).

While microaggressions seem innocuous, the literature (Sue, 2010a) suggests that there are four pathways through which microaggressions might negatively affect individuals' health:

1. biological—microaggressive experiences may cause physiological reactions (blood pressure, heart rate, etc.) or changes in the immune system;
2. cognitive—microaggressive experiences require and occupy attentional resources to discern the meaning of the stressor;

3. emotional—anger, rage, anxiety, depression, or hopelessness may dominate the person;
4. behavioral—the coping strategies or behavioral reactions utilized by the person may either help adjustment or make the situation worse.

Indeed, research suggest that microaggressions may have negative impacts on one's physical and mental health (e.g., Nadal, Griffin, Wong, & Rasmus, 2014; Schmitt, Branscombe, Postmes, & Garcia, 2014; Wong-Padoongpatt, Zane, Okazaki, & Saw, 2017). For example, studies consistently find relationships between perceived discrimination and happiness, life satisfaction, self-esteem, and hypertension (Williams, Neighbors, & Jackson, 2003). Another study found microaggressions to have a cumulative effect that can be quite devastating on the recipients' psychological well-being (Solórzano et al., 2000). Nadal et al. (2014) found that people who experience racial microaggressions tend to experience more negative mental health symptoms such as depression, anxiety, negative affect, and lack of behavioral control, while Nadal, Griffin, Wong, Davidoff, and Davis (2017) found racial microaggressions to be significantly correlated with poorer physical health conditions such as general health problems, pain, lower energy levels, and fatigue. Certainly, the rapid growth of research attention on microaggressions over the past decade has led to the realization that microaggressions are salient for various oppressed groups and that microaggressions have immense negative health consequences.

Although there has been tremendous growth in our understanding of microaggressions and their impacts over the past 10 years (for a review, see Nadal, Whitman, Davis, Erazo, & Davidoff, 2016; Wong, Derthick, David, Saw, & Okazaki, 2013), almost all the work has been about microaggressions committed by members of a dominant group (e.g., men, White, and heterosexual) toward a target or oppressed group (e.g., women, People of Color, and LGBTQ people), and there has been virtually no work on within-group microaggressions (Nadal, Hamit, Lyons, Weinberg, & Corman, 2013; Nadal, Sriken, Davidoff, Wong, & McLean, 2013). That is, what about microaggressions that happen between individuals who are members of the same social group, such as with the scenario described in the beginning of this chapter? Also, what about microaggressions from members of an oppressed group that are directed toward another marginalized group (e.g., when non-Black People of Color discriminate against Black people)? Even further, what about microaggressions that individuals commit against their own selves, such as when an LGBTQ person feels embarrassed to admit one's sexual orientation or gender identity? Before we delve deeper into these understudied types of microaggressions, let us first discuss internalized oppression as it is a key concept to understanding these more nuanced forms of microaggressions.

Internalized Oppression

According to David and Derthick (2014),

> Oppression occurs when one group has more access to power and privilege than another group, and when that power and privilege is used to maintain the status quo (i.e., domination of one group over another). Thus, oppression is both a state and a process, with the state of oppression being an unequal group access to power and privilege, and the process of oppression being the ways in which inequality between groups is maintained. (p. 3)

It is commonly known that social group oppression—whether blatant or subtle—exists and operates on the interpersonal and institutional levels (David & Derthick, 2017). According to theory (Fanon, 1965; Freire, 1970; Memmi, 1965) and empirical findings (e.g., Clark & Clark, 1939; David & Nadal, 2013; David & Okazaki, 2006a), living and being socialized in a systemically oppressive climate may lead oppressed individuals to eventually believe, accept, or succumb to their alleged inferiority. In other words, members of socially oppressed groups may eventually internalize the oppression that they face, creating yet another level in which oppression may exist and operate: internalized. The three levels of oppression—interpersonal, institutional, and internalized—feed off each other, which creates a vicious feedback loop and seemingly inescapable "system of oppression" that destroys individuals, families, and communities for generations (David & Derthick, 2017). That is, all three levels of oppression work together to enact oppression and maintain a state of oppression.

As aforementioned, internalized oppression is when oppressed individuals or groups come to oppress themselves (and others like them) because of the oppression they have experienced (David & Derthick, 2017). The manifestation of internalized oppression varies between groups and even among individuals within the same group. For instance, internalized sexism, hetereosexism, ableism, and racism are different from each other, and internalized racism may look different for various racial groups (see David, 2014). Even further, internalized oppression is an individual-differences variable (David & Okazaki, 2006a) in that not all oppressed individuals internalize the oppression they face, and even people who have internalized oppression may also vary in terms of intensity and the extent to which it affects their lives (David, 2013). Nevertheless, although there are group and individual differences regarding the existence, manifestations, and implications of internalized oppression, research seems to suggest that some characteristics of internalized oppression are commonly experienced.

One consistent characteristic of internalized oppression is that it can be manifested subtly and blatantly (e.g., for a review, see David, 2014). The subtle type of internalized oppression is the attitudes and feelings a person may have about themselves, the group they belong to, and other groups. *Subtle internalized oppression* is when the negative views of the oppressor become unconsciously part of the oppressed person's internal belief system and perception of themselves and others. For example, some folks may feel embarrassed, ashamed, and inferior about their group characteristics (e.g., skin tone and language), believe that their group should change to become better or "more civilized" (e.g., assimilationist attitudes), or perceive some groups as inherently or deservedly better and dominated groups as inherently or deservedly inferior (e.g., believing in the myth of meritocracy). Such inferiorizing attitudes and feelings may be expressed unintentionally—and perhaps even well intentionally—to others verbally and behaviorally. Some verbal examples include people who advise or encourage their loved ones to use bleach to whiten their skin, and a transgender who mocks another transgender person for not "passing." Behavioral examples include immigrants who teach their American-born children "English only" because they believe their heritage language is disadvantageous or when a gay man outwardly denigrates gay people to hide his sexual orientation. Also, research suggests that these subtle manifestations of internalized oppression can exist and operate outside of awareness, intention, or control. (e.g., Chae et al., 2014; David, 2010; David & Okazaki, 2010). In contrast, the blatant type of internalized oppression is overt behaviors that express or is reflective of the oppressive attitudes and beliefs that people have already internalized. Some examples of *blatant internalized oppression* include People of Color who declare "White Power" or who consciously and deliberately subscribe to White supremacist rhetoric (e.g., Chew, 2017), immigrants who purposefully lie about their heritage or deny their proficiency in their native language in order to dilute their "other-ness" or demonstrate their "American-ness" (Nadal, 2011), and LGBTQ individuals who engage in conversion therapy (e.g., Kantor, 2015).

Internalized oppression may also be expressed intrapersonally, interpersonally, and institutionally (David & Derthick, 2017). The most frequently known manifestation of internalized oppression is *intrapersonal*—when individuals hold derogatory or inferiorizing attitudes or feelings toward one's self and when one enacts such beliefs toward one's own self (e.g., use of skin-whitening products). When inferiorizing attitudes, beliefs, and behaviors are expressed to other people, then internalized oppression is manifested *interpersonally* (e.g., when immigrants belittle other immigrants for being not assimilated enough). When such inferiorizing attitudes and practices become normalized—perhaps even to the point where social norms, policies, or laws are developed to legitimize them—internalized oppression becomes *institutionalized*. An example of this is seen in the Philippines, where there are laws establishing English as the official language for school instruction instead of their Indigenous languages.

As is now clear, internalized oppression that is expressed interpersonally or institutionally is when internalized oppression is projected toward other oppressed groups or other members of one's own group. Thus, interpersonal and institutional internalized oppression is when internalized oppression becomes *lateral (or horizontal) oppression*—when oppressed groups use the biased views and/or institutions of the dominant society to marginalize other groups (i.e., between-group) or people in their own group (i.e., within-group; David & Derthick, 2017). Some examples of *within-group lateral oppression* are when immigrants derogate other immigrants for speaking English with an accent (e.g., Castillo, Cano, Chen, Blucker, & Olds, 2008; Castillo, Conoley, Brossart, & Quiros, 2007; David & Okazaki, 2006b) or when a gay person denigrates another person for being gay (e.g., Szymanski & Chung, 2001). An example of *between-groups lateral oppression* (or horizontal hostility; e.g., White & Langer, 1999) is when some Asian Americans see themselves as "model minorities" and uphold stereotypical views of Black, Latina/o/x, and Native Americans as lazy; such beliefs may result in supporting anti-affirmative action policies and blaming other groups for any disparities. The different manifestations of internalized oppression and the various levels in which they may operate are summarized with examples in Table 8.1.

Internalized Microaggressions

Now that we have reviewed microaggressions and internalized oppression, let us put them together and return to the questions we brought up in the beginning of the chapter: What about microaggressions between individuals who are members of the same group? Also, what about microaggressions committed by an oppressed group toward another marginalized group? Further, what about when oppressed individuals microaggress against their own selves? Because we believe these more nuanced forms of microaggressions can be conceptualized as internalized microaggressions, we now present a theoretical framework that locates internalized microaggressions in the larger scholarship on oppression and internalized oppression.

Although there has been an increase of psychological literature on "microaggressions" and "internalized oppression," a *PsycINFO* search indicated that there were no known publications that covered both terms combined. Nevertheless, it does not mean that internalized microaggressions have not been studied. Indeed, scholars (e.g., Castillo, Cano, et al., 2008; Castillo, Conoley, et al., 2007; Chavez-Duenas, Adames, & Organista, 2013; David & Okazaki, 2006a; Lee & Ahn, 2009; Llamas & Consoli, 2012) have used terms such as *within-group discrimination* or *intragroup marginalization* to refer to the hostility, derogation, and prejudices that happen between individuals of the same social group. Scholars (e.g., Bombay, Matheson, & Anisman, 2014; Freire, 1970;

Table 8.1 Levels and Manifestations of Internalized Oppression.

Levels	Manifestations			
	Subtle		Blatant	
Intrapersonal	e.g., A Native American who feels inferior, unattractive, or inadequate for being Native American.		e.g., An Asian person who deliberately hides or denies one's Asian heritage.	
Lateral oppression	Between-groups	Within-group	Between-groups	Within-group
Interpersonal	E.g., A Black American who politely tells his Black friends that he believes that "All Lives Matter."	E.g., A Latina/o/x American who jokingly teases other Latina/o/x Americans about their accents.	E.g., An Arab American who proclaims, "White Power" and participates in White supremacist rallies.	E.g., A Black American who pledges to never marry a Black person because she thinks Black people are not attractive.
Institutional	E.g., A Latin American country that finds acceptable and normal that TV shows and movies almost always portray Black people as villains.	E.g., An Asian community wherein it has become normal and encouraged for members to use skin-whitening products.	E.g., A Hispanic organization that officially endorses anti-affirmative action and other racial equity policies.	E.g., An Asian country where English is the official language in schools and government functions instead of their own language.

Prilleltensky, 2003; Szymanski & Chung, 2001; White & Langer, 1999) have also used the term *lateral oppression* or *horizontal oppression* (or some derivative such as "lateral violence" or "horizontal hostility") to refer to both within-group and between-groups discrimination. Further, myriad scholars have been using the more general concept of internalized oppression to explain not just within-group and between-groups discrimination but also to encompass instances when oppressed individuals oppress their own selves (for a review, see David, 2014). Even further, given that most types of oppression today are of the subtle kind (i.e., microaggressions), it is likely that most forms of internalized oppression today are the subtle kind of oppression. In other words, a big portion of the kinds of oppression talked about in the internalized oppression literature today is probably microaggressions, which are then expressed toward one's own self and toward other people and groups. Therefore, the literature on internalized oppression—particularly subtle internalized oppression—is relevant as we can conceptualize subtle internalized oppression as internalized microaggressions.

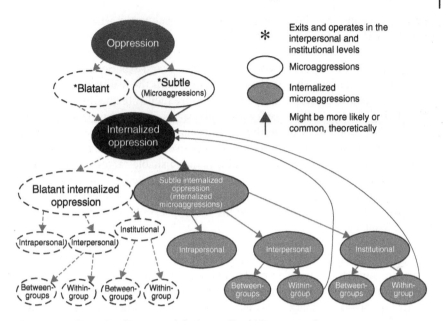

Figure 8.1 A Conceptual Framework for Internalized Microaggressions.

Research seems to suggest that subtle oppression is more commonly expressed today compared to blatant forms (e.g., David & Derthick, 2017; Dovidio & Gaertner, 2000). In Figure 8.1, we see that oppression may be expressed subtly or blatantly (i.e., a solid arrow connects oppression with subtle oppression compared to a dashed arrow connecting oppression with blatant oppression). We also see that blatant and subtle oppression may be internalized. However, as indicated by the thick solid arrow between subtle oppression and internalized oppression, it is theoretically plausible for subtle oppression such as microaggressions to be more likely to be internalized. According to Sue (2010b), "Microaggressions reflect the active manifestation of oppressive worldviews that create, foster, and enforce marginalization. To be confined to the margins of existence in mainstream life is to be oppressed ..." (p. 6). Further, Sue also noted that "Microaggressions are the everyday verbal, nonverbal, or environmental slights, snubs, or insults, whether intentional or unintentional, that communicate hostile, derogatory, or negative messages to target persons based solely upon their marginalized group membership" (p. 3). Thus, microaggressions are a specific type—the subtle kind—of oppression. However, because microaggressions are subtle and vague, it is often not clear who the perpetrator is and if oppression even took place, an experience Sue et al. (2007) called *attributional ambiguity*. Therefore, targets of microaggressions may be more susceptible to making internal attributions instead of external ones. As David and Derthick (2014) explained:

> ... because microaggressions are perpetrated and experienced subtly and often unconsciously, the victim often questions the reality of the oppression. Thus, victims of microaggressions frequently blame themselves for being "overly sensitive" or "crazy" and dismiss (if not excuse) the behavior of the perpetrators. Nevertheless, microaggressions produce equally distressing psychological consequences as overt oppression, perhaps even more so, because of the lack of a distinguishable target to which one can direct anger (Sue, 2010a). When one is denied the opportunity to (identify and) confront the source of oppression, the anger is directed inwardly (or) at those who remind the oppressed individual of him- or herself. (p. 5)

Instead of clearly identifying an event as oppression coming from someone or something outside one's self, targets of microaggressions might be more prone to point to something inside or about themselves (e.g., oversensitivity) as the reason for their experience. This is one way in which microaggressions and internalized oppression are linked: Microaggressions—because of their subtlety and vagueness—are the types of oppression that might be more likely to be internalized.

Just as oppression may be expressed blatantly and subtly, internalized oppression may also be expressed blatantly and subtly. *Subtle internalized oppression* is hidden, unconscious, unintentional, perhaps even well-intentioned slights, insults, "jokes," or behaviors that communicate derogatory or inferiorizing messages toward one's self and others "who remind the oppressed individual of him- or herself" (David & Derthick, 2014, p. 5). This subtle form of internalized oppression may be conceptualized as internalized microaggressions. If we revisit Sue's (2010b) definition of microaggressions—"everyday verbal, nonverbal, or environmental slights, snubs, or insults, whether intentional or unintentional, that communicate hostile, derogatory, or negative messages to target persons based solely upon their marginalized group membership" (p. 3)—nowhere is it stated that "target persons" must be other people or people outside of one's group. Further, nowhere does it state that perpetrators of microaggressions are always members of dominant groups. Therefore, microaggressions may be committed by oppressed individuals toward one's self (intrapersonal), toward other people of the same social group (within-group lateral oppression), and toward members of other oppressed social groups (between-groups lateral oppression). It is when microaggressions are done by oppressed persons or groups and targeted intrapersonally and laterally (within or between) that they become internalized microaggressions.

As Sue et al. (2007) explicated, there are three types of microaggressions: microassaults, microinsults, and microinvalidations. Similarly, internalized microaggresions (or subtle internalized oppression) may also be manifested as microassaults, microinsults, and microinvalidations. First, internalized microassaults are explicit, conscious, and purposeful verbal or nonverbal expressions by an oppressed person or group that hurt, derogate, inferiorize, or exclude one's self, other people of the same group, or another oppressed group. Second, internalized microinsults are often subtle, unconscious, or unintentional verbal or nonverbal expressions by an oppressed person or group that convey rude, insensitive, demeaning, or insulting messages about one's self, other people of the same group, or another oppressed group. Third, internalized microinvalidations are characterized by verbal or nonverbal expressions by an oppressed person or group that exclude, negate, or nullify one's own thoughts, feelings, or experiential reality, or those of other people in the same group or other oppressed groups. And just like internalized oppression, internalized microaggressions may also exist and operate in the intrapersonal, interpersonal, and institutional levels. In Table 8.2, we provide examples of how the different types of internalized microaggressions may occur systemically in various levels.

Clinical and Community Impacts of Internalized Microaggressions

Now that we have established that microaggressions and internalized oppression are linked in two key ways (i.e., through the internalization of oppression and manifestation of internalized oppression), we end this chapter with a brief discussion of how internalized microaggressions may impact individuals and communities. First, the literature on internalized oppression (for a review, see David, 2014) seems to suggest that internalized oppression is detrimental to the mental, physical, and emotional health of oppressed people. For instance, research shows that internalized oppression is negatively correlated with various indicators of well-being and mental health such as anxiety, depression, life satisfaction, and self-esteem (e.g., David, 2013; David & Okazaki, 2006b; Hatzenbuehler, 2009). Further, internalized oppression has even been linked with shorter telomere length (Chae et al., 2014), suggesting that internalized oppression is related to faster deterioration of organs and, thus, sooner death. Even further, research seems to suggest that it is the subtle or covert form of internalized oppression such as feelings of shame, embarrassment, and having inferiorizing beliefs about one's social group—internalized microaggressions—that are especially related to poorer mental health and

Table 8.2 Levels and Types of Internalized Microaggressions.

Levels	Types of Internalized Microaggressions					
	Microassault		**Microinsult**		**Microinvalidation**	
Intrapersonal	E.g., A brown-skinned person deciding to use skin-whitening products at home and to get skin-whitening treatments from a clinic.		E.g., A woman feeling like an "impostor" and questioning her qualifications in a job she has experience in and is well trained for.		E.g., A transgender woman who disregards her experience of discrimination by convincing herself that she is just overly sensitive and paranoid.	
Lateral oppression	*Between-groups*	*Within-group*	*Between-groups*	*Within-group*	*Between-groups*	*Within-group*
Interpersonal	E.g., A Black person calling an Asian person "chink" or an Asian person calling a Latino person a "wetback."	E.g., A woman who uses terms such as *whore* and *slut* to refer to women with different sexual behaviors than her.	E.g., An Asian American who implicitly regards Native or Indigenous People as less intelligent and less "advanced."	E.g., A Latino immigrant who covertly regards newly emigrated Latinas/os as less intelligent or "backward."	E.g., An Asian American person who disregards racist policies and says that other minority groups simply need to get a job to get out of poverty.	E.g., A Latino parent telling his children they have nothing to complain about because they are lucky to be in the United States.
Institutional	E.g., An African American organization that endorses exclusionary immigration laws due to their belief that immigrants (Latinos/as and Asians) reduce employment opportunities for Black people.	E.g., A Native American company that requires their mostly Native employees to wear "professional" attire to work instead of their traditional clothes.	E.g., An Asian American company that has a "tradition" of holding Luau-themed parties every year and that has instituted "Aloha Fridays" in the workplace every week.	E.g., A woman's baseball team that has a team motto that they proclaim at every practice and every game: "Don't throw like a girl, don't run like a girl!"	E.g., A gay and lesbian organization where it has become an accepted norm to consider bisexual people as simply "confused."	E.g., A Native American organization that regards federal recognition and blood quantum certification as the only indicators of Indigenous identity and membership.

well-being (David, 2010). Nevertheless, although we have learned plenty about internalized oppression already, it is still a relatively understudied phenomenon (David & Derthick, 2014; Pyke, 2010), particularly with regard to internalized oppression's institutional-level manifestations and implications.

Another mental health impact of internalized microaggression is through the within-group division it creates. Indeed, the relatively scarce research on the mental health effects of within-group discrimination seem to consistently suggest that people who experience it more often also tend to have poorer mental health and well-being (e.g., Lee & Ahn, 2009; Mata-Greve, 2016; Williams et al., 2003). In fact, these studies seem to suggest that experiencing discrimination—many, if not most, of which are likely to be microaggressions (e.g., Nadal, Hamit, et al., 2013; Nadal, Sriken, et al., 2013)—from other members of one's group might be more painful than discrimination from out-groups, as within-group discrimination causes feelings of betrayal and exclusion and elicits a sense of not belonging or disconnect from people who one might expect to be accepting, understanding, and supportive. Thus, within-group discrimination may dismantle one's social support network, making one more vulnerable to experiencing psychological distress and poor mental health. Further, the lack of group unity that is created by within-group discrimination may render oppressed groups even more powerless (e.g., Nadal, Hamit, et al., 2013; Prilleltensky, 2003), which not only has important mental health implications but community implications as well because lack of unity may make groups more susceptible to exploitation and further subjugation. For instance, a sense of powerlessness may lead to nonparticipation, demobilization, and the belief that even if one engages, one will not be heard, considered, or impactful. Indeed, more attention needs to be devoted to how various social groups (race, gender, etc.) experience within-group discrimination and what its clinical and community impacts might be.

Regarding community implications, internalized microaggressions may also create between-group divisions and lack of solidarity among various oppressed groups (Prilleltensky, 2003; White & Langer, 1999). Between-groups discrimination—many, if not most, of which are expressed through microaggressions—creates further divisions between different groups of people that prevents them from uniting in their similar struggles. Microaggressions between different oppressed groups may instead lead oppressed groups to fight among themselves instead of fighting the actual problem which is oppression (David & Derthick, 2017). Other oppressed groups can become the ransom for one person or one group to feel like a part of the dominant structure or to "look better" in the eyes of society. In this way, both within-group and between-groups lateral microaggressions function together as a negative feedback loop whereby oppressed groups participate in their own marginalization and the marginalization of others. Combine this with intrapersonal microaggressions, then we have all of the manifestations of internalized microaggressions working together and feeding off each other systematically to keep the oppressive status quo in place (David & Derthick, 2017; Prilleltensky, 2003). Given the seeming ubiquity, immense negative impact, and insidiousness of subtle oppression (i.e., microaggressions), it is clear that there is a lot of work for researchers, educators, activists, and community leaders to do. We must create opportunities for people to learn more about both microaggressions and internalized oppression in order for individuals to comprehend how both concepts combine to negatively impact their lives. Parents, family members, and educators may consider teaching their children, students, and other young people about internalized microaggressions so that young people can understand how they can minimize or combat internalized oppression. Researchers can further study not only the detrimental ways that internalized microaggressions damage people's psychological and physical health but also how they may even lead to severe physical illness or even death. Either way, it sure looks like we all have our work cut out for us; so, let us get to it.

References

Bombay, A., Matheson, K., & Anisman, H. (2014). *Origins of lateral violence in aboriginal communities: A preliminary study of student-to-student abuse in residential schools*. Ottawa, ON: Aboriginal Healing Foundation. Available online at: http://www.ahf.ca/downloads/lateral-violence-english.pdf.

Castillo, L. G., Cano, M. A., Chen, S. W., Blucker, R. T., & Olds, T. S. (2008). Family conflict and intragroup marginalization as predictors of acculturative stress in 54 Latino college students. *International Journal of Stress Management, 15*(1), 43–52. doi:10.1037/1072-5245.14.1.43.

Castillo, L. G., Conoley, C. W., Brossart, D. F., & Quiros, A. E. (2007). Construction and validation of the intragroup marginalization inventory. *Cultural Diversity and Ethnic Minority Psychology, 13*, 232–240. doi:10.1037/1099-9809.13.3.23.

Chae, D. H., Nuru-Jeter, A. M., Adler, N. E., Brody, G. H., Lin, J., Blackburn, E. H., & Epel, E. (2014). Discrimination, racial bias, and telomere length in African–American men. *American Journal of Preventive Medicine, 46*, 103–111.

Chavez-Duenas, N. Y., Adames, H. Y., & Organista, K. C. (2013). Skin-color prejudice and within-group racial discrimination: Historical and current impact on Latino/a populations. *Hispanic Journal of Behavioral Sciences, 36*, 3–26.

Chew, E. (2017). *Singaporean blogger has expressed her love for Trump and the need to make America great again*. Retrieved from http://www.yomyomf.com/singaporean-blogger-has-expressed-her-love-for-trump-and-the-need-to-make-american-great-again/.

Constantine, M. G., & Sue, D. W. (2007). Perceptions of racial microaggressions among Black supervisees in cross-racial dyads. *Journal of Counseling Psychology, 54*, 142–153.

Clark, K. B., & Clark, M. P. (1939). The development of consciousness of self and the emergence of racial identification in negro pre-school children. *Journal of Social Psychology, 10*, 591–599.

David, E. J. R. (2010). Testing the validity of the Colonial Mentality Implicit Association Test (CMIAT) and the interactive effects of covert and overt colonial mentality on Filipino American mental health. *Asian American Journal of Psychology, 1*, 31–45.

David, E. J. R. (2013). *Brown skin, white minds: Filipino -/ American postcolonial psychology (with commentaries)*. Charlotte, NC: Information Age Publishing.

David, E. J. R. (Ed.) (2014). *Internalized oppression: The psychology of marginalized groups*. New York, NY: Springer.

David, E. J. R., & Derthick, A. O. (2014). What is internalized oppression, and so what? In E. J. R. David (Ed.), *Internalized oppression: The psychology of marginalized groups* (pp. 1–30). New York, NY: Springer.

David, E. J. R., & Derthick, A. O. (2017). *The psychology of oppression*. New York, NY: Springer.

David, E. J. R., & Nadal, K. L. (2013). The colonial context of Filipino American immigrants' psychological experiences. *Cultural Diversity and Ethnic Minority Psychology, 19*(3), 298–309.

David, E. J. R., & Okazaki, S. (2006a). The Colonial Mentality Scale (CMS) for Filipino Americans: Scale construction and psychological implications. *Journal of Counseling Psychology, 53*, 241–252.

David, E. J. R., & Okazaki, S. (2006b). Colonial mentality: A review and recommendation for Filipino American psychology. *Cultural Diversity & Ethnic Minority Psychology, 12*, 1–16.

David, E. J. R., & Okazaki, S. (2010). Activation and automaticity of colonial mentality. *Journal of Applied Social Psychology, 40*, 850–887.

Dovidio, J. F., & Gaertner, S. L. (2000). Aversive racism and selective decisions: 1989–1999. *Psychological Science, 11*, 315–319.

Fanon, F. (1965). *The wretched of the earth*. New York, NY: Grove.

Freire, P. (1970). *Pedagogy of the oppressed*. New York, NY: Continuum.

Hatzenbuehler, M. L. (2009). How does sexual minority stigma "get under the skin"? A psychological medication framework. *Psychological Bulletin, 145*, 707–730.

Kantor, M. (2015). *Why a gay person can't be made un-gay: The truth about reparative therapies*. Santa Barbara, CA: Praeger/ABC-CLIO.

Lee, D. L., & Ahn, S. (2009). Discrimination against Latina/os: A meta-analysis of individual-level resources and outcomes. *The Counseling Psychologist, 40*(1), 28–65. doi:10.1177/0011000011403326.

Llamas, J. D., & Consoli, M. (2012). The importance of Latina/o college students: Examining the role of familial support in intragroup marginalization. *Cultural Diversity and Ethnic Minority Psychology, 18*(4), 395–403. doi:10.1037/a0029756.

Mata-Greve, F. (2016). *Effects of within-group discrimination on mental health symptoms in Latinos* (Dissertations (2009 -)). Paper 634. Retrieved from http://epublications.marquette.edu/dissertations_mu/634.

Memmi, A. (1965). *The colonizer and the colonized.* Boston, MA: Beacon.

Nadal, K. L. (2011). *Filipino American psychology: A handbook of theory, research, and clinical practice.* Hoboken, NJ: Wiley.

Nadal, K. L., Griffin, K. E., Wong, Y., Davidoff, K. C., & Davis, L. S. (2017). The injurious relationship between racial microaggressions and physical health: Implications for social work. *Journal of Ethnic & Cultural Diversity in Social Work: Innovation in Theory, Research & Practice, 26,* 6–17.

Nadal, K. L., Griffin, K. E., Wong, Y., Hamit, S., & Rasmus, M. (2014). The impact of racial microaggressions on mental health: Counseling implications for clients of color. *Journal of Counseling & Development, 92,* 57–66. doi:10.1002/j.1556-6676.2014.00130.x.

Nadal, K. L., Hamit, S., Lyons, O., Weinberg, A., & Corman, L. (2013). Gender microaggressions: Perceptions, processes, and coping mechanisms of women. In M. A. Paludi (Ed.), *The psychology of business success, Juggling, Balancing, and Integrating Work and Family Role and Responsibilities* (Vol. 1, pp. 193–220). Santa Barbara, CA: Praeger.

Nadal, K. L., Sriken, J., Davidoff, K., Wong, Y., & McLean, K. (2013). Microaggressions within families: Experiences of multiracial and multiethnic people. *Family Relations, 62,* 190–201.

Nadal, K. L., Whitman, C. N., Davis, L. S., Erazo, T., & Davidoff, K. C. (2016). Microaggressions toward lesbian, gay, bisexual, transgender, queer and genderqueer people: A review of the literature. *Journal of Sex Research, 53,* 488–508.

Pierce, C. M., Carew, J., Pierce-Gonzalez, D., & Willis, D. (1978). An experiment in racism: TV commercials. In C. M. Pierce (Ed.), *Television and education* (pp. 62–88). Beverly Hills, CA: Sage.

Prilleltensky, I. (2003). Understanding, resisting, and overcoming oppression: Toward psychopolitical validity. *American Journal of Community Psychology, 31*(1/2), 195–201.

Pyke, K. D. (2010). What is internalized racial oppression and why don't we study it? Acknowledging racism's hidden injuries. *Sociological Perspectives, 53*(4), 551–572. doi:10.1525/sop.2010.53.4.551.

Schmitt, M. T., Branscombe, N. R., Postmes, T., & Garcia, A. (2014). The consequences of perceived discrimination for psychological well-being: A meta-analytic review. *Psychological Bulletin, 140*(4), 921–948. doi:10.1037/a0035754.

Solórzano, D., Ceja, M., & Yosso, T. (2000). Critical race theory, racial microaggressions, and campus racial climate: The experiences of African American college students. *The Journal of Negro Education, 69,* 60–73.

Sue, D. W. (2010a). *Microaggressions in everyday life: Race, gender, and sexual orientation.* Hoboken, NJ: Wiley.

Sue, D. W. (2010b). Microaggressions, marginality, and oppression: An introduction. In D. W. Sue (Ed.), *Microaggressions and marginality: Manifestations, dynamics, and impact* (pp. 3–22). Hoboken, NJ: Wiley.

Sue, D. W., Capodilupo, C. M., Torino, G. C., Bucceri, J. M., Holder, A., Nadal, K. L., & Esquilin, M. (2007). Racial microaggressions in everyday life: Implications for clinical practice. *American Psychologist, 62*(4), 271.

Szymanski, D. M., & Chung, Y. B. (2001). The lesbian internalized homophobia scale: A rational/theoretical approach. *Journal of Homosexuality, 41*(2), 37–52.

White, J. B., & Langer, E. J. (1999). Horizontal hostility: Relations between similar minority groups. *Journal of Social Issues, 55*(3), 537–559.

Williams, D. R., Neighbors, H. W., & Jackson, J. S. (2003). Racial/ethnic discrimination and health: Findings from community studies. *American Journal of Public Health, 93*(2), 200–208.

Wong, G., Derthick, A. O., David, E. J. R., Saw, A., & Okazaki, S. (2013). The what, the why, and the how: A review of racial microaggressions research in psychology. *Race and Social Problems*, 1–20. doi:10.1007/s12552-013-9107-9.

Wong-Padoongpatt, G., Zane, N., Okazaki, S., & Saw, A. (2017). Decreases in implicit self-esteem explain the racial impact of microaggressions among Asian Americans. *Journal of Counseling Psychology.* doi:10.1037/cou0000217.

9

"I Didn't Know That Was Racist": Costs of Racial Microaggressions to White People

D Anthony Clark and Lisa Spanierman

No. White individuals are not the targets of racial microaggressions. White folks are not targets because the United States is a White-privileging, *racialized social system* "in which economic, political, social, and ideological levels are partially structured by the place of actors in racial categories or races" (Bonilla-Silva, 1997, p. 469). The racialized social system in the United States controls discourse about racial identities and racial inequalities and thus reinforces a "common sense" about a White-defined "reality." In short, members of the White racial category sit atop a racialized hierarchy of economic, civic, and psychological advantages. Since at least until 1790, when the first U.S. Congress declared that citizenship was limited to "free white persons," the dominant racial category has been "White" (Jacobson, 1998). All Americans today, Whites included, are socialized into semifluid racial categories constituted at the crossroads of the economy, politics, and culture. In the 21st-century United States, only Whites are the perpetrators of racial microaggressions, which contribute to the web of societal, organizational, and individual acts of racism that reproduce the conditions of White advantage from one generation to the next. And yet, their perpetrating racial microaggressions come with affective, behavioral, and cognitive costs to Whites (e.g., a narcissistic lack of empathy for human misery). How to frame these costs as a subject of empirical research is the subject of this chapter.

The Socioeconomic Context in Which Whites Perpetrate Racial Microaggressions

The costs of perpetrating racial microaggressions to White folks must be understood in a wider economic context that provides material, civic, and

Microaggression Theory: Influence and Implications, First Edition. Edited by Gina C. Torino, David P. Rivera, Christina M. Capodilupo, Kevin L. Nadal, and Derald Wing Sue.
© 2019 John Wiley & Sons, Inc. Published 2019 by John Wiley & Sons, Inc.

psychological benefits to them. *There is an asset advantage to Whiteness,* which is evident in home ownership, income and savings, education, and entrepreneurship (Wiedrich et al., 2016). When we frame household wealth by race, for instance, the median wealth of White households in 2009 was 20 times that of Black households and 18 times that of Latinx households (Kochhar, Fry, & Taylor, 2011). Since 1983, median wealth declined by 75% for African American households and 50% for Latinx households. At the same time, median wealth increased by 14% for White households (Asante-Muhammad, Collins, Hoxie, & Nieves, 2016). Economic opportunities and upward mobility greatly favor Whites. While median American household wealth declined generally, for example, it grew to an astounding 71% among the top 1% (Pew Research Center, 2014). Not surprisingly, 96% of the persons representing the wealthiest 1% of Americans are White. In comparison, Black households comprise only 1.4% of the wealthiest 1% of all Americans (Moore, 2016). Black folks in general were worse off financially in 2016 than they were in 2000 (Long, 2017). The racial wealth gap is growing and not narrowing. Should current trends in terms of overall family wealth and assets continue, public policy researchers estimate that in 2020, White households will own 85 times more wealth than Black households and 68 times more wealth than Latinx households (Asante-Muhammad, Nieves, Collins, & Hoxie, 2017).

Not only is there a material asset advantage to Whiteness, but there are material civic advantages as well. None are more evident than those in the criminal justice system. Racial disparities favor White folks, for instance, in incarceration and felony disenfranchisement. A study commissioned by The Sentencing Project found that African Americans are five times more likely than Whites to be incarcerated in state prisons across the United States (Nellis, 2016). Although evidence suggests that Black and White individuals consume marijuana at similar rates, for instance, Black folks are four times more likely to be arrested, convicted, and thus *felonized* for doing so (American Civil Liberties Union, 2013).

The material civic advantages of Whiteness inform the exercise of constitutional rights, including those rights allegedly guaranteed by the First and Second Amendments. We were struck, for instance, by the stark differences in the law enforcement response to the Ferguson, Missouri, protest in 2014 and the counterprotest the following year. Unarmed Black (and other) folks exercising their constitutional rights to peaceably assemble the government for a redress of their grievances after Michael Brown was gunned down in the street by a Ferguson police officer were met with a military-like intervention (see Figure 9.1).

During the counterprotests the following year in support of the status quo in law enforcement, mercenary-looking armed White "oath keepers" apparently posed no threat to community stability (see Figure 9.2). Imagining a mercenary-looking armed Black man yucking it up with a group of relaxed law enforcement officers is nearly as impossible as visualizing militarized police

Figure 9.1 Photograph by Getty Images News Photographer Scott Olson. © Scott Olson/GettyImages

Figure 9.2 Photograph by St. Louis-Based Freelance Photographer Michael Thomas. © Michael Thomas/GettyImages

officers confronting an unarmed White man exercising his First Amendment rights. We witnessed a similar phenomenon in 2017 with the limited police response to the White supremacist and neo-Nazi rally in Charlottesville, Virginia, where a woman in support of racial justice was murdered and others were injured.

In sum, Whites in the aggregate come out on top in material measures from economic security to incarceration and felony disenfranchisement to exercising constitutionally protected civil rights.

The Psychosocial Benefits of a White-Privileging Racialized Social System

What about those White folks who do not experience the economic or civic assets that privilege Whites over Communities of Color? In what ways do a White-privileging, racialized social system work for them? A wide range of psychological perks, privileges, and wages enable White folks in the lower stratums of household wealth to distinguish themselves from Communities of Color and instead identify with White individuals who are most advantaged by the economic assets of Whiteness (Du Bois, 1998; Hund, Krikler, & Roediger, 2011; Lipsitz, 2006; Liu, 2017; Roediger, 2007; Spanierman, Garriott, & Clark, 2013). These White perks, privileges, wages, and investments run deep.

Communities of Color long ago "discovered" the psychological benefits of whiteness. Any White person who has read bell hooks' (1992) *Representation of Whiteness in the Black Imagination*, for example, understands that Black folks exchange knowledge about the advantages of Whiteness "gleaned from close scrutiny of White people," not only for security purposes but also to make sense of their contradictions (p. 165). Du Bois (1998) used the phrase "public and psychological wage" in 1935 to identify the immaterial benefits that distinguished working-class Whites from their Black working-class counterparts (p. 700). Du Bois explained that the public and psychological wage was linked to an enhanced social status available to all White folks, such as the expectation of receiving "respectful" treatment (e.g., courtesy and public deference) from Black folks and admittance to various public spaces that Persons of Color were barred from enjoying (e.g., parks, swimming pools, and movie theaters). Extending Du Bois's observations about the public and psychological benefits of Whiteness, Roediger (2007) argued in his award-winning *Wages of Whiteness* that "the pleasures of whiteness could function as a 'wage' for white workers [and] status and privileges conferred by race could be used to make up for alienating and exploitative class relationships" (p. 13). Psychological wages of Whiteness thus reproduce feelings of White superiority as a form of affective, behavioral, and cognitive compensation for working-class Whites in return for acquiescing to the rule of White elites.

The boundaries of Whiteness and its economic, civic, and psychological advantages are ever-shifting. In the current moment of 21st-century working life, who might acquire the wages of Whiteness have and arguably will continue to change with unpredictable shifts in who can be White, because the social construction of Whiteness is contingent and context-dependent (e.g., Barrett & Roediger, 2008; Frankenberg, 1993; Lopez, 1996; Roediger, 2006). This is how various groups, such as Irish (Ignatiev, 1995), Italian (Guglielmo & Salerno, 2003), and Jewish (Brodkin, 1998) Americans, moved from racialized "otherness" into the dominant White racial category and its perks, whereas others have been and continue to be excluded even when they request membership (see, for instance, Ozawa *v.* United States, 1922; see also Lesser, 1986; Tehranian, 2000).

Context matters, and it is within the hierarchical context of a racialized social system with White folks on top with a disproportionate collection of advantages that set the stage for White individuals to perpetrate racial microaggressions. Doing so, though, also comes with costs. Thus, we draw on the existing psychological literature in the pages that follow that sheds light on the psychosocial costs of racism to White individuals and how these costs take form when Whites perpetrate racial microaggressions. We first introduce conceptual literature and empirical research about the cognitive, affective, and behavioral costs of racism to Whites. Next, we use Spanierman, Poteat, Beer, and Armstrong's (2006) five costs of racism types to address the link between costs of racism to Whites broadly to costs of racial microaggressions. In closing, we briefly discuss the implications for future racial microaggressions research, education and training, and organizational policy.

Psychosocial Costs of Racism to Whites

Spanierman and Heppner (2004) developed psychosocial costs of racism to Whites theory from conceptual scholarship in psychology and education (see Bowser & Hunt, 1981; Goodman, 2011; Kivel, 2011). In an edited text, *Impacts of Racism on White Americans* (Bowser & Hunt, 1981), social scientists catalogued certain psychological consequences of racism for White folks. These consequences ranged from moral ambivalence in which actions may contradict one's value of justice (Dennis, 1981) and inauthenticity (Terry, 1981) to distress associated with learning about racism (Karp, 1981) and mental instability and maladjustment (Pettigrew, 1981).

Extending Goodman's (2011) and Kivel's (2011) work on costs of oppression to dominant group members, Spanierman and Heppner (2004) framed costs of racism to White individuals with the tripartite model of affective, behavioral, and cognitive dimensions. Affective costs comprise emotional reactions that arise from living in a racialized social system (e.g., irrational fear of People of Color, guilt about one's White privilege). Behavioral costs of racism involve limited or restrictive actions such as censoring oneself in interracial contexts (e.g., Picca & Feagin, 2007) or living only where other White people live (e.g., Bonilla-Silva, Goar, & Embrick, 2006). Cognitive costs of racism include distorted thinking about oneself (e.g., individualized sense of entitlement), People of Color (e.g., relying on stereotypes), or society (e.g., denying the existence of racism). Spanierman and Heppner (2004) developed the *Psychosocial Costs of Racism to Whites Scale* to measure these negative consequences. Focusing on affective, or emotional, costs, the scale assesses *White empathy* (i.e., anger and sadness about the existence of racism), *White guilt* (i.e., remorse and accountability for one's racial privilege), and *White fear* (i.e., irrational fear of People of Color). To date, the most interesting empirical studies in this area have used cluster analysis to examine *costs of racism types* in combination. Researchers identified five types: antiracist, empathic but unaccountable, fearful guilt, oblivious, and insensitive and afraid. Moreover, these types distinguished White students' responses to racial issues on a university campus (Kordesh, Spanierman, & Neville, 2013; Spanierman, Todd, & Anderson, 2009). In what follows, we integrate Spanierman and Heppner's (2004) costs of racism to Whites theory and racial microaggressions theory to explore what might be the costs of perpetrating racial microaggressions to Whites.

Costs of Racism to Whites and Racial Microaggressions

Because racial microaggressions are a form of contemporary racism—subtle and often unintentional slights and indignities (Sue et al., 2007)—costs of racism to Whites theory is transferable to a discussion about the costs of racial microaggressions to White perpetrators and bystanders. In his first book addressing microaggressions in everyday life, Sue (2010) applied Spanierman and Heppner's conceptual framework to what he termed *the psychological costs of microaggressions to perpetrators*. Among the affective costs, he featured fear, anxiety, and apprehension, as these emotions relate to fear of appearing racist. Regarding behavioral costs, he emphasized avoidance (e.g., interacting with People of Color and talking about race). He highlighted the self-deceptive nature of cognitive costs, such as denying the existence of societal racism to continue to "function in good conscience" (p. 128). Finally, he reintroduced Goodman's (2011) and Kivel's (2011) moral and spiritual costs of racism to Whites referring to "losing one's humanity for the sake of the power, wealth, and status attained from the subjection of others" (p. 132). Below, we describe further Spanierman et al.'s (2006) *five costs of racism types* and apply them to understand potential costs to White perpetrators of racial microaggressions and to bystanders who witness them.

Insensitive and Afraid Type

Whites who evidence the *insensitive and afraid* type exhibit the lowest levels of White empathy and White guilt among all five types. They are the most anxious in terms of irrational fear of People of Color. Research has shown that this insensitive and afraid type has the lowest levels among all the types of: multicultural education, cultural sensitivity, racial awareness, support for affirmative action, and exposure to people of differing racial backgrounds (Spanierman et al., 2006). Were a target to confront an insensitive and afraid White individual who delivered or witnessed a racial microaggression, the insensitive and afraid type likely would respond defensively and angrily. They might explode with a barrage of racist microassaults and perhaps even claim they were a victim of reverse racism. In short, any challenges to racial microaggressions could be experienced by the insensitive and afraid perpetrator or bystander as threatening their dominant position in the racialized social system.

Oblivious Type

The *oblivious type*, also referred to as unempathic and unaware, is characterized by low levels of White empathy and White guilt with some measure of White fear. This type embraces color-blind racial ideology (see Neville, Lilly, Duran, Lee, & Browne, 2000), which means they are likely to deny racism and use a deficit framework to rationalize the pervasive racial disparities that characterize U.S. society. Spanierman et al. (2006) found that persons in this type were unaware of White privilege, had little multicultural education, and reported having very few cross-racial friendships. In situations where targets or White-ally bystanders in some way confronted an oblivious perpetrator or otherwise brought the "content" of their racially microaggressive act to their attention, those exhibiting the oblivious type likely would reply with a clueless, color-blind retort, such as "Why are you being so sensitive?"

Fearful Guilt Type

The fearful guilt type reflects high levels of White guilt and White fear, with low White empathy. This type is associated with at least some multicultural education and high awareness of racial privilege. In situations where the *fearful guilt* type perpetrates or witnesses a racial microaggression, a target's response may paralyze them. They may be overcome with remorse and experience anxiety about being perceived as racist. Thus, they likely would retreat back into their White enclave feeling badly but safe once again.

Empathic but Unaccountable Type

The *empathic but unaccountable type* exhibits high White empathy, without the accompanying White guilt described below in the antiracist type. Similar to the antiracist type below, these individuals exhibit racial diversity in their friendship group and acknowledge individual acts of racism. Yet they lack awareness of their own racial privilege in a White-privileging racialized social system. While the empathic but unaccountable type likely would demonstrate some concern for a target's feelings, in circumstances where a target shares them, White individuals demonstrating the qualities of this type might say something like, "You misunderstood my meaning. I meant to give you a compliment." Empathic but unaccountable White individuals commonly will express disappointment in themselves and feel badly about the racial microaggression when someone points it out, yet they probably will not feel that they need to change the institutions that allow racial microaggressions to flourish.

Antiracist Type

Among all five types, the *antiracist type* reflects the highest levels of White empathy and White guilt and the lowest White fear. Spanierman et al. (2006) found that these White individuals reported the highest levels among all five types of multicultural education, racial diversity among friends, cultural sensitivity, and support for affirmative action. Individuals in this type demonstrated the lowest color-blind racial ideology scores than all other types. Thus, they understand institutional racism and White privilege in a racialized social system. When confronted by either a target or White-ally bystander, those reflecting the *antiracist* type likely would empathize with the target's perspective and feelings, see the error in their utterance, apologize sincerely, feel a sense of accountability, and attempt to repair the rupture.

Two Racial Microaggressions Scenarios

More research is needed to examine our speculation regarding the costs of racial microaggressions to White perpetrators and bystanders that we introduced above. Anticipating that more research may follow, we dissect two racial microaggression scenarios to demonstrate possible responses to perpetrating or witnessing racial microaggressions by costs of racism type.

Scenario: Stupid White Man

Readers may be familiar with American actor, stand-up comedian, and Japanese translation specialist David Ury's (2013) YouTube sensation "What Kind of Asian Are You?" Ury's film-short opens with dancer and actress Stella Choe dressed to exercise and stretching while balanced on a fence as actor Scott Beehner approaches in a slow jog, stops to run in place, and greets Choe with "Hey there." Choe responds, "Hi," and the following conversation ensues:

> BEEHNER: Nice day, huh?
> CHOE: Yeah, finally, right?

BEEHNER: Where you from? Your English is perfect.

CHOE: San Diego. We speak English there.

BEEHNER (not getting it and slowing down the rhythm of his question to emphasize each part): Where ... are you ... from?

CHOE: Well I was born in Orange County, but I never actually lived there.

BEEHNER: I mean, before that.

CHOE: Before I was born?

BEEHNER: Well, where are your people from?

CHOE: Well, my great grandma was from Seoul.

BEEHNER: Korean! I knew it! I was like, 'She's either Japanese or Korean.' But I was leaning more towards Korean.

CHOE: Amazing.

The exchange between Choe and Beehner is a commonly reported experience among East Asian Americans who elicit active albeit probably unconsciously seemingly scripted responses from White folks (e.g., Alvarez, Juang, & Liang, 2006; Ong, Burrow, Fuller-Rowell, Ja, & Sue, 2013; Sue et al., 2007; Wang, Leu, & Shoda, 2011). Sue (2010) referred to this form of racial microaggression as "alien in one's own land" to signal that Asian and Latinx Americans are considered perpetual foreigners regardless of how many generations have lived in the United States. The late historian Ronald Takaki recalled a similar experience in his book *A Different Mirror*:

> I had flown from San Francisco to Norfolk and was riding in a taxi. The driver and I chatted about the weather and the tourists. The sky was cloudy, and twenty minutes away was Virginia Beach, where I was scheduled to give a keynote address to hundreds of teachers and administrators at a conference on multicultural education. The rearview mirror reflected a white man in his forties. "How long have you been in this country?" he asked. "All my life," I replied, wincing. His question was one I had been asked too many times, even by northerners with Ph.D's. "I was wondering because your English is excellent!" Then I explained: "My grandfather came here from Japan in the 1880s. My family has been here, in America, for over a hundred years." He glanced at me in the mirror. To him, I did not look like an American. (Takaki, 1993, p. 3)

Takaki continued:

> Questions like the one that my taxi driver asked me are always jarring. But it was not his fault that he did not see me as a fellow citizen: what had he learned about Asian Americans in courses called U.S. history? He saw me through a filter—what I call the Master Narrative of American History. (p. 4)

Thus, the master narrative produces racial microaggressions and racial microaggressions in turn reinforce the master narrative (see also, Feagin's white racial frame, 2013).

What might happen, though, had the dialogue between Choe and Beehner or the taxi driver and the historian unfolded differently? When Choe responded to the "where are you from?" refrain with the subtle dig, "We speak English there," she opened the possibility for Beehner to realize the absurdity of his line of inquiry. This is where the five costs of racism types (Spanierman et al., 2006) might be helpful in theorizing the transferability between the costs of racism and the costs of racial microaggressions to Whites. For instance, Beehner might be understood as the oblivious type. Because he likely was unaware of the master narrative or White racial frame in scripting his question, he was not equipped to recognize Choe's subtle attempt to stop the interrogation that inscribed Choe as an alien in her own country. Had he evidenced the insensitive and afraid type, however, he probably would have blasted Choe with an onslaught of microassaults intended to cause harm. But what if Beehner had some understanding of the White-privileging racialized social system that scripted his nonsense? Might he have been overwhelmed with the emotions of Spanierman et al.'s (2006) fearful guilt type and run away with his tail between his legs? Or perhaps he could reflect the most prevalent of the five types: empathic but unaccountable. Rather than continuing his interrogation uninterrupted as an oblivious type, he may have responded with, "I didn't mean it that way. I'm just trying to get to know you." And finally, in the rarest of the types, what might have happened had Beehner embodied the characteristics of the antiracist? The conversation likely would have followed an entirely different line because he would have realized he was perpetrating a racial microaggression when Choe responded with "San Diego. We speak English there," which would have driven the point home.

Scenario: Microaggressions on a Plane

Readers who have followed the growing scholarly literature on racial microaggressions likely recall Sue's testimony about an experience he had with racial microaggressions on a plane. Identifying as an Asian American in the *American Psychologist* under a heading that reads "the invisibility and dynamics of racial microaggressions," Sue wrote:

> I ... recently traveled with an African American colleague on a plane flying from New York to Boston. The plane was a small "hopper" with a single row of seats on one side and double seats on the other. As the plane was only sparsely populated, we were told by the flight attendant (White) that we could sit anywhere, so we sat at the front, across the aisle from one another. This made it easy for us to converse and provided a

larger comfortable space on a small plane for both of us. As the attendant was about to close the hatch, three White men in suits entered the plane, were informed they could sit anywhere, and promptly seated themselves in front of us. Just before takeoff, the attendant proceeded to close all overhead compartments and seemed to scan the plane with her eyes. At that point she approached us, leaned over, interrupted our conversation, and asked if we would mind moving to the back of the plane. She indicated that she needed to distribute weight on the plane evenly. (Sue et al. 2007, p. 275)

Sue further explained that both he and his African American colleague complied with the flight attendant's request, but that while doing so he experienced increasing "resentment, irritation, and anger." Feeling his "blood pressure rising, heart beating faster, and face flush with anger," Sue asked the flight attendant "in a forced calm voice: 'Did you know that you asked two Passengers of Color to step to the rear of the bus'?" What followed was neither the inevitable nor only possible response from the White flight attendant, which was, as Sue experienced it, "righteously indignant" and "defensive" (Sue et al., 2007, p. 275).

In this case of microaggressions on a plane, the indignant and defensive flight attendant who was confronted by the target of a racial microaggression responded from either the oblivious or insensitive and afraid type. According to Spanierman et al. (2006), both types would exhibit color-blind racial ideology, assume that the targets are overly sensitive, and experience little empathy for them. Working from a racially color-blind perspective, an oblivious-type flight attendant would focus on "proving" that she was not racist and that Sue and his colleague were being overly sensitive. An insensitive and afraid flight attendant would reflect more overt racist attitudes and greater defensiveness, and may, when challenged, perpetrate deliberate microassaults against Sue and his colleague.

What about bystanders who witness racial microaggressions on a plane targeting Passengers of Color? Spanierman et al.'s (2006) five types might be similarly suggestive. In a widely reported preflight incident in Chicago (e.g., Holley, 2017; KHOU, 2017; Mazza, 2017), United Airlines staff removed a White couple, according to the airline, "for making others feel uncomfortable ... and for saying some inappropriate things to customers" (Holley, 2017). The White man apparently had asked a couple sitting behind him and his female companion where they were from and another couple two rows in front if they had a bomb in their luggage. Apparently, the couple in front were Pakistani Americans and the couple to their rear were Indian Americans—all brown and "other" by his White ocular inspection. As flight crew members escorted the perpetrator and his White female companion from the flight, a seated passenger's recording captured the voice of one passenger saying, "Goooodbyeee raaacists!" and unmistakable cheers from others.

Based on empirical research on the five costs of racism types, we think it unlikely that a majority of the United Airlines flight was filled with White antiracist type passengers. Instead, it is probable that most White passengers were empathic and unaccountable or oblivious types. We imagine that empathic but unaccountable individuals would feel bad for the target and appalled to witness a racial microaggression, but likely would not feel accountable to act. Oblivious types might not have reacted to the "Where are you from?" question, but might note the racism in the question about the bomb. Regardless, they likely would not experience an emotional reaction and might turn to their neighbor, minimizing the incident by proclaiming airline officials overreacted. The fearful guilt type likely would feel terrible about witnessing an act of racism in this confined space, might speak out, and would want very much to distance themselves from the racist perpetrators. Alternatively, they may feel so overwhelmed with anxiety and other emotions that they are paralyzed and unable to act. Finally, the insensitive and afraid type might scream out in support of the perpetrator to join in solidarity.

As we hope we demonstrated above, there are a variety of different types of White folks who for myriad reasons experience the racialized social system differently and who therefore express racial microaggressions differently. We must also consider the different responses racial-microaggressive-perpetrating White folks have when they are confronted by both the targets who experience the full weight of the racialized social system and White-ally bystanders who witness and call attention to their racial microaggressive acts. Extending the conceptual microaggressive moment to include what comes before and after the utterance is critical, as is situating racial microaggressions conceptually in the context of the cultural, economic, educational, legal, political, and social institutions that constitute the White-privileging racialized social system.

Implications

Below, we offer future directions for microaggressions research that focuses on White perpetrators and bystanders. Additionally, we discuss implications for education and training.

Research

The next generation of racial microaggressions research should include a focus on White individuals to uncover antecedents and consequences of perpetrating racial microaggressions. We envision a variety of methodological approaches to acquire a deeper understanding of the nuanced associations between White individuals' affective, cognitive, and behavioral responses to perpetrating and witnessing racial microaggressions. Experimental designs, for example, might produce interesting findings about what costs of racism are elicited among White perpetrators or bystanders when made aware of racial microaggressions. Qualitative research could help understand the attitudinal antecedents and correlates of racial microaggressions among White perpetrators, as well as subsequent consequences, or costs. Multiple methodological approaches have the potential to inform the design of impactful educational interventions to prevent future microaggressive behavior in a range of social contexts.

Two empirical studies reflect the sort of research we envision. One psychological investigation is especially informative. To measure White participants' self-reported likelihood of delivering racial microaggressions, Kantor et al. (2017) asked Black undergraduate participants to rate the degree to which they would experience a series of statements as racial microaggressions. They asked non-Hispanic White undergraduate participants to report the likelihood they would express each item in the same series of statements and had them complete measures of racial prejudice. They found that White participants who reported a higher likelihood of committing racial microaggressions scored higher on several measures of prejudice and modern racism. The authors make an important observation: "These findings provide empirical support that microaggressive acts are rooted in racist beliefs and feelings ... and may not be dismissed as simply subjective perceptions of the target."

Regarding investigations of White bystanders to racial microaggressions that target People of Color, a recent sociological study involving more than 500 White Canadian first-year university students is instructive. Using an online survey, Baker (2017) asked participants whether they had witnessed a racist comment or behavior. Nearly half indicated they were witnesses to racism and subsequently were directed to an open-ended question, "Could you briefly describe what happened?" Baker used qualitative methods to analyze 170 open-ended responses. Findings suggested "racialized jokes" as commonplace experiences among White Canadian youth in his sample who found such jokes appropriate and thus were "unwilling to call out acts of racism despite their belief that [racism is] inappropriate and unwarranted" (p. 376).

Education and Training

If research does indeed illuminate the costs of racial microaggressions to White perpetrators and bystanders in terms of the five types, then findings can be applied in at least two ways. For example, we might use research findings to design education and training interventions specifically for White perpetrators and bystanders to increase awareness of the range of their possible defensive and emotional reactions and arm them with strategies to counter such defensiveness. Mindfulness training, for example, has reduced racism and prejudice attitudes (Lueke & Gibson, 2015, 2016) and could be employed in the context of White perpetrators of racial microaggressions. For White bystanders, we envision training along lines similar to the protocols for those who witness bullying or sexual harassment—Speak up! Stand up! Act! Armed with a range of potential responses, empathic but unaccountable and fearful guilt White individuals may be more likely to address microaggressions in the moment. Should research suggest the interplay between costs of racism type and racial microaggressions, as we suspect it will, multicultural educators might design different interventions for different types of White individuals to meet them where they are and maximize the potential for change.

Conclusion

Alongside ongoing research into the resistant and resilient responses to racial microaggressions among People of Color, scientist-practitioners also must focus on understanding the experiences of White perpetrators and bystanders. This effort must work from an understanding that racial microaggressions are the interpersonal manifestations of a racialized social system, which is evidenced in wide-ranging racial disparities in wealth and other measures of well-being that clearly advantage Whites. Costs of racism to White individuals provide one promising framework. A deeper and nuanced understanding of the antecedents and consequences to perpetrating or witnessing racial microaggressions could aid efforts to reduce the countless, daily interpersonal acts of racism that take a serious toll on the psychological well-being of Persons of Color. Having a training model rooted in empirical research that can anticipate the different types of costs of racism to White perpetrators and witnesses, and their different reactions to having attention called to racial microaggressions, might help design interventions that foster nondefensive and empathic responses that replace divisiveness and lead to bringing people together and better, healthier relationships.

References

Alvarez, A. N., Juang, L. P., & Liang, C. T. H. (2006). Asian Americans and racism: When bad things happen to "model minorities." *Cultural Diversity and Ethnic Minority Psychology, 12*(3), 477–492.

American Civil Liberties Union. (2013, June). *Billions of dollars wasted on racially biased arrests.* Retrieved from https://www.aclu.org/sites/default/files/field_document/1114413-mj-report-rfs-rel1.pdf.

Asante-Muhammad, D., Collins, C., Hoxie, J., & Nieves, E. (2016). *The ever-growing gap: Without change, African–American and Latino families won't match white wealth for centuries.* Washington, DC: Institute for Policy Studies.

Asante-Muhammad, D., Nieves, E., Collins, C., & Hoxie, J. (2017). *The road to zero wealth: How the racial wealth divide is hollowing out America's middle class.* Washington, DC: Institute for Policy Studies and Prosperity Now.

Baker, J. (2017). Through the looking glass: White first-year university students' observations of racism in St. John's, Newfoundland and Labrador, Canada. *Sociological Inquiry, 87*(2), 362–384.

Barrett, J. E., & Roediger, D. (2008). How white people became white. In P. S. Rothenberg (Ed.), *White privilege: Essential readings on the other side of racism* (3rd ed., pp. 35–40). New York, NY: Worth Publishers.

Bonilla-Silva, E. (1997). Rethinking racism: Toward a structural interpretation. *American Sociological Review, 62*(3), 465–480.

Bonilla-Silva, E., Goar, C., & Embrick, D. G. (2006). When whites flock together: The social psychology of white habitus. *Critical Sociology, 32*(2–3), 229–253.

Bowser, B. P., & Hunt, R. G. (Eds.). (1981). *Impacts of racism on White Americans.* Beverly Hills, CA: Sage.

Brodkin, K. (1998). *How Jews became white folks and what that says about race in America.* New Brunswick, NJ: Rutgers University Press.

Dennis, R. W. (1981). Socialization and racism: The White experience. In B. J. Bowser & R. G. Hunt (Eds.), *Impacts of racism on White Americans* (pp. 71–85). Beverly Hills, CA: Sage.

Du Bois, W. E. B. (1998[1935]). *Black reconstruction in America 1860–1880.* New York, NY: The Free Press.

Feagin, J. R. (2013). *The white racial frame: Centuries of racial framing and counter-framing.* New York, NY: Routledge.

Frankenberg, R. (1993). *White women race matters: The social construction of Whiteness.* Minneapolis, MN: University of Minnesota Press.

Goodman, D. J. (2011). *Promoting diversity and social justice: Educating people from privileged groups* (2nd ed.). Thousand Oaks, CA: SAGE.

Guglielmo, J., & Salerno, S. (2003). *Are Italians White? How race is made in America.* New York, NY: Routledge.

Holley, P. (2017, February 22). *"This is not Trump's America!" Passengers rejoice when man accused of racism is kicked off flight. Washington Post.* Retrieved from https://www.washingtonpost.com.

Hooks, B. (1992). *Black looks: Race and representation.* New York, NY: Routledge.

Hund, W. D., Krikler, J., & Roediger, D. (Eds.). (2011). *Wages of whiteness and racist symbolic capital.* Berlin, Germany: Lit Verlag.

Ignatiev, N. (1995). *How the Irish became White.* London, United Kingdom: Routledge.

Jacobson, M. F. (1998). *Whiteness of different color: European immigrants and the alchemy of race.* Cambridge, MA: Harvard University Press.

Kantor, J. W., Williams, M. T., Kuczynski, A. M., Manbeck, K. E., Debreaux, M., & Rosen, D. C. (2017, August). A preliminary report on the relationship between microaggressions against Black people and racism among white college students. *Race and Social Problems*. Advance online publication. doi:10.1007/s12552-017-9214-0.

Karp, J. B. (1981). The emotional impact and a model for changing racist attitudes. In B. J. Bowser & R. G. Hunt (Eds.), *Impacts of racism on White Americans* (pp. 87–96). Beverly Hills, CA: Sage.

KHOU. (2017, February 22). *Man kicked off flight to Houston for racist remarks*. Retrieved from http://www.khou.com.

Kivel, P. (2011). *Uprooting racism: How White people can work for racial justice* (3rd ed.). Philadelphia, PA: New Society Publishers.

Kochhar, R., Fry, R., & Taylor, P. (2011, July). *Wealth gaps rise to record highs between whites, blacks, Hispanics*. Retrieved from http://www.pewsocialtrends.org/2011/07/26/wealth-gaps-rise-to-record-highs-between-whites-blacks-hispanics.

Kordesh, K., Spanierman, L. B., & Neville, H. A. (2013). White students' racial affect: Gaining a deeper understanding of the antiracist type. *Journal of Diversity in Higher Education*, 6(1), 33–50.

Lesser, P. H. (1986). Always "Outsiders": Asians, naturalization, and the Supreme Court. *Amerasia Journal*, 12(1), 83–100.

Lipsitz, G. (2006). *The possessive investment in Whiteness: How White people profit from identity politics* (Rev. ed.). Philadelphia, PA: Temple University Press.

Liu, W. M. (2017). White male power and privilege: The relationship between white supremacy and social class. *Journal of Counseling Psychology*, 64(4), 349–358.

Long, H. (2017, September 15). *African Americans are the only U.S. racial group earning less than in 2000. The Los Angeles Times*. Retrieved from http://latimes.com.

Lopez, I. H. (1996). *White by law: The legal construction of race*. New York, NY: New York University Press.

Lueke, A., & Gibson, B. (2015). Mindfulness meditation reduces implicit age and race bias: The role of reduced automaticity of responding. *Social Psychological and Personality Science*, 6(3), 284–291.

Lueke, A., & Gibson, B. (2016). Brief mindfulness meditation reduces discrimination. *Psychology of Consciousness: Theory, Research, and Practice*, 3(1), 34–44.

Mazza, E. (2017, February 23). *"Goodbye, racist!": Passengers cheer as unruly man gets booted from plane. Huffington Post*. Retrieved from http://www.huffingtonpost.com.

Moore, A. (2016). *The decadent veil: Black America's wealth illusion*. Retrieved from http://www.huffingtonpost.com/antonio-moore/the-decadent-veil-black-income-inequality_b_5646472.html.

Nellis, A. (2016). *The color of justice: Racial and ethnic disparity in state prisons*. Retrieved from http://www.sentencingproject.org/wp-content/uploads/2016/06/The-Color-of-Justice-Racial-and-Ethnic-Disparity-in-State-Prisons.pdf.

Neville, H. A., Lilly, R. L., Duran, G., Lee, R. M., & Browne, L. (2000). Construction and initial validation of the color-blind racial attitudes scale (CoBRAS). *Journal of Counseling Psychology, 47*(1), 59–70.

Ong, A. D., Burrow, A. L., Fuller-Rowell, T. E., Ja, N. M., & Sue, D. W. (2013). Racial microaggressions and daily well-being among Asian Americans. *Journal of Counseling Psychology, 60*(2), 188–199.

Ozawa *v.* United States, *260 U.S. 178* (1922).

Pettigrew, T. F. (1981). The mental health impact. In B. J. Bowser & R. G. Hunt (Eds.), *Impacts of racism on White Americans* (pp. 97–118). Beverly Hills, CA: Sage.

Pew Research Center (2014, December). *The American middle class is losing ground.* Retrieved from http://www.pewsocialtrends.org/2015/12/09/the-american-middle-class-is-losing-ground.

Picea, L. H., & Feagin, J. R. (2007). *Two-faced racism: Whites in the backstage and fronstage.* New York, NY: Routledge.

Roediger, D. R. (2006). *Working toward whiteness: How America's immigrants became white: The strange journey from Ellis Island to the suburbs.* New York, NY: Basic Books.

Roediger, D. R. (2007). *The wages of whiteness: Race and the making of the American working class* (New ed.). New York, NY: Verso.

Spanierman, L. B., Garriott, P. O., & Clark, D. A. (2013). Whiteness and social class: Intersections and implications. In W. M. Liu (Ed.), *The Oxford handbook of social class in counseling* (pp. 394–410). New York, NY: Oxford University Press.

Spanierman, L. B., & Heppner, M. J. (2004). Psychosocial Costs of Racism to Whites Scale (PCRW): Construction and initial validation. *Journal of Counseling Psychology, 51*(2), 249–262.

Spanierman, L. B., Poteat, V. P., Beer, A. M., & Armstrong, P. I. (2006). Psychosocial costs of racism to Whites: Exploring patterns through cluster analysis. *Journal of Counseling Psychology, 53*(4), 434–441.

Spanierman, L. B., Todd, N. R., & Anderson, C. J. (2009). Psychosocial costs of racism to Whites: Understanding patterns among university students. *Journal of Counseling Psychology, 56*(2), 239–252.

Sue, D. W. (2010). *Microaggressions in everyday life: Race, gender and sexual orientation.* Hoboken, NJ: Wiley.

Sue, D. W., Capodilupo, C. M., Torino, G. C., Bucceri, J. M., Holder, A. M. B., Nadal, K. L., & Esquilin, M. (2007). Racial microaggressions in everyday life: Implications for clinical practice. *American Psychologist, 62*(4), 271–286.

Takaki, R. (1993). *A different mirror: A history of multicultural America.* Boston, MA: Little, Brown & Co.

Tehranian, J. (2000). Performing whiteness: Naturalization litigation and the construction of racial identity in America. *The Yale Law Journal, 109*(4), 817–848.

Terry, R. W. (1981). The negative impact on White values. In B. J. Bowser & R. G. Hunt (Eds.), *Impacts of racism on White Americans* (pp. 119–151). Beverly Hills, CA: Sage.

Ury, D. [helpmefindparents]. (2013, May 23). *What kind of Asian are you? [Video file]*. Retrieved from https://youtu.be/DWynJkN5HbQ.

Wang, J., Leu, J., & Shoda, Y. (2011). When the seemingly innocuous "stings": Racial microaggressions and their emotional consequences. *Personality and Social Psychology Bulletin, 37*(12), 1666–1678.

Wiedrich, K., Sims, L., Jr., Weisman, H., Rice, S., & Brooks, B. (2016). *The steep climb to economic opportunity and vulnerable families: Findings for the 2016 assets and opportunities scorecard.* Retrieved from http://assetsandopportunity .org/assets/pdf/2016_Scorecard_Report.pdf.

Part III

Manifestation of Microaggressions

10

The 360-Degree Experience of Workplace Microaggressions: Who Commits Them? How Do Individuals Respond? What Are the Consequences?

Jennifer Young-Jin Kim, Duoc Nguyen, and Caryn Block

In this chapter, we explore how microaggressions manifest in the workplace. We examine the types of microaggressions that occur, when microaggressions are likely to occur in the employment cycle, who is likely to commit them, how individuals respond to these microaggressions, and the negative consequences of contending with microaggressions for both individuals and organizations. Finally, we address what organizations can do to mitigate these negative effects. While there has been much research on microaggressions, less is known about the specific types of microaggressions that manifest in the workplace. And the workplace is unique in a number of important ways. When microaggressions occur during leisure activities, such as going to dinner, people can choose to walk away from those who are committing the microaggressions. The workplace is different. People cannot stop working without dire consequences. Furthermore, during the work week, employees spend a majority of their waking hours at their jobs (Bureau of Labor Statistics, 2017). Thus, a substantial amount of an individual's time as an adult is spent with people at work, be it coworkers, supervisors, or subordinates.

Moreover, for many people who are White, the workplace is the first time that they will interact closely with People of Color. In fact, there is an entire industry on diversity and inclusion training to help organizations figure out how to support people from different backgrounds to work more productively together. In addition, overt forms of discrimination in the workplace are illegal. Yet, despite these diversity and inclusion efforts and despite legal mandates, organizations still struggle to include People of Color and women, especially in the most senior positions. One reason for this may be that discrimination is still occurring, but in more subtle forms (e.g., Cortina, 2008;

Microaggression Theory: Influence and Implications, First Edition. Edited by Gina C. Torino, David P. Rivera, Christina M. Capodilupo, Kevin L. Nadal, and Derald Wing Sue.
© 2019 John Wiley & Sons, Inc. Published 2019 by John Wiley & Sons, Inc.

Jones, Peddie, Gilrane, King, & Gray, 2016). Subtle discrimination has been defined as "actions that are ambiguous in intent to harm, difficult to detect, low in intensity, and often unintentional but nevertheless deleterious to target employees" (Jones et al., 2016, p. 1589). And the effects of subtle discrimination can be quite detrimental to employees, having a negative impact on their work-related stress, job satisfaction, turnover intentions, and performance. In fact, a recent meta-analysis by Jones et al. (2016) found that the experience of subtle discrimination had similar deleterious effects on individuals and has the experience of overt discrimination. Additionally, subtle discrimination is likely to be a much more common experience for women and People of Color than overt discrimination (Cortina, 2008). Yet, the vast majority of the research on discrimination in the workplace has focused on understanding and preventing overt forms of discrimination. Surprisingly, we are only beginning to understand the subtle forms that discrimination can take in the workplace. The Theory of Microaggressions can provide a useful framework for advancing our understanding of how subtle forms of discrimination may manifest at work.

Racial microaggressions are defined as verbal or behavioral treatment that conveys hostility toward members of various racial groups that manifest in three different forms: microassaults, microinsults, and microinvalidations (Sue, Capodilupo, et al., 2007). Microassaults are explicit verbal or nonverbal messages meant to hurt the intended victim through behaviors such as name-calling, avoidant behavior, or purposeful discrimination. Microinsults express rudeness, insensitivity, or demean a person's heritage or identity. Microinvalidations exclude or invalidate the psychological feelings, or the experiential reality of a person.

More recently, microaggression research has been extended to include women (Capodilupo et al., 2010) and lesbian, gay, bisexual, transgender (LGBT) people (Nadal, 2013). This research has revealed that while People of Color, women, and LGBT individuals experience some of the same types of microaggressions, they also experience microaggressions that are unique based on stereotypes held about a particular group. Thus, another way to categorize types of microaggressions is whether they are *general microaggressions* or *stereotype-based microaggressions* (Kim, Yu, Drinka, Nguyen, & Block, 2015). *General microaggressions* are verbal or behavioral treatment that occurs regardless of social identity group membership. An example of a general microaggression is *Denial of experiential reality* suggesting that Asians, Blacks, Latina/os, LGBT people, or women all share similar experiences within their respective groups (Johnston & Nadal, 2010; Nadal, 2013; Rivera, Forquer, & Rangel, 2010; Sue, Bucceri, Lin, Nadal, & Torino, 2007; Sue, Capodilupo, & Holder, 2008). On the other hand, *stereotype-based microaggressions* are specific types of verbal or behavioral treatment based on the content of stereotypes perceivers hold about specific groups of people regarding their race, gender, or identity. Some examples of stereotype-based microaggressions include *Alien in own land*, suggesting that Asians and Latina/os are foreigners (Rivera et al., 2010; Sue, Bucceri, et al., 2007); *Assumption of criminality*, suggesting that Blacks (Sue, Nadal, et al., 2008) and Latina/os (Rivera et al., 2010) are potential criminals, prone to violent behavior; and *Assumptions of traditional gender roles*, suggesting that women should occupy roles that are in accordance to traditional gender roles (e.g., stay-at-home mom).

Microaggressions in the workplace take both of these forms. While some of the microaggressions identified in the workplace represent general mistreatment, others are based on stereotypes about different social identity groups, particularly as they relate to workplace performance. Both types of microaggressions manifest in different phases of the employment cycle beginning with the pre-employment phase.

Microaggressions in Pre-employment

The first step in getting a job is applying for it. One way that microaggressions occur in the workplace is in the pre-employment process through a discrepancy in interview callback rates for job candidates with similar credentials but racially different sounding names. Ideally, job candidates with similar credentials on resumes should have an equal chance of getting a job interview. Despite this ideal, not all resumes have similar chances of getting a callback for an interview from recruiters or HR professionals. Racial information associated with different names on resumes has been shown to have a significant effect on callback rates. Audit studies use fictitious yet representative resumes in response to real-job postings. These studies typically send out resumes with similar credentials except for the variable of interest—name of the applicant. Audit studies have shown that resumes with ethnic or racial names receive significantly lower callback rates for job interviews compared to resumes with white-sounding names with similar credentials (Bertrand & Mullainathan, 2004; Oreopoulos, 2011). For example, resumes with White-sounding first names (e.g., Emily or Greg) had a higher callback rate than resumes with African American–sounding names (e.g., Jamal or Aisha; Bertrand & Mullainathan, 2004). In fact, resumes with White-sounding names were *twice* as likely to receive a callback for a job than resumes with African American–sounding names. Likewise, when resumes were manipulated with Asian versus White-sounding forenames and surnames, resumes with White-sounding names (e.g., Greg Johnson) received a 39% higher callback rate than resumes with Asian-sounding names (e.g., Hina Chaudhry; Oreopoulos, 2011). Similarly, resumes with White-sounding names (e.g., John Martin) had a higher callback rate even when compared to resumes with Asian-sounding surnames paired with a White-sounding forename (e.g., Allen Wang; Oreopoulos, 2011).

Not only are resumes with racial and ethnic names disadvantaged in the pre-employment stage, but so are resumes with female names (Moss-Racusin, Dovidio, Brescoll, Graham, & Handelsman, 2012). In a randomized experimental design, faculty members from the biology, chemistry, and physics departments at several universities evaluated the resume of either a fictitious female (Jennifer) or male (John) applicant for potential lab manager positions. The results from this study revealed that both male and female professors evaluated the resume with the female name lower on competency, hireability, mentoring, and salary than the resume with the male name. The findings of these audit studies consistently demonstrate that having a racial, ethnic, or female name disadvantaged individuals when applying for jobs.

Asian and African American job applicants seem to be aware of the lower callback rates due to their racial or ethnic identity. In fact, research has spotlighted a technique used by Asians and African American job applicants to make up for the discrepancy in callback rates—resume "whitening" (Kang, DeCelles, Tilcsik, & Jun, 2016). Some of these "whitening" techniques include changing a racial or ethnic name to a more neutral, "American-sounding" name as well as omitting experiences that may signify minority status (e.g., leaving out work experience in Chinatown or "toning down" experiences in Black Students' Association; Kang et al., 2016, study 1). These whitening techniques had a substantial impact on callback rates. Asian and African Americans had higher callback rates when they "whitened" their resumes, changed their names and work experiences, (21% and 25%, respectively) compared to when they did *not* "whiten" their resumes (12% and 10% respectively, Kang et al., 2016, study 3).

Even though recruiters or HR professionals may not see the people who have submitted their resumes, subtle (and possibly unintentional mistreatment) can still occur prior to the job interview. What is clear is that having an ethnic, racial, or female name will result in a significantly lower chance of being called back for a job interview or being perceived as not competent or hirable. One potential reason for lower callback rates is that recruiters and HR professionals do have stereotypes or biases toward people with racial, ethnic, or female names, and these stereotypes or biases manifest when they select candidates to be interviewed. This is an example of a stereotype-based microaggression. Not only is it unfortunate that names can incite biases from recruiters and HR professionals, but it is also unfortunate that organizations will miss out on the opportunity to hire top talent because recruiters and HR professionals are unaware of the biases that they are perpetuating.

Microaggressions in the Workplace

Beyond microaggressions at the pre-employment stage, People of Color and women also have to contend with microaggressions at work once they are hired. The few studies that have directly examined microaggressions in the workplace have mostly taken place in clinical (Constantine & Sue, 2007; Sue, Capodilupo, et al., 2007) and academic settings (Cartwright, Washington, & McConnell, 2009; Pittman, 2012; Sharp-Grier, 2015). Two qualitative studies shed light on the types of microaggressions that individuals contend with in the workplace. One qualitative study on the experiences of executive Black women found that they experienced five types of microaggressions (Holder, Jackson, &, Ponterotto, 2015). *Environmental microaggressions* were reflected in the underrepresentation of Black women in an organization that employed nearly a thousand people, yet only a few Black women were in senior management positions. *Stereotypes of Black women* were microaggressions based on the stereotype of Black women as aggressive employees whose credentials were consistently challenged. *Universal experience* comprised microaggressions that reduced Black women to employees who know "all" other Black people within the organization or have similar experience of the "typical" Black person. *Invisibility* highlighted that when speaking during meetings Black women receive unexpected body language from coworkers (e.g., head facing down and writing) or simply little to no eye contact. *Exclusion* revealed when Black women were not invited to social gatherings where appointments and opportunities were discussed, leading to fewer ways for them to move up within the organization.

In another qualitative study, Asians reported experiencing seven types of microaggressions in the workplace (Kim et al., 2015). *Ascription of math competency* characterized microaggressions that treated Asians as employees who *only* excel at math, statistics, or data analyses. *Submissive/subservience* described the tendency to characterize Asians as passive or docile and therefore not having what it takes to be a leader. *Invalidation of individual differences* consigns Asian individuals to a broad set of homogenous people. *Invisibility* described the experience of Asians who have been overlooked by non-Asians in meetings or during one-on-one interactions. *Inferiority* describes how work produced by Asian employees was viewed as substandard or not taken seriously compared to work produced by their White counterparts (Kim et al., 2015). *Being singled out* describes situations when an individual was singled out because of his or her race. *Demeaning cultural values and communications style* conveys that Asians cultural values and communication styles have been viewed as *less desirable* than the dominant cultural values and communication styles in the workplace.

These qualitative studies demonstrate that some of the microaggressions that manifest in the workplace can be categorized as *general microaggressions* emerging for both Black women and Asian employees (e.g., *invisibility, universal experiences, and invalidation of individual differences*). Other microaggressions were unique to employees based on their racial and gender identity and the stereotypes held about that group, and can be categorized as *stereotype-based microaggressions* (e.g., *stereotypes of Black women, ascription of math competency, and submissive/subservient)*. In addition, findings from these studies suggest that microaggressions are a "360-degree experience" as they can arise in all interactions that surround the employee: interactions from above (supervisors), interactions from below (subordinates), and interactions from the side (from peers and colleagues).

Microaggressions from above: supervisors

Qualitative research has shown that supervisors can be a primary source of microaggressions in clinical settings (Constantine & Sue, 2007), academia (Cartwright et al., 2009), and the workplace (Kim et al., 2015). In clinical settings, supervisors oversee the cases that clinicians have taken on and help clinicians to develop and refine their counseling skills through supervision feedback. However, some types of feedback can be detrimental when laced with microaggressions (Constantine & Sue, 2007). Qualitative interviews have revealed that Black clinicians felt that White supervisors made stereotypical remarks toward Black clinicians when the supervisors told the clinicians to "be on time" for supervision because of the stereotype that Black people tend to be on a different time orientation. In other instances, supervisors told Black clinicians that they were *gifted* at "multicultural stuff." These microaggressions by supervisors reduced Black clinicians to the stereotype of people who are perpetually late or selectively "gifted."

Receiving recognition from supervisors is an important aspect of work as it highlights the contributions of workers within an organization. Ideally, recognition should be consistently provided to employees within the workplace. However, if recognition is inconsistent when People of Color achieve similar milestones as their White counterparts, this inconsistency can be viewed as a microaggression. For example, one African American faculty member recalled that the dean sent out recognition e-mails whenever awards were given or faculty articles were published (Cartwright et al., 2009). She recalled her anticipation of the dean's e-mail when achieving these milestones, "She sends out everyone else's, but forgot to send mine out." (Cartwright et al., 2009, p. 175). Inconsistent recognition by supervisors may lead to employees to feel that they have been snubbed, perceived as unimportant, or treated as invisible at work.

Supervisors may also commit microaggressions by asking seemingly innocuous questions. For example, inquiring of an Asian employee "Why are you so quiet?" during a top-level meeting was perceived as a microaggression (Kim et al., 2015). When people are quiet during meetings, it does not necessarily mean that they are not engaged. Rather, listening to people who are experts in their field rather than speaking up or asking questions immediately could be a sign of respect (Kim et al., 2015). These communication styles were sometimes viewed as deficits or looked down upon. While supervisors may explicitly say that they are tolerant of other cultures, questions such as, "Why are you so quiet?" may implicitly indicate that adhering to one's culture is viewed as a deficit or is not tolerated by supervisors within the organization.

Microaggressions from below: subordinates

In the workplace, people must also contend with microaggressions from those who are in junior roles. In academic settings, faculty members interact frequently with students, who are also a source of microaggressions. Research has shown that Black faculty members sometimes get mistaken for clerical or administrative staff, often being asked by White students to make copies for them (Pittman, 2012). White students also tended to address Black female faculty members as "Miss," rather than "Doctor" (Cartwright et al., 2009). Similarly, some Faculty of Color reported having their credentials challenged by White students in the classroom. Snubs by students can also take the form of course evaluation feedback. One professor, with almost two decades of experience in her field, got feedback from a student regarding her intellect, "She was more intelligent than I thought she'd be." (Sharp-Grier, 2015, p. 29). This remark incited feelings of powerlessness and anger in this faculty member, in line with previous research that has found strong negative emotions such as anger and resentment associated with experiencing microaggressions (Wang, Leu, & Shoda, 2011).

Microaggressions from the side: coworkers

Coworkers and colleagues who are of a similar rank within the organization have also been demonstrated to be a source of microaggressions. For example, research has shown that Faculty of Color felt that they were limited by their race within their department at the university due to treatment by their colleagues (Cartwright et al., 2009). Faculty of Color felt that they had to consistently prove their worth to their peers. For example, when one Faculty of Color wanted to teach other courses beyond the topic of diversity, her peers asked whether she was stepping outside her realm of "expertise." Faculty of Color felt they were treated by their peers as if they were the "diversity specialists," rather than complete faculty members with broader expertise (Cartwright et al., 2009).

In sum, microaggressions can occur in the process of screening resumes for interview callbacks in pre-employment. Audit research has shown that having an ethnic, racial, or female name results in less favorable callback rates and perceptions prior to entering the workforce. Unfortunately, microaggressions continue once People of Color and women enter the workforce. Qualitative studies have shown that People of Color and women endure microaggressions as a "360-degree" experience, contributed to by supervisors, subordinates, and coworkers. These microaggressions include but are not limited to reducing targets to stereotypes such as being selectively "gifted," quiet, or being mistaken as the "help." While acts of microaggressions can be fleeting, they can have lasting harmful effects on the targets in the short- and long-term.

Responding to Microaggressions in the Workplace

Experiencing microaggressions has been associated with a wide range of negative responses for the target. Some of the responses that are elicited are proximal, occurring immediately in the moment, while other responses are more distal, occurring sometime after the microaggression has occurred (Holder et al., 2015; Wang et al., 2011). These responses can impact a number of different domains, including the individual's emotional and cognitive well-being, performance ability, and social capital within the workplace (Ibarra, Ely, & Kolb, 2013; Steele, 1997; Wang et al., 2011). Left unchecked, these responses can lead to harmful individual and organizational consequences, manifested as negative individual job attitudes, and eventually suboptimal organizational outcomes. In this section, we will discuss how seemingly innocuous microaggressions can have a detrimental impact within organizations by focusing on individual responses to microaggressions and the negative consequences associated with these responses.

Proximal Responses: Cognitive and Emotional Labor

When a person experiences a microaggression, he or she can respond in several ways. A typical proximal, or immediate, response to a microaggression involves the affective and cognitive labor that is exercised by an individual to make sense of the microaggression. Dealing with microaggressions can take up the target's cognitive and emotional resources because he or she must first stop to think and determine if the slight is, in fact, a microaggression. This process is made even harder due to the subtle and oftentimes ambiguous nature of microaggressions (Louis et al., 2016; Sue, Capodilupo, et al., 2007). Qualitative studies have shed light on the thought processes that occur for individuals navigating the aftermath of a workplace microaggression (Holder et al., 2015; Louis et al., 2016). For example, Holder et al. (2015) documented an anecdote illustrating the internal thought process of an individual grappling with how to handle a racial microaggression:

> I tend to play the scene over and over again, so before really coming to a conclusion you start to do the process of elimination. Is it that I'm new here? Is it that they're all friends? ... Then you start to really begin to isolate. Then once you get right down to it, this has to be an issue of race. (p. 172)

This process is referred to as hypothesis testing through which the target tries to determine the intent and meaning behind the microaggression (Holder et al., 2015). Additionally, targets must also contend with the aftermath should they choose to confront the behavior, wondering if their response would be interpreted by others as being overly sensitive, that is, playing the "race card" (Endo, 2015; Louis et al., 2016). Thus, experiencing a microaggression entails navigating how to not only interpret the slight but also deal with whether to respond and how that may be received by others. All of these thought processes require cognitive labor and can be draining for the target who could use that cognitive energy elsewhere (Lewis, Mendenhall, Harwood, & Huntt, 2013), such as performing work-related tasks. In fact, one study that examined the negative effects of microaggressions on the target revealed that individuals perceived more negative proximal work outcomes for the target, such as less ability to concentrate on the job and maintain strong relationships with the perpetrator, as the severity of the microaggression increased (Kim et al., 2015). This suggests that microaggressions do elicit proximal responses, which may negatively impact one's ability to perform on the job.

The constant pressure of negotiating microaggressions can also take a toll on the person's emotional state. In fact, when individuals feel that they have been mistreated based on factors such as their race, they experience greater negative emotions, including anger, contempt, anxiety, and shame (Wang et al., 2011). Unsurprisingly, individuals who are regular targets of microaggressions reported experiencing stronger negative emotions: not only must they deal with regular job-related stressors, but they also must contend with additional stressors related to workplace microaggressions (Louis et al., 2016).

Distal Responses: Performance Domain

So far, we have focused on examples of proximal responses that occur immediately following a microaggression. Some responses, however, can occur distally over time, and affect one's ability to perform at an optimal level long-term. When faced with a stereotype-based microaggression specific to one's group, individuals are likely to be reminded of negative stereotypes related to their group, and consequently may experience stereotype threat, a known hindrance to performance (Bergeron, Block, & Echtenkamp, 2006; Steele & Aronson, 1995).

As a response to this threat, some individuals may choose to overcompensate in one way or another, going above and beyond what they would normally do in their job to defy or live up to the stereotype (Block, Koch, Liberman, Merriweather, & Roberson, 2011). One way of defying a stereotype may take the form of an African American college professor who feels the need to appear near perfect and produce impeccable work for fear that anything less would confirm the negative stereotypes associated with African Americans as being lazy or intellectually inferior, and perpetuate microaggressions against that group (Holder et al., 2015; Louis et al., 2016).

Others, however, may choose to live up to the stereotype associated with one's group. For example, many East Asian cultures, including China, Korea, and Japan, are known for their hard work ethic, epitomized by long workweeks wherein professionals clock significantly more hours than the average American (McCurry, 2015). Given this stereotype, Asian professionals may overcompensate to fulfill the perception of their *hardworking* ethic, thereby living up to the high demands placed on Asians (Kim et al., 2015). This process can be cognitively taxing as individuals constantly remain on high alert, taking on more work, and expending additional energy to try and live up to the stereotype about them. In fact, engaging in this "proving process" has been reported to diminish self-confidence and work performance for those who experience microaggressions (Griffin, Pifer, Humphrey, & Hazelwood, 2011), illustrating the detrimental effects associated with expending extra energy to meet or defy stereotypes elicited by microaggressions.

Further exacerbating this problem, experiencing stereotype threat has also been linked to feedback discounting (Roberson, Deitch, Brief, & Block, 2003). Individuals who suffer microaggressions and experience stereotype threat may be more likely to doubt the accuracy and motivation of the feedback source, thereby dismissing the feedback that they receive. This behavior puts individuals at a disadvantage since research has discovered that they are less compliant with directions for performance improvement (Banks, Stitt, Curtis, & McQuater, 1977), which can hinder a person's performance.

Distal Responses: Social Domain

Experiencing microaggressions can also harm one's social capital within the workplace. To succeed at work requires more than being a high performer, it also involves having a strong social connection with potential sponsors and mentors within organizations who can provide the necessary groundwork for gaining traction, visibility, and social support within organizations (Ibarra et al., 2013). Thus, having a strong social network is integral for succeeding within organizations (Brass, 1985; Burt, 1997). In fact, people who are part of a broad network that extends beyond their work group tend to be much more powerful within organizations than others (Blau & Alba, 1982; Brass, 1985). Establishing such a network can be a challenge for women and minorities in organizations as those who are in positions of power, White males, tend to mentor those who are similar to them (Ibarra, 1993). Given that women and minorities usually have a much smaller set of "similar others" with whom to develop professional relationships, their network is constrained even further (Ibarra, 1993).

Ethnic minorities and women, thus, face an uphill battle. They are limited due to there being fewer members of their group with whom they can network (Ibarra, 1993). Moreover, individuals who experience workplace microaggressions are penalized given that their responses can isolate them even more. Individuals may have a harder time trusting the perpetrator who has committed a microaggression, with many choosing to avoid or limit their future interactions with the perpetrator, constricting their social network (Constantine, Smith, Redington, & Owens, 2008; Holder et al., 2015; Louis et al., 2016). To illustrate, one academic mentioned how, wishing to avoid the constant onslaught of racial microaggressions, he decided to avoid coming into the office during normal business hours:

> It got to a point where I did not even want to be in the office, because any comment could come at any time … I'd go to my office at 9:00 p.m. after class and stay till midnight or 1 [o'clock] doing work in a quiet, serene and not hostile environment.
>
> (Louis et al., 2016, p. 467)

One reason for this type of avoidant behavior stems from feeling vulnerable or hopeless in trying to confront the perpetrator, contributing to feelings of pessimism, and learned helplessness in which the targets are resigned to the fact that subtle forms of discrimination will always exist (Hall & Fields, 2015; Louis et al., 2016). As a result, the target finds it easier to disconnect from colleagues who exhibit or even condone microaggressions (DeCuir-Gunby & Gunby, 2016). While this may alleviate the immediate problem by limiting the target's exposure to the perpetrator, it hinders the target's ability to develop a strong social network, which could impede advancement opportunities (Ibarra, 1995; Mehra, Kilduff, & Brass, 1998).

Consequences of Microaggressions

So far, we have discussed distal and proximal reactions to microaggressions in the workplace. Left unchecked, these responses can lead to negative individual consequences that can eventually affect organizational outcomes. In fact, experiencing microaggressions has been linked to lower job satisfaction as a consequence of such responses such as detaching from the group or feeling hopeless in confronting the aggressor as a way of dealing with microaggressions (DeCuir-Gunby & Gunby, 2016). Perceptions of racial microaggressions have also been found to affect the target's work outcomes such as job satisfaction, organizational commitment, and job-related stress (Kim, Nguyen, & Block, 2017; Offermann, Basford, Graebner, DeGraaf, & Jaffer, 2013).

In one of the first studies to examine perceptions of microaggressions in the workplace, Offermann and her colleagues (2013) looked at racial microaggressions committed by a White supervisor on a Black employee, varying the severity level of the microaggression to examine how it influenced observers' perceptions of negative work-related outcomes experienced by the target. Results showed that as the severity of the microaggression increased, so did the perceptions of negative outcomes such as lowered motivation, job satisfaction, organizational commitment, and higher intentions to quit (Offermann et al., 2013), all of which constitute long-term consequences for the individual. This study also found that as severity levels increased, so did the observers' perception of the intent of the perpetrator. Thus, as severity increased, participants viewed the supervisor as being more intentional and aware of his or her behavior.

In sum, dealing with microaggressions often leave minority group members suspicious and distressed as they try and grapple with the intention behind the microaggression (Sue, Capodilupo, et al., 2007; Sue, Nadal, et al., 2008). Additionally, the added stress of experiencing and dealing with microaggressions places undesirable constraints that interfere with or hinder an individual's ability to achieve valued work outcomes, leading to job-searching behavior and eventually, turnover (Cavanaugh, Boswell, Roehling, & Boudreau, 2000). Therefore, workplace microaggression can be a key contributor to the loss of top talent within an organization.

Moreover, microaggressions can extend their insidious effects beyond the workplace. Experiencing microaggressions can take both a physical and psychological toll on an individual (Sue, Capodilupo, et al., 2007). The constant processing of and responding to microaggressions has been associated with exhaustion, insomnia (Hall & Fields, 2015), binge-drinking (Blume, Lovato, Thyken, & Denny, 2012), higher levels of stress (Smith, Hung, & Franklin, 2011), negative emotions (Wang et al., 2011), and poorer mental health, including higher anxiety and depression and lower self-esteem (Nadal, Griffin, Wong, Hamit, & Rasmus, 2014).

Furthermore, contending with microaggressions and its ensuing consequences, including stereotype threat, can cause spillover. Specifically, stereotype threat spillover refers to the situational predicament in which coping with the ensuing stress leaves one in a depleted state, unable to engage in effortful self-control in a variety of domains (Inzlicht & Kang, 2010). This phenomenon is not surprising given how cognitively and emotionally exhausting it can be to not only interpret the microaggression but also respond by trying to defy or live up to the stereotype associated with one's group (Griffin et al., 2011; Holder et al., 2015; Kim et al., 2015). According to the spillover theory, because one is left depleted after dealing with the microaggression, one is less able to exert self-control, resulting in more aggressive behavior when provoked, riskier decision making, and poorer food choices (Inzlicht & Kang, 2010). It is clear that experiencing microaggressions is anything but harmless to those on the receiving end and that the negative impact stemming from microaggressions needs to be acknowledged and addressed.

Why should practitioners be alarmed by all this? Within the context of the organization, it is suggested that having employees who must endure such inequities can lead to a number of negative outcomes, including lowered motivation and morale, absenteeism, and turnover (Cocchiara & Quick, 2004).

Having women and minority talent leave the organization can lead to a drain in the diversity pipeline, leaving organizations with a shortage of qualified individuals to move up the ladder. This can be costly to organizations. For instance, many individuals choose to leave organizations that perpetuate subtle forms of discrimination. Annually, over two million people leave their jobs because of subtle forms of discrimination (Level Playing Field Institute, 2006). This exodus contributes to a massive financial drain as the ensuing estimated cost of recruiting, selecting, and training to replace two million employees is approximately $64 billion (Burns, 2012).

Targets of microaggressions are not the only ones affected. Bystanders or witnesses of microaggressions can also be negatively impacted. Although bystanders may not be the direct subject of a microaggression, similar to the effects of second-hand smoke, witnessing workplace microaggressions can have lasting negative repercussions on the occupational health for bystanders (Chrobot-Mason, Ragins, & Linnehan, 2013). In fact, individuals who simply witnessed microaggressions reported less satisfaction with their colleagues and supervisors, poorer health, and lower self-esteem (Low, Radhakrishnan, Schneider, & Rounds, 2007). Thus, bearing witness to acts of microaggressions can also be stressful for observers, illustrating the far-reaching negative consequences of microaggressions and highlighting why practitioners must work to reduce the occurrence of such incidents.

Retaining a diverse workforce can also help an organization become more competitive. Research has shown that companies in the top quartile for gender or racial diversity are more likely to enjoy financial returns above the industry median (Hunt, Layton, & Prince, 2015). In fact, ethnically diverse companies are 35% more likely to outperform those in the bottom quartile, illustrating the competitive advantage diverse companies have compared to those that are less diverse. Thus, it would be in a company's business interest to thoroughly examine microaggressions experienced by its employees in an effort to reduce the occurrence of such incidents.

Organizational Buffers against Microaggressions

What can organizations do to help reduce detrimental effects of workplace microaggressions? Though this may seem like a considerable task, practitioners can approach the challenge in a variety of ways. At the individual level, practitioners can provide diversity training to reduce incidents of microaggressions by raising people's awareness of such incidents and transmitting knowledge meant to increase participants' multicultural competency (Ferdman & Brody, 1996). Managers should be mindful to not only recognize and reduce microaggressions among their direct reports but also check their own tendency to ensure that they themselves are not the ones committing microaggressions. Doing so, managers can create a safe climate for their team in which people can also feel comfortable discussing microaggressions that they may be experiencing.

It is integral that leadership also monitor employee sentiment by carefully examining data from sources such as exit interviews, employee engagement surveys, and focus groups to understand drivers of disengagement, particularly around diversity and inclusion. Often, both quantitative and qualitative data related to these dimensions will reflect the perspectives of minority groups, and can be a rich source of information for gauging the organization's diversity climate. To ensure that this happens, organizations should move toward increasing the accountability of managers by including diversity management into the manager's competency model.

At the macrolevel, organizations should strive to create and maintain a positive diversity climate by establishing systemic equitable processes. One such practice is resume blinding in which information from resumes such as gender and race are removed. By blinding resumes, recruiters can bypass their biases and hire more diverse candidates. Similarly, practitioners can reduce specific stereotypes associated with certain jobs or roles. Stereotype-based microaggressions can induce stereotype threat when the stereotype is relevant to the task (e.g., African Americans are good caretakers, Asians are good at math, or women have good interpersonal skills). Research has shown that the effects of stereotype-threat can be eliminated by refuting or diminishing the stereotype relevance of the task (Spencer, Steele, & Quinn, 1999) or underscoring similarities shared by the stereotyped and nonstereotyped groups (Kray, Thompson, & Galinsky, 2001). To do so, managers can emphasize characteristics necessary for successful completion of a task or role that is not linked to group stereotypes (Roberson & Kulik, 2007). For example, a manager could emphasize the organization's holistic hiring practice by saying "Our function has a well-balanced team thanks to our company's hiring process" or highlight the skills necessary for a job through statements such as "This project would benefit from having someone with your expertise in team building" rather than "You'd be great with people because you're a woman."

Finally, organizations should work to promote awareness by encouraging diversity training aimed at helping people identify and reduce microaggressions. For example, individuals who display colorblind attitudes, defined as the denial or distortion of race and racism (Apfelbaum, Norton, & Sommers, 2012), are less likely to recognize racial microaggressions in the workplace, perpetuating these forms of subtle discrimination (Offermann et al., 2014). To counteract such attitudes, practitioners should implement training that demonstrates the importance of adopting a color aware attitude, helping people acknowledge the role of racial dynamics, and how they manifest in the workplace (Block, 2015). By doing so, the organization can not only create an inclusive environment by reducing incidents of microaggressions but also signal to its minority members that diversity is truly valued and accepted.

References

Apfelbaum, E. P., Norton, M. I., & Sommers, S. R. (2012). Racial color blindness: Emergence, practice, and implications. *Current Directions in Psychological Science, 21*(3), 205–209.

Banks, W. C., Stitt, K. R., Curtis, H. A., & McQuater, G. V. (1977). Perceived objectivity and the effects of evaluative reinforcement upon compliance and self-evaluation in Blacks. *Journal of Experimental Social Psychology, 13*(5), 452–463.

Bergeron, D. M., Block, C. J., & Echtenkamp, A. (2006). Disabling the able: Stereotype threat and women's work performance. *Human Performance, 19*(2), 133–158.

Bertrand, M., & Mullainathan, S. (2004). Are Emily and Greg more employable than Lakisha and Jamal? A field experiment on labor market discrimination. *American Economic Review, 94*, 991–1013.

Blau, J. R., & Alba, R. D. (1982). Empowering nets of participation. *Administrative Science Quarterly*, 363–379.

Block, C. J. (2015). The impact of color-blind racial ideology on maintaining racial disparities in organizations. In H. A. Neville, M. E. Gallardo, & D. W. Sue (Eds.), *What does it mean to be color-blind? Manifestation, dynamics, and impact* (pp. 263–286). Washington, DC: American Psychological Association.

Block, C. J., Koch, S. M., Liberman, B. E., Merriweather, T. J., & Roberson, L. (2011). Contending with stereotype threat at work: A model of long-term responses. *The Counseling Psychologist, 39*(4), 570–600.

Blume, A. W., Lovato, L. V., Thyken, B. N., & Denny, N. (2012). The relationship of microaggressions with alcohol use and anxiety among ethnic minority college students in a historically White institution. *Cultural Diversity and Ethnic Minority Psychology, 18*(1), 45–54.

Brass, D. J. (1985). Men's and women's networks: A study of interaction patterns and influence in an organization. *Academy of Management Journal, 28*(2), 327–343.

Bureau of Labor Statistics (2017). *American time use survey—2016 results.* Retrieved from https://www.bls.gov/news.release/pdf/atus.pdf.

Burns, C. (2012). *The costly business of discrimination: The economic costs of discrimination and the financial benefits of gay and transgender equality in the workplace.* Washington, D.C.: Center for American Progress. Retrieved from https://www.americanprogress.org/wp-content/uploads/issues/2012/03/pdf/lgbt_biz_discrimination.pdf.

Burt, R. S. (1997). The contingent value of social capital. *Administrative Science Quarterly*, 339–365.

Cartwright, B. Y., Washington, R. D., & McConnell, L. R. (2009). Examining racial microaggressions in rehabilitation counselor education. *Rehabilitation Education*, 23(3–4), 171–181.

Cavanaugh, M. A., Boswell, W. R., Roehling, M. V., & Boudreau, J. W. (2000). An empirical examination of self-reported work stress among U.S. managers. *Journal of Applied Psychology*, 85(1), 65–74.

Capodilupo, C. M., Nadal, K. L., Corman, L., Hamit, S., Lyons, O. B., & Weinberg, A. (2010). The manifestation of gender microaggressions. *Microaggressions and marginality: Manifestation, dynamics, and impact, 193–216*. Hoboken, NJ: Wiley.

Chrobot-Mason, D., Ragins, B. R., & Linnehan, F. (2013). Second hand smoke: Ambient racial harassment at work. *Journal of Managerial Psychology*, 28(5), 470–491.

Cocchiara, F. K., & Quick, J. C. (2004). The negative effects of positive stereotypes: Ethnicity-related stressors and implications on organizational health. *Journal of Organizational Behavior*, 25(6), 781–785.

Constantine, M. G., Smith, L., Redington, R. M., & Owens, D. (2008). Racial microaggressions against Black counseling and counseling psychology faculty: A central challenge in the multicultural counseling movement. *Journal of Counseling & Development*, 86(3), 348–355.

Constantine, M. G., & Sue, D. W. (2007). Perceptions of racial microaggressions among black supervisees in cross-racial dyads. *Journal of Counseling Psychology*, 54(2), 142–153.

Cortina, L. M. (2008). Unseen injustice: Incivility as modern discrimination in organizations. *Academy of Management Review*, 33, 55–75.

DeCuir-Gunby, J. T., & Gunby, N. W. (2016). Racial microaggressions in the workplace: A critical race analysis of the experiences of African American educators. *Urban Education*, 51(4), 390–414.

Endo, R. (2015). How Asian American female teachers experience racial microaggressions from pre-service preparation to their professional careers. *The Urban Review*, 47(4), 601–625.

Ferdman, B. M., & Brody, S. E. (1996). Models of diversity training. In *Handbook of Intercultural Training* (2nd ed., pp. 282–303). Thousand Oaks, CA: Sage.

Griffin, K. A., Pifer, M. J., Humphrey, J. R., & Hazelwood, A. M. (2011). (Re) defining departure: Exploring Black professors' experiences with and responses to racism and racial climate. *American Journal of Education*, 117(4), 495–526.

Hall, J. M., & Fields, B. (2015). "It's Killing Us!" Narratives of Black adults about microaggression experiences and related health stress. *Global Qualitative Nursing Research*, 2(0).

Holder, A., Jackson, M. A., & Ponterotto, J. G. (2015). Racial microaggression experiences and coping strategies of Black women in corporate leadership. *Qualitative Psychology*, 2(2), 164–180.

Hunt, V., Layton, D., & Prince, S. (2015). Why diversity matters: New research makes it increasingly clear that companies with more diverse workforces perform better financially. In *Diversity Matters*. London, England: McKinsey & Company. Retrieved from http://boardagender.org/files/MyKinsey-DIVERSITY_MATTERS_2014_-_print_version_-_McKinsey_Report.pdf.

Ibarra, H. (1993). Personal networks of women and minorities in management: A conceptual framework. *The Academy of Management Review, 18*(1), 56–87.

Ibarra, H. (1995). Race, opportunity, and diversity of social circles in managerial networks. *The Academy of Management Journal, 38*(3), 673–703.

Ibarra, H., Ely, R. J., & Kolb, D. M. (2013). Women rising: The unseen barriers. *Harvard Business Review, 91*(9), 60–66.

Inzlicht, M., & Kang, S. K. (2010). Stereotype threat spillover: How coping with threats to social identity affects aggression, eating, decision making, and attention. *Journal of Personality and Social Psychology, 99*(3), 467–481.

Johnston, M. P., & Nadal, K. L. (2010). Multiracial microaggressions: Exposing monoracism in everyday life and clinical practice. In D. W. Sue (Ed.), *Microaggressions and marginality: Manifestation, dynamics, and impact* (pp. 123–144). Hoboken, NJ: John Wiley & Sons.

Jones, K. P., Peddie, C. I., Gilrane, V. L., King, E. B., & Gray, A. L. (2016). Not so subtle: A meta-analytic investigation of correlates of subtle and overt discrimination. *Journal of Management, 42*(6), 1588–1613.

Kang, S. K., DeCelles, K. A., Tilcsik, A., & Jun, S. (2016). Whitened resumes: Race and self-presentation in the labor market. *Administrative Science Quarterly, 61*(3), 469–502.

Kim, J., Nguyen, D., & Block, C. (2017, April). *Perceptions of microaggressions towards Asians in the workplace*. Paper presented at the annual meeting for Society for Industrial and Organizational Psychology, Orlando, FL.

Kim, J., Yu, H., Drinka, G., Nguyen, D., & Block, C. (2015, May). *Racial microaggressions experienced by Asians and Asian Americans in the workplace*. Poster presented at the annual meeting for Association for Psychological Science, New York, NY.

Kray, L. J., Thompson, L., & Galinsky, A. (2001). Battle of the sexes: Gender stereotype confirmation and reactance in negotiations. *Journal of Personality and Social Psychology, 80*(6), 942.

Level Playing Field Institute. (2006). *The cost of employee turnover due solely to unfairness in the workplace*. The Corporate Leader Survey. Retrieved from http://www.lpfi.org/wp-content/uploads/2015/05/cl-executive-summary.pdf.

Lewis, J. A., Mendenhall, R., Harwood, S. A., & Huntt, M. B. (2013). Coping with gendered racial microaggressions among Black women college students. *Journal of African American Studies, 17*(1), 51–73.

Louis, D. A., Rawls, G. J., Jackson-Smith, D., Chambers, G. A., Phillips, L. L., & Louis, S. L. (2016). Listening to our voices: Experiences of Black faculty at predominantly White research universities with microaggression. *Journal of Black Studies, 47*(5), 454–474.

Low, K. S. D., Radhakrishnan, P., Schneider, K. T., & Rounds, J. (2007). The experiences of bystanders of workplace ethnic harassment. *Journal of Applied Social Psychology, 37*(10), 2261–2297.

McCurry, J. (2015, February). *Clocking off: Japan calls time on long hours work culture.* The Guardian. Retrieved from https://www.theguardian.com/world/2015/feb/22/japan-long-hours-work-culture-overwork-paid-holiday-law.

Mehra, A., Kilduff, M., & Brass, D. J. (1998). At the margins: A distinctiveness approach to the social identity and social networks of underrepresented groups. *Academy of Management Journal, 41*(4), 441–452.

Moss-Racusin, C. A., Dovidio, J. F., Brescoll, V. L., Graham, M. J., & Handelsman, J. (2012). Science faculty's subtle gender biases favor male students. *Proceedings of the National Academy of Sciences, 109*(41), 16474–16479.

Nadal, K. L. (2013). *That's so gay! Microaggressions and the lesbian, gay, bisexual, and transgender community.* Washington, D.C.: American Psychological Association.

Nadal, K. L., Griffin, K. E., Wong, Y., Hamit, S., & Rasmus, M. (2014). The impact of racial microaggressions on mental health: Counseling implications for clients of color. *Journal of Counseling and Development, 92*(1), 57–66.

Offermann, L. R., Basford, T. E., Graebner, R., DeGraaf, S. B., & Jaffer, S. (2013). Slights, snubs, and slurs: Leader equity and microaggressions. *Equality, Diversity and Inclusion: An International Journal, 32*(4), 374–393.

Offermann, L. R., Basford, T. E., Graebner, R., Jaffer, S., De Graaf, S. B., & Kaminsky, S. E. (2014). See no evil: Color blindness and perceptions of subtle racial discrimination in the workplace. *Cultural Diversity and Ethnic Minority Psychology, 20*(4), 499–507.

Oreopoulos, P. (2011). Why do skilled immigrants struggle in the labor market? A field experiment with thirteen thousand resumes. *American Economic Journal: Economic Policy, 3*(4), 148–171.

Pittman, C. T. (2012). Racial microaggressions: The narratives of African American faculty at a predominantly White university. *The Journal of Negro Education, 81*, 82–92.

Rivera, D. P., Forquer, E. E., & Rangel, R. (2010). Microaggressions and the life experience of Latina/o Americans. In D. W. Sue (Ed.), *Microaggressions and marginality: Manifestation, dynamics, and impact* (pp. 59–84). Hoboken, NJ: John Wiley & Sons.

Roberson, L., Deitch, E. A., Brief, A. P., & Block, C. J. (2003). Stereotype threat and feedback seeking in the workplace. *Journal of Vocational Behavior, 62*(1), 176–188.

Roberson, L., & Kulik, C. T. (2007). Stereotype threat at work. *Academy of Management Perspectives, 21*, May, 24–40.

Sharp-Grier, M. L. (2015). "She Was More Intelligent Than I Thought She'd Be!": Status, stigma, and microaggressions in the academy. In *Racial battle fatigue: Insights from the front lines of social justice advocacy* (pp. 29–54). Santa Barbara, CA: Praeger/ABC-CLIO.

Spencer, S. J., Steele, C. M., & Quinn, D. M. (1999). Stereotype threat and women's math performance. *Journal of Experimental Social Psychology, 35*(1), 4–28.

Smith, W. A., Hung, M., & Franklin, J. D. (2011). Racial battle fatigue and the miseducation of Black men: Racial microaggressions, societal problems, and environmental stress. *The Journal of Negro Education,* 63–82.

Steele, C. M. (1997). A threat in the air: How stereotypes shape intellectual identity and performance. *The American Psychologist, 52*(6), 613–629.

Steele, C. M., & Aronson, J. (1995). Stereotype threat and the intellectual performance of African Americans. *Journal of Personality and Social Psychology, 69*(5), 797–811.

Sue, D. W., Bucceri, J., Lin, A. I., Nadal, K. L., & Torino, G. C. (2007). Racial microaggressions and the Asian American experience. *Cultural Diversity and Ethnic Minority Psychology, 13*, 72–81.

Sue, D. W., Capodilupo, C. M., & Holder, A. M. B. (2008). Racial microaggressions in the life experience of Black Americans. *Professional Psychology: Research and Practice, 39*(3), 329–336.

Sue, D. W., Capodilupo, C. M., Torino, G. C., Bucceri, J. M., Holder, A. M. B., Nadal, K. L., & Esquilin, M. (2007). Racial microaggressions in everyday life: Implications for counseling. *American Psychologist, 62*, 271–286.

Sue, D. W., Nadal, K. L., Capodilupo, C. M., Lin, A. I., Torino, G. C., & Rivera, D. P. (2008). Racial microaggressions against Black Americans: Implications for counseling. *Journal of Counseling & Development, 86*(3), 330–338.

Wang, J., Leu, J., & Shoda, Y. (2011). When the seemingly innocuous "stings": Racial microaggressions and their emotional consequences. *Personality and Social Psychology Bulletin, 37*(12), 1666–1678.

11

Microaggressions: Toxic Rain in Health Care

Silvia L. Mazzula and Rebecca R. Campón

The United States is plagued with racial and ethnic health disparities that detrimentally impact marginalized populations. The challenge to addressing health disparities is complex and multilayered. Currently, much of what is known are the observed and measureable differences in health outcomes, prevalence, and burden of disease between groups (e.g., White vs. Asian; low- vs. high-income) (Centers for Disease Control and Prevention [CDC], 2013; Rivera, Mazzula, & Rangel, 2017; U.S. Department of Health and Human Services [USDHHS], 2011). For example, whereas obesity is a major public health concern affecting approximately 78.6 million North Americans (Ogden, Carroll, Kit, & Flegal, 2014), non-Hispanic Blacks carry the greatest burden (47.8%) compared with Latinx (42.5%—also high), non-Hispanic Whites (32.6%), and Asian (10.8%) populations. Racial/ethnic health disparities exist in various other diseases (e.g., non-Hispanic Blacks have the highest prevalence rate of hypertension) (CDC, 2013).

The observable differences in prevalent rates of health outcomes provide important information to identify the at-risk groups, to inform future research investigating the underlying mechanisms affecting particular populations, and to develop targeted solutions to alleviate and address these disparities. However, in order to arrive at comprehensive and relevant solutions and interventions, it is necessary to address health disparities from an individual-, social-, and systems-level.

In this chapter, we provide an overview of individual determinants of health as context for the chapter. We then discuss social and system-level determinants that are sociodemographic (e.g., lack of insurance) to the more nuanced sociocultural determinates related to discrimination, specifically microaggressions. We conclude the chapter by presenting microaggressions as toxic and hazardous to recipients. As psychologists by training, we infuse a psychological perspective in understanding social determinants of health as well as our

Microaggression Theory: Influence and Implications, First Edition. Edited by Gina C. Torino, David P. Rivera, Christina M. Capodilupo, Kevin L. Nadal, and Derald Wing Sue.
© 2019 John Wiley & Sons, Inc. Published 2019 by John Wiley & Sons, Inc.

own research on the impact that microaggressions have on marginalized populations (Nadal, Mazzula, Rivera, & Fujii-Doe, 2014; Rivera, Forquer, & Rangel, 2010).

Individual Determinants of Health

Much of the attention has been focused on individual choices and behaviors (e.g., eating healthy foods, and exercising), as well as on the family history of disease. Accordingly, it is rational to promote healthy lifestyles and choices. Even with familial history of health conditions, individuals can mitigate the impact of disease by regular medical checkups and by refraining from unhealthy choices that increase risk, such as illicit drug use, unhealthy eating habits, sedentary lifestyle, and so forth.

However, individual behaviors are intrinsically connected to societal and structural determinants of health. In 2013, the Centers for Disease Control and Prevention identified three main categories as social determinants of health: education and income, access to healthier food retailers, and unemployment (2013). For example, educational systems, income, and access to healthy food play an important role in the decisions and choices that people make toward a healthy lifestyle. People who live in impoverished neighborhoods have less access to healthy food compared to those who live in more affluent communities (Matthews, Gallo, & Taylor, 2010). Similarly, school systems with a lack of adequate resources have an impact on the health of their students. Therefore, attending to health disparities not only involves helping individuals to make healthy decisions but also involves including system-level mechanisms to ensure this is possible—that is, attending to structural determinants of health. We argue there are two distinct forms of structural determinants of health: sociodemographic and social cultural.

Structural Sociodemographic Determinants of Health

There are various documented structural sociodemographic determinants of health. Sociodemographic determinants are those that are based on demographic characteristics of a given population, rather than individual psychological or cultural factors. For example, access to health care is an often cited determinant. In 2013, the National Healthcare Disparities Report (USDHHS) showed 26.4% of Americans had difficulty getting health care. When looking at differences from a sociodemographic racial and ethnic background, studies show that racial/ethnic minority populations report more barriers to access than their White counterparts (for review, see Mazzula & Torres, 2016; Rivera et al., 2017). For example, data show that over 93% of White and Black adults had their blood pressure measured compared with only 80% of Latinx groups (USDHHS, 2011).

Access to health insurance is another barrier. A total of 28.4 million individuals under 65 years of age in the United States are uninsured (National Center for Health Statistics, 2015). The CDC shows that Latinx and non-Hispanic Blacks are more likely to be uninsured compared with Asian or non-Hispanic White groups (2013). Latinx groups fair worse than other racial/ethnic groups; in 2013, 35.2% of the Latinx reported barriers related to health insurance (USDHHS). Insurance is a major health and financial concern as uninsured individuals are more likely to seek emergency versus preventive services.

Other structural sociodemographic barriers such as language and citizenship status explain racial/ethnic disparities in treatment access, as well as service utilization (Mazzula & Rangel, 2011; Ortega, Rodriquez, & Vargas Bustamante, 2014; USDHHS, 2011). A less discussed aspect of citizenship, however, is the psychological distress, anxiety, and "fear" that is experienced by individuals who are residents or lack proper documentation (Leyro, 2015).

Taken together, these structural sociodemographic stressors pose significant health concerns for those affected, from lack of treatment to poor prognosis. From a psychological perspective, stress has a negative impact on the immune system and increases risk for health problems (Djuric et al., 2010). These structural sociodemographic determinants can be stressful for individuals in general. However, when looking at these determinants across the lifespan and as chronic stressors, it is easy to say that we are experiencing a public health crisis in the United States, with specific groups being at risk, including racial/ethnic minorities, those from poor socioeconomic backgrounds, and undocumented individuals.

In addition, there are sociodemographic determinants related to race that impact health outcomes. These include, for example, institutional racism or sexism that create barriers in access based on racial/ethnic background or gender. Disparities in access to health care, as well as the quality of health care received, can be attributed to institutional racism. Racial minorities are commonly affected by low-wage jobs with no insurance benefits. Institutional racism also explains limited access to health care, lack of quality health care, racial disparities in medical treatment, and lack of linguistic and cultural competent care. Institutional racism has permeated all systems of care in the United States for years.

Sociocultural Determinants of Health

Whereas structural sociodemographic determinants of health have received significant of attention, albeit still limited, a strong body of research considers sociocultural determinants as major players in peoples' health, particularly discrimination and racism. Racial and ethnic minority populations continue to experience consistent discrimination and racism (Carter, Forsyth, Mazzula, & Williams, 2005; Carter et al., 2013) that has an adverse effect on the health (inclusive of mental health and well-being) of racial and ethnic minorities in the United States (Carter et al., 2005; Chung & Epstein, 2014; Lee & Ahn, 2012). Studies show that these experiences impact overall negative outlook in life (Nadal et al., 2014) and at times also raise the level of stress and traumatic stress reactions (Carter et al., 2013). Studies also show that perceived discrimination is linked to negative coping skills such as drinking and poor eating habits (Lee, Ayers, & Kronenfeld, 2009).

An emerging body of research shows that more nuanced interactions and aggressions have a similar negative impact on racial and ethnic minority populations (and other marginalized groups). Research is extending the knowledge base of discrimination to include microaggressions as these more nuanced experiences (Nadal et al., 2014). Originally coined by American psychiatrist Chester M. Pierce, microaggressions are "subtle, stunning, often automatic, and nonverbal exchanges which are 'put downs' of blacks by offenders" (Pierce, Carew, Pierce-Gonzalez, & Wills, 1977). Since then, Sue and colleagues have redefined microaggressions as "brief and commonplace daily verbal, behavioral, or environmental indignities, whether intentional or unintentional, that communicate hostile, derogatory, or negative racial slights and insults towards the target person or group" (Sue et al., 2007, p. 273).

Whereas microaggressions were originally meant to capture subtle aggressions based on race, researchers and scholars have found these experiences to be relevant to various marginalized groups, such as women, lesbian, gay, bisexual, transgender, and queer (LGBTQ) people, religious minorities, and individuals with disabilities (Capodilupo et al., 2010; Huynh, 2012; Keller & Galgay, 2010; Nadal, 2013; Nadal et al., 2011; Rivera et al., 2010; Sue, 2010).

While this tome provides a comprehensive account of the meaning and concept of microaggressions, we briefly restate these as they can be categorized along three lines (Sue et al., 2007): microassaults, or more overt or conscious verbal or nonverbal behaviors, such as name calling or avoidant behavior that may not be perceived as a bias by the perpetrator; microinsults, communications (verbal or behavioral) that demean peoples' heritage or identity; and microinvalidations, statements that negate peoples' experiences, thoughts, and feelings regarding their identity as a marginalized person. Examples of microaggressions include racist or homophobic remarks (e.g., that is so gay) that are perceived to be jokes rather than intentional aggressions (i.e., microassults); comments toward Latinx or African American individuals such as "You're so articulate," which implies the person is perceived to not speak English or to be well-spoken (i.e., microinsults); and comments that communicate individuals who are marginalized are too sensitive or exaggerating the salience of their identity in interactions that invalidate their experiences (i.e., microinvalidations).

Studies have found other themes for specific marginalized groups. For example, in a study with Latinx populations, Rivera et al. (2010) found recurring themes of "criminality" (i.e., microaggressions in which Latinx are presumed violent, or criminal) and "second-class citizen" (i.e., microaggressions in which Latinx are devalued compared to their White counterparts). Other scholars have found unique themes based on religion (e.g., "pathology of different religious groups" in which religious minorities are pathologized; Nadal, Issa, Griffin, Hamit, & Lyons, 2010) and ability (e.g., "desexualization" in which individuals with disabilities are perceived to be asexual; Keller & Galgay, 2010). Taken together, this body of work highlights the various ways in which microaggressions manifest based on individuals' social, cultural, and political identities.

Microaggressions and Health Outcomes

Research on microaggressions provides strong evidence for its impact on elevated levels of anxiety, anger, and stress (Huynh, 2012) and depression and trauma (Torres & Taknint, 2015). Furthermore, data is indicating that the cumulative experience of being a victim of microaggressions predicts negative mental health, specifically negative affect, and depression. Other studies have begun to examine whether microaggressions manifest differently when within-group differences are considered. For example, among Latinx, we found (see Nadal et al., 2014) that Latinas experience more microaggressions in the workplace or in academic settings compared to their Latino counterparts. With respect to self-reported ethnicity, we also found that people who self-identify as Dominican are more exoticized and that Puerto Ricans are more likely to be treated as criminals or second-class citizens (Nadal et al., 2014). These studies show the pervasive and toxic impact of microaggressions on its victims.

Microaggressions in Health Care

The health-care environment is a complex system of people, laws, policies, and money shaped by U.S. culture. It is difficult to navigate this system as a health-care provider, and even more so as a consumer. Unfortunately, for individuals from underrepresented backgrounds, health care does not escape the hands of systemic barriers that impact the lives of marginalized populations. We argue that the trickle-down effect of institutional forms of oppression breeds environments where microaggressions are left unacknowledged, invalidated, and uncontested.

We recognize that people are socialized within inherently racist systems. As a result, all people experience implicit bias that effects how they interact with others. However, given the vast research on institutional racism, it is plausible to say that as a country, we have failed to take steps to mitigate these realities. As a result, many Americans operate under the disillusioned reality in which microaggressions occur with such frequency that it is easy to shrug it off as "that's just how things are." This delusion is a dangerous one, as it leads to inaction and to accepting the status quo. In many ways, institutional racism "allows" microaggressions to exist and occur without consequences, creating a culture that is toxic for marginalized populations.

Research has found that physicians have been targets of racism (Paul-Emile, Smith, Lo, & Fernández, 2016), and the lack of clear guidelines to address these encounters in health care continues to be challenging. Less is known or established to deal with covert transgressions or microaggressions. In healthcare systems, microaggressions are multidimensional and transcend power differentials. For example, a patient can microaggress against her or his doctor and vice versa. Visible marginalized populations, regardless of their social status or power cannot escape from being a target in the toxic environment of our current health-care system. That is, perhaps, one of our greatest challenges in an environment designed to help people recover and heal.

Microaggressions can occur daily toward individuals, yet their subtlety makes them difficult to address, particularly in health-care systems that lack clear guidelines and policies to understand, see, and address more overt forms of institutional discrimination. Consider the example of a White elderly male patient seen by a young Black female physician. The routine exam goes as usual, however, the White patient asks a few questions or makes statements that creates discomfort for the physician. For example, he might say, "Where did get your medical degree? I haven't seen Black doctors around here." Was that a microaggression? It is possible the patient indeed has not seen other Black doctors. However, the message behind the statement could also be that Black people do not belong in the health-care field. Would the patient have asked about a doctor's medical credentials had the doctor been a White male? The same Black female physician may see another patient, this time a middle-aged female who remarks "you people wouldn't understand, but I am really in a lot of pain, all over." Again, the physician is left wondering if it was an insult or hostility due to her race or if the statement reflected the patients' mental or physical health status (brain damage, intoxication, etc.). Microaggressions add additional emotional stressors to the job of a Physician of Color to perform their job of protecting and treating the health of their patients.

Anecdotal accounts show health-care professionals begin experiencing microaggressions in training programs. One author recalls being in a meeting with the director of psychology at her internship site when in conversation mentioned, "Well, I just don't see how you are prepared to do clinical work coming from a counseling program, we'll have to learn from each other, I'll have to keep my eye on you." Whereas the encounter captured more overt hostility toward fields of study, she also experienced what researchers coin "second-class citizen" microaggressions (i.e., a common microaggressions in which Latinx are devalued). The interaction also included microinsults that demeaned her heritage and identity as a Latina, such as "you seem like you are a tough girl" (as finger snapping was acted out) and verbally mimicking stereotypical Latina accents and "attitude" (e.g., head rolling acted out). The conversation was disguised in a playful way suggesting the two were "pals." Interactions such as these leave trainees in vulnerable positions given the power differential. While little research exists on the frequency of microaggressions experienced by trainees, we venture to say these occur quite often. More research to document these experiences and the specific health risks it poses on trainees is needed.

Similarly, when patients experience microaggressions from their providers, they are even more problematic given the power differentials and patients' vulnerability and health-care needs. Oftentimes, cultural values and communication styles are pathologized during nuanced interactions. For example, health-care providers may assume that individuals of Latinx or Asian descent who are quiet, don't speak up, or give eye contact may not understand English or have poor social skills, leading providers to impose Western–American cultural ideals by stating "Why are you so quiet? Speak up, you should be more verbal." The opposite may also occur if a Person of Color and their family members are "loud," animated and gesturing while talking, leading providers to make statements such as "This is a hospital/clinic/office, you don't have to speak so loudly. Just calm down." Whereas all people, regardless of their racial or ethnic background may hear comments such as these, we argue that People of Color may experience them regularly and result in miscommunication, misdiagnosis, and poorer quality of care. Research is needed to document and mitigate these transgressions.

In general, microaggressions inhibit individuals from expressing themselves openly and trusting their provider, adding additional barriers to health care. If patients feel that they are not respected, they can become silent and limit their ability to explain their symptoms clearly. Many times the health-care environment makes the Patient of Color so uncomfortable that they do not return. Whereas scholars have documented the role race in patients' premature termination or underutilization of services, further research is needed to understand these more nuanced interactions in general, and in health-care specifically. Similar research is needed to understand and adequately address microaggressions experienced by providers and trainees.

The Psychological Hazards of Microaggressions

Perhaps the most understudied concept in the race literature is the psychological impact that results from experiences with discrimination in general, and with microaggressions specifically. Borrowing from the body of literature on internalized racism, we argue that microaggressions can be internalized and result in psychological damage to its targets. People of Color encounter, regularly, both implicit and explicit messages that they do not belong, that they are different, and that they are "less than." These messages are received from not only systems of care but also from the mass media, television, movies, celebrities, and even literature. Being bombarded with such messages, especially when reinforced by family members with implicit messages from childhood (i.e., "this light-skinned doll is so much prettier, nice and clean, don't you want this one?") to young adulthood (i.e., approving White or light-skinned romantic partners, etc.) leads an individual to turn these values and beliefs into their personal schemas (Campón & Carter, 2015). One study on internalized racism (Campón & Carter, 2015) found the accumulation of messages that reinforce, for example, that people are "different" and that they must do their best to be more like the "others" (Whites) weighs heavily on a Person of Color. In this study, Campón and Carter found that people may in turn actively seek to be accepted by White society by avoiding associations with their own race or ethnicity groups, changing their appearance and/or adopting White cultural standards. It was also found that internalized racism further contributes to feelings of inferiority.

We argue that the same way in which individuals internalize racism, microaggressions are internalized and have a negative impact on the psyche of People of Color and their identity. Everyday slights and subtle and nuanced degrading messages wear on the Person of Color, adding to the accumulate effect of the basic message "you are not as good as the other." Microaggressions harbor feelings of initial shock, confusion, and anger. A critical defining characteristic of microaggressions is that targets are left wondering "did that really just happen or is it just me—maybe I'm not good enough, maybe I shouldn't be a doctor?" When individuals begin to question their personal attributes, merits, and personhood, we argue it also begins to reshape their identity. Due to their subtly, microaggressions are often left in the hands of the target to resolve. When health-care systems or leaders do not provide policies, guidelines, or spaces for health-care professionals or patients to discuss these microaggressions, the messages are absorbed.

Similar to internalized racism, we argue that internalizing microaggressions is not a conscious process. Individuals do not willing decide "hey, I am going to internalize and believe all these awful messages people are trying to convey about me." Rather, similar to how individuals look to others for social acceptance and socialization, people also learn about their place in the world from those who surround them. According to Campón and Carter (2015), people "appropriate" the values, beliefs, and cultural tools of the surrounding society and culture—that is, the process in which an individual morphs when coming into contact with their environment. Thus, Campón and Carter's work on internalized racism concluded that if we live in a society in which racism is embedded into its very core and expressed across systems, then in theory, we too have appropriated these racist ideals without conscious effort. That is, just as we learn how to eat, talk, and relate to one another through observation, modeling, and messages from our family and society as children, we also learn how to treat people of different groups, and we quickly learn (without being explicitly taught) who has privilege and who does not.

One of us recalls about how when she was four or five years old receiving a brown-skinned (mimicking a Latinx) doll as a gift and upon unwrapping it, she became excited and started to play with the doll. However, the reaction of the adults was extreme: there was lot of commotion and the brown-skinned doll later vanished. No one told her anything explicitly, except that she was going to get a "new doll." The implicit message was clear: something must have been "wrong" with the brown-skinned doll and the new White doll she received was "better." Whereas this is one anecdotal account (from one of the authors), we have found similar messages received by our clients, students, and colleagues. These nuanced messages are pervasive and occur regularly throughout one's life. Thus, we argue that the experiences with microaggressions are also internalized and become part of ones' personal schema.

When microaggressions occur in health care, they reinforce feelings of inferiority, whether they are conscious or unconscious, and subsequently influence individuals' actions. For example, a health-care provider who happens to be a Person of Color may not speak up during rounds or treatment meetings if they have been microaggressed by their supervisor or manager. If they have already internalized feelings of inferiority or have been made to feel inferior, they may keep silent, which may in turn be perceived as lacking the adequate knowledge or skill set. People of Color walk a fine line, if they speak up, they may be rejected with an insult or demeaned, and if they keep silent, they may equally experience a negative consequence—that is, they find themselves in a "catch 22," a defining characteristic of microaggressions (Sue et al., 2007).

We argue that when People of Color internalize microaggressions, their ability to view themselves as they really are is compromised. Whereas researchers have documented that internalized racism leads to higher rates of depression and anxiety (Campón & Carter, 2015), there is no literature to date that directly discusses the potential impact of internalized microaggressions on People of Color. We predict that similar negative health outcomes would be found in those that endorse high levels of internalized microaggressions. Future research in this area is needed, particularly given the pervasive and nuanced nature of microaggressions.

Given our contention that internalized microaggressions compromise individuals' schemas, we predict that microaggressions may contribute to other forms of psychological hazards such as the "imposter syndrome," originally coined by Pauline Clance and Suzanne Imes in 1978. The imposter syndrome (also termed *impostor phenomenon*) describes high-achieving individuals who have difficulty internalizing their accomplishments or skills and experience fear of being exposed as an imposter or fraud. For example, a person may have the skills, credentials, and capability to be a medical provider but may think (and believe) that they have "fooled" others or the system when they enter these spaces. Subconsciously, or consciously, they believe that in fact they are not qualified to do the work their position entails and that it will be only a matter of time before everyone will "find them out." Studies have shown that People of Color who endorse imposterism also report high levels of anxiety and depression (Cokley et al., 2017). Many medical and health professional students experience this during their training and many Providers of Color experience it even *after* graduating, having their licensures/certifications, and years of experience.

We hypothesize that microaggressions compound the effects of the imposter syndrome, particularly among People of Color. If a Person of Color is experiencing imposterism (e.g., doubting their ability and skill set he/she has picked from a graduate or a training program or even a job), then being slighted, insulted, and/or demeaned has the potential to confirm their doubts. Health-care providers and Trainees of Color (and other marginalized groups) often enter spaces where they are the "only one" of their racial or ethnic group or where they have been historically underrepresented. Imposterism is likely to occur among first-generation professionals and minority populations (Clance & Imes, 1978). Thus, for People of Color, this intersection places them at higher risk.

Whereas self-doubt is a common reaction, self-doubt among racial and ethnic minorities and women is a complex reaction to internalized racism and confirmed by experiences with microaggressions. Health-care providers and Trainees of Color are all susceptible to experiencing microaggressions in a health-care setting. It is like a toxic rain, pouring down the branches of the embedded racism trees that are deeply rooted in our society. It is this rain that gives seed to microaggressions and worsens the psychological hazards of the imposter syndrome. Thus, simply teaching health-care providers and trainees to be more confident dismisses these social–political realities. What is needed are leaders and supervisors who are aware of these realities and enforce guidelines and policies that hold microaggressions perpetrators accountable and responsible for their actions.

Recommendations

In general, awareness and understanding of microaggressions, and the extent to which these occur in health-care settings, are a good start toward dismantling and addressing these encounters that impact the lives of minority populations: providers, trainees, and patients. Clear policies, guidelines, and laws must also be implemented and enforced by health-care leadership and administrators to protect victims of microaggressions.

Recently, several strategies have been published for addressing discrimination experienced by health-care providers and trainees and how to cope as targets of bias and racism (Whitgob, Blankenburg, & Bogetz, 2016). Similar efforts and strategies are needed that include the more nuanced experiences with microaggressions. A centralized set of guidelines and policies, specific to the complex health systems and health provider network, to address microaggressions that occur among colleagues, trainees, provider-to-patient, and patient-to-doctor would reinforce that such encounters exist and indicate the health-care system is committed to preventing the detrimental effects on its victims. Three additional systemic issues related to research, service, and workforce must be attended to in order to move this conversation forward.

Culturally Responsive Research and Scholarship

To date, much of the research and scholarship on microaggressions has focused on mental health. Therefore, there is a dearth of research that advances the knowledge base on the physical health impact of microaggressions. More broadly, however, there is an overall lack of culturally responsive research and scholarship to inform relevant services, treatment, and practice. The medical model is grounded in the Western notions of healing and cultural values that may not be consistent with those of some racial and ethnic minority populations in the United States. The mismatches give rise to opportunities for microaggressions to occur. Accordingly, future research that is culturally responsive to diverse populations is needed to develop robust assessment tools, interventions, training, and services for victims of microaggressions.

Given the overall lack of culturally responsive research and scholarship to help providers deliver culturally responsive services, support must be in place across the health-care system for training on how to critically analyze research studies and literature and how to determine whether these inform, or not, how to best see and respond to microaggressions.

Culturally Responsive Health-Care Service

The overall lack of culturally responsive research and scholarship can add an additional burden to health-care providers who are genuinely interested in culturally competent services as they have limited information to do so. Similarly, even when there are culturally responsive studies and publications, assessing social cultural determinants of health can take a significant amount of time which at times is outside of what is allowed by most managed care models (Mazzula & Torres, 2016). Therefore, policies and guidelines must be in place to support health-care providers to be able to spend the time needed. These would also help promote the importance of awareness and reality of microaggressions and methods of addressing them in treatment to empower marginalized patients. Health-care systems must also have policies in place to ensure their staff, from first responders to those in leadership positions, receives training and support to provide culturally responsive health-care services.

Workforce Diversity

Addressing microaggressions, and more broadly persistent racial and ethnic health disparities, also rests on workforce diversity. Racial and ethnic minority populations continue to be underrepresented in most health-care professions, especially in high-quality subspecialties. For example, whereas Latinx account for over 17% of the population in the United States, they represent less than 3% of physicians and 1.7% of registered nurses (U.S. Department of Health and Human Services, 2010). African Americans represent 4% of physicians yet make up 14% of the population (Association of American Medical Colleges, 2005).

Various initiatives have been implemented to develop workforce diversity. The Affordable Care Act, Section 5101, for example, recommended establishing a national commission to review the health-care workforce and to determine the workforce needs. The National Institute of Health's Division of Training, Workforce Development, and Diversity (2015) also funds programs to train and develop a diverse research capital. Recently, various professional affinity groups have shown promising efforts toward addressing workforce diversity. For example, the Latina Researchers Network, a multidisciplinary network of researchers, clinicians, and scholars across the United States, supports training, recruitment, and retention of underrepresented populations who can provide culturally responsive services (Arredondo, Gallardo-Cooper, Delgado-Romero, & Zapata, 2014; Mazzula, 2013; Rivera et al., 2017). Whereas the Latina Researchers Network is focused more on culturally responsive research that can inform provision of service, it provides a roadmap for health care to support workface development efforts. Affinity groups specific to the health-care system that include underrepresented health-care providers, who share commonalties based on cultural background, would help validate the lived realities of being targets of microaggressions and can empower the health-care professionals to move these conversations forward.

Workforce development policies, initiatives, and taskforce groups must also consider methods for recruiting diverse populations. These must incorporate a comprehensive understanding of how microaggressions work toward keeping marginalized populations outside of the health-care system (e.g., messages that negate their belonging in such spaces). Given the discussion on the imposter syndrome noted earlier in this chapter, increasing the number of underrepresented physicians and health-care providers would also help combat feelings of being the "only one" or a fraud. Similarly, policies and guidelines must also be in place to maintain a diverse health-care workforce given the documented experiences of microaggressions and discrimination more broadly.

Conclusion

The challenge to addressing health disparities in the United States is complex and multilayered. Evidence continues to support that microaggressions are toxic and hazardous. However, microaggressions can be prevented. We must move past understanding health disparities from a sociodemographic framework of observed and measureable differences in health outcomes to a more nuanced and comprehensive framework that includes individual, social, and system levels. Increasing awareness and understanding of the frequency in which microaggressions occur across the lifespan and their impact on health outcome is a foundational step. Clear policies and guidelines specific to the complex health-care systems are necessary, as is more focused attention to culturally responsive research, treatment services, and workforce diversity efforts. The time now is to end the psychological and physical health hazards of this toxic rain.

References

Arredondo, P., Gallardo-Cooper, M., Delgado-Romero, E., & Zapata, A. (2014). *Culturally responsive counselling with Latinas/os.* Alexandria, VA: American Counseling Association.

Association of American Medical Colleges. (2005). *Minority students in medical education: facts and figures 2005.* Table 41a. Washington, DC: Association of American Medical Colleges.

Campón, R. R., & Carter, R. T. (2015). The appropriated racial oppression scale: Development and preliminary validation. *Cultural Diversity and Ethnic Minority Psychology, 21*(4), 497–506.

Capodilupo, C. M., Nadal, K. L., Corman, L., Hamit, S., Lyons, O. B., & Weinberg, A. (2010). The manifestation of gender microaggressions. In D. W. Sue (Ed.), *Microaggressions and marginality: Manifestation, dynamics, and impact* (pp. 193–216). Hoboken, NJ: Wiley.

Carter, R. T., Forsyth, J. M., Mazzula, S. L., & Williams, B. (2005). Racial discrimination and race-based traumatic stress: An exploratory investigation. In *Handbook of racial-cultural psychology and counseling: Training and practice* (Vol. 2, pp. 447–476).

Carter, R. T., Mazzula, S. L., Victoria, R., Vazquez, R., Hall, S., Smith, S., … Williams, B. (2013). Initial development of the race-based traumatic stress symptom scale: Assessing the emotional impact of racism. *Psychological Trauma: Theory, Research, Practice, and Policy, 5*(1), 1–9.

Centers for Disease Control and Prevention (CDC). (2013). Centers for disease control and prevention health disparities and inequalities report-United States, 2013. *Morbidity and Mortality Weekly Report, 62*(Suppl 3), 1–189.

Chung, H., & Epstein, N. B. (2014). Perceived racial discrimination, acculturative stress, and psychological distress among Asian immigrants: The moderating effects of support and interpersonal strain from a partner. *International Journal of Intercultural Relations, 42*, 129–139.

Clance, P. R., & Imes, S. A. (1978). The imposter phenomenon in high achieving women: Dynamics and therapeutic intervention. *Psychotherapy: Theory, Research & Practice, 15*(3), 241–247.

Cokley, K., Smith, L., Bernard, D., Hurst, A., Jackson, S., Stone, S., ... Roberts, D. (2017). Impostor feelings as a moderator and mediator of the relationship between perceived discrimination and mental health among racial/ethnic minority college students. *Journal of Counseling Psychology, 64*(2), 141–154.

Djuric, M., Djonic, D., Milovanovic, P., Nikolic, S., Marshall, R., Marinkovic, J., & Hahn, M. (2010). Region-specific sex-dependent pattern of age-related changes of proximal femoral cancellous bone and its implications on differential bone fragility. *Calcified Tissue International, 86*(3), 192–201.

Huynh, V. W. (2012). Ethnic microaggressions and the depressive and somatic symptoms of Latino and Asian American adolescents. *Journal of Youth and Adolescence, 41*, 831–846. doi:10.1007/s10964-012-9756-9.

Keller, R. M., & Galgay, C. E. (2010). Microaggressive experiences of people with disabilities. In D. W. Sue (Ed.), *Microaggressions and marginality: Manifestation, dynamics, and impact* (pp. 241–268). Hoboken, NJ: Wiley.

Lee, C., Ayers, S. L., & Kronenfeld, J. J. (2009). The association between perceived provider discrimination, health care utilization, and health status in racial and ethnic minorities. *Ethnicity & Disease, 19*(3), 330–337.

Lee, D. L., & Ahn, S. (2012). Discrimination against Latina/os: A meta-analysis of individual-level resources and outcomes. *The Counseling Psychologist, 40*(1), 28–65.

Leyro, S. (2015). *Legal violence: Crimmigration and the violent effects of deportation.* Paper session at the 32nd annual Winter Roundtable, Teachers College, Columbia University, New York, NY.

Matthews, K. A., Gallo, L. C., & Taylor, S. E. (2010). Are psychosocial factors mediators of socioeconomic status and health connections? *Annals of the New York Academy of Sciences, 1186*(1), 146–173.

Mazzula, S. L. (2013, August). Latinas breaking glass ceilings. In R. Navarro (Chair), *Latina Researchers Network: Latinas in hard to reach places.* Paper presented at the American Psychological Association 121st Annual Convention, Honolulu, HI.

Mazzula, S. L., & Rangel, R. (2011). Cultural consideration for mental health treatment with women of color. In P. Lundberg-Love, K. Nadal, & M. Paludi (Eds.), *Women and Mental Disorders: Treatments and Research* (Vol. 4, pp. 75–91). Santa Barbara, CA: Praeger Publishers.

Mazzula, S. L., & Torres, A. (2016). Latino trends and health policy. From walking on eggshells to commitment. In L. T. Benuto et al. (Eds.), *Enhancing behavioral health in Latino populations: Reducing disparities through integrated behavioral and primary care* (pp. 75–94). Cham, Switzerland: Springer International Publishing.

Nadal, K. L. (2013). *That's so gay! Microaggressions and the lesbian, gay, bisexual, and transgender community*. Washington, DC: American Psychological Association.

Nadal, K. L., Issa, M., Griffin, K. E., Hamit, S., & Lyons, O. B. (2010). Religious microaggressions in the United States. In D. W. Sue (Ed.), *Microaggressions and marginality: Manifestations, dynamics, and impact* (pp. 287–310). New York: Wiley.

Nadal, K. L., Mazzula, S. L., Rivera, D. P., & Fujii-Doe, W. (2014). Microaggressions and Latina/o Americans: An analysis of nativity, gender, and ethnicity. *Journal of Latina/o Psychology, 2*(2), 67–78.

Nadal, K. L., Wong, Y., Issa, M. A., Meterko, V., Leon, J., & Wideman, M. (2011). Sexual orientation microaggressions: Processes and coping mechanisms for lesbian, gay, and bisexual individuals. *Journal of LGBT Issues in Counseling, 5*(1), 21–46.

National Institute of Health Statistics. (2015). *Current programs in the division of training, workforce development, and diversity (TWD)*. U.S. Department of Health and Human Services, Division of Training, Workforce Development and Diversity, Rockville, MD. Retrieved from http://www.nigms.nih.gov/Training/Pages/TWDPrograms.aspx.

Ogden, C. L., Carroll, M. D., Kit, B. K., & Flegal, K. M. (2014). Prevalence of childhood and adult obesity in the United States, 2011-2012. *Jama, 311*(8), 806–814.

Ortega, A. N., Rodriquez, H. P., & Vargas Bustamante, A. (2014). Policy dilemmas in Latino health care and implementation of the affordable care act. *The Annual Review of Public Health, 26*(10), 10.1–10.20.

Paul-Emile, K., Smith, A. K., Lo, B., & Fernández, A. (2016). Dealing with racist patients. *New England Journal of Medicine, 374*(8), 708–711.

Pierce, C. M., Carew, J. V., Pierce-Gonzalez, D., & Wills, D. (1977). An experiment in racism: TV commercials. *Education and Urban Society, 10*(1), 61–87.

Rivera, D. P., Forquer, E. E., & Rangel, R. (2010). Microaggressions and the life experience of Latina/o Americans. In D. W. Sue (Ed.), *Microaggressions and marginality: Manifestations, dynamics, and impact* (pp. 59–83). New York, NY: Wiley.

Rivera, D. P., Mazzula, S., & Rangel, R. (2017). Psychological perspectives on ethnic minority physical health disparities. In A. Blume (Ed.), *Social Issues in Living Color: Challenges and solutions from the perspective of ethnic minority psychology* (pp. 53–76). Santa Barbara, CA: Praeger.

Sue, D. W. (2010). *Microaggressions in everyday life: Race, gender, and sexual orientation.* Hoboken, NJ: Wiley.

Sue, D. W., Capodilupo, C. M., Torino, G. C., Bucceri, J. M., Holder, A. M. B., Nadal, K. L., & Esquilin, M. (2007). Racial microaggressions in everyday life: Implications for counseling. *The American Psychologist, 62*(4), 271–286. doi:10.1037/0003-066x.62.4.271.

Torres, L., & Taknint, J. T. (2015). Ethnic microaggressions, traumatic stress symptoms, and Latino depression: A moderated mediational model. *Journal of Counseling Psychology, 62*(3), 393–401.

U.S. Department of Health and Human Services. (2010). *Movilizandonos por Nuestro Futuro: Strategic development of a mental health workforce for Latinos Consensus statements and recommendations.* USDHHS Office of Minority Health and the National Resource Center for Hispanic Mental Health.

U.S. Department of Health and Human Services. (2011). *HHS action plan to reduce racial and ethnic disparities: A nation free of disparities in health and health care.* Washington, DC: U.S. Department of Health and Human Services.

Whitgob, E. E., Blankenburg, R. L., & Bogetz, A. L. (2016). The discriminatory patient and family: Strategies to address discrimination towards trainees. *Academic Medicine, 91*(11), S64–S69.

12

From Racial Microaggressions to Hate Crimes: A Model of Online Racism Based on the Lived Experiences of Adolescents of Color

Brendesha M. Tynes, Fantasy T. Lozada, Naila A. Smith, and Ashley M. Stewart

There has been rapid growth in research on racial microaggressions since the publication of Sue et al.'s (2007) seminal piece (Wong, Derthick, David, Saw, & Okazaki, 2014). A recent review of the first five years of research noted 59 articles resulted from the authors' search for the keyword *racial microaggression* and 112 for the general term *microaggression* in PsychInfo (Wong et al., 2014). Despite the popularity the topic has garnered, few studies have focused on online racial microaggressions. One reason for this gap in the literature is early concern over whether the construct is applicable to online experiences (Tynes, Rose, & Markoe, 2013). Though the microaggressions literature outlines microassaults in the initial taxonomy of experiences (along with microinsults and microinvalidation), the subtle forms dominate the offline literature. Moreover, scholars have argued that the term *micro* inadequately describes users online experiences and might minimize the nature and impact on People of Color (Gin, Martínez-Alemán, Rowan-Kenyon, & Hottell, 2017; Minikel-Lacocque, 2013). Second, when scholars have studied online experiences, they tend to use different terms such as overt or covert racism, cyber, or online racism (Daniels, 2009), online racial discrimination (Tynes, Giang, Williams, & Thompson, 2008), hate speech (Tynes, 2005), racialized aggression (Gin et al., 2017), and colorblind racism (Yoon, 2016).

This chapter attempts to synthesize these literatures and propose a model of online racism that includes both subtle and explicit forms that represent the range of experiences users may have online. The taxonomy includes three types of online racism: online racial microaggressions, online racial discrimination, and online hate crimes. Heeding the call to have the "microaggressed" define their experiences rather than having others define it for them, we utilize

Microaggression Theory: Influence and Implications, First Edition. Edited by Gina C. Torino, David P. Rivera, Christina M. Capodilupo, Kevin L. Nadal, and Derald Wing Sue.

interview data from a sample of Adolescents of Color. Much of the extant offline microaggressions literature tends to focus on college samples; little is known about adolescents and emerging adults (18–25 year olds) in online settings. This is despite the fact that 97% of teens have access to the Internet, 92% report going online daily, and 24% are online constantly (Perrin, 2015). Similarly, 99% of 18–29 year-olds had access to the Internet as of 2016 (Pew Research Center, 2017). In addition, Adolescents of Color have been noted to spend more time consuming various types of media than their White counterparts (Rideout, Lauricella, & Wartella, 2011) and have experienced an exponential increase in more explicit forms of online racism based on online survey data (Tynes, Seaton, & Zuckerman, 2015). We complement this research with open-ended survey data and interviews that center on adolescent voices, allowing adolescents themselves to describe what it means to experience online racism.

Overview of Current Conceptualizations of Online Racism

Although not consistently or explicitly labeled as such, a number of scholars have theorized about online racism. Online racism is a system of anti-people of color practices that privilege and maintain political, cultural, and economic power for Whites in digital space. These systems create an electronic White racial frame (Feagin, 2006) that "includes racist ideology, stereotypes and emotions" (Daniels, 2009, p. 11). In addition to being ideological, the systems are structural, promoting enduring status hierarchies on the basis of perceived membership in a racial-ethnic group. Perhaps most critical is a persistent dehumanization and de-individualization of People of Color (Neville, Spanierman, & Lewis, 2012) through electronic means. Online racism may be technologically mediated, that is built and expressed in the online infrastructure or back end (e.g., algorithms), or through the interface (e.g., symbol, image, voice, text, and graphic representations). It can also be expressed in interpersonal verbal and nonverbal interactions online (e.g., on social media and multiplayer games). Furthermore, as the online context dramatically shifts the nature of the experience of racism, we note that it does so through the convergence of new and old media. Daniels (2009) notes in her work documenting the transition of White supremacist groups to online spaces, that it is impossible to draw a line of distinction between print and digital media. The two are not discrete categories. This may be the case for different types of media such as news, television, film, advertisements, books, images, and music.

Nevertheless, there are some key distinctions between online and offline forms of racism. First, because of the design of online spaces, narrative structures, dialogue, and settings, users can become immersed in a simulated reality (e.g., games) that allow them to practice doing race and racism. As such, in agreement with Everett and Watkins (2008), we argue online contexts are *racialized pedagogical zones* or spaces that teach and instantiate users into stereotypes about racial groups. Additionally, online racism is arguably more pervasive than off-line racism as it operates as a "never-ending pipeline" that fundamentally changes the way in which People of Color experience racist incidents (Keum & Miller, 2017, p. 311). Rather than having a racist encounter in person that is held and potentially recreated in a person's mind, individuals have a permanent electronic record that they may return to repeatedly (and possibly carry on their person). This allows for increased rumination and revictimization. In addition, because of the interactivity afforded by online interfaces, a potential wide audience can participate in the victimization by further comments, likes, sharing, meming, gaming, and so forth.

Definitions and Current Research on Three Types of Online Racism

Researchers have studied at least three types of online racism that map onto these forms: online racial microaggressions (Clark, Spanierman, Reed, Soble, & Cabana, 2011), which encapsulates covert microinvalidations and microinsults (and overt microassaults); online racial discrimination (Tynes et al., 2008), which describes direct or vicarious overt microassaults, and online hate crimes (e.g., Citron, 2014), which includes online abuse that violates the law.

Online Racial Microaggressions

We define online racial microaggressions as subtle, intentional or unintentional, visual, nonverbal and verbal, representations of racist ideas about People of Color. We argue that online racial microaggressions are electronic representations of racism that are layered, often unconscious and cumulative. These include microinvalidations, microinsults, and microassaults; the latter will be briefly mentioned in the literature here and discussed more extensively in the online racial discrimination section (p. 198). Extending the conceptualization of microinvalidations put forth by Sue et al. (2007), we conceive of online microinvalidations as text, video, images, and symbols that communicate (often unintentionally) that one is an alien in their own country, colorblindness, endorsement in the myth of meritocracy, denial of individual racism, and claims of "reverse discrimination." Further drawing on Sue et al.'s (2007) conceptualization of microinsults, we conceive of online microinsults as text, video, images, and symbols that communicate (often unintentionally) ascription of intelligence, second-class citizen, pathologizing of cultural values, and assumption of criminal status. These electronic communications nullify, exclude, or negate psychological or expressed thoughts.

The online racial microaggressions literature includes work that has replicated the off-line literature. For example, Clark et al. (2011) analyzed data from a weblog in which users expressed views of American Indians and the discontinuation of a university's racialized mascot, Chief Illiniwek. Data were then categorized using the racial microaggressions model (Sue et al., 2007). Researchers found themes advocating for sociopolitical dominance, alleging over-sensitivity (microinsults), waging a stereotype attack (microassaults) as well as those denying racism, employing the logics of elimination and replacement, expressing adoration and conveying grief (microinvalidations). Other studies replicating the off-line microaggression framework include Kettrey and Laster (2014) who examined two thousand comments from the 20 most frequently viewed videos posted to YouTube to reveal patterns they identify as overt racism (microassaults), color-blind racism (microinvalidations), and dissent against racism. Results revealed that racism appeared in 10.7% of the comments, with 6.4% containing overt racism and 5.5% colorblind racism. Comments in which an individual identified as a Person of Color were significantly more likely to elicit overt racism. These comments included racial epithets and threats of death or harm to property, prosegregationist arguments as well as those suggesting People of Color are less intelligent.

By their nature, microaggressions have the power to perpetuate racial stereotypes through microinsults, leading scholars to examine how racial stereotypes are reinforced or challenged online. Guo and Harlow (2014) used a content analysis to examine how popular YouTube videos featuring African Americans, Latinx, or Asians included or reinforced cultural stereotypes about these groups. They also used the number of likes/dislikes and comments to measure the differences between videos that perpetuated stereotypes and those that challenged them. Researchers found that three-fifths of the videos included racial stereotypes. The most common stereotypes about Blacks was "lawbreaker," and second, stereotypical portrayals of physical appearance and language. For Latinx, sexualized women was the most common stereotype and "lawbreaker" the second most common stereotype. For Asians, the most common stereotypes mocked their physical appearance and language pronunciation, and the second most common stereotype sexualized Asian women. Related to these findings, Harrison, Tayman, Janson, and Connolly (2010) examined online articles and commentary on professional Black male athletes on the ESPN.com homepage to assess whether online articles and Internet commentary challenge or reinforce stereotypes. A majority of the articles covering Black male athletes included microinsults, often portraying them as being violent, irresponsible, and guilty of crimes. While the articles never mentioned race, reader comments frequently did so and debated its role in the media's coverage of Black male athletes.

Online Racial Discrimination

Explicit forms of online racism have been described in the literature as online racial discrimination (Tynes et al., 2008) and racialized aggression (Gin et al., 2017). Consistent with Tynes et al's (2010) conception of online racial discrimination, we conceive of individual online racial discrimination as intentional verbal or visual assaults personally directed at an individual on the basis of race, exclusion from sites or conversations communicated via text, video, images, and symbols. Similarly, vicarious online racial discrimination is intentional verbal or visual assaults including jokes on a person's ethnic group that are witnessed via text, videos, images, and symbols. Online racial discrimination has also been called microassaults in the microaggressions literature.

Tynes et al. (2015) have noted an exponential increase in both the individual and vicarious forms of online racial discrimination across three time points from 2010 to 2013 for adolescents in 6th–12th grade. Online survey data revealed that 42% of Students of Color experienced at least one direct (individual) discriminatory incident in the first year, with 55% in the second year, and 58% in the third year reporting such an incident. The most common direct experience is being shown a racist image. For vicarious experiences 64% of Students of Color indicated that they had experienced at least one vicarious discriminatory incident in the first year, with 69% the second year and 68% the third year. Their research has also shown that both of these types of experiences should be measured and that they have a unique impact on adolescent mental health, behavior, and academic outcomes beyond face-to-face experiences (Tynes, English, Del Toro, & Smith, in prep; Tynes et al., 2008).

Scholars have also conceptualized online racial discrimination as racialized aggression. Gin et al. (2017) examined racialized aggression through interviews about the social media accounts of 15 Black, Latinx, Asian, and White college students at a Primary White Institution. Researchers note that participants were struck by the volume of and regularity of overt racism that specifically demeaned Black individuals. They further note the degree of invalidation that took place around the Black Lives Matter movement along with messages questioning Black students' belongingness. In addition, the authors found that statements rationalized violence against Blacks. These comments appeared to be most intense around events such as protests in Ferguson and the police killing of Eric Garner.

Using a sample of 1,023 Black, East Asian, Latinx, South Asian, Middle Eastern, Native American, and multiracial participants ages 18–67, researchers found the Perceived Online Racism Scale had three factors that included personal experience of racial cyber-aggression, online-mediated exposure to racist reality, and vicarious exposure to racial cyber-aggression. They noted that the more personal and vicarious experiences were stronger predictors of mental health outcomes than the online-mediated exposure factor. Further, the vicarious experiences were the only experiences with a unique contribution to psychological distress over and above off-line experiences. Findings also show that items that represented microaggressions did not hold in the model and were removed. Researchers suggest that this may be because the more explicit forms are more salient for the adult population in the study.

Online Hate Crimes

Online hate crimes include, but are not limited to, targeting someone on the basis of their race and engaging in the following activities: stalking, cyber-mobs, harassment, and privacy violations that include identity theft, hacking, and/or publishing nude photos (Citron, 2014). More extreme versions of online racism also have differing labels such as severe behaviors or forms of abuse. A recent study of online harassment by the Pew Research Center found that 23% of harassment that is motivated by race includes a severe behavior (e.g., sustained harassment, physical threats, or stalking; Duggan, 2017). Moreover, 25% of African Americans and 10% of Latinx adults online are harassed because of their race compared with 3% of Whites. Similarly, Baum, Catalano, Rand, and Rose (2011) note that 12.2% of Blacks, 19.6% of American Indian, 10.6% of Latinos, and 7% of Asians have experienced stalking victimization, with one in four victims reporting these experiences via e-mail or instant messaging. They further note that 18–19 year olds and those aged 20–24 report the highest rates of stalking victimization (Baum et al., 2011).

Assessing Online Racism

Much of the literature on online racist experiences utilizes measures that have been both qualitative and quantitative. Qualitative approaches have included ethnographic observation online and off-line (Daniels, 2009; West & Thakore, 2013), in-person interviews designed to capture encounters with racial bias online, online interviews (Tynes, 2007), textual, thematic, and content analysis (Daniels, 2009; Ding, 2015; Gin et al., 2017; Guo & Harlow, 2014; Tynes, 2005), and critical and multimodal discourse analysis (Yoon, 2016). Studies have also used mixed methods (Tynes & Markoe, 2010). Quantitative methods include online surveys using the Online Victimization Scale (Tynes, Rose, & Williams, 2010) and the recently developed Perceived Online Racism Scale (Keum & Miller, 2017). To complement survey data and to address the need for additional research that centers the voices of adolescents, we use online interview data to provide further examples of our proposed model (Figure 12.1).

A Model of Online Racism

We propose a comprehensive model of online racism that draws on the work of Daniels (2009), Feagin (2001, 2006), Jones (1972, 1997), Neville and Pieterse

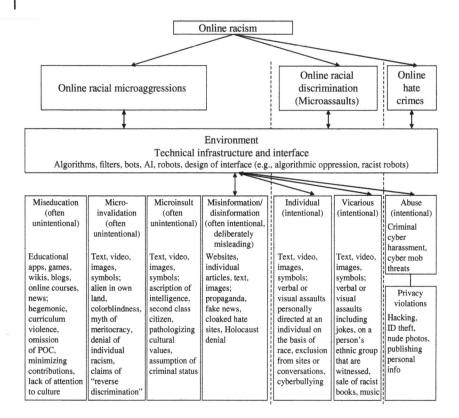

Figure 12.1 Taxonomy of Online Racism.

(2009), Neville et al. (2012), Pérez Huber and Solórzano (2015), Pierce (1995), and Sue et al. (2007). We synthesize and expand existing literature and propose a model that includes *online racial microaggressions* (e.g., miseducation, microinvalidations, microinsults, and mis/disinformation), *online racial discrimination* (e.g., individual and vicarious), and *online hate crimes* (e.g., abuse and privacy violations). We outline examples of each in Figure 12.1 drawn from extant literature and media reports. We also present examples from our own interview data on the experiences of adolescents and emerging adults that specifically represent online racial microaggressions, online racial discrimination, and online hate crimes.

Online Racial Microaggressions

In addition to microinvalidations and microinsults, which are outlined in the offline literature, we propose two new types of microaggressions unique to the online experience: miseducation and mis/disinformation.

Miseducation

Miseducation is the creation of online learning materials that in most cases unintentionally demeans or omits People of Color. It takes place in the design of educational games, educational apps, online courses, and e-books. We extend Allen, Scott, and Lewis's (2013) argument that off-line hegemonic curriculum that ignores contributions of People of Color or trivializes their histories is a type of violence. Miseducation in digital media is exemplified with the creation and release of the controversial game "Playing History 2-Slave Trade." The educational game was created in 2013 by the Danish game company, Serious Games, to educate middle-school-aged children about the trans-Atlantic slave trade. Within the game, the user plays as a young slave boy who is tasked with helping his master buy 300 slaves (including his own sister) and sailing the ship to America to sell all of the slaves for his master. In addition to the inaccurate depictions of the slave trade in the name of "fun" over education, the game relied on additional demeaning activities, such as stacking African slaves as a player would in Tetris to make them fit in the cargo area of the ship (Thomas, 2015).

Through these activities, middle-school users may be introduced to the concept of slavery, but this introduction is devoid of the portrayal of the horrific acts and crimes committed against enslaved African humans by slave traffickers. Throughout the game, the enslavement of Africans is trivialized, and Africans are dehumanized by depicting their bodies as odd shapes to be fit together. In contrast, White slave traffickers are humanized and depicted as being taunted and demeaned by the Africans who call the traffickers "White devils." Similar to Everett and Watkins (2008) conception of games as being racialized pedagogical zones, middle-school users of "Playing History 2" are learning about both historical and current racialized power differentials. Through game play, students are being taught that Black bodies can be bought, sold, contorted, and stacked as objects to meet the needs of White slave traffickers historically and to meet the "educational" and entertainment needs of game users currently. Such an approach misleads the intended audience about the experience of slavery and trivializes the painful history of African-descended people. For these reasons, we argue the model include these types of attempts at educating users and students that may be uninformed and lack a deep understanding of the subject matter.

Microinvalidations

We include microinvalidations as online interactions, texts, video, images, or symbols that often unintentionally discredit an individual's or ethnic group's culture or deny their experience or full citizenship. These interactions gain an added legitimacy online simply by being discussed in such spaces as social media. They are then amplified with likes and shares. In our interview data, we found examples of microinvalidations that were consistent with both online and off-line literature. For instance, Melisa, a 16-year-old Latina female, described how she felt when she encountered online content that disparaged Latinx individuals.

MELISA: I believe it had something to do with our culture and the way we talk.

INTERVIEWER: How did you feel when you saw the comments?

MELISA: Although I was born in America I felt really bad. I still follow the Hispanic cultures and when they talked about it, it didn't feel good. My parents can speak clearly but with an accent. When they mentioned about the way we talk, it didn't seem fair to them or me.

Melisa describes that although she is an American citizen, the content she came in contact with through social media made her feel that she and her family were not valued and looked at as "others" in their own country. She mentions that her parents can speak English, they just do so with an accent. Others' disparaging remarks about the ways that Latinx populations talk made Melisa feel "really bad" and like the comments were not fair to her or her parents as Americans. This assessment is consistent with the microinvalidation feature of making one feel as if they will always be viewed as a foreigner or alien in their own home country.

Microinsults

Similar to microinvalidations, microinsults online are shared through text, video, images, and symbols. They often unintentionally question marginalized groups' intelligence and reproduce stereotypes while perpetrators in some cases claim they were just having fun. Adolescents shared a range of experiences that could be classified as microinsults. Kassidy, a 15-year-old African American adolescent, describes encountering an online joke that may be conceived as a microinsult because of its insinuation of the criminality of African Americans:

INTERVIEWER: You mentioned that people have cracked jokes about people of your race or ethnic group online a few times a year. Tell me about the worst or most recent time this occurred.

KASSIDY: That we're stupid and won't ever get anywhere in life and just end up in jail because that's all we're good at.

INTERVIEWER: How do you feel when you hear things like this?

KASSIDY: I think that it's a stereotype that people play into and not all of us will be that way

Although Kassidy doesn't describe the exact wording or context of the "joke," she does describe the messaging behind the "joke" insinuates that African Americans are of lower intelligence than other groups and that they are more likely to go to jail. Kassidy also reflects that this "joke" is based on stereotypes and assumes that there is homogeneity in the behaviors and experiences of

African Americans. All of these features are consistent with previous conceptions of microinsults in the literature (Sue et al., 2007).

Mis/disinformation

Our model expands the offline microaggressions framework by focusing on mis/disinformation as a form of covert microaggression online. Misinformation is the unintentional or intentional "action of misinforming or condition of being misinformed; or erroneous or incorrect information" (Information and Its Counterfeits, 2017). It is distinguished from disinformation, which is "information that is deliberately false or misleading" (Jack, 2017). Because it is often difficult to determine an actor's intent, scholars tend to use the term *misinformation* rather than disinformation. Propaganda is an additional type of problematic information that at times overlaps with disinformation. It is a deliberate and systematic information campaign usually meant to deceive, usually conducted through press, digital, or broadcast media (Jack, 2017). Material may be made up of primarily accurate information, inaccurate information, or some combination of the two. Importantly, propaganda is designed to provoke a particular attitude or emotion. It often does so through moral appeals. Daniels (2009) referred to cloaked hate sites as overlapping with propaganda in that sites often conceal authorship deliberately mislead their viewers with respect to their political agenda. These sites often use technological features of the Internet such as domain names and Web site address registrations with the suffix ".org" to appear as a legitimate news or educational reference site. One example of a cloaked hate site is "www.martinlutherking.org," a site created and operated by the White supremacist Web site Stormfront. Stormfront uses martinlutherking.org to provide inaccurate information and extremist views about the African American civil rights activist Dr. Martin Luther King, Jr. The information on this Web site is presented in such a way that high school and college students who encounter it do not recognize the information as incorrect or as representing White supremacist ideologies. We argue that being exposed to this misinformation is a type of microaggression that potentially inflicts academic and emotional harm.

Mis/disinformation is a dangerous form of online racial microaggression that may provide the basis of more serious forms of racial discrimination and hate. For example, before the Charleston 9 massacre, Dylann Roof claimed he conducted a Google search on "Black on White" crime (Noble, 2018). The results of the search included sites with misinformation which distorted crime statistics and portrayed this issue as prevalent.

Online Racial Discrimination

Our model proposes we move microassaults from the microaggression subtype to online racial discrimination. As previously noted, these experiences may be individually directed at participants or may be vicariously experienced. We found these experiences in the interview data to be consistent with both adolescent and adult experiences, but like microaggression, legitimized, amplified, and made permanent in digital contexts.

Individual

Solomon, a 13-year-old African American male adolescent, shared an online discrimination experience that also reflected some of his online experiences with peers at school.

> INTERVIEWER: You mentioned that people have said things that were untrue about people in your race or ethnic group online every day. Tell me about the worst or most recent time this occurred.
>
> SOLOMON: Well, it was a conversation, and it was once I think someone mentioned something about because I'm Black and African that's why I have this type of accent in a mean way. And that was it.
>
> INTERVIEWER: What Web site were you on when this conversation happened?
>
> SOLOMON: Either Facebook or Myspace. I can't really remember, but I know it hurt me that day, and I deleted the person off my friends list.
>
> INTERVIEWER: I'm really sorry to hear this happened to you. Can you give me a few more details about this conversation?
>
> SOLOMON: I got bullied a lot back in middle school because of the way I talk, dress, and react. Also I was a smart kid, but I just came here (America) from Nigeria, and I had an accent. It became the main target for kids in my class to talk about and made me feel bad about. I used to keep everything to myself back then, and finally, I told my parents, but it was little they could do stop it. One day, one of my mates, I think it was a guy, they were talking on Facebook or Myspace, and I added them back. Then he started saying my name and something about my accent and you know mean things. And I got frustrated and deleted them, that was all I could do at that moment. And now, I just don't put things like that in mind.

Solomon describes being the target of an individual online racial discrimination based on both his race and his nationality. His accent and the way he talks make him a target among his classmates both online and in face-to-face contexts. Solomon's experience highlights that some People of Color may have extended race-related experiences that are perpetuated face to face and online. This reiterates the idea that the Internet is sometimes used as an additional tool to communicate racist statements and ideologies that are also communicated in offline settings. In Solomon's case, he experienced racial discrimination from peers at school who also expressed racist statements to him through the technological tool of the Internet and social networking sites.

Vicarious

In our data, we found participants commonly witnessed their peers being denigrated because of their race. For example, Ariana, a 14-year-old Latina, describes encountering a violent image toward African Americans online:

> INTERVIEWER: You also mentioned people have shown you a racist image online once. Tell me about the worst or most recent time this occurred.
>
> ARIANA: The one I remember was the KKK.
>
> INTERVIEWER: Can you give me more details about this image?
>
> ARIANA: Well it had a picture of the KKK around a burning cross, but it looked like someone was hanging from the cross.
>
> INTERVIEWER: How did you feel when you saw the image?
>
> ARIANA: I felt disgusted. I was thinking why is there so much racism in the world when all people are the same just with different backgrounds and skin color.

Ariana describes seeing very violent imagery that was not specifically directed at her, but that she was exposed to from visiting the "home page" of the Facebook site. Seeing the image clearly disturbed her, although the image was likely depicting violence toward African Americans instead of a Latinx, a member of her own racial group (given that such an image depicting violence against African Americans by the KKK is common). Consistent with work on vicarious online racial discrimination (Tynes et al., 2010), the vicarious experience of online racial discrimination is impactful, leaving lasting impressions about the electronic content that one encounters. The content may not be directed at the exposed individual, but it may still have emotional consequences for that individual. In this case, Ariana described that she felt "disgusted" and that exposure to racism against another group seemed to lead her to reflect on her own beliefs of everyone being "the same just with different backgrounds and skin color."

Online Hate Crimes

Online hate crimes involve criminal activity that may be punishable by law in certain states or across the United States in federal cases. These experiences were extremely rare in our data. One example includes Karina, a 12-year-old African American girl who describes students improperly accessing the school computers through hacking to display racialized jokes toward African Americans.

> INTERVIEWER: Thank you for sharing that. Can you think of an example of a time someone has made a joke about people of your race online before?
>
> KARINA: They might say that Black people are as dark as night.
>
> INTERVIEWER: Where have you seen those comments before?

KARINA: Like at school we all have different settings but people put things on the screen. They hack it.

INTERVIEWER: I'm sorry, I'm not sure I understand. Can you explain a little more?

KARINA: At school, we have laptops. In the student shared files, we have settings to change our background. Some people hack other people's things and make jokes as their screensaver talking about them.

INTERVIEWER: I understand now. Thanks for explaining.

KARINA: Welcome.

INTERVIEWER: So you have seen someone change another student's background to say they were dark as night?

KARINA: Yes.

Although Karina conceptualizes her experience with students hacking into student files and changing the screensavers to taunt Black students about their skin tone in a derogatory way as a joke, the act of hacking into students' school files can be considered an online hate crime. The features of this incident such as targeting an individual based on their race, and hacking into their information to display harassing information, even if it is meant as a joke, makes it so that this action can be taken as a serious offense.

Implications for Youth Development

Though all components of our comprehensive model may have a detrimental impact on a range of outcomes for developing adolescents and emerging adults, we know the least about online racial microaggression. Social cognitive and racial/ethnic identity development across the lifespan likely affects the interpretation and impact of these experiences. Racial perspective taking is an especially relevant social cognitive skill. It allows individuals to view others and social events from different points of view and includes the ability to understand the role of race in one's own and others' life (Quintana, 2008). According to the racial perspective–taking ability (RPTA) model, which describes how children develop race-related perspective-taking abilities, at ages 10–14, children begin to understand that race/ethnicity has social meaning and recognize its associations with bias and discrimination (Quintana, 1998, 2008). This ability is critical to how microaggressions are processed, as youth can now recognize whether an online incident is a racial microaggression. Below this age, children's ability to recognize discrimination may be restricted to intentional, overt forms of discrimination such as name-calling and social exclusion (Verkuyten, Kinket, & van der Wielen, 1997). Therefore, one implication is that below a certain age, youth may be less equipped to perceive subtle and ambiguous online incidents of microaggression, even though at younger ages, they might be capable of detecting overt forms of discrimination and hate crimes.

Emerging racial/ethnic identity development also facilitates detection of and reactions to microaggressions online. In the fourth and final stage of RPTA development, adolescents integrate and synthesize self-knowledge in order to arrive at a coherent sense of self. In this stage, youth acquire the ability to take the perspective of the group and racial-ethnic identity development begins (Quintana, 1998). A common feature of racial-ethnic identity development theories is that racial-ethnic identity exploration is elicited by salient race-related experiences (Cross & Cross, 2008; Phinney, 1990). Consequently, experiences of racial microaggressions online expose Youth of Color to racialized content and interactions that likely precipitate racial-ethnic identity exploration, prompt youth to question their ethnic identity (Umaña-Taylor et al., 2014), and lead to changes in ethnic identity development over time (Pahl & Way, 2006). Furthermore, the relationship between racial-ethnic identity development and microaggressions online is likely reciprocal in nature (Umaña-Taylor et al., 2014). Research conducted in off-line settings suggests that youth who identify more strongly with their ethnic group are more likely to detect discrimination (Brown & Bigler, 2005). This effect likely extends to online experiences and should be taken into account when understanding the online experiences of microaggressions of adolescents. As such, clinicians, educators, and researchers should consider the ways these developmental processes along with peer relationships and other developmental factors might influence the microaggressions process from incident through to interpretation and impact.

Future Directions

This chapter proposed a comprehensive model of online racism that is rooted in extant research, digital tools, and the lived experiences of adolescents. In doing so, we outlined the nature and impact of online racism. Given the developmental concerns highlighted above, future research should further determine whether and how adolescents make meaning around each component of the proposed model. It is particularly important to determine adolescent reasoning with respect to the four forms of online racial microaggression proposed in the model. Given the recent election and widespread "fake news," it is important to determine from a developmental perspective how adolescents are able to recognize when a site is legitimate along with factors that may influence their decisions. In addition, more research is needed because there tends to be widespread efforts to have students use mobile technology and the Internet in their learning, without regard to whether the online curricula or the technology reproduces white supremacy as with off-line curricula.

The field would also benefit from more research on all aspects of the model—online microaggressions, online racial discrimination, and online hate crimes and their associations with mental and physical health across the lifespan. Academic outcomes, including motivation and performance, will also be important, particularly for K-12 populations. In this case, more mixed method studies of specific regions as well as nationally representative studies will be needed. Both types of studies are also particularly important given the repeated nature of young people's exposure to these experiences and the varied individual and cultural factors that may buffer youth against negative outcomes typically associated with these experiences.

Further research should also begin to explore how to capture these experiences using an intersectional framework (Crenshaw, 1989) that acknowledges the multiple social identities held by adolescent Internet users. A number of studies examining microaggressions off-line have been careful to consider these intersectional experiences that manifest in off-line contexts (Nadal et al., 2015; Suárez-Orozco et al., 2015). These approaches could potentially be applied to online contexts, as well, in order to gain a more nuanced and comprehensive understanding of online racism and microaggressions in particular.

References

Allen, A., Scott, L. M., & Lewis, C. W. (2013). Racial microaggressions and African American and Hispanic students in urban schools: A call for culturally affirming education. *Interdisciplinary Journal of Teaching and Learning, 3*(2), 117–129. Retrieved from http://www3.subr.edu/coeijtl/.

Baum, K., Catalano, S., Rand, M., & Rose, K. (2011). *Stalking victimization in the United States* (No. NCJ 224527). DIANE Publishing. Retrieved from https://victimsofcrime.org/docs/src/baum-k-catalano-s-rand-m-rose-k-2009.pdf?sfvrsn=0.

Brown, C. S., & Bigler, R. S. (2005). Children's perceptions of discrimination: A developmental model. *Child Development, 76*(3), 533–553. doi:10.1111/j.1467-8624.2005.00862.x.

Citron, D. K. (2014). *Hate crimes in cyberspace*. Cambridge, MA: Harvard University Press.

Clark, D. A., Spanierman, L. B., Reed, T. D., Soble, J. R., & Cabana, S. (2011). Documenting weblog expressions of racial microaggressions that target American Indians. *Journal of Diversity in Higher Education, 4*(1), 39–50. doi:10.1037/a0021762.

Crenshaw, K. (1989). Demarginalization the intersection of race and sex: A Black feminist critique of antidiscrimination doctrine, feminist theory and antiracist politics. *University of Chicago Legal Forum, 1*, 139–167.

Cross, W. E., & Cross, T. B. (2008). Theory, research, and models. In S. M. Quintana & C. McKown (Eds.), *Handbook of race, racism, and the developing child* (pp. 16–36). Hoboken, NJ: Wiley.

Daniels, J. (2009). Cloaked websites: Propaganda, cyber-racism and epistemology in the digital era. *New Media & Society, 11*(5), 659–683. doi:10.1177/1461444809105345.

Ding, Z. (2015). *The internet meme as a rhetoric discourse: Investigating Asian/Asian Americans' identity negotiation* (Unpublished master's thesis). Ohio Department of Higher Education, Columbus, OH. Retrieved from http://www.ohiolink.edu/etd/.

Duggan, M. (2017). *Online Harassment 2017*. Washington, D.C.: Pew Research Center. Retrieved from http://www.pewinternet.org/2017/07/11/online-harassment-2017/.

Everett, A., & Watkins, C. (2008). The power of play: The portrayal and performance of race in video games. In K. Salen (Ed.), *The ecology of games: Connecting youth, games, and learning* (pp. 141–166). Cambridge, MA: The MIT Press.

Feagin, J. R. (2001). *Racist America: Roots, current realities, and future reparations*. New York, NY: Routledge.

Feagin, J. R. (2006). *Systemic racism: A theory of oppression*. New York, NY: Routledge.

Gin, K. J., Martínez-Alemán, A. M., Rowan-Kenyon, H. T., & Hottell, D. (2017). Racialized aggressions and social media on campus. *Journal of College Student Development, 58*(2), 159–174. doi:10.1353/csd.2017.0013.

Guo, L., & Harlow, S. (2014). User-generated racism: An analysis of stereotypes of African Americans, Latinos, and Asians in YouTube videos. *Howard Journal of Communications, 25*(3), 281–302. doi:10.1080/10646175.2014.925413.

Harrison, C., Tayman, K., Janson, N., & Connolly, C. (2010). Stereotypes of Black male athletes on the internet. *Journal for the Study of Sports and Athletes in Education, 4*(2), 155–172. doi:10.1179/ssa.2010.4.2.155.

Information and Its Counterfeits. (2017, August 10). *Propaganda, misinformation and disinformation*. Retrieved from http://guides.library.jhu.edu/c.php?g=202581&p=1334961.

Jack, C. (2017). *Lexicon of lies: Terms for problematic information*. Data & Society Research Institute. Retrieved from https://datasociety.net/output/lexicon-of-lies/.

Jones, J. M. (1972). *Prejudice and racism*. Reading, MA: Addison-Wesley.

Jones, J. M. (1997). *Prejudice and racism* (2nd ed.). New York, NY: McGraw-Hill.

Kettrey, H. H., & Laster, W. N. (2014). Staking territory in the "World White Web" an exploration of the roles of overt and color-blind racism in maintaining racial boundaries on a popular web site. *Social Currents, 1*(3), 257–274. doi:10.1177/2329496514540134.

Keum, B. T., & Miller, M. J. (2017). Racism in digital era: Development and initial validation of the perceived online racism scale (PORS v1.0). *Journal of Counseling Psychology, 64*(3), 310–324. doi:10.1037/cou0000205.

Minikel-Lacocque, J. (2013). Racism, college, and the power of words: Racial microaggressions reconsidered. *American Educational Research Journal, 50*(3), 432–465. doi:10.3102/0002831212468048.

Nadal, K. L., Davidoff, K. C., Davis, L. S., Wong, Y., Marshall, D., & McKenzie, V. (2015). Intersectional identities and microaggressions: Influences of race, ethnicity, gender, sexuality, and religion. *Qualitative Psychology, 2*(2), 147–163. doi:10.1037/qup0000026.

Neville, H. A., & Pieterse, A. L. (2009). Racism, white supremacy, and resistance: Contextualizing Black American experiences. In H. A. Neville, B. M. Tynes, & S. O. Utsey (Eds.), *Handbook of African American psychology* (pp. 159–172). Thousand Oaks, CA: Sage.

Neville, H. A., Spanierman, L. B., & Lewis, J. A. (2012). The expanded psychosocial model of racism: A new model for understanding and disrupting racism and white privilege. In N. A. Fouad (Ed.), *APA handbook of counseling psychology* (Vol. 2, pp. 333–356). Washington, DC: American Psychological Association.

Noble, S. U. (2018). *Algorithms of oppression: How search engines reinforce racism.* New York, NY: New York University Press.

Pahl, K., & Way, N. (2006). Longitudinal trajectories of ethnic identity among urban Black and Latino adolescents. *Child Development, 77*(5), 1403–1415. doi:10.1111/j.1467-8624.2006.00943.x.

Pérez Huber, L., & Solórzano, D. G. (2015). Racial microaggressions as a tool for critical race research. *Race Ethnicity and Education, 18*(3), 297–320. doi:10.1080/13613324.2014.994173.

Perrin, A. (2015). *Social media usage: 2005–2015.* Pew Research Center. Retrieved from http://www.pewinternet.org/2015/10/08/2015/Social-Networking-Usage-2005-2015/.

Pew Research Center. (2017). *Internet broadband [Fact Sheet].* Retrieved from http://www.pewinternet.org/fact-sheet/internet-broadband/.

Phinney, J. S. (1990). Ethnic identity in adolescents and adults: Review of research. *Psychological Bulletin, 108*(3), 499–514.

Pierce, C. (1995). Stress analogs of racism and sexism: Terrorism, torture, and disaster. In C. V. Willie, P. P. Rieker, B. M. Kramer, & B. S. Brown (Eds.), *Mental health, racism, and sexism* (pp. 277–293). London, United Kingdom: Routledge.

Quintana, S. M. (1998). Children's developmental understanding of ethnicity and race. *Applied and Preventive Psychology, 7*(1), 27–45. doi:10.1016/S0962-1849(98)80020-6.

Quintana, S. M. (2008). Racial perspective taking ability: Developmental, theoretical, and empirical trends. In S. M. Quintana & C. McKown (Eds.), *Handbook of race, racism, and the developing child* (pp. 16–36). Hoboken, NJ: Wiley.

Rideout, V., Lauricella, A., & Wartella, E. (2011). *Children, media, and race: Media use among White, Black, Hispanic, and Asian American children.* Northwestern

University, Center on Media and Human Development, School of Communication. Retrieved from http://cmhd.northwestern.edu/reports/.

Suárez-Orozco, C., Casanova, S., Martin, M., Katsiaficas, D., Cuellar, V., Smith, N. A., & Dias, S. I. (2015). Toxic rain in class: Classroom interpersonal microaggressions. *Educational Researcher, 44*(3), 151–160. doi:10.3102/0013189X15580314.

Sue, D. W., Capodilupo, C. M., Torino, G. C., Bucceri, J. M., Holder, A., Nadal, K. L., & Esquilin, M. (2007). Racial microaggressions in everyday life: Implications for clinical practice. *American Psychologist, 62*(4), 271–286.

Thomas, D. (2015, September 7). *I played "Slave Tetris" so your kids don't have to. Los Angeles Times.* Retrieved from http://www.latimes.com/.

Tynes, B. M. (2005). Children, adolescents and the culture of online hate. In N. E. Dowd, D. G. Singer, & R. F. Wilson (Eds.), *Handbook of children, culture and violence* (pp. 267–289). Thousand Oaks, CA: Sage.

Tynes, B. M. (2007). Internet safety gone wild? Sacrificing the educational and psychosocial benefits of online social environments. *Journal of Adolescent Research, 22*(6), 575–584. doi:10.1177/074355840730397.

Tynes, B. M., English, D., Del Toro, J., & Smith, N. A. (2017). *The impact of a rising tide of cyberhate: Trajectories of online racial discrimination predict negative psychological outcomes.* (Manuscript under review).

Tynes, B. M., Giang, M. T., Williams, D. R., & Thompson, G. N. (2008). Online racial discrimination and psychological adjustment among adolescents. *Journal of Adolescent Health, 43*(6), 565–569. doi:10.1016/j.jadohealth.2008.08.021.

Tynes, B. M., & Markoe, S. L. (2010). The role of color-blind racial attitudes in reactions to racial discrimination on social network sites. *Journal of Diversity in Higher Education, 3*(1), 1–13. doi:10.1037/a0018683.

Tynes, B. M., Rose, C. A., & Markoe, S. L. (2013). Extending campus life to the Internet: Socialmedia, discrimination, and perceptions of racial climate. *Journal of Diversity in Higher Education, 6*(2), 102–114. doi:10.1037/a0033267.

Tynes, B. M., Rose, C. A., & Williams, D. R. (2010). The development and validation of the online victimization scale for adolescents. *Cyberpsychology: Journal of Psychosocial Research on Cyberspace, 4*(2).

Tynes, B. M., Seaton, E., & Zuckerman, A. (2015, December). *Online racial discrimination: A growing problem for adolescents. Psychological Science Agenda.* Retrieved from http://www.apa.org/science/about/psa/2015/12/online-racial-discrimination.aspx.

Umaña-Taylor, A. J., Quintana, S. M., Lee, R. M., Cross, W. E., Rivas-Drake, D., Schwartz, S. J., & Seaton, E. (2014). Ethnic and racial identity during adolescence and into young adulthood: An integrated conceptualization. *Child Development, 85*(1), 21–39. doi:10.1111/cdev.12196.

Verkuyten, M., Kinket, B., & van der Wielen, C. (1997). Preadolescents' understanding of ethnic discrimination. *Journal of Genetic Psychology, 158*(1), 97–112. doi:10.1080/00221329709596655.

West, R. J., & Thakore, B. K. (2013). Racial exclusion in the online world. *Future Internet, 5*(2), 251–267. doi:10.3390/fi5020251.

Wong, G., Derthick, A. O., David, E. J. R., Saw, A., & Okazaki, S. (2014). The what, the why, and the how: A review of racial microaggressions research in psychology. *Race and Social Problems, 6*(2), 181–200. doi:10.1007/s12552-013-9107-9.

Yoon, I. (2016). Why is it not just a joke? Analysis of internet memes associated with racism and hidden ideology of colorblindness. *Journal of Cultural Research in Art Education, 33*, 92–123.

13

Environmental Microaggressions: Context, Symbols, and Mascots

Jesse A. Steinfeldt, Jacqueline Hyman, and M. Clint Steinfeldt

The theoretical and empirical conceptualization of microaggressions has been deeply explored and expanded in recent years, providing our field with a more comprehensive understanding of the nuanced race-related experiences that are impactful yet often unacknowledged in society. The recent movement to remove Confederate symbols and statues across the United States, for instance, speaks to a previously overlooked and perpetual racism that has silently eroded the fabric of our diverse society since their inception years ago. Statues commemorating historical figures such as Robert E. Lee, Nathan Bedford Forrest, Junipero Serra, and Christopher Columbus have symbolized a rich heritage for some. However, these societally revered and honored monuments also serve as a painful reminder to others of the genocide and atrocities performed against their culture and their ancestors, serving as microaggressions toward members of these marginalized groups. This dynamic has been pervasive over time, and the egregious church shooting at the Emanuel African Methodist Episcopal Church in 2015 in Charleston, South Carolina, provided the impetus for a more critical evaluation of the duality of these controversial symbols (e.g., Confederate flag) from a wider societal perspective. Despite the more recent awareness of the duality of these symbols, conversations about removing these symbols have generated tremendous backlash, particularly among hate groups across the country, as was evidenced by the violent events that took place in Charlottesville, Virginia, in mid-August 2017.

The chapters within this volume attempt to provide an in-depth understanding of different contextual aspects of microaggressions, while the current chapter intends to contribute to this understanding by examining particular manifestations of microaggressions that occur within certain societal contexts. Specifically, we will be examining the dynamic of sports teams that use Native-themed mascots, nicknames, and logos (e.g., *Indians, Seminoles,*

Microaggression Theory: Influence and Implications, First Edition. Edited by Gina C. Torino, David P. Rivera, Christina M. Capodilupo, Kevin L. Nadal, and Derald Wing Sue.
© 2019 John Wiley & Sons, Inc. Published 2019 by John Wiley & Sons, Inc.

Redskins), and the impact that this practice has on not only First Nations individuals but also the impact that this practice has on society at large.

Context of First Nations Cultural Misappropriation in American Society

The use of First Nations culture, symbols, and iconography—particularly for use within sports—is omnipresent in American society. This widespread appropriation is an area within the domain of manifestations of microaggressions that has received little attention to date. It is the purpose of this chapter to provide examples to illustrate how this dynamic fits within the microaggression framework. Within American society, First Nations culture and imagery have been represented in a number of ways: Western movies (e.g., pick almost any John Wayne movie), alcohol and tobacco products (e.g., Red Man Tobacco and Crazy Horse Malt Liquor), food products (e.g., Land O'Lakes Butter), and children's play (e.g., games, toys, songs, and stories), just to name a few (Bird, 1996; Deloria, 1998; King, 2002). These representations do not present accurate information about First Nations culture and people. Instead, they provide stereotypic representations of First Nations culture that drive societal misperceptions about First Nations individuals.

For example, many children in U.S. society have grown up singing songs like *Ten Little Indians*, dressed up as an "Indian Princess" or "Indian Warrior" for Halloween, or they may have played *Cowboys and Indians*, with the *Cowboys* inevitably occupying the desired role of the good guys, while the *Indians* were largely the savage villain to be conquered (Merskin, 2001). Given the way that these practices were introduced as innocuous play, they became hegemonic norms within society that are largely unquestioned. Furthermore, the generational nature of this practice has resulted in American society not only becoming inundated by products, practices, phrases, and sports teams that appropriate First Nations culture, but this generational nature has contributed to the belief that this practice is acceptable to all, including First Nations tribes and individuals (King, Davis-Delano, Staurowsky, & Baca, 2006; King, Staurowsky, Baca, Davis, & Pewewardy, 2002).

The use of First Nations culture, imagery, and their iconography for sports mascots, nicknames, and logos is a common societal practice that perpetuates stereotypes of First Nations people in society (Baca, 2004; Davis, 2002; Russel, 2003; Staurowsky, 1999; Williams, 2006). According to Steinfeldt et al. (2012):

> Sports-related representations of American Indians are considered problematic because they (a) misuse cultural practices and sacred symbols; (b) perpetuate racist stereotypes of American Indians (e.g., the

noble savage, the *bloodthirsty savage,* a historic race that only exists in past-tense status, one singular pan-Indian culture); (c) deny American Indians control over societal definitions of themselves; and (d) create a racially hostile environment for all students. (p. 328)

Furthermore, for many members of U.S. society, these images are often the only exposure they have to First Nations culture (Merskin, 1998; Steinfeldt et al., 2012), which serves to perpetuate existing societal stereotypes of First Nations individual. The common stereotypes of the bloodthirsty savage, the noble savage—along with the stereotypic expectation that this race of people only exist in past-tense historic times—are activated in these situations, and these stereotypes are transferred to an individual's expectations about who contemporary First Nations people are, what they look like, and what they do (e.g., all Indians wear headdresses with feathers). With the dearth of accurate information about—and a critical mass of real-life experiences with—First Nations people, these images fill the void and provide members of society with a narrative about who First Nations people are and what they do. Instead of a diverse and dynamic group of individuals, these images portray unidimensional and static stereotypic representations about First Nations individuals.

Utilizing the framework of environmental microaggressions (e.g., Sue et al., 2007), we can conceptualize this dynamic as a way in which institutions—systems larger than the individual—work to maintain societal structures of oppression and privilege by appropriating First Nations culture. In this instance, First Nations culture, identity, and heritage becomes a commodity—something that can be used out of novelty, convenience, or interest, and then be readily discarded when it exhausts its utility or something more interesting arises.

To illustrate more concretely the way in which such cultural co-optation takes place in everyday situations, it may be helpful to provide a vignette of the misappropriation of First Nations culture—behavior which, regrettably, is all too common. On a typical college campus, a student can put on an "Indian Warrior" costume, complete with face paint, and dance around shirtless in a loin cloth with a feather headdress while attending a Halloween or fraternity-themed party. He can additionally enact all the stereotypic representations he believes about that group of people. Little to no thought is given about any actual people being depicted, nor is much consideration given to whether it is an accurate portrayal. Perhaps it is something the student remembered from a movie or from watching a University of Illinois half time dance by the [now defunct] school mascot, Chief Illiniwek.

The implicit message conveyed within this pervasive environmental microaggression is that the culture being depicted is not something real, legitimate, or lived. Instead, this costumed student has the power to define the reality of the "Indian" he is depicting, thereby replacing the dynamic living individual with static stereotypic misrepresentations of that group. The costume is likely to be met with approval of his peers, who may also be clothed in a similar version of this costume. They may comment humorously about the "fire water" (i.e., alcohol) they are drinking as they become a bunch of "Drunken Indians." He may engage in broken English conversation with others, saying "How!" or "Me Chief Drinksalot!" And if he chooses to add some corresponding actions (e.g., a war whoop, a rain dance, and a tomahawk chop), then his performance will likely be further applauded, perhaps even creating a group dynamic wherein multiple students join in the merriment of acting like a bunch of "Savage Injuns."

With some, any, or all of these stereotypic representations embedded into this costume and corresponding public act, what impact does this have on a First Nations individual at the party? What should he do while this microaggression is being played out? He may be forced to idly watch as his culture is being misportrayed, mocked, and marginalized for the merriment of his peers. He may want to speak up, but self-preservation may be a driving force to prevent him from saying anything—going along with it is likely a safer choice. He may internalize the implicit message that his culture is inferior. His culture is something for his peers to play with and treat without reverence or regard. The internalization of this implicit message can negatively impact his psychological functioning in a variety of different ways (e.g., Fryberg, Markus, Oyserman, & Stone, 2008).

But what is the impact on these costumed students, the perpetrators of this microaggression? They can clown around with this culture, subsequently minimizing this culture as anything valid; the people of this culture are not real. According to Merskin (2001), "These stereotypical representations of American Indians denies that they are human beings, and presents them as existing only in the past and as single, monolithic Indians" (p. 167). When people are reduced to stereotypes, they are not real. They do not have to be listened to. They are easier to hurt.

Furthermore, the systemic process that perpetuates these stereotypic images is neither controlled nor sustained by First Nations communities. "White Americans developed the stereotypes; White Americans produced the collectibles; and White American manufacturers and advertisers disseminated both the images and the objects to a White audience" (Goings, 1994, as cited in Merskin, 2001, p. 161). So the costume shops that advertise and sell this costume—and the manufacturer that makes the costume, along with all involved in—are also complicit in the problem with their systemic impact on conveying the implicit message about reducing First Nations culture and identity to stereotypic form, thus reinforcing its status as inferior.

Native-Themed Mascots, Nicknames, and Logos in Sports

While the use of First Nations cultural symbols and icons has permeated the fabric of society in the myriad ways we enumerated above (extending way beyond the example of Halloween or fraternity party costumes), the most common perpetrator of this dynamic of cultural misappropriation of First Nations imagery, identity, and iconography can be found in sports teams. Sports teams, from youth leagues through high school and college, all the way up to professional teams, commonly use Native-themed mascots, nicknames, and/or logos. Like the majority of athletic participants in U.S. society, the first author has had first-hand experience with Native-themed mascots throughout his athletic career. He remembers playing for a little league baseball team named the *Braves* at the age of 9, then competing against the Sheboygan South *Redmen* in high school, and as a collegiate athlete, playing against the Dartmouth *Big Green* (who had changed their name from the *Indians*) while watching as the Florida State *Seminoles* rose atop the college football standings. Even after competing, as he watches professional sports, he cheers as his hometown Green Bay *Packers* competes against the Washington *Redskins* in National Football League (NFL) games, and his father-in-law dutifully watches his hometown Detroit *Tigers* battle the Cleveland *Indians* in Major League Baseball (MLB) contests.

These Native-themed mascots, nicknames, and logos are embedded into the sporting experience across all levels of competition. Teams with fierce animal nicknames (*Badgers, Wolverines, Tigers*) compete against opponents named after human beings (e.g., *Indians, Redskins, Braves*). This environmental microaggression conveys a subtle but powerful message: First Nations people are inherently relegated to subhuman status. On the plus side, they are portrayed as fierce and powerful, yes, but they are fierce and powerful in the animalistic, and subsequently subhuman, sense when their name and likeness is used to represent a team that competes against other teams that are mostly named after animals. The existence of this system of sports team nicknames conveys the message of First Nations inferiority. Furthermore, because First Nations team names are disproportionately over-represented—without sufficient societal narratives to counterbalance the stereotypic representation conveyed by these mascots, nicknames, and logos—when compared to other human-based sports mascots (e.g., Steinfeldt & Steinfeldt, 2012), the impact becomes even more profound and potentially impactful.

Beyond the problems inherent within the system of nomenclature, there are active ways that this sense of cultural inferiority is conveyed through environmental microaggressions involving Native-themed sporting mascots, nicknames, and logos. At a sporting event, the fans of opposing teams often generate denigrating chants about their opponent to intimidate and create an advantage for their own team. For example, the North Dakota State University (NDSU) *Bison* are rivals with the University of North Dakota (UND) *Fighting Sioux* (recently renamed the *Fighting Hawks*). In recent contests, when the NDSU football team would get a first down, the NDSU fans would vulgarly chant in unison "Sioux ... Suck ... Dick!" (Springer, 2016). Even though the UND team changed their team nickname from the Native-themed nickname of *Fighting Sioux* to *Fighting Hawks* in 2015, this chant still remained ingrained in the NDSU fans. Afterward, the NDSU President called for an end to this "hateful chant" that his students would frequently yell during games against UND, but the impact of that microaggression cannot be undone. The intent is for the NDSU fans to use this chant to denigrate the largely White fan base of their rivals from UND, without much thought about how that might impact the actual Sioux people. So while the NDSU fans may not intend for actual Sioux (i.e., Dakota, Nakota, Lakota) tribal members to be the recipients of that vulgar chant, their intent does not match the outcome: being exposed to this environmental microaggression while attending a UND/NDSU football game can adversely impact the psychological functioning of a First Nations individual (LaRocque, McDonald, Weatherly, & Ferraro, 2011).

Beyond verbal manifestations of these microaggressions, fans also utilize motivational images to provide an advantage for their team at the expense of the opposing team. When their team is playing against an opponent with a Native-themed mascot, nickname, or logo, they may try to use clever imagery of their own team mascot, nickname, or logo dominating the opponent. It might be an image of a *Pirate* holding the severed head of an *Indian* when the Bay Port *Pirates* play the Berlin *Indians*, or a *Bear* mauling a *Chief* when the Chicago *Bears* play the Kansas City *Chiefs*. Or it might be when the McLain High School *Tigers* played the Hillsboro *Indians* in 2016. The cheerleaders may create a banner for the team to run through that says, "Hey Indians, Get Ready for a Trail of Tears Part 2" (Payne, 2016). The trivial way in which that traumatic and genocidal event is utilized within a sporting event sends a powerful implicit message. The history and experience with cultural genocide and attempted extermination is relatively insignificant, but it is significant insomuch as it can be used to attempt to intimidate an almost entirely White group of athletes from Hillsboro School who happen to be called *Indians*. Again, a First Nations individual who is witnessing this unfold sees their cultural history and heritage be minimalized and used for social gain by a group of people who likely don't understand the full scope and impact of American government policies that led to the Trail of Tears and other similar traumatic events.

Native-Themed Sports Logos: Societally Embedded Visual Microaggressions

We will return to additional examples of environmental microaggressions, but it is first necessary to discuss visual microaggressions because emerging empirical research indicates that images associated with Native-themed mascots, nicknames, and logos can have a negative psychological impact (e.g., Fryberg et al., 2008; LaRocque et al., 2011). For example, Fryberg et al. (2008) conducted a series of empirical examinations into the impact of Native-themed nicknames and logos on the psychological functioning of participants, both First Nations students and White students. First Nations high school and college students who were exposed to images of Native-themed logos reported significantly fewer achievement-related selves, along with lower levels of self-esteem and community worth when compared to members of the control group who were not exposed to these images. The authors' conclusion was that seeing these stereotypical representations of First Nations people (e.g., *noble savage*; *the caricatured image of Chief Wahoo*) being used by sports teams can make First Nations people feel worse about themselves, and it can facilitate the internalization of negative views of themselves and their own communities. Furthermore, consistent exposure to these images from the White majority culture contributes to First Nations people perceiving that they have a limited range of future goals to choose from, thereby internalizing the narrow and prejudicial view that society has of them and limiting the possibilities they see for what they can become. There is a second consciousness that is born beyond self-perception, where one is forced to view themselves from the lens of the dominant culture, and measure their worth with the metrics of a society that, "looks on in amused contempt and pity" (Du Bois, 1968, p. 3). Understanding this phenomenon can help address dynamics of visual racism experienced by First Nations people when exposed to Native-themed mascots, nicknames, and logos. If others see me as a member of an inherently flawed group—an impending failure or irredeemable burden on society—then it becomes harder to see through that clouded lens of negativity, particularly when there is a general absence of positive images of people who look like me in society. As a result, that reflected and limited view of oneself can become readily more internalized, negatively impacting one's developmental trajectory and subsequent psychological functioning. Across all of the findings of their studies, Fryberg et al. (2008) concluded that the presence of these Native-themed logos—which are omnipresent in society at all levels of sports—can effectively threaten the psychological functioning of First Nations people in a number of different ways.

Native-themed mascots, nicknames, and logos can enact visual microagggressions that perpetuate stereotypic representations and reinforce institutional racism, thereby negatively impacting the psychological functioning of those who come across these logos. LaRocque et al. (2011) empirically assessed this dynamic in their study. In doing so, they also attempted to determine if categories of images had a differential impact. Oftentimes proponents of Native-themed mascots, nicknames, and logos will not only minimize opposition (e.g., Steinfeldt et al., 2012), they will also often claim that these images are inherently benign (e.g., neutral images), but sometimes people do cross the line (e.g., controversial images) and that is when some people could take offense. In the LaRocque et al. (2011) study, the authors investigated the impact of two categories of mascot images on both White participants and First Nations participants. The first category of images was referred to as *neutral*, based on societal expectations that these images are omnipresent and readily visible (e.g., team logos that are present on uniforms, shirts, and other areas on campus and beyond). The other category of images was referred to as *controversial* in that they represented images and logos that depicted caricatured or demeaning images of Indigenous people and misuse of tribal names (e.g., *Sioux-venirs*, caricatured images of Indigenous-themed logos).

Results indicated that First Nations participants reported significantly higher levels of psychological distress and negative affect after viewing both the controversial and the neutral images, when compared to their baseline scores. White participants also reported higher levels of negative affect compared to their own baseline scores after viewing the "controversial" images. However, when White participants viewed the "neutral" images, there was no significant difference in response as compared to their baseline. That is, although both groups seemed to be negatively impacted by the "controversial" images, only First Nations participants experienced more psychological distress after viewing the "neutral" images. These results also contributed to the authors concluding that the term *neutral* was not applicable to these Native-themed logo images because these images negatively impacted the psychological functioning of First Nations people.

As these results suggest, First Nations students can be negatively impacted by simply walking around campus and seeing the omnipresent "neutral" images (LaRocque et al., 2011). These images, which are school-sanctioned, aggressively marketed, and widely disseminated in the local community and beyond, appear on buildings, shirts, media sources, and in many other places. These visual macroaggressions are hegemonically woven into the fabric of society, which renders their effect more insidious, and consequently even more powerful. Seeing the Cleveland *Indians* "Chief Wahoo" image on Sports Center or the UND *Fighting Sioux* logo in the local newspaper is a daily occurrence that draws little attention from most people; furthermore, most people do not have awareness of the potential for these images to be psychologically impactful. Yet, for a First Nations person, the act of turning on ESPN, opening the newspaper, or simply walking around on campus where these images are around every corner can have an inherently negative impact on his/her psychological functioning, yet the same act may not even rise to the level of awareness of other people. The fact that this reality exists primarily among Persons of Color solidifies its categorization as a racial microaggression, in that it selectively impacts some individuals negatively while others remain oblivious to this dynamic. Thus, this systematic and everyday visual assault from these race-based visual microaggressions reinforce the dynamics of institutional racism, while perpetuating ideologies that subjugate Communities of Color.

Sports Mascots: We Are the Indians!

Native-themed sports mascots, nicknames, and logos represent a disproportionately large portion of the "Human" mascot category. The category of "Animal" mascots would include nicknames like the *Tigers, Bears, Wolverines, Badgers*, and so on, while the category of "Human" mascots would include nicknames like the *Fighting Irish, Pirates, Vikings*, and *Indians*. However, there are a number of differences between different kinds of "Human" mascots that create negatively unique ramifications associated with using Native-themed mascots, nicknames, and logos. Steinfeldt and Steinfeldt (2010) provide a comprehensive comparative analysis of categories of differences between types of human mascots, centering on issues related to: (a) de facto representation, (b) societal control over image use and presentation, and (c) dynamics of ethnic slurs inherent in the use of Native-themed mascots, nicknames, and logos.

To begin with, the *Vikings* nicknames do not represent contemporary Scandinavians in the same way that the *Indians* nicknames represent contemporary First Nations people. This is based on a critical mass of contemporary societal representations of Scandinavians as compared to a lack of these accurate portrayals of First Nations people. On the other hand, the lack of accurate portrayals of First Nations people in society allows these mascot images to fill that societal void—these Native-themed mascots, nicknames, and logos serve as de facto representations, portraying First Nations people as past tense people from historic times who wear loin cloths, shoot bow and arrows, and speak in broken English ("How, White Man!"). In comparison, *Vikings* are in fact people of the past, but they do not represent contemporary Scandinavians, so their mascot portrayal in sports teams has considerably less negative impact.

Second, there is a difference between the *Fighting Sioux* and the *Fighting Irish* (Steinfeldt & Steinfeldt, 2010). It is true that the *Fighting Irish* mascot from the University of Notre Dame (and also used by hundreds of youth and high school teams in America) represents a stereotypic representation of Irish people, one in which they are combative (and potentially often drunken) individuals. However, the University of Notre Dame has the power to regulate and control the way their *Fighting Irish* image is being used. If an opposing team chooses to denigrate the issue (e.g., Stanford University Marching Band), Notre Dame can push back on this portrayal. Notre Dame can also create and put forward imagery that is consistent with their self-identification with this mascot, nickname, and logo image.

On the other hand, First Nations people do not have this same power. Native-themed mascots, nicknames, and logos are often used without their consent, and rarely (if ever) with compensation to them. In general, sports fans readily identify with the nickname, mascot, and/or logo of their favorite team, and they formulate an identity that is intertwined with their support for and affiliation with the team. Letters sent out to supporters of the Florida State *Seminoles* often refer to the recipient as a fellow *Seminole*. Fans of the Cleveland Indians refer to themselves as *Indians* or *Sons of Wahoo* (in reference to the image of *Chief Wahoo*, the team mascot and logo that appears on their hats, jerseys, and merchandise). This practice operates without compensation to or full consent from First Nations individuals. Being an "Indian" allows a Cleveland fan to define what it means to be an Indian, without regard to the input of First Nations individuals.

Related to this point about the lack of societal control, the language that is used by contemporary sports media also serve to disempower First Nations communities, to reinforce the microaggression, and perpetuate the stereotypic representations. Headlines like "Red Robins scalp Indians in solid GNC 6-0 shutout" (Sherek, 2017) serve to reinforce stereotypes of First Nations people (i.e., bloodthirsty savage). This manifestation of an environmental microaggression perpetuates stereotypic representations and reinforces the narrative of racial inferiority among First Nations individuals, serving as a reminder of the U.S. government's policies of extermination and genocide, which were based on the premise that *savage Indians* were not fully human. These experiences all negatively impact the psychological functioning of First Nations people.

Finally, the presence of the *Redskins* team nickname and logo presents a heightened level of concern with this microaggression. The term *Redskin* is considered to be a racial slur, an epithet that is considered to be harmful and denigrating to First Nations communities. Yet this team name is embraced and used at all levels of competition, from youth sports through high school sports and all the way up the ladder of societal visibility to the Washington *Redskins* of the NFL. The prospect of comparably named sports teams (e.g., the New Jersey *Jews*, the Charlotte *Chinks*, or the New York *Negroes*) would be considered an absurdity in contemporary times that would be quickly condemned and replaced. However, the *Redskins* slur remains omnipresent in the sporting world, subjecting First Nations individuals to constant psychological harm. Furthermore, when calls to address and remove the *Redskins* mascots are made, they are met with derision and refusal, thus validating the perception that First Nations people are invisible members of an inferior race whose objections need not be considered.

Psychological Dilemmas of Responding

When faced with the prospect of speaking up against Native-themed mascots, nicknames, and logos, a First Nations individual is presented with a difficult task. Oftentimes, the costs of speaking up outweigh the benefits, and so the dynamics of self-preservation may silence opposition. Exacerbating this difficulty is the general lack of critical consciousness within U.S. society, given the hegemonic way these images are embedded within society, inundating consumers of sports from early childhood on with the normalcy of these images. The nature of these unintentional expressions of bias results in the proponent of these Native-themed mascots, nicknames, and logos feeling strongly sincere in their belief that they are acting without racial bias. Thus, the onus of responsibility is put on the First Nations individual to prove how these images could possibly be harmful, and the oppressed bear the burden of proof for their own oppression.

Reactions to the prospect of harm coming from Native-themed mascots, nicknames, and logos often involve minimization, denial, or even attack (Steinfeldt et al., 2012). Proponents will often raise accusations of being "overly sensitive" or they will lament the "PC culture" that is overreacting. Oftentimes, the tradition, history, and duration of these images in society is used as an argument (i.e., "We have had this mascot for so many years—if they were such a problem, why are people only complaining now?"). This perspective overlooks the possibility that past people had previously raised the issue but were similarly invalidated, among a host of other explanations.

In terms of attack, Steinfeldt et al. (2012) analyzed online forum comments from newspapers in a community that had a Native-themed nickname and logo. They found that participants were likely to disparage and verbally attack opponents to Native-themed nicknames and logos, often using vitriolic and threatening language to attempt to squelch opposition. Steinfeldt et al. (2012) also conducted a qualitative study in which they interviewed social justice activists who advocated for the removal of Native-themed mascots, nicknames, and logos in their communities. These participants reported dangerous experiences with people who did not agree with their opposition. Their stories entailed vandalism to their property, threats of violence to them and their children, and physical altercations and attacks at the hands of individuals who disagreed with their opposition to the community's Native-themed mascot, nickname, and logo. As mentioned earlier in the chapter, self-preservation may be a valid reason for not speaking up—the cost is often too high. Without the chance to address the issue and be validated, First Nations individuals are forced to endure the microaggression and deal with the consequences.

Conclusion

First Nations communities face difficulties in effectively advocating for removing these stereotypic representations for a number of reasons. Although such difficulties are commonly experienced among populations that experience microaggressions, First Nations people face several impediments that are specific to sports culture. To begin with, sport is a powerful and popular institution in the United States. It serves as a primary socializing agent through widespread participation among American youth at an early age, and sports is a multibillion dollar entertainment industry that sits at the center of many social circles. Through this broad participation and consumption of sports, affiliation with sports teams generates a long-lasting sense of identity. When the omnipresent image of a Native-themed mascot, nickname, or logo receives critical perspectives to its potential for harm, that opposition is often minimalized, resisted, and rejected. Furthermore, First Nations individuals represent less than 1% of the population, with nearly a quarter of the population living below the poverty line (Merskin, 2001; U.S. Census Bureau, 2006). Consequently, it becomes difficult for First Nations people to have the power and resources to advocate for the challenge of comparable images (e.g., *Li'l Black Sambo*; *Frito Bandito*) that other racial groups have successfully removed. As a result, this microaggression becomes a daily reality, and the corresponding feeling of powerlessness further contributes to the negative psychological impact.

References

Baca, L. R. (2004). Native images in schools and the racially hostile environment. *Journal of Sport & Social Issues, 28*, 71–78.

Bird, S. E. (Ed.). (1996). *Dressing in feathers: The construction of the Indian in American popular culture*. Boulder, CO: Westview.

Davis, L. R. (2002). The problem with Native American mascots. *Multicultural Education, 9*, 11–14.

Deloria, P. J. (1998). *Playing Indian*. New Haven, CT: Yale University Press.

Du Bois, W. E. B. (1968). *The souls of black folk; essays and sketches*. Chicago: A. G. McClurg, 1903. New York, NY: Johnson Reprint Corp, 1968.

Fryberg, S. A., Markus, H. R., Oyserman, D., & Stone, J. M. (2008). Of warrior chiefs and Indian princesses: The psychological consequences of American Indian mascots. *Basic and Applied Social Psychology, 30*, 208–218.

Goings, K. W. (1994). *Mammy and Uncle Mose: Black collectibles and American stereotyping*. Bloomington, IN: Indiana University Press.

King, C. R. (2002). Defensive dialogues: Native American mascots, anti-Indianism, and educational institutions. *SIMILE: Studies in Media and Information Literacy Education, 2*(1). doi:10.3138/sim.2.1.001.

King, C. R., Davis-Delano, L., Staurowsky, E., & Baca, L. (2006). Sports mascots and the media. In A. A. Raney & J. Bryant (Eds.), *Handbook of sports and media* (pp. 559–575). Mahwah, NJ: L. Erlbaum and Associates.

King, C. R., Staurowsky, E. J., Baca, L., Davis, L. R., & Pewewardy, C. (2002). Of polls and prejudice: *Sports Illustrated's* errant "Indian Wars." *Journal of Sport & Social Issues, 26*, 381–402.

LaRocque, A., McDonald, J. D., Weatherly, J. N., & Ferraro, F. R. (2011). Indian sports nicknames/logos: Affective difference between American Indian and non-Indian college students. *American Indian and Alaska Native Mental Health Research: The Journal of the National Center, 18*, 1–16.

Merskin, D. (1998). Sending up signals: A survey of Native American1 media use and representation in the mass media. *Howard Journal of Communication, 9*(4), 333–345.

Merskin, D. (2001). Winnebagos, Cherokees, Apaches, and Dakotas: The persistence of stereotyping of American Indians in American advertising brands. *The Howard Journal of Communications, 12*, 159–169.

Payne, M. (2016, October). *Ohio high school cheerleaders taunt opposing "Indians" with "Trail of Tears" banner*. Retrieved from https://www.washingtonpost.com/news/early-lead/wp/2016/10/29/ohio-high-school-cheerleaders-taunt-opposing-indians-with-trail-of-tears-banner/?utm_term=.88ddfa433a03.

Russel, S. (2003). Ethics, alterity, incommensurability, honor. *Ayaangwaamizin: The International Journal of Indigenous Philosophy, 3*, 31–54.

Sherek, D. (2017, January). *Racially charged headline causes uproar*. Retrieved from http://www.wjfw.com/storydetails/20170127190544/%20%20racially_charged_headline_causes_uproar.

Springer, P. (2016, November). *President calls for end of "hateful" chant at Bison football games*. Retrieved from http://www.grandforksherald.com/news/4138709-ndsu-president-calls-end-hateful-sioux-chant-bison-football-games.

Staurowsky, E. J. (1999). American Indian imagery and the miseducation of America. *Quest, 51*, 382–392.

Steinfeldt, J. A., Foltz, B. D., LaFollette, J. R., White, M. R., Wong, Y. J., & Steinfeldt, M. C. (2012). Perspectives of social justice activists: Advocating against native-themed mascots, nicknames, and logos. *The Counseling Psychologist, 40*, 326–362.

Steinfeldt, J. A., & Steinfeldt, M. C. (2010). Gender role conflict, athletic identity, and help-seeking among high school football players. *Journal of Applied Sport Psychology, 22*(3), 262–273.

Steinfeldt, J. A., & Steinfeldt, M. C. (2012). Components of a training intervention designed to produce attitudinal change toward native-themed mascots, nicknames, and logos. *Counselor Education and Supervision, 51*, 17–32.

Sue, D. W., Capodilupo, C. M., Torino, G. C., Bucceri, J. M., Holder, A., Nadal, K. L., & Esquilin, M. (2007). Racial microaggressions in everyday life: implications for clinical practice. *American Psychologist, 62*(4), 271–286.

U.S. Census Bureau. (2006). *We the people: American Indians and Alaska American Indians in the United States*, Washington, DC. Retrieved from http://www.census.gov/prod/2006pubs/censr-28.pdf.

Williams, D. M. (2006). Patriarchy and the "Fighting Sioux": A gendered look at racial college sports nicknames. *Race, Ethnicity, & Education, 9*, 325–340.

Part IV

Microaggressions and Social Policies and Practices

14

Microaggressions and Student Activism: Harmless Impact and Victimhood Controversies
Derald Wing Sue

Since publication of "Racial Microaggressions in Everyday Life: Implications for Clinical Practice" in the *American Psychologist (AP)* (Sue et al., 2007), the conceptual taxonomy of microaggressions has taken the professional field and general public by storm (Wong, Derthick, David, Saw, & Okazaki, 2013). Although the article was published only 10 years ago, there has been a proliferation of research on microaggressions that is grounded in its theory and classification. The original article has garnered 2,701 citation counts in fields as diverse as psychology, sociology, education, law, and political science; there are now over 11,900 publications on the topic of microaggressions, nearly all after the article made its appearance in 2007 (Google Scholar, April 27, 2018, search). Wong et al. (2013) consider the *AP* article "seminal" and that it marked "the point when racial microaggressions gained widespread psychological research attention." Microaggression theory has become part of mainstream discourse (print, television, and talk radio) and the social media (Internet blogs, Tumblr, and Facebook). Nowhere has the impact of microaggressions been more keenly felt than in higher education. Numerous protests have taken place recently following academic officials' insensitivity to complaints of racist, anti-gay, and anti-Semitic incidents on our finest college campuses (Anderson & Svrluga, 2015).

In response to student protests, backlash against microaggression awareness has emerged. Critics (a) minimize the harmful impact of microaggressions, (b) claim that the focus on microaggressions (theory, research, and initiatives) fosters a dangerous culture of victimhood, (c) warn that it imperils free speech, and (d) advocate creating a moratorium on microaggression initiatives (safe spaces, trigger warnings, removal of offensive historical names and symbols, hiring of chief diversity officers, and creating required microaggression training programs for educators). Although some of these criticisms are not without merit, a critical analysis of existing research reveals that microaggressions are

Microaggression Theory: Influence and Implications, First Edition. Edited by Gina C. Torino, David P. Rivera, Christina M. Capodilupo, Kevin L. Nadal, and Derald Wing Sue.

detrimental to the psychological and physical well-being of targets, that they are quantitatively and qualitatively different from personal insults (i.e., insults not based on group membership), and in fact liberates and empowers marginalized groups in society.

Microaggression Discourse in Higher Education

The rapidly emerging "language of microaggressions" in mainstream discourse and in nearly all mediums of communication has been likened to a prairie fire. Microaggression examples and explanations have flooded the airwaves through television, talk radio, public service announcements (music television [MTV]), and editorial and opinion pieces in newspapers and magazines, blogs, social media, and political conversations (Lukianoff & Haidt, 2015; Martin & Petrey, 2015). MTV's multi-year "Look Different" campaign, for example, was among the first to run a series of public service announcements that portrayed "enacted microaggression scenes" to educate and to provide tools for millennials to discuss hidden racial, gender, and LGBT bias (Townsend, 2014). These educational clips ran for a period of time between regular programing and can still be found on the MTV "Look Different" Web site. In 2010, "The Microaggression Project," an Internet blog, published reader anecdotes of true-life incidents of microaggressions with the help of Tumblr and Facebook; it has generated thousands of stories attesting to their existence and the psychological impact on targets (Microaggression blog (2016). www.microaggressions.com, retrieved March, 2017).

The microaggression movement was keenly felt in higher education where racial discrimination protests erupted across college campuses throughout the country (Hartocollis & Bidgood, 2015). Complaints of racial insensitivity in the form of microaggressions were voiced on many campuses. Soon other marginalized groups voiced their discontent as well and noted the hostile and invalidating campus climates they were subjected to, making learning difficult. The protests against racist, anti-gay, and anti-Semitic incidents, for example, even led to the resignation of the University of Missouri system president and its chancellor (Anderson & Svrluga, 2015).

Public opposition to racial injustices is something that many Americans hoped we had moved beyond with the election of the first Black president of the United States in 2008 (Neville, Awad, Brooks, Flores, & Bluemel, 2013). On the contrary, not since the Third World and Civil Rights movements of the 1960s and 1970s have we witnessed such an explosion of racial protests. The complaints of racial bias on college campuses were also fueled by multiple incidents of Black men killed by White police officers, and the rise of the "Black Lives Matter" movement (Neville, Gallardo, & Sue, 2016). When politicians and law enforcement officers responded with the counter slogan "All Lives Matter," they set off a firestorm of protests with many labeling the response as a microaggression itself. They believed the all-inclusive phrase invalidated, diluted, and undermined the legitimacy of the "Black Lives Matter" message: *in our society, the lives of Black Americans are less valued than that of Whites.* For many People of Color, it was clear that racism was alive and well, that it had morphed into various forms of microaggressions, that it continued to oppress and harm, and that White Americans simply did not understand how their hidden biases were expressed (Sue, 2017).

Behind many campus protests were complaints of "microaggressions" being delivered by well-intentioned fellow students, professors, and administrators who often unknowingly engaged in racial or group-based insults and putdowns that took a heavy psychological and educational toll on targets. Fed up with being constant recipients of racial microaggressions, a group of African American students created the "I, Too, Am Harvard" (2014) photo campaign on YouTube, which had an enormous impact across college campuses. They portrayed the faces and voices of Black students at Harvard University describing their experiences with microaggressions: being ignored and unheard, having their opinions devalued, being seen as less competent and capable, and of not belonging or being wanted.

Due to the speed of social media, a chain reaction occurred in which Students of Color throughout the United States and even in different countries took up the call and created social media projects of microaggressive experiences on their own college campuses. The "I, Too, Am ..." projects were echoed at Berkeley, NYU, Wellesley, Iowa, Princeton, University of Wisconsin, Madison, and at institutions outside of the United States (Auckland and Oxford) (Campbell & Manning, 2014). It is surely accurate to say that the concept of "microaggressions" struck a responsive chord with People of Color and many marginalized groups in our nation.

As protests against bias and discrimination mounted on campuses, calls for administrators to take action against microaggressions manifested in the renaming or removing offensive monuments, hiring of Chief Diversity Officers, providing safe places for Students of Color to discuss their concerns, and instituting training for faculty and staff in understanding microaggressions (Eligon, 2016; Sinclair, 2016). The University of California system even went so far as to encourage sensitivity training for employees on all 10 California campuses.

The Microaggression Backlash

Despite the widespread acceptance of the theory and taxonomy of microaggressions in racial/ethnic psychology, it is not without detractors. Like any new concept that acquires so much visibility and generates so many social change implications, critics differed in their views of microaggressions. These scholars minimized the harmful impact of microaggressions (Schacht, 2008; Thomas,

2008), concluded that the concept fostered a dangerous culture of dependency and victimhood (Campbell & Manning, 2014), questioned whether empirical studies supported the theory, called for a moratorium on microaggression initiatives on college campuses (Lilienfeld, 2017), and warned of dangers it posed to First Amendment Rights to free speech (Lukianoff & Haidt, 2015). Critics accused universities of cowering to the unwarranted demands of protestors, perpetuating an infantilized culture, and "coddling minority" students (Lukianoff & Haidt, 2015). The conservative right ridiculed microaggression examples as ridiculous and nonsensical, and asserted that Students of Color were simply overly sensitive and immature in their responses. Furedi (2015) labels it the "anti-microaggression" backlash.

These detractors took issue with Students of Color who claimed that microaggressions made them feel "unsafe" in class and college campuses, that they represented traumatic forms of oppression, and that they were psychologically harmful. Indeed, they characterized protesters as crybabies and complainers, who needed to simply toughen up and learn how to deal with minor incivilities, just like everyone else. Critics implied that microaggressions were simply petty annoyances, and that Students of Color needed to learn how to deal with "unpleasant offenses in the real world." The microaggression movement, they contend, was simply a ploy to gain sympathetic attention, use their victim roles to control others, and avoid personal responsibility for handling them (Campbell & Manning, 2014; Saffron, 2015).

These criticisms are predicated on several underlying assumptions: (a) Microaggressions are trivial, relatively harmless, and insignificant offenses. (b) They are no different from the everyday incivilities experienced by anyone (regardless of race, gender, or sexual orientation). (c) They imply that the complainants are somehow to blame for making such a fuss and the solution is to "grow up," develop a thicker skin, and stop "whining." Microaggression theory, they assert, allow People of Color to *play victims* who are weak, helpless, and vulnerable, and thus require "special treatment and protection." The following sections examine these three assumptions in closer detail in order to assess their validity.

Harmless Impact Controversy

The belief that microaggressions are negligible slights and insignificant offenses has been voiced not only in the general public but also by social scientists as well. This line of thinking, for example, equates racial microaggressions to the everyday incivilities that everyone encounters. A rude clerk who behaves poorly toward a customer, a waiter/waitress who provides slow service to patrons, and a teacher who makes fun of a student are all offensive behaviors. While distressing, critics argue, these acts are part of life, and most of us learn how to handle them without complaining. Schacht (2008) contends that insults and rudeness are characteristic of all human interactions. Thomas (2008) labels microaggressions as "macrononsense" and says they "hardly necessitate the hand-wringing reactions" described by Students of Color. And Lukianoff and Haidt (2015) believe our educational system is teaching Students of Color "to catastrophize" and to "have zero tolerance" for being offended.

These assertions are not supported in light of the overwhelming body of research on the detrimental impact of racial, gender, and sexual orientation/ identity microaggressions. Microaggressions have been found to assail the mental health of recipients (Hernandez, Carranza, & Almeida, 2010; Sue, Capodilupo, & Holder, 2008), increase depression and negative affect (Nadal, Griffin, Wong, Hamit, & Rasmus, 2014), and lower emotional well-being (Ong, Burrow, Fuller-Rowell, Ja, & Sue, 2013). Perpetual exposure to microaggressions leads to a chronic state of "racial battle fatigue" (Smith, Hung, & Franklin, 2011). Further, researchers have identified microaggressions as creating a hostile and invalidating campus climate (Solórzano, Ceja, & Yosso, 2000; Yosso, Smith, Ceja, & Solórzano, 2009), which is found to perpetuate stereotype threat (Steele, Spencer, & Aronson, 2002; Torres, Driscoll, & Burrow, 2010) and to impede learning through depletion of cognitive resources (Harwood, Huntt, Mendenhall, & Lewis, 2012; Kohli & Solórzano, 2012; Salvatore & Shelton, 2007).

In a study of three community colleges, researchers found that microaggressions occurred frequently in classrooms, that instructors were most often the perpetrators, and they likened microaggressions to "toxic rain" falling corrosively onto educational environments and affecting the learning and emotional well-being of students (Suarez-Orozco et al., 2015). But it is not simply the detrimental impact on the psychological well-being and educational performance of targets that is at issue here: research indicates that microaggressions take a heavy toll on the physical health of recipients (Clark, Anderson, Clark, & Williams, 1999; Frost, Lehavot, & Meyer, 2013), reduce work productivity (Dovidio, 2001), impair employee performance (Hunter, 2011), and in the long term, create inequities in education, employment, and health care (Purdie-Vaughns, Davis, Steele, & Ditlmann, 2008).

Microaggressions versus Nongroup-Based Incivilities

But, what makes microaggressions different from ordinary every day forms of incivility? In a study that tested the impact of microaggressions versus general insults on Asian Americans, it was found that when targets interpreted the slights as race-based instead of a "general nonrace-based" slight, the experience had a significantly greater harmful impact (Wang, Leu, & Shoda, 2011). The investigators posit that one of the major differences was in the target's lower social status that heightened and reminded them of their second-class status in society. Contrary to the beliefs of critics, microaggressions and nongroup-based general incivilities differ significantly in both quantity and quality in the following ways (Ong et al., 2013; Smith et al., 2011; Sue, 2010; Wang et al., 2011):

First, using race as an example, microaggressions are constant and continual in the life experience of People of Color. They can occur and recur from the moment of birth until the time of death. In contrast, non-race-based insults are time-limited and tend to be infrequent. Thus, a White person who encounters a rude service worker may be angered in the moment, but the negative impact is transitory. For People of Color, however, these encounters are frequent from the time they awake in the morning until the time they go to bed. A lifetime of microaggression leaves long-term detrimental psychological and physical effects (Sue, 2010).

Second, microaggressions are cumulative and any single one may represent the straw that breaks the camel's back. When an African American female student is mistaken for a cafeteria worker and angrily "blows up," observers may perceive this as an overreaction to an innocent mistake. They are unaware that these "mistakes" are common occurrences in the life experience of the Black student. As stated by Maya Angelou, these affronts are not isolated incidents but cumulative and exhausting; they represent the old adage, "death by a thousand cuts" (Angelou, 2009).

Third, microaggressions are energy depleting because they often send double messages that must be deciphered. One study found frequent cognitive disruptions and conflicts that occur among African Americans when encountering possible microaggressions (Sue, Nadal, et al., 2008). The energy-depleting thought processes went something like this: "Did what I think happen, really happen? Was this an intentional or unintentional slight? If a racially based slight, what should I do or say? If I say something, what will be the consequences?" Participants often described their dilemmas as "You're damned if you do and damned if you don't." If targets say something they risk negative consequences, especially if there is a significant power differential. If they remain silent, however, targets often feel like they are "cowards" or that they have sold out their integrity. Participants often describe dealing with microaggressions to be cognitively and emotionally exhausting.

Fourth, microaggressions are constant reminders of the person's second-class status in society. They are reminded, for example, that they live in a country where People of Color are not represented in Fortune 400 companies, that they continue to occupy the lower rungs of the employment ladder, that history books continue to ignore or portray them in pathological ways, and that positive role models on television and the media are few (Sue, 2010). General offenses that are nongroup-based do not generate these humiliating associations.

Last, microaggressions symbolize profound historical injustices (enslavement of African Americans, incarceration of Japanese Americans, and the taking away of land from Indigenous peoples of this country). Just as Jews consider the Holocaust to represent historical trauma, many People of Color experience a deep-seated and lasting sense of injustice with respect to atrocities in the past. Thus, to tell a Person of Color that "America is a land of opportunity" is at best a historical inaccuracy, and at worst a microaggression that denies and invalidates their racial reality.

Victimhood Controversy

Critics who equate microaggressions with minor slights bemoan the fact that we have now entered into a dangerous societal state of victimhood (Brooks, 2015). Campbell and Manning (2014) argue that the microaggression movement signals the development of a new moral culture in society; a culture that glorifies victimhood, fosters dependency and helplessness, teaches our young to become intolerant of minor offenses, and uses public complaints of microaggressions as a means of social control. To support their contention, they present a biased historical account of the evolution of western morality, while ignoring its applicability to disempowered groups. The authors trace two evolutionary stages beginning with a "culture of honor" followed by a "culture of dignity." They lament the emergence of a new "culture of victimhood" that they blame on microaggression theory, and warn about its detrimental social consequences.

The *honor culture*, as they describe, is rooted in the personal status of physical bravery that demands retaliation when a person's reputation is maligned. To be honorable is to protect one's integrity, to refuse to be dominated or impugned, and to seek personal retribution when insulted. In early times, when legal authority was weak or absent, honor and justice could only be obtained through individual personal action (usually "physical bravery"). Campbell and Manning provide the example of the 1804 duel between Aaron Burr, the United States Vice President, and Alexander Hamilton over an exchange of insults. Hamilton accepted Burr's challenge in order to protect his honor and was subsequently killed. In an honor culture, relying on others for assistance may be perceived as a sign of weakness or even of cowardice.

As state authority and governing law became stronger in the modern world, the honor culture gave way to *a culture of dignity*, in which the inherent worth of a person was less important on how others perceive the individual, but depended on one's internal sense of integrity and efficacy. Slights and insults might prove offensive, but belief in one's own self-worth allowed him or her to let such affronts slide, to seek nonviolent compromise with the offender, or in serious transgressions (i.e., breaking the law), to seek help from authorities (law). In a dignity culture, value is placed upon restraint, toleration, and being impervious to minor slights and insults (i.e., developing a thick skin). The authors contend that the dignity culture as exemplified in the mid-20th century fostered toleration, peaceful confrontation, and ties of cultural closeness and intimacy: the glue that binds a society together.

Now in the 21st century, microaggression theory, which has been instrumental in the recent public airing of complaints (campus protests, social media, etc.), portends the emergence, so the authors believe, of a culture of *victimhood*, at odds with both the culture of honor and the culture of dignity. Microaggressive grievances at colleges and campuses are divisive and detrimental to the well-being of society by tearing the fabric of commonality, destroying a sense of societal unity, and undermining personal responsibility to resolve "minor" interpersonal grievances. In the honor culture, an affront would be settled by individual action and aggression. Appealing for help, advertising one's grievances, and portraying one's victimization would be dishonorable. On the other hand, members from a dignity culture would not hesitate to appeal to third parties for relief, but would consider it disgraceful to do so over "minor and merely verbal offenses." According to Campbell and Manning, in the dignity culture, people would confront an offender to discuss the issue or ignore the remarks completely, signs of efficacy and toughness.

In the victimhood culture, however, minor complaints like microaggressions are blown out of proportion (catastrophizing) and made public, represent attempts to garner sympathy by stressing marginalization (playing victims), are really means of controlling offenders by making them defensive and guilty, and demand third-party interventions. The social consequences (especially on college campuses) are disharmony, conflict, lack of intimacy, and the supplanting of individual toleration/negotiation with requests for third-party interventions (excessive dependency).

Power and Privilege: The Lack of an Equal Status Relationship

There are serious flaws not only in the postulation of victimhood culture, but in the authors' formulation of the honor and dignity ones as well. First, the authors seem oblivious to how honor and dignity cultures apply to a narrow spectrum of society, those with power and privilege. Aaron Burr and Alexander Hamilton engaged in a duel, but both men were of equally high social status. Throughout history, those accorded lower status in society have had an altogether different experience. For example, being a woman in medieval times, a Person of Color, or a White peasant from a low social class did not allow the person to seek personal retribution or even to voice dissent of any kind (Rini, 2015). It is ludicrous to entertain the notion that an enslaved Black man who is insulted by a White slave owner could challenge the person to a duel, or even mildly complain about it. To do so would have resulted in his death!

Second, the critics appear oblivious to the lived reality of People of Color. African Americans, for example, in responding to their forced enslavement and oppression have historically adopted ritualized accommodation and subordination behaviors toward Whites in which they hid or indirectly expressed hostility, aggression, and fear in order to create as few waves as possible (Boyd-Franklin, 2003). To retain the most menial jobs, to minimize retaliation, and to protect self and loved ones, they have had to conceal their anger and resentment not only over the open racism they experienced but also over the many microinsults and microinvalidations thrown their way (Pierce, Carew, Pierce-Gonzalez, & Willis, 1977; Sue, 2003).

Third, even if help or justice could be sought from a third party, the word of the disempowered had no social standing, and laws unfairly advantaged one group over another. In the history of the United States, for example, racial segregation, interracial marriage, ownership of land, voter restriction, and many other exclusionary laws were normative.

Fourth, it appears that equating microaggression theory with victimization is a false one and a misnomer. Indeed, Paulo Freire in *Pedagogy of the Oppressed* (1968) argues that the first step to liberation and empowerment is "naming" an oppressive event, condition, or process so it no longer holds power over those that are marginalized. It demystifies, deconstructs, and makes the "invisible" visible. Understanding the manifestation, dynamics, and impact of microaggressions is (a) liberating and empowering because it provides a language for People of Color to describe their experiences, (b) reassures them that they are not "crazy," (c) forces majority group members to consider the roles they play in the perpetuation of oppression, and (d) demands individual, institutional, and societal change (Sue, 2010). Students of Color who challenge fellow students, professors, and administrators about their hidden biases, and who demand that biased programs, policies, and practices be changed are not the actions of victims who are weak, helpless, and crybabies.

Fifth, victimhood accusations possess hidden assumptions that characterize complainants as the problem; they are overly sensitive, whiners, snivelers, immature, and self-pitying. People of Color are blamed for their own victimization, and publicly bringing attention to microaggressions is somehow due to personal failures or inadequacies. Critics believe that Students of Color must learn to grow up, stand on their own two feet, and be able to handle annoyances without complaining. Such accusations and labels are highly reminiscent of what happened during the civil rights protests of the 1960s on college campuses and in Communities of Color, when Students and Citizens of color were accused of being spoiled brats, unprepared to deal with the real world, ungrateful, lacking in respect for authority, and even coming from criminal "elements" (Caplan, 1970).

Social scientists have labeled this the "riffraff theory" of protesters, and it was often applied by those in power and privilege (university administrators, law enforcement, and politicians) to portray protesters as having personal flaws, thereby invalidating the legitimacy of their complaints (Caplan, 1970; Fogelson, 1970). Ironically, a series of studies on the characteristics of past protesters found them to be better educated, more integrated into the social and political fabric of their communities, possessing greater ethnic pride and identity, as well as a stronger sense of self-efficacy, and actually mentally healthier than nonprotesters (Forward & Williams, 1970; Turner & Wilson, 1976).

It seems difficult for critics of student protesters to entertain an alternative explanation for the many demonstrations on college campuses, for example, that microaggressions are not insignificant, that they harm and oppress, and that those voicing complaints are not somehow misguided or flawed. For example, Students of Color who demand change are usually those with high aspirations and who believe strongly in their ability to achieve their goals; however, it is environmental forces (biased programs, policies, and practices in an institution) rather than their own personal inadequacies that block their path to bettering themselves in the educational and outside world (Caplan & Paige, 1968). To be asked to simply accept the status quo is tantamount to asking Students of Color to passively and silently accept a life of oppression and discrimination (Sue, 2017).

Sixth, if there is anything that history has taught us about the attainment of equal rights for marginalized groups in our society, it is that collective action not just individual action is required for social change. The concept of microaggressions has resulted in a shared understanding among marginalized groups that they are not alone, and social media has allowed them to communicate and relate to one another instantaneously. Critics of microaggression theory bemoan publicly airing grievances on social media and warn that it is corrosive and divisive to society by fostering accusations and counteraccusations (Lukianoff & Haidt, 2015). Rini (2015), however, takes issue with this stand and presents an especially insightful critique of the culture of victimhood, asserting that it is not new, but actually the moral culture of the disempowered. That culture, she asserts, is a "culture of solidarity," where the oppressed are unable to enforce their honor, dignity, or humanity to those with power and privilege. In referring to those most silenced and oppressed, she states, "They publicize mistreatment not because they enjoy the status of victim, but because they need the support of others to stand strong and because ultimately public discomfort is the only route to redress" (p. 2).

Implications: Free Speech, Safe Spaces, and Trigger Warnings

Accusing microaggression complainants of playing the victim role and fostering a culture of victimhood dismisses and negates the legitimacy of grievances, blames the targets of microaggressions for their own victimization, and absolves perpetrators and our society from the responsibility to take action. Contrary to describing the movement against microaggressions as the beginning of a culture of victimhood, a more accurate description is that it is a culture of liberation/empowerment (Freire, 1968; Sue, 2010), and an expression of a culture of solidarity among those most silenced and marginalized in our society (Rini, 2015).

The question that we must ask is, "How do we maintain the delicate balance between protecting marginalized groups from the constant onslaught of harmful microaggressions, and at the same time, get well-intentioned unknowing perpetrators and institutions from continuing their harmful ways?" This is not an easy question to answer. Many Students of Color, for example, have demanded that college administrators ban microaggressions and punish students and faculty for their indiscretions. Except for extreme cases, it is not punishment that provides the answer but education. Some universities have recommended and instituted awareness training for faculty and staff about the manifestation, dynamics, and impact of microaggressions.

When the University of California system instituted such a program, however, a strong outcry among faculty about first amendment rights and "free speech" arose (Martin & Petrey, 2015). Although free speech is an important right in our society, there have always been limits, especially when it harms. In a comprehensive study of diversity and free speech on college campuses, PEN America (2016) acknowledged that there were occasionally troubling instances of speech curtailment. But overall, they found (a) little support that college campuses have become "hotbeds of speech intolerance," (b) that free speech concerns are often a "red herring" diverting attention away from issues of inequality, (c) that the harmful impact of microaggressions are genuine and must be addressed, and (d) that student protests are not incursions on free speech, but rather manifestations of it. They observed that power and privilege, and the historical traditions in institutions can unwittingly stifle and silence the voices of those most marginalized on college campuses. Free speech and charges of "political correctness" should never give cover to bias or bigotry regardless of whether it is intentional or not.

Because microaggressive words and actions, and institutional policies and practices, may silence, harm, and oppress marginalized students on college campuses, calls for microaggression initiatives in many forms have been proposed. Two of these include the idea that universities have a responsibility to create "safe spaces" for socially marginalized students on college campuses, and the other is to provide "trigger warnings" for potentially traumatic or offensive materials covered in classes. The former suggests that educational institutions and the campuses do not tolerate harassment, hate speech, and violence directed toward Students of Color, lesbian, gay, bisexual, transgender, and queer (LGBTQ) students, and other socially devalued group members. It is intended to provide a safe campus environment that allows marginalized group members to gather together and to share their experiences. Trigger warnings involve a statement, written or verbal, about material (lecture, content in readings, videos, etc.) that may prove distressing or traumatic to some students. In academia, for example, it is most likely to make its appearance on syllabus for a particular course. Originally, trigger warnings were used to caution students about graphic depictions of sexual assaults and other sensitive materials that would affect students who might suffer from posttraumatic stress. The use of these statements has broadened to include coverage of other racial, sexual orientation, gender, and religious issues as well.

Safe spaces and trigger warnings come in many different forms, and they can look quite different from one institution to another. In some situations, they may prove effective, but in others they may be more problematic than helpful. There is no "one size fits all" solution in developing campus initiatives that address microaggressions. One can argue over whether creating safe spaces, trigger warnings, removal of offensive names and monuments, or requiring microaggression training represent effective solutions. But it is clear that the onus of responsibility for eradicating or minimizing microaggressions on college campuses falls squarely on the heads and shoulders of university administrators and professors; it is they who are in the best positions of power and privilege to effect change.

References

Anderson, N., & Svrluga, S. (2015, November 10). Can colleges protect free speech while also curbing voices of hate? *The Washington Post*. Retrieved from https://www.washingtonpost.com.

Angelou, M. (2009). *Now I know why the caged bird sings*. New York, NY: Ballantine Books.

Boyd-Franklin, N. (2003). *Black families in therapy*. New York, NY: Guildford Press.

Brooks, A. C. (2015, December 26). The real victims of victimhood. *New York Times*. Retrieved from https://wwwnytimes.com.

Campbell, B., & Manning, J. (2014). Microaggressions and moral cultures. *Comparative Sociology, 13*, 692–726.

Caplan, N. S. (1970). The new ghetto man: A review of recent empirical studies. *Journal of Social Issues, 26*, 59–73.

Caplan, N. S., & Paige, J. M. (1968). A study of ghetto rioters. *Scientific American, 219*, 15–21.

Clark, R., Anderson, N. B., Clark, V. R., & Williams, D. R. (1999). Racism as a stressor for African Americans. *American Psychologist, 54*, 805–816.

Dovidio, J. F. (2001). On the nature of contemporary prejudice: The third wave. *Journal of Social Issues, 57*, 829–849.

Eligon, J. (2016, February 3). University of Missouri struggles to bridge its racial divide. *New York Times*. Retrieved from https://wwwnytimes.com.

Fogelson, R. M. (1970). Violence and grievances: Reflections on the 1960s riots. *Journal of Social Issues, 26*, 141–163.

Forward, J. R., & Williams, J. R. (1970). Internal-external control and black militancy. *Journal of Social Issues, 26*, 75–92.

Freire, P. (1968). *Pedagogy of the oppressed*. New York, NY: Bloomsbury Academic.

Frost, D. M., Lehavot, K., & Meyer, I. H. (2013). Minority stress and physical health among sexual minority individuals. *Journal of Behavioral Medicine, 38*, 1–8.

Furedi, F. (2015, November 23). *Microaggression theory an assault on everyday life*. Retrieved from http://frankfuredi.com/site/article/818.

Google Scholar. (2018, April 27). Scholar.google.com.

Hartocollis, A., & Bidgood, J. (2015, November 11). Racial discrimination protests ignite at colleges across the U.S. *The New York Times*. Retrieved from https://wwwnytimes.com.

Harwood, S., Huntt, M. B., Mendenhall, R., & Lewis, J. (2012). Racial microaggressions in the residence halls: Experiences of students of color at a predominantly White university. *Journal of Diversity in Higher Education, 5*, 159–173.

Hernandez, P., Carranza, M., & Almeida, R. (2010). Mental health adaptive responses to racial microaggressions: An exploratory study. *Professional Psychology: Research and Practice, 41*, 202–209.

Hunter, R. L. (2011). *An examination of workplace microaggressions and their effects on employee performance*. Gonzaga University ProQuest Dissertation. (1503508).

I, Too, Am Harvard. (2014). Retrieved from www.itooamharvard.tublr.com.

Kohli, R., & Solórzano, D. G. (2012). Teachers, please learn our names!: Racial microaggressions and the K-12 classroom. *Race, Ethnicity and Education, 15*, 441–462.

Lilienfeld, S. (2017). Microaggressions: Strong claims, inadequate evidence. *Psychological Science, 12*, 138–169.

Lukianoff, G., & Haidt, J. (2015). The coddling of the American mind. *The Atlantic, 316*(2), 42–52.

Martin, G., & Petrey, M. (2015, September 9). Righto: UC's trigger warnings and microaggression labels outrage conservatives. *California Magazine*. Retrieved from https://alumni.berkeley.edu/california-magazine/just-in/2015-09-29/righto-ucs-trigger-warnings-and-microaggressions-labels.

Nadal, K. L., Griffin, K. E., Wong, Y., Hamit, S., & Rasmus, M. (2014). The impact of racial microaggressions on mental health: Counseling implications for clients of color. *Journal of Counseling and Development, 92*(1), 57–66.

Neville, H. A., Awad, G. H., Brooks, J. E., Flores, M. P., & Bluemel, J. (2013). Color-blind racial ideology: Theory, training, and measurement implications in psychology. *American Psychologist, 68*, 455–466.

Neville, H. A., Gallardo, M. E., & Sue, D. W. (2016). *The myth of racial color blindness.* Washington, DC: American Psychological Association.

Ong, A. D., Burrow, A. L., Fuller-Rowell, T. E., Ja, N. M., & Sue, D. W. (2013). Racial microaggressions and daily well-being among Asian Americans. *Journal of Counseling Psychology, 60*(2), 188–199.

PEN America (2016). *And campus for all: Diversity, inclusion, and freedom of speech at U. S. Universities.* New York, NY: PEN America.

Pierce, C., Carew, J., Pierce-Gonzalez, D., & Willis, D. (1977). An experiment in racism: TV commercials. In C. Pierce (Ed.), *Television and education* (pp. 62–88). Beverly Hills, CA: Sage.

Purdie-Vaughns, V., Davis, P. C., Steele, C. M., & Ditlmann, R. (2008). Social identity contingencies: How diversity cues signal threat or safety for African Americans in mainstream institutions. *Journal of Personality and Social Psychology, 94*, 615–630.

Rini, R. (2015). *The splintered mind: Microaggression and the culture of solidarity.* Retrieved from http://schwitzsplinters.blogspot.com/2015/09/microaggression-and-culture-of.html.

Saffron, J. (2015). *Erasing the past will not improve the future.* The John William Pope Center for Higher Education Policy. Retrieved from http://www.popecenter.org/commentaries/article.html?id=3294&utm_source.

Salvatore, J., & Shelton, J. N. (2007). Cognitive costs of exposure to racial prejudice. *Psychological Science, 18*, 810–815.

Schacht, T. (2008). A broader view of racial microaggression in psychotherapy. *American Psychologist, 63*, 273.

Sinclair, K. (2016, February 3). Student demands: An update. *New York Times.* Retrieved from https://wwwnytimes.com.

Smith, W. A., Hung, M., & Franklin, J. D. (2011). Racial battle fatigue and the miseducation of black men: Microaggressions, societal problems and environmental stress. *Journal of Negro Education., 80*, 63–82.

Solórzano, D., Ceja, M., & Yosso, T. (2000). Critical race theory, racial microaggressions, and campus racial climate: The experiences of African American college students. *Journal of Negro Education, 69*, 60–73.

Steele, C. M., Spencer, S. J., & Aronson, J. (2002). Contending with group image: The psychology of stereotypes and social identity threat. In M. Zanna (Ed.), *Advances in experimental social psychology* (Vol. 23, pp. 379–440). New York, NY: Academic Press.

Suarez-Orozco, C., Casanova, S., Martin, M., Katsiaficas, D., Cuellar, V., Smith, N. A., & Dias, S. I. (2015). Toxic rain in class: Classroom interpersonal microaggressions. *Educational Researcher, 44*, 151–160.

Sue, D. W. (2003). *Overcoming our racism: The journey to liberation.* San Francisco, CA: Jossey Bass.

Sue, D. W. (2010). *Microaggressions in everyday life: Race, gender & sexual orientation.* Hoboken, NJ: Wiley.

Sue, D. W. (2017). Microaggressions and "evidence": Empirical or experiential reality? *Psychological Science, 12,* 170–172.

Sue, D. W., Capodilupo, C. M., & Holder, A. (2008). Racial microaggressions in the life experience of Black Americans. *Professional Psychology: Research and Practice, 39*(3), 329.

Sue, D. W., Capodilupo, C. M., Torino, G. C., Bucceri, J. M., Holder, A. M. B., Nadal, K. L., & Esquilin, M. E. (2007). Racial microaggressions in everyday life: Implications for clinical practice. *American Psychologist, 62,* 271–286.

Sue, D. W., Nadal, K. L., Capodilupo, C. M., Lin, A. I., Rivera, D. P., & Torino, G. C. (2008). Racial microaggressions against Black Americans: Implications for counseling. *Journal of Counseling and Development, 86,* 330–338.

Thomas, K. R. (2008). Macrononsense in multiculturalism. *American Psychologist, 63,* 274–275.

Torres, L., Driscoll, M. W., & Burrow, A. L. (2010). Racial microaggressions and psychological functioning among highly achieving African-Americans: A mixed-methods approach. *Journal of Social and Clinical Psychology, 29*(10), 1074–1099.

Townsend, M. (2014). *MTV launches "Look Different" campaign to help youth fight racial, gender and LGBT inequality.* Retrieved from www.glaad.org/blog/mtv-launches-look-different-campaign.

Turner, C. B., & Wilson, W. J. (1976). Dimension of racial ideology: A study of urban black attitudes. *Journal of Social Issues, 32,* 152–193.

Wang, J., Leu, J., & Shoda, Y. (2011). When the seemingly innocuous "stings": Racial microaggressions and their emotional consequences. *Personality and Social Psychology Bulletin, 30,* 1–13.

Wong, G., Derthick, A. O., David, E. J. R., Saw, A., & Okazaki, S. (2013). The what, the why, and the how: A review of racial microaggression research in psychology. *Race and Social Problems.*

Yosso, T. J., Smith, W. A., Ceja, M., & Solórzano, D. G. (2009). Critical race theory, racial microaggressions, and campus racial climate for Latina/o undergraduates. *Harvard Educational Review, 79,* 659–691.

15

"Radical by Necessity, Not by Choice": From Microaggressions to Social Activism

Michelle Fine, Maria E. Torre, David Frost, and Allison Cabana

In the 1970s, Pierce and colleagues introduced the term *microaggressions* as the "subtle, stunning often automatic, and non-verbal exchanges which are 'put downs'" (Pierce, Carew, Pierce-Gonzalez, & Willis, 1978, p. 66). In 2007, Sue et al. published their landmark essay "Racial Microaggressions in Everyday Life" in *The American Psychologist*. Since then, there has been a virtual explosion of scholarly work in the field. Activist movements have mobilized around the construct, and an array of public reactions (including substantial conservative backlash) have been voiced (e.g., Friedersdorf, 2015; Runyowa, 2015). There is no doubt that the significance of this strain of scholarship has been enormous—marked by substantial scholarly citations, popular references in mainstream and alternative news outlets, and the proliferation of movements and counter-movements (which are arguably all grounded in microaggressions). Within the academy, there has also been much attention to the conceptual streamlining of the construct, vis-à-vis discrimination (Williams & Mohammed, 2009), minority stress (Meyer, 2015), and intersectionality (Lewis & Neville, 2015).

Sue et al. (2007) articulated the relationship between microaggressions to structure and history, citing: "Although the civil rights movement had a significant effect on changing racial interactions in this society, racism continues to plague the United States" (p. 271). Sue et al. elaborate on the concepts *microassault, microinsult,* and *microinvalidation;* they stress the *invisibility* of microaggressions (to the perpetrator and sometimes the target) and *dynamics* of racial microaggressions from the perspective of the target. In doing so, they challenge language traditionally treated as banal, innocent, and normative, and assert that hurtful words and behaviors (regardless of intention) matter. The writers are particularly clever about acknowledging the "Catch-22 of responding to microaggressions" (p. 279), describing the clashing of realities when individuals confront others on their microaggressive behaviors. Ironically,

Microaggression Theory: Influence and Implications, First Edition. Edited by Gina C. Torino, David P. Rivera, Christina M. Capodilupo, Kevin L. Nadal, and Derald Wing Sue.
© 2019 John Wiley & Sons, Inc. Published 2019 by John Wiley & Sons, Inc.

their own work has been vulnerable to these very critiques; many scholars deny and distort microaggression scholarship—perhaps a reflection of a clashing of privileged and unprivileged worldviews or perspectives.

Without a doubt, there has been well-orchestrated ideological critique that has tried to silence evidence of oppression by delegitimizing the scholarly and pedagogical fields of microaggressions, Ethnic Studies, Critical Whiteness studies, Queer Studies, Feminist programs, and faculty/students working in Solidarity with Palestine (to name just a few "hot spots" for conservative assault). Concurrently, it is also true that within psychology (and within progressive movements), activists have raised important questions about the extent to which Microaggression Theory has been (mis)used to erase structural and historic violence, and instead reduce oppression to psychological pain or trauma. Some researchers and scholars argue that a focus on "victimization" may weaken structural analyses, dilute radical struggles, and feed a narrow "identity politics" (Bar-Tal, Chernyak-Hai, Schori, & Gundar, 2009; Kelley, 2017). As Kelley (2017) writes, "Trauma is real. But reading Black experience through trauma can lead to thinking of ourselves as victims rather than agents" (p. 10). While this was never the intent of Sue and colleagues' original piece, such analyses can oversimplify complex agentic lives.

We enter this conversation with great respect for the scholars and activists who have set forth a microaggression analysis; who have made visible the "invisible" and made public the private injuries that racial/sexual/gender minorities have had to endure. Nadal has effectively migrated microaggression theory from the academy into circulation through social media—amplifying the visibility and wounding of people who sit at racial/gender/sexual intersects when comments are expressed as presumably "innocent" but experienced as assaults. Microaggression theory validates the experiences of those who have been targets and educates those who have been (un)witting perpetrators. Consider, for instance, a BuzzFeed article inspired by Nadal's compelling photo exhibit of microaggressions within the LGBT community (Nigatu, 2014). In his collage of images and words, Nadal displays "the everyday encounters of subtle discrimination that people of various marginalized groups experience throughout their lives." Interested in educating the public, animating a radical contestation of "normativity," and documenting the psychic and physical health consequences of microaggressions, Nadal initiated a project that would make visible and circulate in popular culture the banal ways in which microaggressions adversely affect those targeted. In his book, *That's So Gay! Microaggressions and the Lesbian, Gay, Bisexual and Transgender Community*, Nadal (2013) articulates how cumulative microaggressions that may seem innocent to perpetrators can accumulate into symptoms of depression, distress, and physical health concerns. Such a body of work is a remarkable accomplishment in "revolting" times.

The purpose of this chapter is to bridge the microaggressions literature with our own scholarship on how structural violence moves under the skin of young people and transforms into social action. Our work draws not only from microaggression theory but also from broader frameworks of minority stress theory and studies on everyday discrimination. We are rooted in a framework developed by Fine and Ruglis (2009) that calls for interrogating "circuits of dispossession and resistance" (p. 20). Simply stated, we study how structures and histories of oppression affect groups of young people; how dispossession in one arena (e.g., school or family) bleeds into other arenas (e.g., homelessness or health); and how resistance can be mobilized not only within groups but also across groups in solidarity.

Throughout the chapter, we refer to our project *What's Your Issue?*— a national participatory survey by/about lesbian, gay, bisexual, transgender, queer (LGBTQ+)[1] and gender expansive (GE) youth—of various self-identities and racial backgrounds. Using this data (and a discussion about the process of the project), we ask two questions in this chapter:

1. Under what conditions does the experience of structural oppression (whether measured as microaggressions, discrimination, and/or minority stress) provoke activist engagements?
2. Under what conditions does an analysis of in-group oppression foster both in-group and cross-group solidarities?

What's Your Issue?

In 2014, María Elena Torre and Michelle Fine were asked to meet with three philanthropists—all lesbian and each of different racial and ethnic backgrounds—who knew our work on critical participatory action research in women's prisons and with highly marginalized youth. While their philanthropic portfolios focused on the needs of LGBTQ+ and GE Youth of Color, they were deeply frustrated that the small pool of existing national research on the experiences of LGBTQ+ youth (a) focused primarily on depression, bullying, suicide, and HIV; (b) rarely included "BTQ+" or GE youth; (c) drew from largely White and "out" samples; (d) failed to include young people exiled to the social margins; and (e) was never designed by, or from the perspective of young people.

These philanthropists knew that LGBTQ+/GE Youth of Color were in the forefront of a wide range of community organizing projects; yet, they were concerned that in mainstream LGBTQ political forums (e.g., campaigns for marriage equality or ending *Don't Ask, Don't Tell* policies in the military), LGBTQ+ youth were portrayed largely as victims or deficient. Worse, LGBTQ+ youth's

---

[1] We use LGBTQ+ to refer to people who identify as lesbian, gay, bisexual, transgender, queer, questioning, intersex, asexual, or other identities that are either not heterosexual or cisgender.

rich knowledge and understandings of the complex structural intersections of sexuality, gender, immigration, housing, mass incarceration, family violence, street violence, inadequate health care, aggressive policing, and serious miseducation were silenced. While these funder philanthropists supported activist groups, organizations, and sheltering spaces (e.g., UndocuQueer, Foster by Gay, BreakOUT! and Detroit Represent!), the experiences of these young people were not included in the empirical tales traditionally circulated by mainstream LGBTQ+ advocates for equal rights. They worried that the effects of respectability politics and desires for assimilation were, in the words of our youth colleague and coresearcher, Shear Avery, "cis-tematically"[2] excluding these stories from the narratives of human rights "Equality" campaigns, shoving LGBTQ+ young people into yet another closet.

The funders knew that gender expansive, trans, and queer youth were disproportionately homeless, in foster care, and involved with juvenile justice; that many young people find the binaries of gay/lesbian and heterosexual, as well as male and female, to be psychically violent "straight" jackets. They knew that the very identity politics that had ushered victories in the courts and at the ballot box also erased the "inconvenient truths" about gender and sexual fluidity, flexibility, and contingency of young sexual bodies. With very important exceptions of scholars who did this work (e.g., Birkett et al., 2014; Diamond, 2013; Greene, 2008; Irvine, 2010; Kosciw et al., 2014; Payne & Smith, 2014; Tate, Youssef, & Bettergarcia, 2014), the field needed more intersectional research on the landscape of structural violence against LGBTQ+ and gender queer Youth of Color. Thus, these funders sought a national participatory project that could gather narratives and responses from a much wider berth of queer, trans, and gender nonconforming young people living at the margins—specifically those young People of Color who might tell a different story about the desires, betrayals, dreams, demands, and radical imaginaries. And with that, *What's Your Issue?* (or WYI) was born.

Building the Advisory Board/Designing a National Participatory Survey

A national Participatory Action Research (PAR) project is a daunting (and perhaps even naive) endeavor. So to ground ourselves in and across place, we invited a very diverse research coalition (by geography, race/ethnicity, sexuality, gender expression, and lived experience) to sketch the design.[3] We set out

---

[2] Shear Avery uses the blended word of "cisgender" and "systemically" to signify the ways that cisgenderism and rigid gender binaries are oppressive in most systems and institutions (S. Avery, personal communication, June 24, 2016).

[3] We struggled over constructing "comparative categories"; we reject the normative social science tradition of damage-based evidence, pointing to group level differences as "disparities" that "stick" to some bodies and not others. However, working closely with queer youth

to create the WYI survey as a queer survey of radical wills (and won'ts), with LGBTQ+/GE young people, primarily young LGBTQ+/GE People of Color, through a critical praxis of participatory research.

To begin, we recruited and facilitated a national advisory collective of half youth and half adults—nearly all LGBTQ+ and gender expansive. Most were working at the intersections of racial/sexual justice, immigration and sexuality, and disability and sexuality. Youth were from rural and urban areas, high schools and youth centers, foster care agencies, and Gay Straight Alliances. While our primary colleagues were young people, we also sought to include expertise and representation from some adult artists, activists, educators, and researchers. All of us were deeply situated in place—eager and anxious to analyze how circuits of oppression and resistance migrate across place and time.

We contacted groups of youth activists across the country—some who were focused on LGBTQ+ issues, but others who were also involved in activities like spoken word, immigration struggles, social media, and public radio. We worked together with squatting youth and DREAMers, young people in foster care, and those who were precariously housed. We provided funding for food and supplies used in "survey-making parties" across the country where young people generated survey themes, developed items, and eventually edited the multiple drafts of the survey in Tucson, Seattle, rural Montana, New Orleans, Miami, and across the country. We drew items from "traditional" youth surveys and sat those items next to "homegrown" items created by youth to tap issues of meaning, urgency, debate, desire, and controversy in the lives of LGBTQ+ and GE youth in their communities. A full copy of the final survey is available at whatsyourissue.com.

Preliminary Analyses of Precarity, Microaggressions, and Survivance

We present below the data from a sample of almost 6,000 LGBTQ+/GE young people about discrimination, coping, and activism. As a framework, however, we want readers to understand the conditions of structural precarity in which queer and trans young people, particularly queer and trans Youth of Color, have been situated in the contemporary political economy of neoliberalism, while also now navigating the era of Trump. To nest these lives within a structural framework, we created a Precarity Index, assessing the extent to which a young person would rate themselves as unstably housed, experiencing food insecurity, vulnerable to police, at risk of being pushed out of school, worried about Immigration Control Enforcement (or ICE), and/or anxious about

---

movements, we collectively decided we could not white-out the devastating consequences of punishing young people for transgressing the social political mandates of heteronormativity, racism, or misogyny all of which propel banishment from families, exile from church, abuse from police, alienation in schools, and violence on the streets for far too many.

Percentage of LGBTQ & GE Youth Reporting Experiences of Precarity and Discrimination in the Last 12 Months

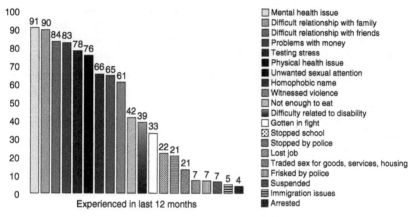

Figure 15.1 Precarity and Discrimination Experiences.

relationships in schools, bathrooms, bullying, with intimate adults and peers. With extraordinary help from organizations across the nation working with youth in general, youth on the rim, and LGBTQ+/GE youth, our survey sample draws from every state in the nation, Puerto Rico, and Guam and includes 3,012 trans/nonbinary respondents and 2,350 cisgender respondents; 3,467 who identify as White only, and 2,302 as Youth of Color.

We created the Precarity Index to assess the cumulative, over time, and horizontal, across sectors, experiences of precarity (e.g., unstable housing, pushed out of school, food insecurity, financial distress). We found important, if unsurprising, group-level differences, presented in Figure 15.1. When the data is disaggregated by gender (trans/nonbinary/genderqueer/GNC vs. cisgender) and race/ethnicity (Youth of Color vs. White only), we find that Youth of Color experience significantly more Precarity than White youth ($p = .000$) and Trans/Gender nonbinary/Gender fluid youth experience significantly more Precarity than Cisgender youth ($p = .004$). When researchers "find" significant differences by race/ethnicity or gender/sexuality, they/we must acknowledge that these differences derive in large part from real, structural conditions of discrimination—not from some "demographic fantasy" about the group itself. These differences are systemic results of the betrayal, exile, and moral exclusion from all sorts of institutional barriers like labor industries, economy, schooling, housing, and family love.

Further, our results indicate that age matters. While our findings may be conflated by younger respondents who may still be living at "home," an analysis of our sample of 14–24 year olds found our older respondents were significantly

Table 15.1 Correlations Between Precarity/Discrimination and Health Indicators.

Health indicator	Precarity index	Discrimination
General health (Higher = Better)	−.349[**]	−.276[**]
k6, psychological distress (Higher = Worse)	.430[**]	.437[**]
Suicidal ideation (Higher = More frequent)	.355[**]	.346[**]
Traded sex for goods, services, or housing (0 = No, 1 = Yes)	.310[**]	.218[**]

Note: [**] Correlation is significant at the .001 level.

more likely to experience structural precarity than younger respondents. Such findings cast a shadow of skepticism on the "It gets better" message coined by Dan Savage (a cisgender gay White male writer) that has spread across mainstream media—focusing, perhaps naively, on hope without a political analysis of the conditions and consequences of structural oppression.

While it comes as no surprise, it is disturbing to confirm, again, that structural precarity is highly negatively correlated with physical health and psychological well-being, and positively correlated with suicidal ideation and involvement in survival sex (see Table 15.1). State-sponsored, institutionally enforced, and family-reproduced levels of punishment of queer youth have severe consequences for our collective well-being.

Turning now toward microaggressions, there is a parallel, and an unsurprising but devastating, pattern: trans and nonbinary youth and Youth of Color systematically (or cis-tematically) and significantly experience more everyday

Table 15.2 Experiences of Discrimination by Gender.

Gender identity	Race	Mean	Std. deviation	N
Trans, genderqueer, GNC	White	2.1078	.96162	1,736
	POC	2.4120	1.09700	1,112
	Total	2.2265	1.02722	2,848
Cisgender	White	1.7427	.89894	1,209
	POC	2.0052	1.02702	869
	Total	1.8525	.96310	2,078
Total	White	1.9579	.95332	2,945
	POC	2.2335	1.08555	1,981
	Total	2.0687	1.01749	4,926

discrimination and other indicators of microaggressions (people staring, being misgendered, assuming incorrect gender, and less respect) than cisgender and White participants (significant and sizeable main effects for gender and race/ethnicity, but no interaction). Microaggressions accumulate from intimate and stranger adults in authority, and from peers along these vectors of oppression. Whether we probe about police, teachers, health-care providers, religious leaders, or peers, trans and nonbinary youth and Youth of Color report feeling far less respect than cisgender and White participants.

The Paths from Oppression to Activism

While the patterns displayed above are as predictable as they are horrific, there is an important empirical turn in the road. For a significant core of LGBTQ+ youth, the cumulative consequences of oppression provoke various forms of activism. We draw from the quantitative and qualitative material to unpack this relationship. First, from the survey, scores on the everyday discrimination scale are significantly and positively associated with engagement in and varied forms of activism ($r = .22$, $p = .000$). Greater experiences of discrimination are associated with more types (focused on race, environmental, LGBTQ & GE issues, etc.) of activism one gets involved in and the more activism behaviors they report (writing letters, signing petitions, saying something on social media, etc.). Further, the correlations are stronger for trans/nonbinary youth than cis youth (see Figure 15.2) and for Youth of Color than White youth (see Figure 15.3). Our analysis suggests that Youth of Color and trans/nonbinary youth embody a well-resourced, experience-filled, and accelerated capacity to convert discrimination into activism. Youth of Color and trans/nonbinary youth

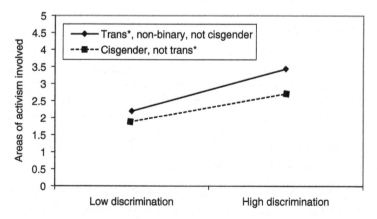

Figure 15.2 Associations between Discrimination and Activism by Gender.

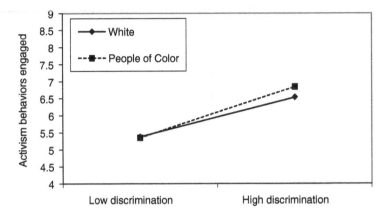

Figure 15.3 Associations between Discrimination and Activism by Race.

hold experiences, memories, and narratives that provide a framework in which they can identify patterns of discrimination—allowing them to move from "victim" to "agent" with a kind of psychological agility.

Since discrimination and activism were linked quantitatively, we were encouraged to turn to the qualitative data where we begin to see *how* these two variables embrace. We reviewed all responses to two open-ended items from the survey: Tell us a story about your proudest moment, and if you were to create a political banner, what would it say? We offer, provisionally, three critical psychological moves between oppression and liberation/self-acceptance/activism: (a) claiming self/insisting on the right to transgress; (b) speaking back to power/challenging dominant hierarchies; and (c) embracing collective movements and solidarities.

Claiming Self/Celebrating Transgression

Anzaldúa (1987) once wrote, "Wild tongues cannot be tamed, they can only be cut out" (pp. 53–54). In the thousands of qualitative responses, we heard an overwhelming sense of pride and joy from youth speaking aloud with wild tongues, demanding humanity and recognition, and the right to transgress to family, church, friends, stepping out of shadows, or simply to self. Below are some of the vibrant and multifaceted answers that participants provided— matched with their self-identifiers—when they were asked, "What would you say has been your proudest or happiest moment?"

- *When I was 21, I came out to my parents and while it was definitely not my happiest moment, looking back now I would have to say it's my proudest. I had to work hard and overcome a lot of things internally to be who I am today.*

We were in a hotel room for my sister's volleyball tournament and I handed them a manila folder with a letter I had been writing for the past six months. Coming out to first generation immigrant Christian parents is not an easy feat. I broke their hearts when I told them who I was and while we are still in the process of figuring out how to love and understand each other, I'm glad I can die unapologetic about who I am or what I stand for. (Lesbian, cis female, and Chinese American)

- *When I graduated with my "male" color [graduation] gown and my chosen name being called. All my family and school [were] there, and it reaffirmed everything I went through. I also felt proud because the majority of the people there didn't support me and I was throwing it in their faces.* (Trans man publicly, gender fluid, nonbinary personally, White)

Other participants staked out claims and complexity in form of self-banners, responding to the prompt, "If you were designing a banner about you what would it say?"

- *I break my chains all by myself.* (Queer, likes all girls and trans guys, femme boy, Black.)
- *Queer, Trans, Asian, Disabled; Scientist, Artist, Actor. Imagine me complexly.* (I have no idea anymore, really. Bigender and Japanese.)
- *Transgender, nonbinary, autistic, proud.* (Pansexual, demiboy, White.)
- *Womyn, queer, immigrant, Mexican... How much more powerful could I get in this country?* (Dykeness, cisgender, Mexican to the core, Maya/Aztec.)
- *Just because I am a man with a vagina doesn't mean I can't be proud about it.* (Gay, male, transman, Caucasian.)
- *Recovering Catholic Republican, now queer and homeless. "And they'll know we are Christians by our love."* (Bisexual, cmanc/transman, Whiter than a Republican debate in the Alaskan panhandle.)

When we give young people, especially those who are trans or nonbinary, the opportunity to describe themselves in their own words, we affirm that their voices matter, in a society where they are told otherwise. When they feel normalized, validated, and affirmed, they transform their struggles and traumas into empowerment and activism.

Speaking Back to Those Who Oppress: Challenging Cis-Tems of Dispossession and Humiliation

While many young people who took the survey reported engaging in activism through relentless re-claiming of complex selves, others spoke of direct contestation of dominant hierarchies—busting open normative binaries and refusing with rage the intimate and structural betrayals they endure. These participants are the trans-generational babies of Sylvia Rivera, the renowned Stonewall veteran, gay liberation and transgender activist, and founding member of Gay Liberation Front and Gay Activist Alliance—carrying her words into the 21st century: "Hell hath no fury like a drag queen scorned" (as cited in Osorio, 2017). In the spirit of fury and wicked sarcasm, a number of young people designed banners brilliantly and expeditiously, in the middle of a lengthy survey, to speak back with sharp tongues to people and systems (or "cis-tems") of oppression. For instance, one young person proclaimed: "*If I were designing a sign/banner about me, I would probably say along the lines of 'I'm a borderline, hard of hearing, learning disabled genderfluid girl. GET OVER IT!'*" Others shared similar sentiments:

- *Flexing my complexion over White supremacy.* (Gay, boy, multiracial, Brazilian, Latino, Asian, Black.)
- *People's opinion doesn't matter to me.* (I'm not active, girl, African American.)
- *Lesbians have more orgasms than straight women.* (Pansexual, primarily women, female, White, but my father is mulatto, and my grandparents were Black.)
- *I was born gay, were you born an asshole?* (Natural, queer, woman, White.)
- *Speaking words of wisdom, let them pee.* (Demisexual, a mess, man.)
- *How am I still here?* (Blackity Black, I'm Black yall, and Afrolatinx.)
- *Hug a Gay Mormon: We Exist!* (I am a boy who is attracted to other boys for emotional and physical reasons. I am Caucasian, and my family stems from Europe... I am LDS but have Jewish heritage, practice both Jewish and Christian holidays, White.)
- *We were all born naked and the rest is drag.* (Goldstar, platinum, double mile day, male with some drag queer influences, sombrero AF, Latino, Native.)
- *Don't judge a book by its genitals.* (I like girls mostly. But I'm not entirely comfortable with sex. Most of the time I feel male, but sometimes it's more blurry. I have constant bad feelings about my chest regardless, GNC, White.)
- *Skin color is not probable cause.* (Queer, nonbinary, Black.)
- *A critical mind is a terrible thing to systematically destroy.* (Pansexual/bisexyal, ugh, agender, Black/White, White/Hispanic, Cuban.)
- *We're here. We're queer. Can I go back to bed?* (Queer, cis, femme, White.)

With a sharp sense of entitlement to justice (and a caustic and healthy suspicion about dominant hierarchies), these young people rehearse, queer, and challenge traditionally popular, mainstream tropes (e.g., "Speaking words of wisdom"; "Don't judge a book"; "A mind is a terrible thing to waste") as they charge hypocrisy and seduce morality from those who would dare to judge or deny them. Again, they write as if in translation of James Baldwin (1972), "People who treat other people as less than human must not be surprised when the bread they have cast on the waters comes floating back to them, poisoned" (p. 192).

Embodying Activisms/Embracing Solidarities

Finally, some young people directly translate discrimination to solidarity, recognizing the vast circuits of dispossession and circuits of resistance they share with other movements (Fine & Ruglis, 2009). While many are not formally educated about the work of the activists that came before them, these young people act in the world as if inspired by James Baldwin, who once was quoted saying:

> You think your pain and your heartbreak are unprecedented in the history of the world, but then you read. It was [books] that taught me that the things that tormented me most were the very things that connected me with all the people who were alive, who had ever been alive. (Howard, 1963, p. 89)

And so, their banners stitch their bodies into the waves of social movements:

- *My PGP (preferred gender pronoun) is PRISON ABOLITION.* (Queer, GNC, butch, White.)
- *I am #tamirrice. I am #sandrabland. I am #john crawford.* (Straight?, nonbinary, two spirit, GNC, Peruvian.)
- *Vietnamese queer femme sorceress mermaid out to abolish the American state.* (Queer, nonbinary, gender nonconforming, genderqueer, Southeast Asian/Vietnamese.)
- *Reparations for slavery and femme labor.* (Queer, femme, Black.)
- *Radical by necessity not choice.* (Gay as hell, queer, pansexual, fluid, female, Korean, Asia.)
- *I am more than the identities that White supremacy has created for me.* (Queer, cis woman, Pakistani American.)
- *Yellow Peril supports Black Power.* (Lesbian, cis, biracial, Japanese/White.)
- *Action that does not benefit PoC is ALWAYS white supremacy #AbolishMarriage.* (Queer, nonbinary, GNC, White/Arab.)
- *Disability is about a system of oppression, not about me being broken.* (Straight, transman, White.)
- *I didn't choose to be Asian or mixed or autistic or queer. But I'm damn proud of it and I'll be telling the people who try to make me suppress that until I see justice for every battle.* (Panromantic, woman, cisgender, GNC, half Korean, half Jewish.)

These young people see the world at an angle—allying themselves with movements far and near; they boldly process personal discriminations and microaggressions into public struggles across communities, dedicated to "justice for every battle."

We catalogue and present these comments so that readers may also appreciate the prism of queer lines of vision, hear how delicately humor is laced with pain, notice how embodiments of hate and refusals are stitched into the responses of young people who dare to transgress the man-dates of hetero-normativity, gender binaries, and white nationalism, by choice or not, with pride and perhaps fear, often alone, sometimes with friends and family, increasingly with allies online, and pouring onto the streets in waves of protests.

Theorizing "Conversion Strategies": Metabolizing Oppression into Activism

Queer and trans youth, particularly Youth of Color, report cumulative experiences of state violence, social discrimination, and intimate/stranger microaggressions. They also narrate individual and collective insistence on radical recognition and intersectionality, and they model stunning "conversion" struggles as they morph oppression into varied forms of activism. The quantitative and qualitative material gathered force us to reject psychology's simplistic reliance on the tired and deceiving trilogy of internalization, self-hatred, and resilience. Assimilation is not the goal; acceptance and tolerance are not the desire; radical transformations of social arrangements are the demand. Rather than inclusion, these young people shoved to the margins stand tall, as they seek recognition and justice. They do not simply internalize or resist, but they *metabolize* oppression and betrayal, claiming their complex humanity and asserting the right to transgress. They contest dominant representations and challenge the hypocrisies of race/ethnicity, (dis)ability, gender, sexuality and class categories, and stratifications. And they embrace ferociously solidarities with other "Others" under siege.

As the evidence demonstrates, they are microaggressed and discriminated against disproportionately in schools, on the streets, in subways, in airports, by public agencies, by the police, and also often violated/betrayed at home. And second, they are also despised for the strength of their convictions; their lack of desire to assimilate and critique of dominant hierarchies and hypocrisies; the fact that they will not bow to the mandates of the current colonial project. Indeed, they embody and "flaunt" their differences with words and bodies that transgress; they align in solidarity with groups they are supposed to repel, and they model a bold commitment to dis-order.

Federici (2004), feminist activist and educator, published a groundbreaking book entitled *Caliban and the Witch: The Body and Primitive Accumulation* in which she argues that the killing and burning of witches was foundational to establishing capitalism as a system that domesticated women's reproductive labor. The title draws from two Shakespearean characters: Caliban, the rebel who resists slave labor, and the Witch who refuses to submit to patriarchy and capitalism. In Federici's analysis, for capitalism to survive, the twinned refusals of women and slaves had to be annihilated; their transgressions had to be punished, publicly; they had to be shamed and tamed. At this moment in history, in the United States, immigrant and undocumented youth, Muslims, African Americans, and queer and trans youth (especially those of color) are the "witches" being hunted and mounted on the wall for display, by a nation struggling to reclaim White supremacy, Christian fundamentalism, and heteronormativity. These young people are twice punished for transgression, and still they refuse to comply. Our research suggests that young people targeted by state-sponsored, socially reinforced, and sometimes family-enacted microaggressions are indeed wounded by the betrayals, but have also developed clever tactics, alone, online, and in movements, to "convert" oppression to activism.

References

Anzaldúa, G. (1987). *Borderlands: la frontera* (Vol. 3). San Francisco, CA: Aunt Lute Press.

Baldwin, J. (1972). *No name in the street*. New York, NY: Dell.

Bar-Tal, D., Chernyak-Hai, L., Schori, N., & Gundar, A. (2009). A sense of self perceived collective victimhood in intractable conflicts. *International Review of the Red Cross, 91*, 229–248.

Birkett, M., Russell, S. T., & Corliss, H. L. (2014). Sexual-orientation disparities in school: The mediational role of indicators of victimization in achievement and truancy because of feeling unsafe. *American Journal of Public Health, 104*, 1124–1128.

Diamond, L. M. (2013). Sexual-minority, gender-nonconforming, and transgender youths. In D. Bromberg & W. O. Donohue (Eds.), *Handbook of child and adolescent sexuality: Developmental and forensic psychology* (pp. 275–300). Oxford: Elsevier Press.

Federici, S. (2004). *Caliban and the witch*. Brooklyn: Autonomedia.

Fine, M., & Ruglis, J. (2009). Circuits and consequences of dispossession: The racialized realignment of the public sphere for US youth. *Transforming anthropology, 17*, 20–33.

Friedersdorf, C. (2015, September). *Readers lament the rise of victimhood culture*. *The Atlantic*. https://www.theatlantic.com/politics/archive/2015/09/readers-lament-the-rise-of-victimhood-culture/405784.

Greene, B. (2008). African American lesbians and gay men. In H. Neville (Ed.), *The psychology of African Americans: A handbook*. Thousand Oaks, CA: Sage.

Howard, J. (1963, May). Doom and glory of knowing who you are. *LIFE, 54*, 86–90.

Irvine, A. (2010). We've had three of them: Addressing the invisibility of lesbian, gay, bisexual, and gender nonconforming youths in the juvenile justice system. *Columbia Journal of Gender & Law, 19*, 675–701.

Kelley, R. D. G. (2017, January). *Black study, Black struggle. Boston Review of Books*. Retrieved from http://bostonreview.net/forum/robin-d-g-kelley-black-study-black-struggle.

Kosciw, J. G., Grestak, E. A., Palmer, N. A., & Boesen, M. J. (2014). *The 2013 National School Survey: The experiences of lesbian, gay, bisexual, and transgender youth in our nation's schools.* Washington, DC: GLSEN.

Lewis, J., & Neville, H. (2015). Construction and initial validation of the gendered racial microaggressions scale for black women. *Journal of Counseling Psychology, 62,* 289–302.

Meyer, I. H. (2015). Resilience in the study of minority stress and health of sexual and gender minorities. *Psychology of Sexual Orientation and Gender Diversity, 2,* 209–213. Washington, DC: American Psychological Association.

Nadal, K. L. (2013). That's so gay! In *Microaggressions and the lesbian, gay, bisexual and transgender community.* Washington, DC: American Psychological Association.

Nigatu, H. (2014, February). *19 LGBT microaggressions you hear on a daily basis. BuzzFeed.* Retrieved from https://www.buzzfeed.com/hnigatu/19-lgbt-microaggressions-you-hear-on-a-daily-basis.

Osorio, R. (2017). Embodying truth: Sylvia Rivera's delivery of "Parrhesia" at the 1973 Christopher Street liberation day rally. *Rhetoric Review, 36,* 151–163.

Payne, E., & Smith, M. (2014). The big freak out: Educator fear in response to the presence of transgender elementary school students. *Journal of Homosexuality, 61,* 399–418.

Pierce, C., Carew, J., Pierce-Gonzalez, D., & Willis, D. (1978). An experiment in racism: TV commercials. In C. Pierce (Ed.), *Television and education* (pp. 62–88). Beverly Hills, CA: Sage Publications.

Runyowa, S. (2015, September) *Microaggressions matter. The Atlantic.* https://www.theatlantic.com/politics/archive/2015/09/microaggressions-matter/406090.

Sue, D. W., Capodilupo, C. M., Torino, G. C., Bucceri, J., Holder, A., Nadal, K. L., & Esquilin, M. E. (2007). Racial microaggressions in everyday life. *American Psychologist, 62,* 271–286.

Tate, C. C., Youssef, C. P., & Bettergarcia, J. N. (2014). Integrating the study of transgender spectrum and cisgender experiences of self-categorization from a personality perspective. *Review of General Psychology, 18,* 302–312.

Williams, D. R., & Mohammed, S. A. (2009). Discrimination and racial disparities in health: Evidence and needed research. *Journal of behavioral medicine, 32,* 20–47.

Part V

Microaggressions: Interventions and Strategies

16

Microaggressions: Workplace Interventions

Aisha M. B. Holder

Workplace discrimination remains a persistent and serious problem in the United States despite several decades of legislation prohibiting these occurrences. According to the Equal Employment Opportunity Commission (EEOC), 32,309 charges of race-based workplace discrimination, 20,857 age-based, and 26,934 sex-based charges were filed in 2016 (EEOC, 2016a). These numbers have remained fairly consistent over the last 20 years and continue to have a deleterious impact on individuals and organizations. Several studies have linked discrimination to negative physical and psychological health outcomes such as cardiovascular concerns, anxiety, psychological distress, and increased depressive symptomatology (Clark, Anderson, Clark, & Williams, 1999; Lewis et al., 2006; Hammond, Gillen, & Yen, 2010). The consequences of discrimination for organizations range from monetary costs of litigation (Goldman, Gutek, Stein, & Lewis, 2006) to negative job outcomes (Bergman, Palmieri, Drasgow, & Ormerod, 2012; Chan, Lam, Chow, & Cheung, 2008). Financial consequences of workplace discrimination are staggering. In 2016, the EEOC secured more than $482 million for victims of discrimination in private, state, and local governments, and federal workplaces (EEOC, 2016b). Such workplace discrimination contributes to decreased organizational commitment, poorer supervisor relationships, and lower confidence in employees' ability to achieve professional goals (Gifford, 2009).

To address the issue of workplace discrimination, many organizations have made significant investments, especially through diversity initiatives, to reduce the experience of discrimination for their employees. Diversity training, for example, has developed over the years to an estimated eight-billion-dollar industry (Hansen, 2003). Despite critical efforts made with time and money, organizations continue to be plagued with discriminatory behavior. One reason for persistent inequalities in the workplace is the tendency to focus on overt or "old-fashioned" forms of discrimination at the expense of subtle, implicit,

Microaggression Theory: Influence and Implications, First Edition. Edited by Gina C. Torino, David P. Rivera, Christina M. Capodilupo, Kevin L. Nadal, and Derald Wing Sue.

contemporary manifestations of discrimination. Workplace discrimination is often thought of as more overt occurrences described as when "differential and unfair treatment is clearly exercised with visible structural outcomes" and manifests in ways that are intentional and easily recognizable, and are directed at individuals based on his or her stigmatized characteristics (Van Laer & Janssens, 2011, p. 1205). This type of discrimination is generally considered socially unacceptable and can be directly addressed through legal and organizational policies. However, the presence of everyday, subtle, and seemingly innocuous experiences of workplace discrimination can compromise an organization's ability to cultivate inclusive high-performing work cultures that drive success and facilitate opportunities for employees to realize their full potential.

A common and frequently expressed form of modern discrimination can be communicated through microaggressions. First coined by psychiatrist Chester Pierce, microaggressions are defined as "everyday verbal, nonverbal, and environmental slights, snubs, or insults, whether intentional or unintentional, which communicate hostile, derogatory, or negative messages to target persons based solely upon their marginalized group membership" (Sue, 2010). The consequences of microaggressions are viewed to be just as significant, if not more so, as the effects of overt discrimination (Jones, Peddie, Gilrane, King, & Gray, 2016). Indeed, the ambiguous nature of microaggressions makes it difficult to identify and assess whether an offense was committed (Hebl, Foster, Mannix, & Dovidio, 2002). As a result, microaggressions can be more disorienting and stressful to marginalized populations in comparison to explicit manifestations of discrimination. In addition, uncertainty about the best way to respond also contributes to distress when one encounters microaggressions (Sue, 2010).

Options for addressing subtle forms of discrimination in the workplace are less apparent. While several organizations have clear policies and procedures in place for reporting discriminatory practices and protecting against forms of retaliation, there are fewer options for employees to report casual and inadvertent demeaning occurrences that are too often minimized. Experiences of subtle discrimination, like microaggressions, can be more damaging than overt discrimination because of their frequency and chronic effects, whereas overt discrimination may occur less often (Van Laer & Janssens, 2011). For example, consider how many times a Black woman may experience being called the "N" word in the workplace compared to incidents where she is expected to speak for, and on behalf of, all People of Color or simultaneously experiences invisibility and hypervisibility—all examples of microaggressions.

What then are some strategies organizations can employ to reduce the presence of workplace microaggressions and their damaging consequences? The following analysis falls into two broad sections. The first section will offer best practices for utilizing training to address microaggressions, and the second one will explore more systemic interventions that can be integrated into organizational practices to address these subtle forms of discrimination.

Diversity Training

Diversity training represents a long-standing practice that companies have relied upon to reduce bias and discrimination in the workplace. Early diversity training initiatives in the 1960s and 1970s focused on legislation and compliance (Arand & Winters, 2008). Following landmark legislation such as Title VII of The Civil Rights Act of 1964 that prohibit employment discrimination based on race, color, religion, sex, and national origin, many companies introduced diversity training, primarily in response to several discrimination lawsuits filed by the EEOC that resulted in financial losses and negative publicity for them. Diversity training content focused on laws and company policies. Such training experiences during this era were often not well received by participants in part because they perpetuated the notion that women and People of Color were receiving preferential treatment, and that training content had little connection to ways in which behavioral change would improve business (Arand & Winters, 2008). Compliance-based training evolved in the 1980s to focus on helping women and People of Color assimilate into existing corporate cultures (Fernandez, 1981). By the late 1980s to 1990s, diversity training shifted to include all employees focusing on sensitivity and awareness and appreciation of differences. Later and until now, paradigms of diversity training have focused on positioning diversity and inclusion as key ingredients to achieve business success.

Let us now consider some objectives that can be explored in workplace diversity training to addresses microaggressions.

Enhance Awareness of Biases

The process of exploring biases can be a difficult one resulting in a defensive stance that does not promote learning and change. This process can produce anger, anxiety, hostility, and painful experiences for participants. The suggestion that individuals of privileged identities whether it be race, gender, or sexual orientation, for example, could have unknowingly committed a discriminatory act causes cognitive dissonance and defensiveness (Rozas & Miller, 2009). Sue and Sue (2013) referenced these reactions as "emotional roadblocks" that interfere with productive dialogue that can lead to a deeper understanding. It is important to emphasize that microaggressions are most similar to aversive discrimination because they generally occur below the level of awareness of well-intentioned people (Sue & Capodilupo, 2008; Sue et al., 2007). A person can engage in discriminatory behavior while maintaining a conscious sense that he or she would never discriminate against someone on the basis of a diversity characteristic like race or gender (Jimenez, Pasztor, Chambers, & Fujii, 2015). While everyone is susceptible to committing implicit forms of discrimination, it is important to note the role of power inherent in privileged identities, such as White, male, and heterosexual, in determining standards by which marginalized groups are compared (Sue, 2010).

A starting point for this discussion in a diversity training session about microaggressions might be for employees to reflect on what inclusive work environments mean to them and what best practices they have observed in creating and maintaining inclusive work environments. This question highlights the point that inclusion means different things for different people. It also emphasizes the importance for employees to understand the lens they use to filter or process their experiences in the workplace in pursuit of becoming culturally competent leaders. Ultimately, inclusive workplaces should represent arenas where employees can leverage their talents to contribute to the success of their institutions, feel respected, and be their authentic selves.

The Implicit Association Test (IAT) can be an effective tool to provide a tangible demonstration of one's implicit bias. The IAT is a computer-based measure that requires participants to quickly categorize two target concepts with an attribute (e.g., the concepts of Black and White with the attribute "pleasant"). Faster responses are interpreted as stronger associations than slower responses that represent more difficult pairings. The IAT is thought to measure implicit attitudes—"introspectively unidentified (or inaccurately identified) traces of past experience that mediate favorable or unfavorable feeling, thought, or action toward social objects" (Greenwald & Banaji, 1995, p. 8). Given that the IAT requires participants to make a series of quick judgments, researchers believe that IAT scores may reflect attitudes that people may be hesitant or unwilling to reveal publicly (Greenwald, McGhee, & Schwartz, 1998). Because the design of the IAT addresses the problem of the tendency of respondents to answer questions in a way that will be viewed favorably by others, it can be useful in addressing individuals' attitudes toward stigmatized groups (Devine, 2001).

In using the IAT in training sessions, it is important for facilitators to have a firm understanding of how the test works. Also, it is crucial to convey the difference between having implicit biases and being prejudiced toward others. The IAT may reveal biases that an individual does not necessarily endorse or believe to be consistent with his or her value system. Nonetheless, it is important to acknowledge that implicit biases can predict behavior. Thus, it is imperative for employees to enhance awareness of their hidden biases and understand how they influence actions. A best practice to suggest to employees before taking the IAT or other assessment that measures implicit bias is to not share their specific results but rather share thoughts, reflections, and observations with fellow group members after having completed the test. Facilitators can offer suggestions on how employees can address undesired biases toward certain groups that surfaced after completing IAT. It is important for employees to not underestimate the power of being more aware of their implicit biases and how they can impact judgments and actions. Facilitators can also suggest seeking information and experiences that can counter undesired preferences for particular groups.

When facilitating diversity training discussions that enhance awareness of biases, it is important to establish ground rules in the beginning of the training in order to create a safe space for productive dialogue. Examples of ground rules include using "I" statements to encourage participants to speak from their own experience instead of generalizing. Participants must also respectfully challenge ideas and ask questions without engaging in personal attacks. Another best practice is to encourage participants to be committed to active engagement and listening, noting that change happens with everyone's participation. It is important to also consider organizational levels and the types of relationships among participants in training sessions (Bell, Goodman, & Ouellett, 2016). Various levels of power in organizational hierarchy can influence individuals' confidence about whether it is safe to talk about their experiences in a group setting. Direct reports can have concerns that what they share in training sessions could be used against them by a manager, resulting in adverse consequences for their career. Conversely, managers can be afraid of losing credibility by appearing ignorant and less informed which can compromise their credibility.

Increase Knowledge of Microaggressions

There continues to be stark differences in the realities between privileged and stigmatized populations. For example, studies reveal that African Americans believe that racism is a persistent problem that impacts every realm of their lives, while most Whites believe that racism is an experience of the past (Sue, 2010). This perception was particularly heightened following the election of Barack H. Obama as the 44th President of the United States where many believed that America was now a postracial society. Workplace diversity training should educate employees about the shift from overt forms of discrimination to more contemporary, subtle forms of discrimination like microaggressions. Employees should know that although microaggressions were initially studied in the context of racial indignities, today microaggressions are examined in the context of various groups marginalized on the basis of gender, sexual orientation, socioeconomic status, and physical disability (Sue, 2010). Additionally, diversity training content should include the taxonomy of microaggressions that fall into three major categories: microinsults, microinvalidations, and microassaults (Sue, 2010). Microinsults are characterized by communications that demean a person's racial, gender or sexual orientation, heritage, or identity. An example of a microinsult in the workplace is the assumption that an Asian employee is good in math and science. Microinvalidations are unconscious communications that negate the thoughts, feelings, or experiential reality of individuals such as People of Color and women. One of the damaging aspects of microinvalidations is the power to impose reality upon marginalized populations. Common examples of microinvalidations in the workplace include the myth of a meritocracy where there is the belief that all groups have an equal opportunity to succeed, and there is an equally level playing field. The message is that success in the workplace, for example, is solely the result of personal attributes such as intelligence and hard work, but this is only possible in the absence of systemic oppressions which can derail career advancement. The philosophy of color blindness where there is an unwillingness to see differences based on race, gender, or sexual orientation represents the denial of privilege and power (Sue, 2010) and communicates the message that employees who are People of Color, women, or LGBT should assimilate to the dominant culture. Microassaults are similar to what has been called "old fashioned" discrimination, which is conscious, intentional attitudes and behavior that communicate hostility to marginalized groups. Examples include using racial epithets or the display of sexually explicit material in the workplace. While microassaults can occur in the workplace, organizations generally have clear policies for addressing this type of microaggression.

However, it is just as important to address criticisms of microaggressions in diversity training to bolster employee "buy in" about the existence and impact of microaggressions in the workplace. One of the criticisms of microaggressions is that they are no different from interpersonal slights that all people experience regardless of diversity identity (Schacht, 2008; Thomas, 2008). However, microaggressions are constant and continuous experiences unlike interpersonal slights that may be time limited. Also, unlike interpersonal snubs, microaggressions contain double messages. For example, when a Black employee is frequently told he or she is "articulate," it may appear to be a compliment, however, the meta-communication conveys disbelief that a Black individual has the ability to effectively communicate given the persistent stereotype that Black people are intellectually inferior. Additionally, in contrast to general interpersonal slights, microaggressions are rooted in historical injustices that impact multiple realms of the lives of stigmatized populations. By definition, microaggressions are repetitive patterns that have a cumulative effect on employees in the workplace making them feel devalued and excluded. While each behavior may seem inconsequential, as part of a pattern, this cumulative effect negatively impacts commitment, self-confidence, and productivity at work.

Discuss the Impact of Microaggressions on Management Decisions and Employee Performance

The factors by which we attribute success can be rooted in the unconscious biases we have about marginalized populations. Managers can attribute different reasons for the success of top-rated performers in their departments. For example, when talking about men, they tend to attribute success to permanent features such as being clever, analytical, and quick thinking. When talking about women, managers can attribute success to more situational or temporary factors such as being part of a good team or a particular product doing well in the marketplace, or sheer luck. Managers' expectations of direct reports and direct reports' expectations of themselves are key factors in how well people perform at work. Managers communicate their expectations of direct reports whether conveyed consciously or unconsciously. Employees in turn perform in ways that are consistent with the expectations they have discerned from their managers. Known as the Pygmalion effect, "the way managers treat their subordinates is subtly influenced by what they expect of them" (Livingston, 1988, p. 121). Staff members can excel in response to managers' messages that they are capable of success and expected to excel. Conversely, staff performance can be undermined with subtle messages communicating the opposite. These cues are often subtle such as a manager communicating less frequently with certain employees or providing positive feedback to some and not others with similar performance. This can have consequences for stigmatized populations. Thus, it is imperative to emphasize in diversity training sessions that workplace bias diminishes an organization's ability to fully utilize its employees' skills and abilities. With increased competition, organizations not only need to attract a diverse workforce but also to maximize the potential of all employees to solve increasingly challenging problems.

What Are Some Effective Leadership Behaviors That Can Help Reduce Microaggressions in the Workplace?

A common workplace microaggression is invisibility where the presence of stigmatized group members is disregarded and their contributions are diminished or dismissed entirely. Invisibility conveys the message that they are not recognized for their worth and value as employees. Therefore, it is important for managers to ask themselves to what extent do they solicit opinions and feedback from a wide range of colleagues who might have different perspectives from their own. When addressing employees, consider whether you send messages that encourage participation from everyone. Be explicit in inviting participation and acknowledging that all responses are welcomed and important. Are you conveying verbal and nonverbal cues signaling that you are being attentive to the speaker? Consider the degree to which you consistently and equitably acknowledge employees who were first to come up with a good idea or colleagues for doing a good job.

Another common workplace microaggression is exclusion from work-related meetings, social gatherings with colleagues, and access to informal networks, mentors, and sponsors. A factor that contributes to these exclusionary practices is the limited contact and familiarity that members of privileged groups have with marginalized groups. In diversity training sessions, participants can consider to what extent they make efforts to share unwritten rules of the organization with colleagues who historically may not have had access to circles of power. To what extent do you get to know all of your colleagues? Are you conscious about how your relationship with people on your team may be perceived or may impact work projects? Examine whether you disseminate appropriate levels of information to direct reports. Take a few minutes to get to know your colleagues by engaging in appropriate nonbusiness-related conversations to show some interest in them as individuals. In fact, since experiences of microaggressions in the workplace can increase feelings of mistrust, it is important to demonstrate such interest and a willingness to understand these occurrences.

Not Just for Business: A Case for Addressing Microaggressions

The business case approach has been used in diversity training to illustrate how diversity and inclusion drive business success and profitability. Inclusive teams lead to better innovation and outperform heterogeneous teams (Hewlett, Marshall, & Sherbin, 2013). Inclusion promotes innovation and creative ideas, as well as better solutions for clients. Addressing microaggressions reduces employee turnover because it results in employees feeling included, valued, and respected. However, research has shown that focusing only on monetary and economic justifications for diversity may create barriers to promoting deeper understanding and integration of individuals from different social identity groups (Dipboye & Colella, 2005; Konrad & Linnehan, 1999; Kossek, Lautsch, & Eaton, 2006). One can argue that relying solely on the business case approach can minimize or ignore the historical experience of stigmatized groups and the intergroup tensions that exist, thus diminishing opportunities to achieve the benefits of diverse groups (Jones, King, Nelson, Geller, & Bowes-Sperry, 2013). Organizations should not only commit to diversity and to remedy discrimination in the workplace solely to advance their bottom line but to demonstrate a genuine care about people and their experiences in the workplace (Greening & Turban, 2000; Turban & Greening, 1997). Perceived organizational sincerity can increase the effectiveness of organizational programs and not have them appear to be superficial efforts (Smith, Botsford, King, Knight, & Hebl, 2010).

While workplace diversity training is a strategy for addressing microaggressions, it is not sufficient for creating sustainable organizational change. Training can be helpful in shifting attitudes, but it falls short in terms of implementing inclusive practices throughout an organization. There is greater commitment and effectiveness when diversity and inclusion are integrated into organizational functions and roles.

Systemic Interventions

Recruitment

A common microaggression in the workplace is the lack of representation of historically marginalized individuals, particularly in senior-level roles. This reality stands in contrast to the often touted company mission of inclusion and meritocracy. A typical reason offered to explain lack of representation is that organizations have a difficult time finding diverse talent. Therefore, an important start for organizations if they are to explore more systemic interventions for dealing with microaggressions is to examine how they search for talent. Management engagement is vital for attracting diverse talent. When managers are actively involved in bolstering diversity in their organizations, they begin to think of themselves as diversity champions (Dobbin & Kalev, 2016). For instance, research has shown that managers are more willing to participate in college recruitment programs targeting women and minorities when they are charged with helping their organization find a variety of promising talent. They become determined to return to the workplace with candidate recommendations from underrepresented groups (Dobbin & Kalev, 2016). Research has found that 5 years after a company launches a college recruitment program targeting female employees, the share of White women, Black women, Latina women, and Asian American women in management positions increases by about 10% on average. A program focused on minority recruitment can increase the proportion of Black male managers by 8% and Black female managers by 9% (Dobbin & Kalev, 2016). This kind of strategy can help in building a diverse candidate slate for open positions.

Another effective organizational tool for reducing discrimination in recruitment is the use of structured employment interviews. Structured interviews represent a standardized way of comparing job candidates. An employer creates an interview protocol with questions focused on a set of competencies related to open positions. In contrast, unstructured interviews are characterized as free form discussions that can allow for more subjectivity in how candidates are evaluated. Indeed, the use of structured interviews has been shown to leave stigmatized individuals less vulnerable to interpersonal discrimination and has demonstrated fewer racial differences in ratings than unstructured interviews (Arvey & Faley, 1988; Huffcutt & Roth, 1988). Research has also shown that providing structure during interviews can reduce interpersonal discrimination because it provides nonstigmatized interviewers with a behavioral protocol that lowers their anxiety in interviews with stigmatized individuals (Avery, Richeson, Hebl, & Ambady, 2009).

Leadership and Manager Accountability

Organizations that are most successful in achieving managerial diversity have human resources systems and practices that hold managers and executives accountable for meeting diversity objectives such as actively developing women and People of Color (Corporate Leadership Council, 2002). One of the downfalls of diversity initiatives designed to address discrimination in the workplace is when they are positioned as ad hoc efforts instead of integrated into core functions of an institution, including how managers are evaluated. Managing diversity should be viewed as an integral part of leadership and represent a core competency used to assess management's performance and inform promotion and compensation decisions. Strong performance on diversity-related efforts should be viewed as strategically as performance in a core operating business with a clear vision, defined metrics to track progress and increased investments toward initiatives that produce results (Rice, 2012). Measurement tools include 360° feedback, peer reviews, employee attitude surveys, and performance reviews that include diversity objectives and periodic reviews of employee demographics (Giscombe & Mattis, 2002). Managers should be expected to know the people in their departments and have clear plans for developing their direct reports. It is important to have transparency, objectivity, and accountability in tracking how employees gain access to key assignments and leadership development opportunities, both of which are critical for career advancement. These efforts can help organizations develop sustainable talent pipelines and succession plans that include diverse talent and ultimately contribute to increasing representation of marginalized individuals. Organizations that are progressive in developing diverse talent use a different strategy by emphasizing results, utilizing objective measures of competency, and by focusing on measurable track records (Thomas & Gabarro, 1999).

Sponsorship

Marginalized employees are often excluded from formal and informal networks in the workplace, which can have adverse implications for career advancement. Access to influential networks provides insights into informal and unwritten rules and values of an organization.

When decision makers in an organization are significantly different from the persons whose competence they are judging, natural biases can emerge and impact decisions. The notion of competence can be quite subjective depending on the perceiver. This is particularly important for marginalized populations like People of Color and women who are often subjected to the microaggression of being intellectually inferior. Evaluators in organizations can advocate aggressively for employees who are most like them which is particularly problematic given that circles of power in the workplace continue to be dominated by White males. This instance is where the power of sponsorship can play a critical role in promoting equity in the workplace. This special type of relationship goes beyond the scope of mentoring that tends to focus on career advice and providing feedback (Ibarra, Carter, & Silva, 2010). Sponsorship is when an individual in the company uses his or her influence with senior management to advocate for the success of protégés. Sponsorship involves elevating a protégé's visibility in arenas of power, advocating for key assignments and promotions, and placing one's own reputational capital on the line to facilitate a protégé's continued advancement (Hewlett, Jackson, Cose, & Emerson, 2012). Behaviors of effective sponsors include connecting protégés to other organizational leaders. Providing "air cover" or sense of safety is important in sponsorship relationships. It can encourage protégés to take risks and provide the critical feedback often needed to enhance workplace performance (Hewlett et al., 2012).

Mentoring Programs

Mentoring is an effective tool for addressing exclusionary practices in the workplace some of which have resulted from discriminatory practices and microaggressions. Mentoring is important in facilitating career success and has been linked to career advancement, increased compensation, and greater career satisfaction (Bova, 2000). The challenge with mentoring is that not everyone has equal access to mentors. These relationships tend to be informal and unstructured, and senior leaders who are often majority White and male tend to gravitate toward employees with similar backgrounds, whether racial cultural identity, gender, or socioeconomic status. Mentors can help in maximizing a protégé's potential by providing career advice and insight about the political landscape of a company. They also provide psychosocial support through encouragement, acceptance, friendship, and role modeling that influences a protégé's professional identity and competence (Chao, Walz, & Gardner, 1992; McGlowan-Fellows & Thomas, 2004). Mentors help protégés build a large and diverse network of relationships (Thomas, 1990). Organizations can sponsor formal and informal mentoring opportunities to provide employees, particularly stigmatized groups, with access to senior-level leaders. Formal programs include organizations creating matches between mentors and protégés, monitoring the relationship and measuring the program's effectiveness. Informal mentoring activities can include networking events, conversations, and panel discussions that provide exposure and visibility.

Employee Resource Groups

Affinity groups represent another strategy for addressing workplace microaggressions. Employee networking groups are an inclusive group of employees who voluntarily work together to advance an organization's diversity strategy. The initiatives and activities of these groups should support and be aligned to an organization's people and talent agendas as well as its business goals and diversity strategy. Employee resource groups provide social support, professional development, and access to role models. A key component to the success of affinity groups is to have an executive sponsor, usually a senior-level person in the organization, who engages members of the group, provides support and advocacy for issues and challenges with other senior managers, and champions the missions and goals of these groups.

Conclusion

In conclusion, interventions designed to address microaggressions in the workplace cannot be effective without commitment from senior leaders. Management must be consistently explicit and clear about its commitment to inclusion, as well as ways in which diversity vision and goals are integrated into business practices and measured for effectiveness. Senior leaders have an opportunity in their daily roles to reflect and respond to how they show up in their organizations as role models of inclusion and to consider how they define diversity and inclusion. Imagine if senior leaders embraced opportunities to think about their employees' personal experiences of what it means to be an outsider as a way of informing their understanding of inclusion (Groysberg & Connolly, 2013) and to deepen their understanding and compassion for marginalized populations. Senior leaders must hold managers accountable for results related to diversity and inclusion. When employees understand that senior leadership is serious about eradicating discrimination in their organizations, they are more likely to embrace efforts designed to enhance inclusion.

References

Arand, R., & Winters, M. F. (2008). A retrospective view of corporate diversity training from 1964 to the present. *Academy of Management Learning & Education, 7*(3), 356–372. doi:10.5465/AMLE.2008.34251673.

Avery, D. R., Richeson, J. A., Hebl, M. R., & Ambady, N. (2009). It does not have to be uncomfortable: The role of behavioral scripts in Black–White interracial interactions. *Journal of Applied Psychology, 94*, 1382–1393. doi:10.1037/a0016208.

Arvey, R. D., & Faley, R. H. (1988). *Fairness in selecting employees* (2nd ed.). Reading, MA: Addison-Wesley.

Bell, L. A., Goodman, D. J., & Ouellett, M. L. (2016). Design and facilitation. In M. Adams & L. A. Bell (Eds.), *Teaching for diversity and social justice* (pp. 55–94). New York, NY: Routledge.

Bergman, M. E., Palmieri, P. A., Drasgow, F., & Ormerod, A. J. (2012). Racial/ethnic harassment and discrimination, its antecedents, and its effect on job-related outcomes. *Journal of Occupational Health Psychology, 17*, 65–78.

Bova, B. (2000). Mentoring revisited: The Black woman's experience. *Mentoring & Training, 8*, 5–16. doi:10.1080/713685511.

Chan, D. K.-S., Lam, C. B., Chow, S. Y., & Cheung, S. F. (2008). Examining the job-related, psychological, and physical outcomes of workplace sexual harassment: A meta-analytic review. *Psychology of Women Quarterly, 32*, 362–376.

Chao, G. T., Walz, P., & Gardner, P. D. (1992). Formal and informal mentorships: A comparison on mentoring functions and contrast with nonmentored counterparts. *Personnel Psychology, 45,* 619–636. doi:10.1111/j.1744-6570.1992.tb00863.x.

Clark, R., Anderson, N. B., Clark, V. R., & Williams, D. R. (1999). Racism as a stressor for African Americans. *American Psychologist, 54,* 805–816. doi:10.1037/0003-066X.54.10.805.

Corporate Leadership Council. (2002). *The role of leadership in diversity efforts.* Washington, DC: Corporate Executive Board.

Devine, P. G. (2001). Implicit prejudice and stereotyping: How automatic are they? *Journal of Personality and Social Psychology, 81*(5), 757–759. doi:10.1037/0022-3514.81.5.757.

Dipboye, R. L., & Colella, A. (2005). *Discrimination at work: The psychological and organizational bases.* Mahwah, NJ: Lawrence Erlbaum.

Dobbin, F., & Kalev, A. (2016). Why diversity programs fail. *Harvard Business Review, 94,* 52–60.

EEOC. (2016a). *Charge statistics FY 1997 through FY 2016.* Retrieved from https://www.eeoc.gov/eeoc/statistics/enforcement/charges.cfm.

EEOC. (2016b). *What you should know: EEOC's fiscal year 2016 highlights.* Retrieved from https://www.eeoc.gov/eeoc/newsroom/wysk/2016_highlights.cfm.

Fernandez, J. P. (1981). *Racism and sexism in corporate life.* Lexington, MA: Lexington Books.

Gifford, G. T. (2009). *Stigma in the workplace: Testing a framework for the effects of demographic and perceived differences in organizations* (Unpublished doctoral dissertation). University of Nebraska, Lincoln.

Giscombe, K., & Mattis, M. C. (2002). Leveling the playing field for women of color in corporate management: Is the business case enough? *Journal of Business Ethics, 37,* 103–119.

Goldman, B. M., Gutek, B. A., Stein, J. H., & Lewis, K. (2006). Employment discrimination in organizations: Antecedents and consequences. *Journal of Management, 32,* 786–830. doi:10.1177/0149206306293544.

Greening, D. W., & Turban, D. B. (2000). Corporate social performance as a competitive advantage in attracting a quality workforce. *Business & Society, 39,* 254–281.

Greenwald, A. G., & Banaji, M. R. (1995). Implicit social cognition: Attitudes, self-esteem, and stereotypes. *Psychological Review, 102,* 4–27. doi:10.1037/0033-295x.102.1.4.

Greenwald, A. G., McGhee, D. E., & Schwartz, J. K. L. (1998). Measuring individual differences in implicit cognition: The implicit association test. *Journal of Personality and Social Psychology., 74,* 1464–1480. doi:10.1037/0022-3514.74.6.1464.

Groysberg, B., & Connolly, K. (2013). Great leaders who make the mix work. *Harvard Business Review, 91*, 68–76.

Hammond, W. P., Gillen, M., & Yen, I. H. (2010). Workplace discrimination and depressive symptoms: A study of multi-ethnic hospital employees. *Race and Social Problems, 2*(1), 19–30. doi:10.1007/s12552-010-9024-0.

Hansen, F. (2003). Diversity's business case: Doesn't add up. *Workforce, 82*(4), 28–32.

Hebl, M. R., Foster, J. B., Mannix, L. M., & Dovidio, J. F. (2002). Formal and interpersonal discrimination: A field study of bias toward homosexual applicants. *Personality and Social Psychology Bulletin, 28*, 815–825.

Hewlett, S. A., Jackson, M., Cose, E., & Emerson, C. (2012). *Vaulting the color bar: How sponsorship levers multicultural professionals into leadership.* Los Angeles: Center for Talent Innovation.

Hewlett, S. A., Marshall, M., & Sherbin, L. (2013). How diversity can drive innovation. *Harvard Business Review, 91*, 30–30.

Huffcutt, A. I., & Roth, P. L. (1988). Racial group differences in employment interview evaluations. *Journal of Applied Psychology, 83*, 179–189. doi:10.1037/0021-9010.83.2.179.

Ibarra, H., Carter, N. M., & Silva, C. (2010). Why men still get more promotions than women. *Harvard Business Review, 88*, 80–126.

Jimenez, J., Pasztor, E. M., Chambers, R. M., & Fujii, C. P. (2015). *Social policy and social change: Toward the creation of social and economic justice.* Thousand Oaks, CA: Sage.

Jones, K. P., King, E. B., Nelson, J., Geller, D. S., & Bowes-Sperry, L. (2013). Beyond the business case: An ethical perspective of diversity training. *Human Resource Management, 52*, 55–74. doi:10.1002/hrm.21517.

Jones, K. P., Peddie, C. I., Gilrane, V. L., King, E. B., & Gray, A. L. (2016). Not so subtle: A meta-analytic investigation of the correlate of subtle and overt discrimination. *Journal of Management, 42*, 1588–1613.

Konrad, A. M., & Linnehan, D. (1999). Affirmative action: History, effects and attitudes. In G. Powell (Ed.), *Handbook of gender and work* (pp. 429–452). Thousand Oaks, CA: Sage.

Kossek, E. E., Lautsch, B. A., & Eaton, S. C. (2006). Telecommuting, control, and boundary management: Correlates of policy use and practice, job control, and work-family effectiveness. *Journal of Vocational Behavior, 68*, 347–367. doi:10.1016/j.jvb.2005.07.002.

Lewis, T. T., Everson-Rose, S. A., Powell, L. H., Matthews, K. A., Brown, C., Karavolos, K., et al. (2006). Chronic exposure to everyday discrimination and coronary artery calcification in African-American women: The SWAN heart study. *Psychosomatic Medicine, 68*, 362–368.

Livingston, J. S. (1988). Pygmalion in management. *Harvard Business Review, 66*, 121–130.

McGlowan-Fellows, B., & Thomas, C. S. (2004). Changing roles: Corporate mentoring of black women. *International Journal of Health, 33*, 3–18.

Rice, J. (2012). Why make diversity so hard to achieve? *Harvard Business Review, 90*, 40–40.

Rozas, L., & Miller, J. (2009). Discourses for social justice education: The web of racism and the web of resistance. *Journal of Ethnic & Cultural Diversity in Social Work, 18*(1–2), 24–39. doi:10.1080/15313200902874953.

Schacht, T. E. (2008). A broader view of racial microaggression in psychotherapy. *American Psychologist, 63*, 273. doi:10.1037/0003-066X.63.4.273.

Smith, A., Botsford, W. E., King, E. B., Knight, J. L., & Hebl, M. R. (2010). *The view from outside: How reputation influenced public evaluations of an organization's commitment to diversity.* Unpublished manuscript.

Sue, D. W. (2010). *Microaggressions in everyday life: Race, gender, and sexual orientation.* Hoboken, NJ: Wiley.

Sue, D. W., & Capodilupo, C. M. (2008). Racial, gender, and sexual orientation microaggressions: Implications for counseling and psychotherapy. In D. W. Sue & D. Sue (Eds.), *Counseling the culturally diverse: Theory and practice.* Hoboken, NJ: Wiley.

Sue, D. W., Capodilupo, C. M., Torino, G. C., Bucceri, J. M., Holder, A. M. B., Nadal, K. L., & Esquilin, M. (2007). Racial microaggressions in everyday life: Implications for clinical practice. *American Psychologist, 62*, 271–286. doi:10.1037/0003-066X.62.4.271.

Sue, D. W., & Sue, D. (2013). *Counseling the culturally diverse: Theory and practice* (6th ed.). Hoboken, NJ: Wiley.

Thomas, D. A. (1990). The impact of race on managers' experiences of developmental relationship (mentoring and sponsorship): An intra-organizational study. *Journal of Organizational Behavior, 2*, 479–492. doi:10.1002/job.4030110608.

Thomas, D. A., & Gabarro, J. J. (1999). *Breaking through: The making of minority executives in America.* Boston, MA: Harvard Business School Press.

Thomas, K. R. (2008). Macrononsense in multiculturalism. *American Psychologist, 63*, 273.

Turban, D. B., & Greening, D. W. (1997). Corporate social performance and organizational attractiveness to prospective employees. *Academy of Management Journal, 40*, 658–672. doi:10.2307/257057.

Van Laer, K., & Janssens, M. (2011). Ethnic minority professionals' experiences with subtle discrimination in the workplace. *Human Relations, 64*, 1203–1227. doi:10.1177/0018726711140926.

17

"Compliments" and "Jokes": Unpacking Racial Microaggressions in the K-12 Classroom

Rita Kohli, Nallely Arteaga, and Elexia R. McGovern

"Wow! You speak English so well."
– A comment made to a second generation Latino middle school student by his teacher.
"That's so great that *you* got an A on that paper!"
– A comment made to a young Black woman in high school by her White classmate.
"Why are *you* stressing? You don't need to study. Asians are naturally good at math."
– A statement made laughingly to an Asian American student in math class by a White peer.
"Are you sure you are in the right class? Auto shop is down the hall."
– A question posed by an AP English teacher to a Mexican American student on the first day of class, while laughing.
"I hope you don't have a bomb in your backpack."
– A comment made to a South Asian turban-wearing high schooler by a peer, while laughing.

Each of these quotes has been shared with us in our work as educators and educational researchers over the years from K-12 Students of Color. These comments, veiled as compliments or jokes, are what critical scholars of race have conceptualized as racial microaggressions—micro, covert manifestations of racism. Compliments, which are "polite expression[s] of praise or admiration" (McKean, 2005) and jokes, which are things people say to stir amusement or laughter, are typically understood as well-intentioned, positive communication. While intent may have a place in understanding racialized interactions, to challenge racism, however, it is important to center racially

Microaggression Theory: Influence and Implications, First Edition. Edited by Gina C. Torino, David P. Rivera, Christina M. Capodilupo, Kevin L. Nadal, and Derald Wing Sue.

charged experiences from the lens of those who are marginalized (Pérez Huber & Solórzano, 2014).

Several of the Students of Color who were targets of the comments shared that when they expressed discomfort, the perpetrator claimed positive intent—they were just offering praise, or being funny. These Students of Color, however, expressed feeling othered, criminalized, or viewed as intellectually incapable. The statements and questions in the quotes above—seemingly innocuous to some—are harmful manifestations of institutionalized racism—racial discrimination systematically enacted by laws, structures, and practices of institutions (Omi & Winant, 2014). Stereotypes of the perpetual "foreigner," the "dumb Mexican" (Valencia, 2002), or the "Muslim terrorist" (Ali, 2014) are ideologies rooted in historical and current-day policies and practices that position Communities of Color as inferior to Whites and fueled these microinteractions. Additionally, as these racial microaggressions reflect institutionalized racism, they also maintain it by subordinating Students of Color within the moment and beyond.

Using a framework of critical race theory (CRT), in this chapter we emphasize that racial microaggressions in K-12 schools are mechanisms of institutionalized racism. We analyze three case studies where Students of Color experienced microforms of racism that were framed as "compliments" or "jokes." In each of these cases, we unpack the structural root of the microaggression to understand its legacy and trauma. Our aim is to bring attention to the dynamic relationship between macro- and microracism and offer strategies for researchers and practitioners of K-12 schools to better reflect upon and transform the way Students of Color experience their education.

Critical Race Theory

Racism is the creation or maintenance of a racial hierarchy, supported through institutional power (Solórzano, Allen, & Carroll, 2002). CRT is a framework that emerged out of critical legal studies in the 1970s to illuminate racism as an ever-present barrier in U.S. racial progress (Crenshaw, 1995; Delgado & Stefancic, 2000). An interdisciplinary theory, CRT challenges ideology, policy, and practice that uses individualized explanations for racial inequity such as colorblindness and meritocracy, and instead, points to structural causes for U.S. racial hierarchies (Crenshaw, 1995). As a theory, CRT acknowledges the intersectionality of race and class oppression, explaining that race and racism were created as tools of economic exploitation (Harris, 1993). It, additionally, weaves its analysis with other factors of subordination such as sexism (Solórzano & Delgado Bernal, 2001), nativism (Pérez Huber, 2011), and ableism (Annamma, Connor, & Ferri, 2013). It is important to note that the purpose of CRT is not simply to understand racial power but also to transform it (Crenshaw, 2011).

CRT has been applied to the field of education to illuminate how, from Americanization schools (Spring, 1994) to segregation (Irons, 2004), and extreme racial inequity in education today, K-12 schools have maintained a history driven by racialization and racism (Ladson-Billings & Tate, 1995). Since its initial theoretical purpose within education discourse, CRT has expanded to include empirical research that further highlights the nuances of racism within education (Parker, 2015). Even so, racism, in its macro or micro forms, remains undertheorized in K-12 school-based research (Kohli, Pizarro, & Nevárez, 2017).

Racial Microaggressions as Racism

While overt racism continues to exist in U.S. society, everyday or mundane acts of racism also maintain the status quo (Bonilla-Silva, 2012) because they are directly linked to macrostructures of racial injustice (Essed, 1997; Holt, 1995; Lewis, 2003). Rooted in factors associated with race, such as language and culture (Smith, Yosso, & Solórzano, 2007), CRT scholars have defined racial microaggressions as follows: (a) *Subtle verbal and nonverbal assaults* directed toward People of Color, often carried out automatically or unconsciously; (b) *Layered assaults*, based on one's race, gender, class, sexuality, language, immigration status, phenotype, accent, or name; and (c) *Cumulative assaults* that take their toll on People of Color. In isolation, racial microaggressions may not have much meaning or impact; however, as repeated slights, the effect can be profound (Kohli & Solórzano, 2012).

Chester Pierce first coined the term *racial microaggressions* to describe racial offenses that are "done in automatic, preconscious, or unconscious fashion" (Pierce, 1974, p. 515). As he articulated, these microforms of racism exist as "often automatic, and non-verbal exchanges, which are 'put downs' of blacks by offenders" (Pierce, 1978, p. 66). Davis (1989) built upon Pierce's work to clarify that, from the lens of the victim, racial microaggressions are not just personal slights, but instances of racialized harm. He operationalizes them as "stunning automatic acts of disregard that stem from unconscious attitudes of white superiority and constitutes verification of black inferiority" (Davis, 1989, p. 1576).

Starting in 2001, CRT scholars of education have also built upon the concept of racial microaggressions to discuss the covert forms of systemic racism that exist in educational institutions (Allen & Solórzano, 2001; Smith et al., 2007; Solórzano, Allen, & Carroll, 2002). These scholars have argued that although often dismissed or overlooked, racial microaggressions have tangible consequences for People of Color (Smith et al., 2007). Racial microaggression research in education has primarily focused on the experiences of Students of Color in higher education who attend predominantly White institutions (Smith et al., 2007; Solórzano et al., 2002). There is, however, limited research examining the impact of racial microaggressions in K-12 schools (Carter Andrews, 2012; Kohli & Solórzano, 2012; Pérez Huber, 2011).

Method

Adapting case study methodology (Baxter & Jack, 2008) and counterstory-telling (Yosso, 2005), this chapter involves excerpts of qualitative interviews from various research projects and personal communications, presented as narratives. CRT builds upon the value and process of firsthand accounts of legal testimony and the oral traditions of Communities of Color to challenge dominant narratives through counterstories (Yosso, 2005). The narratives and analysis we share are constructed through the recollection of those who are marginalized, as a means to reframe to dominant views, myths, values, and norms shaped by stereotypes and racism. They are told from the vantage point of those oppressed to reveal structures and practices that facilitate and reproduce inequality (Yosso, 2005).

In this way, our case studies are stories conveyed and analyzed to center the perspective of the participants. Pulled from (a) a research project with teacher Candidates of Color reflecting on their racialization as K-12 students (Kohli, 2014); (b) a study of Students of Color reflecting on the racial microaggressions they experienced in school relating to their names (Kohli & Solórzano, 2012); and (c) the personal experiences of one of the authors, each case study reveals a unique nuance about racial microaggressions in K-12 schools, particularly as it relates to racialized "compliments" and "jokes." In each of the following cases, we present and analyze the narrative using a CRT lens to bridge the racial microaggressions to macroinstitutionalized racism and other forms of oppression.

Case #1: "Your vocabulary is extraordinary!"

Ashley was one of few African American students in her predominantly White elementary school. Sometimes, when she would win at tetherball or have conflict on the playground, to degrade her, peers would call her the "n-word" without any consequences from the school staff. Within a school racial climate—defined as a school's norms and values of race and interracial interactions (Byrd & Chavous, 2011)—of tolerated overt racism, students and teachers would also pay Ashley racialized "compliments." Students would often remind her how much they liked her, saying, "You're a cool Black person!" or "You're a White-Black girl" or "A proper Black person." They would tell her, "You talk proper," "you're clean," and "you're not ghetto." Her teachers would state, "Well, Ashley's different," that "Ashley's very articulate; her vocabulary is extraordinary!" When she reached high school, with much social pressure to adhere to the standards of beauty of her peers, she began straightening her hair. Her classmates would often respond to her looks, comparing her to other Black people by saying things such as, "but you—your hair is so nice and it's so clean."

Why Are These Comments Racial Microaggressions and Not Compliments?

Ashley was the target of many comments that were framed as "compliments." Her classmates and teachers felt she was smart, articulate, and clean. What was embedded in their comments, however, was that they found her smart, articulate, and clean relative to how they perceived other African Americans— unintelligent, inarticulate, and unclean. Entrenched in their seeming praise were deep-seated expressions of racism, racialized stereotypes, and hierarchical ideologies. Furthermore, layered onto these racist perceptions of Black intelligence and hygiene were also gendered perceptions of Eurocentric standards of beauty. Ashley's acceptability as a Black woman in her predominantly White K-12 school was heightened when she adhered to white norms, as she was praised when she processed and straightened her natural hair.

The comments that Ashley describes are unfortunately not uncommon.[1] Framed as praise, these layered assaults were meant to distance her from others in her community, and they were hurtful to Ashley's self- and community perception because they were fueled by (and perpetuated) anti-Blackness (Dumas & ross, 2016). The cumulative nature of racial microaggressions took their toll on Ashley and she started to internalize racism—a phenomenon that manifests when People of Color subconsciously or consciously adapt racial hierarchies of White superiority (Cross, Parham, & Helms, 1991; Pérez Huber & Solórzano, 2014). The impact of racism can sometimes be minimal and temporal, but it can also have a profound effect on the way an individual sees themselves, their culture, and the world around them (Steele, 1997). In Ashley's case, a repeated exposure to racial microaggressions caused her to accept and subscribe to racial stereotypes and attitudes of superiority to her family and community. She shared, "I felt that all black people that aren't like me are worthless. And when I would hear things from white people that [I now know] were racist and nasty, 'You talk proper, or you're not ghetto, or you're clean, or your hair is nice' I would take that as a positive. I was proud to be that way."

To understand the negative impact racial microaggressions could have on the perceptions of Students of Color, it is important to interrogate its root causes. Often, the perpetrator of racism is seen as the sole problem, in

---

[1] These forms of racial microaggressions are deep-seated and normalized within our society. In an interview during something as visible as the 2008 presidential campaign, former Vice President Joe Biden publicly "complimented" President Barak Obama as "articulate, bright and clean" (Thai & Barrett, 2007).

Ashley's case—her classmates and teachers. However, within a limited analysis, we might blame and remove particular actors, yet allow the broader climate that enabled racial microaggressions to continue. Instead, it is important to understand that the microaggressions that Ashley experienced in her K-12 education stem from and are empowered by macro forms of racism. The everyday racism said to her has a foundation in overt racialized U.S. policies and practices such as slavery, eugenics, segregation, and the development of the prison industrial complex, where many lawmakers, scientists, researchers, and educators have historically and currently articulated a biological, mental, and intellectual inferiority of people of African descent to justify their subordination (Bonilla-Silva, 2012; Hilliard, 1999; Irons, 2004). These institutionalized forms of racism manifest intersectionally and in daily ideology related to things such as standards of beauty and hair texture (Hooks, 1989), language patterns (Perry & Delpit, 1998), and perceptions of academic efficacy (Lane, 2017). While racism is woven into all facets of U.S. life, a danger of racial microaggressions is its covert nature. It can be hard to identify or call out microaggressions because they are at times framed as praise, yet they can cause lasting harm, particularly if Students of Color internalize the ideologies behind them (Kohli & Solórzano, 2012). It is within highly racialized context that we must interpret the seeming "compliments" to Ashley about her physical and intellectual attributes.

Case #2: "I wouldn't want to call you Gandhi by accident or something"

Nirupama went to a high school that was primarily Latinx and East Asian, with very few South Asian students. On her first day of tenth grade, she went to biology class. At a new school where she did not know many students, she sat quietly at her desk until it was time for roll call. When the White male teacher got to her name, he asked her to pronounce it very slowly. She responded "Ni-ru-pa-ma." He responded by laughing, "Thanks, because I wouldn't want to call you 'Gandhi' by accident or something." Nirupama recalls that the whole class of students erupted into laughter at his comment, and she felt humiliated. For the rest of the school year, her classmates continued to call her "Gandhi."

Why Is This a Racial Microaggression and Not a Joke?

Already an ethnic minority in her school, the teacher exacerbated Nirupama's isolation by comparing her identity to Gandhi, one of few South Asians referenced in K-12 history textbooks. This seeming "joke" was a tokenization of her Indian identity, equating her first name as a current young woman to the last name of a historic, world-recognized male leader, just because they broadly share a common cultural origin. When a child goes to school and their name is mispronounced or changed, it can negate the thought, care, and significance of the name, and thus the identity of the child. Additionally, this "joking" conflation is a disregard of the complexity and nuance of the billion people who share Indian culture, making this experience, albeit in micro form, an incident of racism.

The teacher's racial microaggression led Nirupama to feel humiliated within the moment. It also was embedded within, and simultaneously perpetuated, a hostile school racial climate where other students felt comfortable repeating the racialized "joke" throughout the school year. Although her peers were primarily Students of Color, unable to benefit from this racism (Omi & Winant, 2014) and likely experiencing racism within their own schooling, the action of the teacher fostered a dynamic where Students of Color were complicit in Nirupama's alienation and racialization. Whether the students had internalized the racial hierarchy (Kohli & Solórzano, 2012), or if they were just laughing along in a moment, expanding the analysis of racism to a broader institutional perspective offers insights into the relationship between the actors and the social context.

It may be easy to individualize this experience and blame the students as "bullies" or the teacher as a "bad apple" for the racism that Nirupama experienced. And while they should be held accountable, there are also larger, historical, and institutionalized structures that enable the power of microaggressions that are important to recognize if we are to understand and eradicate racial microaggressions at their roots. The sentiment that non-Western names are odd or an unwelcome inconvenience has historical and legal underpinnings. For centuries, enslaved Africans were forced to shed their names and were given the names of their masters (Irons, 2004). The names of Indigenous people were replaced with Anglo and Christian names until the 1920s (Bonnin, 1921). And more recently, in 2009, during House testimony on voter identification legislation, a Texas lawyer argued that voters of Asian descent should adopt names that are "easier for Americans to deal with" (Ratcliffe, 2009). From the inception of systemic schooling in the United States, Students of Color have been invisiblized within curriculum (Loewen, 2008), unreflected in the teaching force (Sleeter, 2008), and neglected within cultural frameworks of success (Yosso, 2005). Living in a racialized society, Nirupama woke up that day and walked into a school within a system that, for centuries, has not been designed to serve her. The joking disregard of Nirupama's name by her teacher is not something specific to him or just an unfortunate choice of words; it is backed by a legacy of racist ideology and practice, and also works to further institutionalize racism within the school culture. It is in this context of historical and current racial hierarchies that we must understand the teacher's choice to publicly disregard Nirupama's culture and identity. Similarly, it is in this context that we must begin to unpack the actions of Nirupama's classmates, Students of Color, as it relates to racism.

Case #3: "They don't steal anything, do they?"

One of the authors, Ms. Arteaga, was a Latina who attended a working-class, Southern California high school that was labeled a "dropout factory" in a popular, internationally viewed documentary. The stigma placed on her education was something that deeply impacted Ms. Arteaga's perception of herself, her school, and her community. As an adult, she became an English teacher in an urban, comprehensive public high school not too far from where she grew up. After 4 years of teaching, she was re-assigned to work at a continuation high school for students who had struggled to succeed in traditional high school contexts. When she went to sign the paperwork, a group of employees of the Human Resources (HR) department of her district offered unsolicited advice that she should not accept the placement and would be better off applying at other school districts. They thought they were doing her a favor, stating that teaching anywhere else was better than this predominantly Black and Latinx high school; that "the students were nothing but trouble." But Ms. Arteaga, however, had explicit interest in working with the population the school served. Her first day there, she was greeted by the assistant principal who shared the sentiments of the HR personnel. He warned her that she needed to be "extra cautious while working with the students." She quickly learned that the teachers at the school also shared deficit perceptions of the Students of Color on campus.

While Ms. Arteaga never attended a continuation school, she saw herself in her students, and felt troubled by the racial climate of the school. She put in effort to earn their respect and develop meaningful relationships; thus, you would often find students working on homework or socializing in her room outside of class time. One lunch period a few months into the school year, another teacher walked into the classroom and saw Ms. Arteaga eating lunch and working with several Students of Color. This teacher "joked" laughingly, "Wow, you let THEM eat lunch with you! They don't steal anything do they?" The students and Ms. Arteaga did not laugh back.

Why Is This a Racial Microaggression and Not a Joke?

The students in Ms. Arteaga's class were attending a continuation school. They had been pushed out of traditional school settings, were often labeled as "troublemakers" or "problem students," but continued to persist in their educational goals. On the day of the incident, they were spending their lunch hour working on their classwork, committed to their learning. While the teacher made the comment in a joking tone, under the veil of humor laid a stereotype that was rampant at the school—that continuation students were "thieves" and criminals. Said between adults, in front of the youth, the teacher expressed this racist sentiment about Black and Latinx students with an intention of camaraderie. While the tone was casual and warm, the content was racialized, and the incident was experienced as a racial microaggression against the Students of Color. We also assert that Ms. Arteaga experienced trauma from the comment, what we call here a second-hand racial microaggression (Pizarro & Kohli, 2017).

In psychological research, secondary trauma—or vicarious trauma—is the emotional stress that occurs when hearing about or witnessing someone else's first-hand trauma (Hesse, 2002). This is particularly impactful to those who have experienced firsthand trauma, as it can feel like a re-experience of their own personal trauma (McInerney & McKlindon, 2014). Similarly, we argue that when Teachers of Color witness racial microaggressions targeted at Students of Color, they can experience that microaggression secondhand. For Teachers of Color who feel a racial or cultural connectivity to students, and have endured similar microaggressions in their past, secondhand racial microaggressions take a toll on their well-being even when they are not the direct or intended target.

These microforms of racism directed at the Students of Color are also tied to macroracism structurally embedded within the broader schooling system. As evidenced by the acceptability and banality of the racialized stereotypes, the school operated as a hostile racial climate, where the teachers, school administrators, and district staff did not believe in the worth or integrity of students, and thus, could not truly stand as advocates for their academic and life success. Continuation schools were designed to provide alternative pathways and opportunities for students who were not succeeding in traditional schools, but unfortunately, these settings have turned into pushout factories, often the last step along the school-to-prison pipeline (Annamma, 2015). With a typically unrigorous and culturally disconnected education, and high attrition rates (many leaving for juvenile hall), Black and Latinx students are overrepresented in continuation schools and are often socialized not to believe in their academic capabilities (Malagon & Alvarez, 2010; Winn, 2011). It is in this racially disparate context of low expectations and pathways to prison that we must understand the comment made in Ms. Arteaga's classroom—a racialized comment that cannot be understood as a "joke" because it both reflects and perpetuates a cycle of Student of Color criminalization.

Interventions and Strategies

In this chapter, we provide three case studies to uncover how "compliments" and "jokes" in K-12 schools can sometimes exist as racialized microassaults. These forms of everyday racism are particularly harmful because, while it is systemically mediated by institutional racism, their mundane-ness can be invisibilizing (Pérez Huber & Solórzano, 2014). Even the most sincere and well-intended racialized comments can have long-lasting effects that can jeopardize the physiological, psychological, and academic well-being of Students of Color.

Understanding how racial microaggressions operate and analyzing their underlying root is essential if we are to move toward disrupting racism in schools. And because racial microaggressions are an intersection of individually acted and institutionally supported racism, the interventions must also exist on those levels.

Individual Responses to Racial Microaggressions

Whether you are a bystander or the target, it is hard to know what one should say or do when confronted with racial microaggressions. Because of the mask of positivity in the form of praise or humor, it can be difficult to articulate what needs to be challenged without disrupting a perceivably cordial interaction and being framed as "angry," "too sensitive," or "too politically correct," all additional examples of microaggressions that are mechanisms used to shut down challenges to racism. And while the onus to end racism should not fall upon People of Color and there is no prescribed response to mitigate its power or impact, Students of Color, their families, and their teachers have articulated the need to name and respond to racial microaggressions.

A primary step in mitigating the detrimental impact of a racial microaggression is to be able to identify that it is happening. If one can classify something as racism, even internally, it is easier to prevent its message from shaping one's perception. A secondary step in addressing racial microaggressions on an individualized level is articulating that racism to the perpetrator, as naming racism can—at times—facilitate a climate of reflection. The power dynamic and broader racial climate of a context, however, shape if and how target(s) or bystander(s) of racial microaggressions feel agency to respond.

Unfortunately, because of limited explicit racial discourse and colorblind approaches in formal educational contexts (Bonilla-Silva, 2012), it can be difficult to pinpoint the racial undertones in a particular setting. Similar to psychological research on racial socialization that has connected explicit racial discourse to improved self-esteem in Children of Color (Gaskin, 2015), racial literacy is a skill that can offer an ability to identify what is problematic in the interaction, to thwart an internalization of its effects, and to challenge the injustice, no matter how micro in form. Racial literacy is one's ability "to probe the existence of racism and examine the effects of race and institutionalized systems on their experiences and representation in US society," including the "ability to read, discuss, and write about situations that involve race or racism" (Sealey-Ruiz, 2013, p. 386). Considering the need for students to navigate racism that covertly diminishes their educational and career opportunities, the literature points to the importance of racial literacy to shift their understanding from an individualized to an institutional analysis of racism (Epstein & Gist, 2015). Having this skill allows Students of Color the ability to connect, as we did throughout this chapter, the microaggression to larger macro systems of institutional racism. This process helps to deindividualize situations, remove themselves as responsible for any pain or failure they may feel, and rearticulate the situation with a clear vision of the role of power within inequity (Pérez Huber & Solórzano, 2014).

Building the racial literacy of Students of Color within schools is not easy, however. It requires meaningful and open discussions of race and racism in the classroom (Sealey-Ruiz, 2013). Rogers and Mosley (2006), in a study with second graders, demonstrated how racial literacy development is an interactive process requiring teachers adept at guiding students through a development of race and racism discourse. While teachers' racial literacies vary widely, teachers with high ability to navigate and discuss race have made a considerable difference in students' ability to process and confront racism. What this means is that for individual actors in K-12 schools to have the skills to confront racial microaggressions, students, families, teachers, and staff must be able to comfortably and skillfully discuss race and racism. This can involve including racial literacy as a qualification in the hiring process of teachers, creating professional development sessions that address issues of race, culture, power, and inequity, and engaging in regular racial discourse in the curriculum.

Institutional Responses to Racial Microaggressions

In addition to the responses of individual actors, eliminating the presence of racial microaggressions in schools would require the end of policies and practices of racism. While many facets of structural racism exist beyond the control of school administrators or teachers because they extend historically and societally, there are still things that schools can do to protect students from their impact on school grounds. Creating a positive racial climate is an important component to preventing Students of Color from enduring the harm of racial microaggressions. School racial climate is a school's norms and values around race and interracial interactions (Byrd & Chavous, 2011). Student and teacher demographics, classroom and professional development curriculum, discipline practices, and cultural responsiveness are all aspects of school racial climate and can dictate how and if racism has a place in the everyday policies and practices of a campus. Diversifying the teaching staff, building upon the community cultural wealth of Students of Color (Yosso, 2005), and having regular reflections and open discussions of racial equity and racism on campus are all things that can support a positive racial climate.

An additional piece of shifting school racial climate is allowing Students of Color to create or access third spaces/counterspaces—places where they can feel supported and validated in their racialized experiences (Nuñez, 2011). Building from higher education research on Students of Color who are constantly dealing with racial microaggressions in their education, studies have shown that these safe havens can be an important strategy for their academic survival (Grier-Reed, 2010). In K-12 settings these practices can also be incredibly useful, providing or cocreating spaces where students can critically analyze microaggressions to not internalize or normalize these practices. Like Ms. Arteaga's classroom, this can be as simple as opening up the classroom during lunch or before or after school.

Discussion and Implications

In this chapter, we present several case studies that articulate some of the nuances of racial microaggressions, as they exist in K-12 schools. Despite the intent of the perpetrator, a seeming compliment or joke can have detrimental impact on People of Color if it embodies racialized stereotypes. As discussions of microaggressions become more popularized and part of mainstream discourse, our fear is that they get watered down and framed as insults that are enacted individually and can be addressed by reprimanding that person— telling him/her that what they said is wrong. We write this chapter to emphasize that the power of racial microaggressions comes from legacies of racism. It is not just the words that are said, but it is the ideologies that are represented in the words and are supported by historical and current policies of dehumanization, domination, and exclusion. Thus, eliminating the existence of racial microaggressions in K-12 education requires strong racial literacies and positive racial climates where equity, community cultural wealth, and racial justice are constantly reflected in the everyday structures, practices, and interactions of schools.

References

Ali, A. I. (2014). A threat enfleshed: Muslim college students situate their identities amidst portrayals of Muslim violence and terror. *International Journal of Qualitative Studies in Education, 27*(10), 1243–1261.

Allen, W. R., & Solórzano, D. (2001). Affirmative action, educational equity and campus racial climate: A case study of the University of Michigan Law School. *Berkeley La Raza LJ, 12,* 237.

Annamma, S. A. (2015). Disrupting the school-to-prison pipeline through disability critical race theory. In L. D. Drakeford (Ed.), *The race controversy in American education* (pp. 191–211). Santa Barbara, CA: Praeger.

Annamma, S. A., Connor, D., & Ferri, B. (2013). Dis/ability critical race studies (DisCrit): Theorizing at the intersections of race and dis/ability. *Race Ethnicity and Education, 16*(1), 1–31.

Baxter, P., & Jack, S. (2008). Qualitative case study methodology: Study design and implementation for novice researchers. *The Qualitative Report, 13*(4), 544–559.

Bonilla-Silva, E. (2012). The invisible weight of whiteness: The racial grammar of everyday life in contemporary America. *Ethnic and Racial Studies, 35*(2), 173–194.

Bonnin, G. (1921). *American Indian stories.* Washington DC: Hayworth.

Byrd, C. M., & Chavous, T. (2011). Racial identity, school racial climate, and school intrinsic motivation among African American youth: The importance of person–context congruence. *Journal of Research on Adolescence, 21,* 849–860.

Carter Andrews, D. J. (2012). Black achievers' experiences with racial spotlighting and ignoring in a predominantly White high school. *Teachers College Record, 114*(10), 1–46.

Crenshaw, K. (1995). *Critical race theory: The key writings that formed the movement.* New York: The New Press.

Crenshaw, K. W. (2011). Twenty years of critical race theory: Looking back to move forward. *Connecticut Law Review, 43*(5), 1253–1352.

Cross, W. E., Jr., Parham, T. A., & Helms, J. E. (1991). *The stages of Black identity development: Nigrescence models.*

Davis, P. C. (1989). Law as microaggression. *The Yale Law Journal, 98*(8), 1559–1577.

Delgado, R., & Stefancic, J. (2000). *Critical race theory: The cutting edge.* Philadelphia: Temple University Press.

Dumas, M. J., & ross, k. m. (2016). "Be real black for me": Imagining blackCrit in education. *Urban Education, 51*(4), 415–442.

Epstein, T., & Gist, C. (2015). Teaching racial literacy in secondary humanities classrooms: Challenging adolescents' of color concepts of race and racism. *Race Ethnicity and Education, 18*(1), 40–60.

Essed, P. J. (1997). Racial intimidation: Socio-political implications of the usage of racist slurs. In S. H. Riggins (Ed.), *The language and politics of exclusion: Others in discourse* (pp. 131–152). Thousand Oaks, CA: SAGE Publications, Inc.

Gaskin, A. (2015). *Racial socialization: Ways parents can teach their children about race.* CYP News: American Psychological Association.

Grier-Reed, T. L. (2010). The African American student network: Creating sanctuaries and counterspaces for coping with racial microaggressions in higher education settings. *Journal of Humanistic Counseling, Education, and Development, 49*(2), 181–188.

Harris, C. I. (1993). Whiteness as property. *Harvard Law Review,* 1707–1791.

Hesse, A. R. (2002). Secondary trauma: How working with trauma survivors affects therapists. *Clinical social work journal, 30*(3), 293–309.

Hilliard III A. G. (1999). Language, diversity, and assessment—Ideology, professional practice, and the achievement gap. In C. T. Adger, D. Christian, & O. Taylor (Eds.), *Making the connection: Language and academic achievement among African American students* (pp. 125–136). McHenry, IL: Delta Systems Co.

Holt, T. C. (1995, February). Marking race, race-making, and the writing of history. *American Historical Review, 100*, 1–20.

hooks, b. (1989). *Talking back: Thinking feminist, thinking black.* New York: South End Press.

Irons, P. H. (2004). *Jim Crow's children: The broken promise of the Brown decision.* New York: Penguin.

Kohli, R. (2014). Unpacking internalized racism: Teachers of color striving for racially just classrooms. *Race Ethnicity and Education, 17*(3), 367–387.

Kohli, R., Pizarro, M., & Nevárez, A. (2017). The "new racism" of K-12 schools: Centering critical research on racism. *Review of Research in Education, 41*(1), 182–202.

Kohli, R., & Solórzano, D. G. (2012). Teachers, please learn our names!: Racial microaggressions and the K-12 classroom. *Race Ethnicity and Education, 15*(4), 441–462.

Ladson-Billings, G., & Tate, W. F. (1995). Toward a critical race theory of education. *Teachers College Record, 97*(1), 47.

Lane, M. (2017). Reclaiming our queendom: Black feminist pedagogy and the identity formation of African American girls. *Equity & Excellence in Education, 50*(1), 13–24.

Lewis, A. E. (2003). Everyday race-making: Navigating racial boundaries in schools. *American Behavioral Scientist, 47*(3), 283–305.

Loewen, J. W. (2008). *Lies my teacher told me: Everything your American history textbook got wrong.* New York: The New Press.

Malagon, M., & Alvarez, C. (2010). Scholarship girls aren't the only Chicanas who go to college: Former Chicana continuation high school students disrupting the educational achievement binary. *Harvard Educational Review, 80*(2), 149–174.

McInerney, M., & McKlindon, A. (2014). *Unlocking the door to learning: Trauma-informed classrooms & transformational schools.* Education Law Center. Retrieved from http://www.vtnea.org/uploads/files/Trauma-Informed-in-Schools-Classrooms-FINAL-December2014-2.pdf.

McKean, E. (2005). *The new oxford American dictionary* (Vol. 2). New York: Oxford University Press.

Nuñez, A. M. (2011). Counterspaces and connections in college transitions: First-generation Latino students' perspectives on Chicano studies. *Journal of College Student Development, 52*(6), 639–655.

Omi, M., & Winant, H. (2014). *Racial formation in the United States.* Routledge.

Parker, L. (2015). Critical race theory in education and qualitative inquiry: What each has to offer each other now? *Qualitative Inquiry, 21*(3), 199–205.

Pérez Huber, L. (2011). Discourses of racist nativism in California public education: English dominance as racist nativist microaggressions. *Educational Studies, 47*(4), 379–401.

Pérez Huber, L., & Solórzano, D. G. (2014). Racial microaggressions as a tool for critical race research. *Race Ethnicity and Education, 18*(3), 297–320.

Perry, T., & Delpit, L. D. (1998). *The real Ebonics debate: Power, language, and the education of African-American children.* Boston: Beacon Press.

Pierce, C. (1974). Psychiatric problems of the Black minority. *American Handbook of Psychiatry, 2,* 512–523.

Pierce, C. M. (Ed.). (1978). *Television and education* (pp. 62–88). Beverly Hills, CA: Sage.

Pizarro, M. & Kohli, R. (2017). *"I'm not crazy!": Teachers of color and the impact of racial battle fatigue.* Manuscript submitted for publication.

Ratcliffe, R. G. (2009, April 8). *Lawmaker defends comment on Asians. Houston Chronicle.* Retrieved from http://www.chron.com/news/houston-texas/article/ Texas-lawmaker-suggests-Asians-adopt-easier-names-1550512.php.

Rogers, R., & Mosley, M. (2006). Racial literacy in a second-grade classroom: Critical race theory, whiteness studies, and literacy research. *Reading Research Quarterly, 41,* 462–495.

Sealey-Ruiz, Y. (2013). Building racial literacy in first-year composition. *Teaching English in the Two Year College, 40*(4), 384.

Sleeter, C. (2008). Preparing white teachers for diverse students. In M. Cochran-Smith, S. Feiman-Nemser, & J. McIntyre (Eds.), *Handbook of research in teacher education: Enduring issues in changing contexts* (3rd ed., pp. 559–582). New York, NY: Routledge.

Smith, W. A., Yosso, T. J., & Solórzano, D. G. (2007). Racial primes and black misandry on historically white campuses: Toward critical race accountability in educational administration. *Educational Administration Quarterly, 43*(5), 559–585.

Solórzano, D., Allen, W. R., & Carroll, G. (2002). Keeping race in place: Racial microaggressions and campus racial climate at the University of California, Berkeley. *Chicano-Latino Law Review, 23,* 15.

Solórzano, D. G., & Delgado Bernal, D. (2001). Examining transformational resistance through a critical race and Latcrit theory framework. *Urban Education, 36*(3), 308–342.

Spring, J. (1994). *The American school 1642–1993.* New York, NY: McGraw Hill Inc.

Steele, C. M. (1997). A threat in the air: How stereotypes shape intellectual identity and performance. *American Psychologist, 52*(6), 613.

Thai, X., & Barrett, T. (2007). *Biden's description of Obama draws scrutiny.* CNN, posted February, 9.

Valencia, R. R. (2002). "Mexican Americans don't value education!" On the basis of the myth, mythmaking, and debunking. *Journal of Latinos and Education, 1*(2), 81–103.

Winn, M. (2011). *Girl time: Literacy, justice, and the school-to-prison pipeline.* New York, NY: Teachers College Press.

Yosso, T. J. (2005). Whose culture has capital? A critical race theory discussion of community cultural wealth. *Race Ethnicity and Education, 8*(1), 69–91.

18

Microaggressions in Higher Education: Embracing Educative Spaces

Kathryn S. Young and Myron R. Anderson

Unfortunately, microaggressions are everywhere. Research has documented microaggressions in clinical spaces, classrooms, boardrooms, everyday life, and so forth (Hunter, 2011; Suarez-Orozco et al., 2015; Sue et al., 2007). Microaggressions have been documented relating to race, class, gender, sexuality, ability, and other important identity categories (Alleyne, 2004; Constantine, Smith, Redington, & Owens, 2008; Evans & Broido, 2002; Renn, 2010; Sandler, 1986; Sue, 2010; Swim, Hyers, Cohen, & Ferguson, 2001; Tatum, 2000). These spaces and identities intersect in specific ways in institutions of higher education in the form of hierarchical microaggressions. Hierarchical microaggressions are "the everyday slights found in higher education that communicate systemic valuing (or devaluing) of a person because of the institutional role held by that person" (Young, Anderson, & Stewart, 2015, p. 6). They are important to learn how to reduce for several reasons: (a) Microaggressions limit learning (Harwood, Huntt, Mendenhall, & Lewis, 2012; Kohli & Solórzano, 2012; Salvatore & Shelton, 2007); (b) Microaggressions create a toxic campus climate (Solórzano, Ceja, & Yasso, 2000; Yosso, Smith, Ceja, & Solórzano, 2009); (c) Microaggressions affect people's sense of belonging (Suarez-Orozco et al., 2015); and (d) Microaggressions lower the retention of students, staff, and faculty (Turner, González, & Wood, 2008). This chapter focuses on the manifestations of microaggressions between employees at universities (faculty/staff, tenured/nontenured faculty, faculty/administration, new employees/long-standing employees, etc.) and offers proactive and reactive solutions to reduce microaggressions on university campuses.

Microaggression Theory: Influence and Implications, First Edition. Edited by Gina C. Torino, David P. Rivera, Christina M. Capodilupo, Kevin L. Nadal, and Derald Wing Sue.
© 2019 John Wiley & Sons, Inc. Published 2019 by John Wiley & Sons, Inc.

Understanding Hierarchical Microaggressions

Hierarchical microaggressions manifest predominantly in four ways: valuing based on role, changing accepted behavior based on role, actions related to role, and terminology related to role. These microaggressions matter because people are given identities associated with their role and status. These microaggressions intersect with other identity-based microaggressions in the form of microaggressive intersectionalities.

Valuing Based on Role

Valuing or devaluing a person because of the role they were hired into ascribes privileges to certain roles and oppressive structures to others. For example, a new faculty member is listened to over a staff member with more experience; recommendations made by a junior faculty member are ignored when the same idea is rearticulated by a senior faculty member, who is listened to by the committee. These comments send an organizational message that contributions are valued in relation to the role of the contributor, based on their position in the academic hierarchy: "The message sent to the devalued employee is that s/he is less capable, less important, less valued" (Young et al., 2015, p. 7).

Changing Accepted Behavior

When a person changes how she/he/they act depending on the role of the person she/he/they are interacting with, this demonstrates how institutional hierarchy matters in the interactions. For example, when a faculty member speaks differently or stops speaking to an administrative assistant once finding out that the administrative assistant is a student worker; when a faculty member listens respectfully to the Dean about a policy change, then berates a subordinate faculty member for accepting that same policy change. People higher in the academic hierarchy sometimes interact differently with people in "lesser" roles. They change what is considered acceptable behavior in the interaction pattern once knowing the perceived social distance. This happens within the staff/faculty divide and also in the pretenure/posttenure divide. "Equals" often interact differently than those who are not considered hierarchically on par, sending messages of exclusion and devaluation to those who experience hierarchical microaggressions.

Actions Related to Role

Related to the second theme but resulting in a nonverbal and/or behavioral change is that of ignoring, excluding, being surprised, and/or interrupting those in "lesser" roles. These actions might include stopping someone from speaking, ignoring their entrance into a space, finishing sentences for someone, and expressing surprise at a good idea. These actions help the person lower in the hierarchy to "feel like they are invisible or not worth the faculty member's time or interest" (Young et al., 2015, p. 8). These actions also take place in staff/ staff, tenured/nontenured faculty, faculty/administration, new employees/ long-standing employees with the common denominator being that one person is in a "higher" role within the university. These actions devalue the position and the person who holds that position.

Terminology

The words chosen to talk about someone's role and the qualifiers to that role, formally or informally, indicate their relative power within the institution. These qualifiers might include words like "just a" as in, you are *just* an "adjunct" or "his/her" or "my" as in "He is *my* administrative assistant." Just is a word that makes the person less than others in a similar role, and his/her/my indicates ownership. In either case, the people who hold the role have been turned into objects of the university. You are an adjunct, you are an administrative assistant: "A person who works at a university wants to hold a position, not become a position" (Young et al., 2015, p. 8).

Microaggressive Intersectionalities

Microaggressive intersectionalities refer to the phenomenon of being negatively "ismed"—in relation to race, class, gender, or another social identity (Young & Anderson, 2015). In addition to the hierarchical microaggressions listed above, employees also must contend with how their role interacts with their other identities such as race, class, gender, education level. Even though there are women in positions of power in organizations, there remain moments in their work lives where their race or gender or race and gender are called into question in subtle ways in relation to the role they hold at the university. This becomes even more problematic when they cannot tell if it is racism (Sue, 2010). Is it sexism? Is this about the organizational role I hold? Or is it something else, a combination of racism, sexism, and hierarchical microaggressions all at play (Young & Anderson, 2015)?

Given the swirling mix of possibilities for microaggressions in higher education, how can institutions of higher education use the organizational context of a university to lessen microaggressions from happening in the first place? We suggest two courses of action: being proactive, and if (and when) microaggressions happen, address them in a meaningful way—being reactive. We share with you the case of one university that has put in place many strategies to reduce the occurrence of microaggressions. These strategies include the introduction of policies, procedures, and programs designed to both proactively and reactively reduce microaggressions on the campus.

Background

About MSU Denver

MSU Denver, founded in 1965, is an urban land grant university that takes a proactive and balanced approach to diversity. Diversity is reflected in the curriculum, in activities of the university, and in the composition of faculty, staff, and students. MSU Denver's student population is 68.4% White, 18.2% Hispanic or Latino, 6.2% African American, 3.5% Asian, 2.6% Bi- or Multi-racial, 0.8% American Indian or Alaskan Native, and 0.3% Native Hawaiian or Pacific Islander. The 1,900 faculty and staff is 77% White, 9% Hispanic or Latino, 4% African American, 6% Asian, 2% Bi- or Multi-racial, 1% American Indian or Alaskan Native, and 1% Other. Furthermore, MSU Denver's administrative staff population is 64% White, 19% Hispanic or Latino, 6% African American, 6% Asian, 3% Bi- or Multi-racial, 1% American Indian or Alaskan Native, and 1% Other. MSU Denver is a very diverse institution and believes that placing a high value on diversity and inclusivity are essential elements in providing excellence in education. Diversity leads to innovative thinking, but diverse workplaces also "lead to more conflict between different ideas and perspectives" (Klein, 2014). Therefore, if we value diversity, we must plan for conflict and create spaces to engage with it.

Research shows that systems, institutions, and personal attitudes perpetuate workplace bias through laws, policies, processes, and personal value systems within those systems (Dovidio & Gaertner, 1996; Miller & Garran, 2007; Sue, 2010). Microaggressions in higher education can be reduced through creating proactive and reactive educative spaces to transform policies, processes, programs, and value systems. Universities can use their advantage as institutions of higher education to prioritize learning about, maintaining, and sustaining diversity as part of the polices, processes, programs, and value systems.

To that end, MSU Denver was intentional in implementing strategies to educate university personnel about diversity, reducing microaggressions, and providing employees with the tools to reduce and/or remove microaggressions when encountered. To execute these education-based strategies the Office of Diversity and Inclusion (ODI) served as the central educative nexus. The ODI was created by the university in 2006 and was organizationally placed in the Office of the President. This move to physically locate diversity at the top of the academic hierarchy, both conceptually and spatially, evidenced the prioritization of diversity as a key component at the university. This infrastructure backdrop frames the main way to reduce microaggressions in higher education— leadership that values and supports diversity (Griffin, Muñiz, & Espinoza, 2012).

The ODI was charged with tracking campus climate. It developed the "2010 Campus Climate Survey" as an important mechanism to hear directly from their constituents and to serve as a proactive tool to monitor, maintain, and improve the campus climate. The campus climate survey was repeated in 2013, and most recently in 2017. The all-inclusive campus climate survey is administered every four years to allow for a systemic stream of data that takes the "inclusive temperature" of the university. The climate surveys have identified areas that needed to be addressed so that MSU Denver could move forward with one of its core values, "Diversity," and be a leader in creating a welcoming and inclusive environment for all students, staff, and faculty. The campus climate surveys polled all 1,900 faculty and staff at MSU Denver and both received a 63% return rate. The surveys solicited opinions related to the overall climate, attitudes toward diversity, satisfaction with the institution, feeling of comfort and belonging, treatment of various identity groups, and inclusiveness of the workforce. A similar survey captured the experiences of students on campus. Responses to the climate survey indicated a need to better educate the campus about issues related to diversity broadly and microaggressions specifically.

Educate the Campus—Systemic Solutions to Microaggressions

Systematic Practices That Proactively Reduce Microaggressions

University leadership undertook a process to augment the work environment and learning opportunities to systematically make it easier for "our biased minds to get things right" (Morse, 2016, p. 64). MSU Denver works to support a "choice architecture" of continuous learning related to improving campus climate so students, faculty, and staff can choose to "get things right" more often (Beshears & Gino, 2015). Following is a nonexhaustive list of purposefully designed programs to reduce bias on campus through proactively educating the campus (Whittaker, Montgomery, & Martinez Acosta, 2015): the Higher Education Diversity Summit (HEDS), the Tenure Track Supper Club (TTSC), Faculty and Staff Learning Communities (FSLCs), Inclusive Excellence Grants, and Supervisor Trainings.

Higher Education Diversity Summit (HEDS)

The HEDS is a campus initiative for faculty, staff, and students that promotes and increases professional development opportunities through the lens of inclusive excellence (Williams, Berger, & McClendon, 2005). The Summit is held in April of each year to mark the assassination of Dr. Martin Luther King, Jr. (April 4) and acts as a connection between contemporary issues, past leaders, and work on diversity, equity, and social justice. HEDS acts as a catalyst to understand others' experiences on campus. It opens communication about how to be supportive to groups and individuals who traditionally feel marginalized at universities. It acts as a preventative strategy to reduce microaggressions because it educates the campus in the areas of implicit bias, diversity and inclusion, lesbian, gay, bisexual, transgender, and queer (LGBTQ) issues, disabilities, race, gender, socioeconomic status, ageism, organizational climate, microaggressions, and much more. Understanding and removal of microaggressions are an important initiative for the university. Having an annual conference that keeps this educative point in the forefront of university dialogue is a systemic way to continue the education process about microaggressions throughout the workforce.

Tenure Track Supper Club (TTSC)

The TTSC is a faculty retention program that utilizes mentorship as a tool in the retention of minority faculty. Given the disproportionate retention rates of African American faculty at the university, the ODI led the development of the Tenure Track Faculty Mentorship Program for African American and other Faculty of Color. Over the years, the program grew to provide all minority tenure track faculty with the tools necessary to increase their capacity to earn tenure. The program now welcomes tenure track faculty from all underrepresented populations and majority junior faculty, to introduce them to tenured faculty, who serve as mentors, to help them build on the hidden curriculum of higher education, and to demystify the tenure process in order to increase their probability of earning tenure.

Understanding microaggressions and how to remove them from the classroom, the office, from areas of scholarly activity, in-service, during advising, and with daily interactions with students, other faculty, and staff is a core element of this mentorship program. Understanding microaggressions within the academy and developing strategies to reduce and remove them arms each faculty member with additional intellectual, social, and emotional horsepower, removes a key impediment to university progress, and builds community with other faculty, thus smoothing out the path to tenure.

At the onset of the program, African American faculty were earning tenure at 60%, while White faculty were earning tenure at 90%. Today, African Americans are earning tenure at 95%, and White faculty are earning tenure at 95%. The program has a direct link to the Associate to the President for Diversity who is an advocate for Faculty of Color across the institution. This program offers a unique opportunity to create change through dialogue, to begin conversations that can influence the recruitment of minority faculty, to improve campus climate through mentorship, to reduce microaggressions through education, and to create an increasingly inclusive tenure process.

Faculty and Staff Learning Communities (FSLCs)

FSLCs are cross-disciplinary groups of faculty and staff, numbering roughly 8–12 members, engaged in active, collaborative learning throughout the academic year around a specific theme and toward defined outcomes. The ODI sponsors FSLCs that relate to improving campus climate through examining diversity issues. Sponsoring these communities reduces microaggressions as it leads systemic and ground-up engagement with diversity issues. ODI's sponsorship of these learning communities ensures highly trained faculty, who are leading researchers in diversity and inclusion, will lead them. In addition, by incorporating them within the Center for Faculty Excellence and not having them as programs separately delivered by the ODI further supports the university's philosophy of Inclusive Excellence, and places the FSLC's within an educational delivery unit within the university thus promoting buy-in, trust, credibility, stability, and longevity. All of these points are key for consistency and sustainability as the university works to reduce microaggressions systemically.

Diversity Initiative Grants

Diversity Initiative Grants are awarded to faculty and staff for initiatives, programs, and/or events that advance the university's core values of diversity and inclusion. These grants support the creation of culturally enriching and sustaining spaces for acting on the value added by diversity in higher education. The road to increasing culturally enriching and sustaining spaces follows a path of cultural precompetence, cultural self-reflection and reflection of others, professional development, and education through reading, travel, and cultural and professional experiences all of which can be developed as part of these grants (Cross, Bazron, Dennis, & Isaacs, 1989). Diversity initiative grants hope to lead to changes in policies, standards, and practices that increase opportunities for diverse groups. The delivering of these culturally enriching and sustaining spaces to the university community provides an educational platform to transfer knowledge in the area of diversity and inclusion, which is a direct component to reducing microaggressions. Grant programs like this systemically move an organization toward cultural competence and the reduction and removal of microaggressions.

Supervisory Training

The university engages in proactive voluntary approaches to learn about diversity, as in the programs above. It also engages in mandatory, proactive strategies to teach people in positions of authority about their role in promoting diversity as part of the university's mission. People in positions of authority are defined as anyone who has to formally supervise anyone else—from an administrative assistant who supervises one work-study student to the president of the university who supervises everyone. Dobbin and Kalev (2016) argue that managers advocate better for a diverse workplace when managers become part of the problem-solving team. To foster supervisors at the university into anti-microaggression champions, the Associate to the President for Diversity collaborated with a faculty member to develop a 90-minute interactive workshop on microaggressions woven into a mandatory supervisor-training program. This administrative decision squarely places the issues of cultural competence within the broader framework of supervisors' responsibilities within the university and asks them to be problem solvers for questions related to diversity. The 90-minute presentation teaches microaggression awareness and understanding, explains the effects of microaggressions on individuals and on organizations, and teaches how to remove microaggressions. People break into groups to share their own examples of microaggressions on campus, often hierarchical in nature. The groups then share their examples and their solutions. The training ends with developing a shared list of strategies to combat microaggressions. These shared reduction strategies help supervisors think about their role in reducing microaggressions from individual and organizational perspectives.

The supervisor training was so well received that other units in the university began requesting trainings as well. Again, in an effort to empower people and departments to resolve their own microaggressions, the ODI set up a request mechanism allowing for any individual (faculty, staff, or students) or unit throughout the university to request a workshop on microaggressions from the identified experts associated with the office. An online request form on the ODI's website provides easy access for individuals and campus units to request a tailored workshop on microaggressions.

These five programs act as part of the infrastructure of continuous learning related to diversity and campus climate improvement. They address employees at different stages of their university development; all have the goal of encouraging a campus that sees diversity as an asset to be cultivated. Continuous knowledge acquisition related to diversity is a necessary component to addressing microaggressions in higher education, but alone is not enough.

Educate the Workforce—Reactive Solutions to Microaggressions

Despite all the systems in place to reduce microaggressions through proactive educative spaces, this campus, as any campus, will still contend with microaggressions. The ODI responds to referrals from organizational units that work directly with these issues daily (the Ombuds Office, the Equal Opportunity Office, The Office of Student Life, etc.). If a climate issue arises via referrals from one of these units and/or the complaint process, the ODI then meets with the person who entered the referral (most often a faculty or staff member) to decide a course of action, and when deemed appropriate, provides an interactive workshop on microaggressions based on their specific needs facilitated by faculty and administrators from the ODI. Other climate issues are resolved through one-on-one mediation or through other university-sanctioned interventions.

Strategies for Individuals to Reduce Microaggressions on Campus

It is important for universities to think about being proactive and reactive systemically in regards to reducing and removing microaggressions. Additionally, because of the fleeting nature of microaggressions, the better the university educates faculty, administrators, staff, and students, the better they can individually intervene to reduce microaggressions on campus. The strategies below are incorporated into all the different trainings on campus for a shared language and shared expectation of addressing microaggressions on campus.

Importantly, universities, with many built-in hierarchies, must strategize microaggression reduction through the lens of understanding relative power since there are different levels of institutional positions contending for power in any given interaction. These levels of power are important to understand when people are being encouraged to speak up to address microaggressions. We teach that if a student has a problem with a faculty member or feels insulted by a faculty member, the student should go talk to the faculty member. The same applies within departments: Go talk to the Chair, the Dean. So why do more people not go and report microaggressions? Understanding the obstacles might help departments and administrative units put in place alternative ways to share concerns about microaggressions.

When and How to Speak Up

The problem remains; students in classes often want to speak up when they hear a microaggression; staff want to speak up when they experience or witness one; faculty want to speak up when microaggressions happen in staff meetings or in faculty senate, but rarely does anyone speak up. Adam Galinsky, a psychologist, researches when people feel safe enough to speak up (Galinsky, 2016). They do so when they have enough perceived power within the specific context. Those with more perceived power have a wider range of when they can speak up. Those with less perceived power have a narrower range when they feel they can safely speak up. The range expands and narrows depending on the context. There are consequences for speaking up outside of a person's range: "The problem is that when our range narrows, that produces something called the low-power double bind. The low-power double bind happens when, if we don't speak up, we go unnoticed, but if we do speak up, we get punished" (Galinsky, 2016). So how do we help those with less power speak up in a university setting since power differences are built into the very fabric of the institution?

Galinsky's research has shown that certain attributes, such as having allies and demonstrating expertise, give people more power—so creating structures to enhance these attributes help people gain more range and more ability to speak up. Galinsky's research is in line with our own work and many other researchers and writers who examine how to respond to bias (Anderson & Young, 2016; for practical examples see Aguilar, 2006; Teaching Tolerance, n.d.). We share the following list of strategies to increase power and decrease microaggressions on campus.

1. *Have allies.* When people feel like they have social support, others who think like they do, they are more likely to speak up to a microaggression. What can you put in place in a classroom or a department to cultivate allyship?

2. *Advocate for others.* When we advocate for others who are experiencing microaggressions, we expand our range and earn strong allies. What systems can be put in place to encourage advocating for others?

3. *Expertise gives credibility.* Those in power are assumed to have credibility in interactions. When a microaggression happens from someone with credibility, people are quick to dismiss the microaggression. How can a university create spaces where students, staff, and faculty can demonstrate their expertise, thus increasing their credibility when a microaggression happens?

4. *Listen to alternative perspectives.* When a person in a position of power listens to another's perspective, she/he/they are more likely to listen to the pain of the microaggression and not dismiss it. How can honoring multiple perspectives be embedded into classes and into meetings so that when a microaggression happens, the practice of listening to alternative perspectives is already in place?

5. *Interact with people different from you.* People develop empathy for others' experiences when the "otherness" is removed. This is most easily accomplished by interacting with people different from oneself because then they become more human. Universities have so many opportunities to interact across a variety of identity and role characteristics. How can these opportunities be highlighted and supported?

6. *Put yourself in uncomfortable situations.* It is much easier to understand a marginalized experience if you have experienced marginalization. What experiences does a university afford to make oneself safely uncomfortable?

7. *Discuss your own perpetrations of microaggressions.* Act as a model for how to own microaggressive behavior. Show others that it is acceptable at the university to understand the effect of your words and actions on others, to apologize (even publicly), and to learn from the experience. Can you think of an example at your university when a person in a position of power has done so?

8. *Enact diplomacy.* Talking about microaggressions is hard. Listening to microaggressions is hard. Experiencing microaggressions is harder. If called upon to address a microaggressive experience, work to be tactful as emotions are raw. Explicitly note the impact of feelings on all sides of the issue. How can you create space within a microaggressive experience to be diplomatic?

What to Do When Someone Gets It Wrong

In classes, in meetings, and on campus impart the understanding that in diverse environments microaggressions are going to happen. Research suggests that many microaggressions committed are unintentional (Sue et al., 2007) When microaggressions do happen, when someone is microaggressed, campuses can agree on several tenets for the opportunity for education that arises: develop an "agreement to say ouch," embrace the "least dangerous assumption" about the microaggressor, and understand the difference between "intent and impact" for the microaggressee.

An "agreement to say ouch" has a long tradition in Anti-Bias and Inter-Group Relations literatures (e.g., Walsh, 2007). The idea is that if someone feels a microaggression has taken place, the hurt person, a witness, or a bystander can say "ouch." This small word opens the door for blame-free dialogue where the aggressor can know a microaggression just occurred. The group then has a chance to address the issue in the moment using the least dangerous assumption and the difference between intent and impact.

The least dangerous assumption comes from special education and refers to "in the absence of conclusive data educational decisions ought to be based on assumptions which, if incorrect, will have the least dangerous effect on the likelihood that students will be able to function independently as adults" (Donnellan, 1984, p. 141). This same assumption applies to any interaction. What would be the least dangerous assumption about the speaker who just committed a microaggression? Knowing that the microaggression probably came from an unconscious bias, rather than a desire to be hurtful and hateful, helps the person with authority (faculty, administrator, etc.) turn the experience into a teachable moment. Taking advantage of the charge of universities as institutions of learning, the faculty can stop class (or a meeting) and explain why a comment is a microaggression, not in an accusatory way, but in an educative one, where ignorance is just unknowing, not malicious intent.

The experience is still a microaggression, and the speaker needs to understand the difference between intent and impact (for a much deeper analysis of this concept examine the research on blame attribution, for example, Ames & Fiske, 2013). Faculty (administrators and related) can use the moment of "I did not mean to ..." to help the microaggressor understand that not meaning to do something does not mean it did not happen, nor does it mean there has been no impact experienced by others. When those in power model addressing microaggressions in constructive ways, they show students that classroom spaces are safe spaces for dialogue, for making mistakes, and for learning from them. When these same strategies are adopted in staff and faculty meetings, more people know the climate is welcoming and that everyone has a role in continually improving it.

Conclusion

What if, instead of waiting for poor climate or waiting to engage in cultural competence when required by the institution, faculty, staff, and administration undertook a process of self-learning and self-renewal to increase their own personal cultural competence? This would be a "paradigm shift on how we look at cultural competence systemically and infuse this work into the fabric of the organization continuously" (M. Anderson, personal communication, November 1, 2014). Educating university personnel on microaggression awareness, understanding, and removal is a comprehensive and, oftentimes, organic process that we believe is best accomplished systemically and individually, proactively, and reactively.

Systemically, the university promotes proactive educative spaces to employees at all levels of the university infrastructure (i.e., senior leadership, the offices of human resources, and the faculty and staff development offices). Individually, the university provides an avenue for employees to take ownership of the climate in their units by requesting microaggression experts (i.e., the ODI) to come into their departments, units, and classrooms to deliver educational workshops to help participants learn the terminology, work through examples, understand their impact, and develop strategies and skills on how to reduce and remove microaggressions. This work is so important in educational spaces where the stakes are high; if microaggressions persist, they limit learning and retention of students, staff, and faculty from marginalized groups.

We are of the belief that some microaggressions can be prevented through proactive and systemic practices and others need to be removed going forward, after they have been committed via an appropriate reactive and individual response, educating the microaggressor so that she/he/they do not commit similar microaggressions in future interactions with people. This strategy is often referred to as removing one microaggression at a time. Universities need to support employees with the institutional and individual tools for microaggression removal. They must engage the university community in continuous knowledge acquisition related to diversity and inclusion in order to provide the intellectual, social, and emotional foundations to improve organizational climate.

Universities can accelerate this removal and greatly improve work environments by including both systemic-proactive and individual-reactive microaggression removal strategies simultaneously. Implementing this two-tier strategy will create a community of microaggression awareness and understanding leading to the development of anti-microaggression champions positioned throughout the university, working collectively to remove microaggressions, and improve the work environment throughout the university community.

References

Aguilar, L. C. (2006). *Ouch...That stereotype hurts*. Dallas, TX: The Walk the Talk Company.

Alleyne, A. (2004). Black identity and workplace oppression. *Counseling and Psychotherapy Research, 4*(1), 4–8. doi:10.1080/14733140412331384008.

Ames, D. L., & Fiske, S. T. (2013). Intentional harms are worse, even when they're not. *Psychological Science, 24*(9), 1755–1762. doi:10.1177/0956797613480507.

Anderson, M. R., & Young, K. S. (2016, March 15 and 22). *Microaggressions and workplace bullying.* Academic Impressions Webcast. Retrieved from http://www.academicimpressions.com/webcast/microaggressions-and-workplace-bullying.

Beshears, J., & Gino, F. (2015, May). Leaders as decision architects. *Harvard Business Review,* 2–12.

Constantine, M. G., Smith, L., Redington, R. B., & Owens, D. (2008). Racial against black counseling and counseling psychology faculty: A central challenge in the multicultural counseling movement. *Journal of Counseling & Development, 86,* 349–355. doi:10.1177/1745691616659391.

Cross, T. L., Bazron, B. J., Dennis, K. W., & Isaacs, M. R. (1989). *Towards a culturally competent system of care, A monograph on effective services for minority children who are severely emotionally disturbed* (Vol. 1). Washington, DC: Georgetown University, Child Development Center, Child and Adolescent Services System Program, Technical Assistance Center.

Dobbin, F., & Kalev, A. (2016, July–August). Why diversity programs fail and what works better. *Harvard Business Review,* 52–60.

Donnellan, A. M. (1984). The criterion of the least dangerous assumption. *Behavioral Disorders, 9*(2), 141–150. Retrieved from https://eric.ed.gov/?id= EJ305413.

Dovidio, J. F., & Gaertner, S. L. (1996). Affirmative action, unintentional racial biases, and intergroup relations. *Journal of Social Issues, 52*(4), 51–75. doi:10.1111/j.1540-4560.1996.tb01848.x/full.

Evans, N. J., & Broido, E. M. (2002). The experiences of lesbian and bisexual women in college residence halls: Implications for addressing homophobia and heterosexism. In E. P. Cramer (Ed.), *Addressing homophobia and heterosexism on college campuses.* Binghampton, NY: Harrington Park Press.

Galinsky, A. (2016, September). *Adam Galinsky: How to speak up for yourself [Video file].* Retrieved from https://www.ted.com/talks/adam_galinsky_how_to_ speak_up_for_yourself/transcript?language=en.

Griffin, K. A., Muñiz, M. M., & Espinoza, L. (2012). The influence of campus racial climate on diversity in graduate education. *The Review of Higher Education, 35*(4), 535–566. doi:10.1353/rhe.2012.0031.

Harwood, S., Huntt, M. B., Mendenhall, R., & Lewis, J. (2012). Racial microaggressions in the residence halls: Experiences of students of color at a predominantly White university. *Journal of Diversity in Higher Education, 5,* 159–173. doi:10.1037/a0028956.

Hunter, R. L. (2011). *An examination of workplace microaggressions and their effects on employee performance* (Doctoral dissertation). Retrieved from ProQuest Dissertation. (1503508).

Klein, E. (2014, October 14). *Workplace diversity is hard for the exact same reason it's so important.* Retrieved from https://www.vox.com/xpress/2014/10/23/ 7048353/workplace-diversity-is-hard-for-the-exact-same-reason-its-so-important.

Kohli, R., & Solórzano, D. G. (2012). Teachers, please learn our names! Racial microaggressions and the K-12 classroom. *Race, Ethnicity and Education, 15,* 441–462. doi:10.1080/13613324.2012.674026.

Miller, J., & Garran, A. (2007). The web of institutional racism. *Smith College Studies in Social Work, 77*(1), 33–67. doi:10.1300/J497v77n01_03.

Morse, G. (2016, July–August). Designing a bias-free organization: It's easier to change your processes than your people. An interview with Iris Bohnet. *Harvard Business Review,* 63–67.

Renn, K. A. (2010). LGBT and queer research in higher education: The state and status of the field. *Educational Researcher, 39*(2), 132–141. doi:10.3102/0013189X10362579.

Salvatore, J., & Shelton, J. N. (2007). Cognitive costs of exposure to racial prejudice. *Psychological Science, 18,* 810–815. doi:10.1111/j.1467-9280.2007.01984.x.

Sandler, B. R. (1986). *The campus climate revisited: Chilly for women faculty, administrators, and graduate students [final report].* Washington, DC: Fund for the Improvement of Postsecondary Education. Retrieved from https://eric.ed.gov/?id=ED282462.

Solórzano, D., Ceja, M., & Yasso, T. (2000). Critical race theory, racial microaggressions, and campus racial climate: The experiences of African American college students. *The Journal of Negro Education, 69,* 60–73. Retrieved from https://eric.ed.gov/?id=EJ636426.

Suarez-Orozco, C., Casanova, S., Martin, M., Katsiaficas, D., Cuellar, V., Smith, N. A., & Dias, S. I. (2015). Toxic rain in class: Classroom interpersonal microaggressions. *Educational Researcher, 44,* 151–160. doi:10.3102/0013189X15580314.

Sue, D. W. (2010). *Microaggressions in everyday life: Race, gender & sexual orientation.* Hoboken, NJ: Wiley.

Sue, D. W., Capodilupo, C. M., Torino, G. C., Bucceri, J. M., Holder, A. M. B., Nadal, K. L., & Esquilin, M. E. (2007). Racial microaggressions in everyday life: Implications for clinical practice. *American Psychologist, 62,* 271–286. doi:10.1037/0003-066X.62.4.271.

Swim, J. K., Hyers, L. L., Cohen, L. L., & Ferguson, M. J. (2001). Everyday sexism: Evidence for its incidence, nature, and psychological impact from three daily diary studies. *Journal of Social Issues, 57,* 31–53. doi:10.1111/0022-4537.00200.

Tatum, B. (2000). Who am I? The complexity of identity. In M. Adams, W. J. Blumenfeld, H. H. Castaneda, M. Peters, & X. Zuñiga (Eds.), *Readings for diversity and social justice: An anthology on racism, antisemitism, sexism, heterosexism, ableism, and classism.* New York, NY: Routledge.

Teaching Tolerance. (n.d.). *Speak Up Handbook.* Retrieved from http://www.tolerance.org/sites/default/files/general/speak_up_handbook.pdf.

Turner, C. S. V., González, J. C., & Wood, J. L. (2008). Faculty of color in academe: What 20 years of literature tells us. *Journal of Diversity in Higher Education, 1*(3), 139–168. doi:10.1037/a0012837.

Walsh, K. C. (2007). *Talking about race: Community dialogues and the politics of difference.* Chicago, IL: University of Chicago Press.

Whittaker, J. A., Montgomery, B. L., & Martinez Acosta, V. G. (2015). Retention of underrepresented minority faculty: Strategic initiatives for institutional value proposition based on perspectives from a range of academic institutions. *Journal of Undergraduate Neuroscience Education, 13*(3), A136–A145. Retrieved from https://www.ncbi.nlm.nih.gov/pmc/articles/PMC4521729/.

Williams, D. A., Berger, J. B., & McClendon, S. A. (2005). *Toward a model of inclusive excellence and change in postsecondary institutions.* Washington, DC: Association of American Colleges and Universities.

Yosso, T. J., Smith, W. A., Ceja, M., & Solórzano, D. G. (2009). Critical race theory, racial microaggressions, and campus racial climate for Latina/o undergraduates. *Harvard Educational Review, 79,* 659–691. doi:10.17763/haer.79.4 .m6867014157m7071.

Young, K. S., & Anderson, M. R. (2015, November). *Microaggressive intersectionalities: Race, gender and hierarchy in higher education.* Paper presented at the meeting of the American Anthropological Association, Denver, CO.

Young, K., Anderson, M., & Stewart, S. (2015). Hierarchical microaggressions in higher education. *Journal of Diversity in Higher Education, 8*(1), 61–71. doi:10.1037/a0038464.

Part VI

The Future of Microaggression Theory

19

Microaggression Theory: What the Future Holds

Gina C. Torino, David P. Rivera, Christina M. Capodilupo, Kevin L. Nadal, and Derald Wing Sue

Introduction

Microaggression theory and research has gained considerable momentum within the past decade. Since the publication of Sue, Capodilupo, et al.'s (2007) "Racial Microaggressions in Everyday Life: Implications for Clinical Practice," the article has received over 2,700 citations (Google Scholar, April 27, 2018, search). Significant research has been conducted investigating the themes, impact, and responses to microaggressions for a variety of racial and cultural groups including African Americans, Asian Americans, Latinx, Native Americans, multiracial groups, women, oppressed sexual orientation and gender identity groups, intersectional identities, persons with disabilities, Muslim Americans, Jewish Americans, and those with mental illness as well as other groups. Moreover, this research has been conducted across multiple settings including higher education (see Young & Anderson, in this book), K-12 education (see Kohli, Arteaga, & McGovern, in this book), business (see Kim, Nguyen & Block, in this book), health care (see Mazzula & Campon, in this book), and the therapeutic context (see Owen, Tao, & Drinane, in this book) to name a few. Many of the studies conducted utilized the original taxonomy included in the Sue, Capodilupo et al., 2007 piece. This taxonomy has proved to be an excellent starting point for more than a decade of substantial research.

As we look to the future, it seems appropriate to take account of what has been learned since the original taxonomy was published and to refine and elaborate on the original taxonomy accordingly. In addition, it is important to examine the controversies and criticisms of microaggressions, especially on college campuses where students have established new culture mores (see Sue, in this book). Furthermore, as microaggression theory continues to influence research across disciplines, it becomes essential to understand it from multiple lenses

Microaggression Theory: Influence and Implications, First Edition. Edited by Gina C. Torino, David P. Rivera, Christina M. Capodilupo, Kevin L. Nadal, and Derald Wing Sue.
© 2019 John Wiley & Sons, Inc. Published 2019 by John Wiley & Sons, Inc.

(e.g., multidimensionality of racism (MMR) and critical race theory (CRT) in Jones & Rolon-Dow in this book). A call to advance research in relevant areas, such as microaggressions in K-12 education, internalized oppression, everyday interventions, long-term cumulative impact of microaggressions, and many others, can benefit multiple fields, disciplines, and populations. This chapter will outline possible future lines of inquiry including theoretical and conceptual elaboration, research topics and methods, prevention, training, and media advocacy.

Future Areas of Research

In thinking about the future of microaggressions, it seems likely to become an increasingly contested concept that will no doubt frequently be misconstrued, misrepresented, and maligned. The controversy surrounding the concept of microaggressions will be most readily resolved if researchers continue to empirically investigate the phenomenon concurrently with training programs raising awareness about and providing empirically informed guidance and resources for what is clearly a serious and widespread issue. It seems that there are some individuals who are opposed to faculty, staff, and students on campus and the general populace using the term *microaggressions* (e.g., Lilienfeld, 2017). Nevertheless, critics as well as deniers of microaggressions will find it increasingly difficult to minimize or ignore the ever-growing body of empirical evidence establishing that microaggressions take place everyday, everywhere, and that general consciousness of their existence is beneficial to everyone who is negatively affected by them. To this end, we are issuing a call to empirical research communities to launch a coordinated, systematic, transdisciplinary research program using both quantitative and qualitative methodologies to investigate microaggressions, including investigating the effectiveness of microaggression training and education.

It is incumbent upon microaggression theorists and researchers not to create a "closed circle," in which microaggression theory is "unfalsifiable," that is, there is no conceivable empirical means (e.g., no experiment) by which the theory of microaggressions might be refuted (Popper, 1959). For instance, the early criticism of microaggressions purporting that they were no different from everyday indignities that everyone experiences (Schacht, 2008; Thomas, 2008) has not been supported by research, which shows significant psychological and somatic harm related to experiences with microaggressions (e.g., Huynh, 2012; Ong, Burrow, Fuller-Rowell, Ja, & Sue, 2013). Thus, research seems to have established that microaggressions are indeed distinct from everyday slights that do not involve prejudice toward groups that are marginalized in society. If the research had shown otherwise, the validity of microaggressions theory, if not falsified, would have been called into question.

Another possible topic for future research is the prevalence of specific microaggression themes and encounters. For example, let us consider the frequently reported microaggressive question "Where are you from?" typically asked of Asian American/Pacific Islander, Latinx, and Middle Eastern/North African people. This question, which represents the microaggression theme "Alien in Own Land," may seem innocuous when taken at face value. However, the targets of this particular microaggression theme indicate they experience messages of otherness and "outsiderness" quite frequently across contexts, such as in public spaces, education, the workplace, and in the media. In the current sociopolitical climate, this theme is further sanctioned by public policy, such as the proposed southern border wall and the travel ban from several Muslim-majority countries. Given the prevalence of these specific policy issues in the media, it is difficult for targets of this microaggression to avoid these potentially damaging encounters. The pervasiveness and complex nature of this particular microaggression theme warrants further research attention, as it is likely that there are related significant deleterious psychological and physical consequences for the target group member since this particular microaggression has the entire weight of dominant society behind it.

Moreover, microaggressions research would benefit from cross-cultural and international research that transcends national boundaries. For example, are there similarities and/or differences between microaggressions experienced by Mexican Americans in the United States in contrast to individuals living in Mexico? In addition, what is the differential impact across national boundaries? Further areas of potential research include understanding the dynamics of intra- and inter-racial and ethnic microaggressions. To what extent can individuals of the same reference group (e.g., women) microaggress toward one another? Also, what is the differential impact of such microaggressions in contrast to those committed by dominant group members?

Frameworks and Concepts

As the research on microaggressions continues, it is important to clarify frameworks and concepts surrounding terminology. There appears to be a discussion in the literature about what constitutes a micro versus a macro aggression. The term *microaggression* encompasses the interpersonal nature of such aggressions and not the gravity of their impact. Thus in the original definition of the term, micro is synonymous with "everyday" and not as smaller, less than, or inconsequential (Pierce, 1970). In contrast to racial microaggressions, racial macroaggressions represent structural forms of racism that are reflected in the systems that govern our institutions (Pérez Huber & Solórzano, 2015). Macroaggressions impact entire groups or classes of people as they are embedded in systems. Laws and policies around immigration and deportation may be considered macroaggressions as they can restrict or inhibit one's ability to be with their family. Moreover, differential access to health care can be considered a macroaggression as a staggering number of People of Color and poor individuals experience higher levels of adverse health outcomes and lower access to quality health care (Rivera, Mazzula, & Campon, 2017; Wilson & Yoshikawa, 2007). Voting laws and policies that deny early or weekend voting, which disproportionately target Communities of Color (e.g., African American voters in North Carolina during the 2016 presidential election), serve to reduce the number of votes cast from these communities.

Refinement of the Taxonomy

In thinking about the future research on the concept of microaggressions, it may be helpful to refine the taxonomy of the past decade (see Figure 19.1 for the

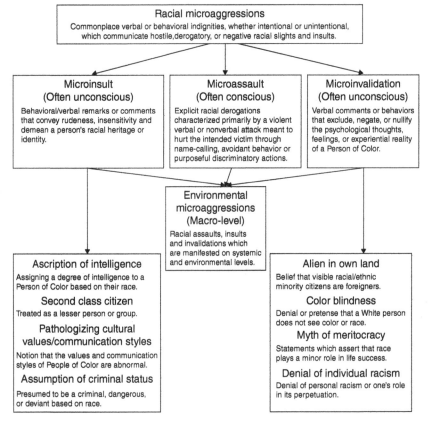

Figure 19.1 Original Taxonomy from 2007: Categories of and Relationships among Racial Microaggressions.

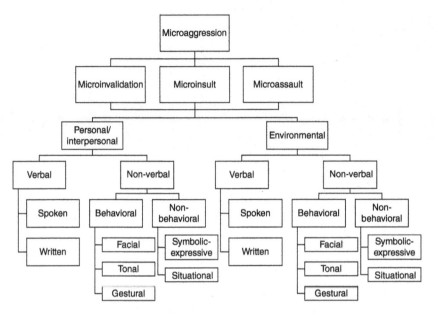

Figure 19.2 Revised Taxonomy of Microaggressions.

original). A further taxonomic specification is provided in Figure 19.2, which elaborates on some of the finer points of the concept. Please note that the "Example Themes" (e.g., "Alien in Own Land") for the types of microaggressions still apply in exactly the same way as in the original, but for reasons of space these could not repeated in Figure 19.2.

The previous taxonomy (Sue, Bucceri, Lin, Nadal, & Torino, 2007) has proven to be highly useful in all theoretical, empirical, and practical contexts. The changes reflected in Figure 19.2 should only be utilized if they prove to be equally or more useful. To employ a metaphor, these changes do not so much constitute a new edition with major revisions as an "expanded sub-edition" with minor revisions. For example, in the revised taxonomy, a new division to contrast with Environmental Microaggressions has been added (Personal/Interpersonal), but this new division simply labels what was already implicit in the original taxonomy. Environmental Microaggressions have been explicitly broken down into either Verbal or Non-Verbal categories (although, again, this was already implicit in the original). In addition, behavioral microaggressions have been given a slightly greater specification (e.g., Facial, Tonal, Gestural), and nonverbal microaggressions have been divided into behavioral and nonbehavioral categories. Finally, nonverbal microaggressions that are not behavioral are either "Symbolic-Expressive" or "Situational" (see Table 19.1 for example). These updates are altogether in keeping with the original taxonomy and simply offer a further elaboration that we hope may be useful in conducting research.

Table 19.1 Elaborated Taxonomy Examples.

		Personal/Interpersonal	Environmental
Verbal	Spoken	White person asks "Where are you from?" to Asian American	Talk Show host says "That's so gay" as a dismissive comment
		A man calls a female coworker "honey" or "sweetie" but calls male coworkers by their first name	Exclusively middle or upper class "White-sounding" voices announcing subways stops
	Written	Instructor corrects First Nations student's paper by changing the capitalization of "Indigenous" to lower-case throughout paper	Film poster: "Mankind Faces Its Greatest Challenge"
		A speaker shares a powerpoint presentation that reads: "No differences between LGBTQ people and normal populations"	Sports channel teletype reads "Chink in Armor" regarding Asian American
Non-Verbal	Behavioral		
	Facial	Rolling eyes when an issue involving sexism comes up	Same as Personal/Interpersonal, only portrayed in media (poster, TV, film, web)
	Tonal	"Scoffing" noise upon hearing a Latinx's question about race	Same as Personal/Interpersonal, only portrayed in media (TV, film, web)
	Gestural	Not paying attention/or looking at one's smart phone when a Black person speaks	Same as Personal/Interpersonal, only portrayed in media (poster, TV, film, web)
	Non-behavioral		
	Symbolic-Expressive	Wearing "Redskins" jacket to a First Nations person's birthday party	Film in which First Nations people are slaughtered with impunity by the "hero"
		Someone wears a t-shirt that says "All Lives Matter"	Restroom signs show male and female icons only
	Situational	Orthodox Jewish person invited by a Christian colleague to a holiday party where no Kosher food is served	Person of Color works at a corporation in which upper management are all White
		Able-bodied person using a restroom stall reserved for those with disabilities	No provision of Spanish language at an event within predominantly Latinx American community

With respect to personal/interpersonal microaggressions, they can be experienced in spoken or written forms. In addition, these types of microaggressions can be directly experienced by the target individual or witnessed in an indirect manner (e.g., seeing another person of your group membership experiencing a microaggression). Environmental microaggressions (especially written) are less commonly experienced, possibly because, being readily documentable or recordable, and therefore potentially later used as evidence in court, they are more susceptible to lawsuits. Nonenvironmental (especially oral and behavioral) microaggressions are less readily documentable (e.g., private conservations). This is yet another topic for future research.

Environmental microaggressions can include situations that involve an absence of a supportive feature or technology for a marginalized group. Often occurring in public spaces, environmental microaggressions, which are physical and structured into the environment include, for example, the lack of language translating at voting booths and no wheelchair access in government buildings. In addition, an example of a situational *interpersonal* microaggression could involve a manager asking an employee who is a Person of Color to join a diversity committee at work. When the employee shows up for the meeting, he sees that he is the only Person of Color and feels as though he is the customary token addition to the committee. Thus, environmental microaggressions, regardless of context, are an exceptionally worthwhile area to concentrate reform efforts. An example of effective reform efforts geared toward reducing environmental microaggressions against transgender and gender nonbinary communities is the implementation of gender nonbinary restrooms and accompanying gender inclusive signage at a growing number of institutions of higher education and other public and private spaces. A by-product of this reform effort includes the education regarding transgender and gender nonbinary communities and issues that is also helping to dispel misinformation and stereotypes that often lead to microaggressions.

This revised taxonomy of microaggressions offers a glimpse into the myriad ways in which microaggressions are enacted and potentially experienced. Although not exhaustive, the revised taxonomy provides a more complex depiction of microaggression encounters and provides a more nuanced conceptualization of the microaggression process that might prove useful for the development of future research questions that can be used to further refine the taxonomy. For example, a few more potential research questions include What is the threshold between thinking and expressing a microaggression? Does the unconsciously biased person keep the fire of bias burning until it is revealed in a public communication or behavior (including the *lack* of behavior, e.g., not "interrupting" and not "intervening" after witnessing a microaggression, e.g., failing to speak out against an overheard gender microinvalidation)? Presuming that more awareness is better, what is the best method for helping to "raise the consciousness" of the person with unconscious bias and/or of the inadvertent microaggressor? What is the longitudinal, cumulative impact of being the recipient of microaggressions?

Another topic that can be further explored empirically is what could be termed "marginalized-on-marginalized" microaggressing. Such a microaggression may occur between members of two marginalized groups (e.g., a First Nations individual microinvalidating a person with mental illness, or vice versa) or even within one's own marginalized group (a Latinx person with internalized racism microinsulting another Latinx person). Some of these topics will be expanded on below.

Development of Additional Themes

We encourage the discovery and conceptual development of new themes. It may be useful to set up a wiki for microaggressions (if a suitable one is not already in place), especially one focused on the exhaustive listing of themes (as well as incidents). For example, Sue, Lin, Torino, Capodilupo, and Rivera (2009) through focus group research, confirmed themes such as "Alien in Own Land" and "Assumption of Criminality." By opening up to contributors from all over the world, a far more comprehensive list of themes could be developed. The popular Web site http://www.microaggressions.com is an effective example of how to utilize the Internet and technology to gather a diverse array of microaggression experiences and provides guidance for the development of similar Internet-based mechanisms.

Such an expanded listing of themes and representative incidents in turn could be used to further refine microaggression theory. Seeing how such themes of prejudice fit together for a dominant group's perception of a particular marginalized group will help to better understand the microaggressive mindset. The metaphorical modeling technique used by cognitive scientist George Lakoff and others may be especially helpful (e.g., Lakoff, 2002). If this method is used, then when completed, these thematic models would take the form of condensed microaggressive "metaphors" that operate behind a number of microaggressive themes. Since these metaphors will more than likely be unfounded and irrational, they will also likely be extremely offensive to the target groups. Nevertheless, these condensed metaphors would be extremely important to talk about during a difficult dialogue on racism, sexism, ableism, and so forth, in the same way that someone with a phobia finds it beneficial to acknowledge to a respectful and supportive other the irrationality of the fear (in order to work through it).

Intersectionalities

All individuals have an intersectional identity whereby their various sociocultural identities are interrelated and synergistically informed by systems of privilege and oppression. While microaggressions research initially focused on a single racial or sociocultural group (e.g., Black American or sexual orientation identity), some research has explored the possibilities of intersectional microaggressions, or the types of discrimination people encounter as a result of their multiple identities (Nadal et al., 2015). As individuals do not inhabit a single group membership, scholarship has begun to explore and highlight the complexities and nuances of intersectional microaggressions for Women of Color (see Lewis & Neville, 2015; Lewis, Williams, Moody, Peppers, & Gadson, in this book), lesbian, gay, bisexual, transgender, queer (LGBTQ) People of Color (Nadal, 2013), and other intersectional identity groups. We would like to encourage the continued investigation of the ways in which such overlapping categories of identity combine to influence one's experience of microaggressions. Such intersectional oppression has been labeled the "matrix of domination" (Collins, 2000), or the matrix of oppression. Table 19.2 provides a listing (not intended to be comprehensive) of specific types of identity groups. The table may prove useful in identifying potential intersectional microaggressions by allowing for the combination of multiple identities.

While it is certainly challenging to conceptualize and investigate all of these possible combinations of intersectional identities, resistance to such complex oppression, as Collins (2000) points out, must itself be complex. Moreover, before intersectional alliances among marginalized group members can be developed (a critical problem for social justice movements), we will need to understand in a more complex manner how the overlapping of identity categories influences one's experience of microaggressions.

Further, understanding intersectionalities may be vital in recognizing how microaggressions may contribute to feelings of trauma (Bryant-Davis, in this book). When people experience microaggressions pervasively and intensely, they may develop trauma symptoms that are similar to people diagnosed with posttraumatic stress disorder. Sometimes the accumulation of microaggressions could be labeled as a trauma itself; other times, microaggressions may simply be triggers to more insidious trauma experienced in the past (Nadal, 2018). Thus, if someone experiences microaggressions based on their multiple marginalized identities, they become susceptible to developing a more complex trauma, experience microaggressions that serve as triggers that exacerbate their trauma, or both.

Finally, when examining the intersectional identities of both the enactors and targets of microaggressions, one may recognize how privilege and power (and lack of power or privilege) may influence how microaggressions are perpetrated or experienced. For instance, when White teachers make negative presumptions about Black students and engage in microaggressions, the microaggression may have a stronger impact because of their racial privilege and the status of being an authority figure (Martin, in this book). When people of the same group engage in within-group microaggressions, it may be due to their internalized oppression (David, in this book). For instance, if a darker-skinned Filipino

Table 19.2 Consider How Intersectional Microaggressions May Occur Based on the Following Identities.

Race/ethnicity	Ability status
Black/African American	Physical disability
Asian American	Mental disability
Latinx American	Able-bodied
Native American	
Middle Eastern	Religion
Multiracial	Muslim
Pacific Islander	Jewish
White American	Hindu
	Buddhist
Gender identity	Agnostic
Cisgender women	Atheist
Cisgender men	Shamanism
Transgender	Indigenous practice
Genderqueer	Christian
Gender non-binary	
	Age
Sexual identity	Youth/children
Bisexual	Young adult
Lesbian	Middle age
Gay	Elderly
Queer	
Pansexual	Immigrant status
Heterosexual	Undocumented immigrant
	Documented immigrants
Social class	Second-Generation immigrant
Poor/low-income	
Working class	Educational Status
Middle class	Less than a High School Diploma
Upwardly mobile	High School Diploma
Upper middle class	Technical School
Upper class	College Educated
	Graduate School

teases another Filipino on their skin color, the bias and subsequent microaggression may be a projection of their own insecurity about their skin color. When people hold both privileged and less-privileged identities, they are capable of being both a perpetrator or a target of microaggressions (Nadal, 2013). For example, while a gay, White cisgender man may understand what it is like to be discriminated against based on his sexual orientation, he may also enact his biases toward People of Color, women, and transgender and gender nonconforming people.

Research Methods

Empirical research conducted on microaggressions to date has utilized quantitative, qualitative, and mixed methods approaches. The earliest microaggressions research was qualitative in nature as the initial concept was under exploration. Early studies focused on understanding the types of microaggressions experienced by various racial cultural groups (Nadal et al., 2012; Sue, Bucceri, et al., 2007) mostly in higher education (Solórzano, Ceja, & Yosso, 2000). Subsequent studies focused on understanding how microaggressions were experienced across a variety of contexts (e.g., counseling) (Nadal, Davidoff, Davis, & Wong, 2014; Keith, Nguyen, Taylor, Mouzon, & Chatters, 2017). Moreover, many psychometric scales have been published in order to accurately measure the extent to which individuals have experienced microaggressions (Balsam, Molina, Beadnell, Simoni, & Walters, 2011; Capodilupo & Torino, 2017; Lewis & Neville, 2015; Nadal, 2011; Wright & Wegner, 2012). Most importantly, the subsequent impact of and reactions to the experience of microaggressions is under investigation (Donovan, Galban, Grace, Bennett, & Felicié, 2013; Grier-Reed, 2010; Huynh, 2012).

To date, microaggressions research has been largely conducted by self-report measures (e.g., interviews or self-report surveys). It would behoove future researchers to expand microaggressions research to other types of experimental designs that go beyond self-report measurement. Understanding the connection between implicit bias (see Dovidio, Pearson, & Penner, in this book) and microaggressions would open up a new line of inquiry. For example, the Implicit Association Test (IAT) measures the strength of associations between concepts by determining response times in a computer-based categorization task (Greenwald, McGhee, & Schwartz, 1998). Associations occur implicitly or unconsciously and oftentimes reveal the extent to which one might have biases for or against particular racial/cultural groups. It seems a promising avenue for future empirical research to examine correlations between dominant group members' implicit associations that involve bias toward a marginalized group and microaggression awareness with respect to that group. (The IAT method is discussed in more depth in the "Training components" section below.)

In addition, integrating microaggressions into studies that incorporate functional magnetic resonance imaging (FMRI) would be another method by which to explore the automatic and unconscious nature of biases. For example, research has indicated that White individuals have elevated amygdala activity responses when exposed to Black faces in contrast to White faces (Ronquillo et al., 2007). There are many potential research questions that involve the connection of implicit and automatic bias to microaggressions, especially in the case of microinvalidations and microinsults that are often unconsciously enacted. We invite researchers to inquire into this underexplored area of investigation.

Practice

Prevention

Another largely underexplored topic that is promising for both future research and practice is the prevention of the formation of prejudice through increased awareness of microaggressions. Research on the impact of microaggressions on children from both dominant and marginalized groups in the family or K-12 settings and media (e.g., television programs, advertising, movies, and Web sites aimed at children) would be highly valuable in understanding how inter-generational stereotypes and bias are transmitted. For example, in this book, Tynes, Lozada, Smith, and Stewart interview adolescent participants about their experiences with online microaggressions to better understand how this concept manifests in virtual settings. Such research would provide invaluable insights into the formation of the values, dispositions, motivations, attitudes, and beliefs behind microaggressions. Furthermore, we encourage the further investigation of the impact of microaggressions on children and adolescents, either through surveying college students about their youth and adolescent experiences (e.g., the research method used by Forrest-Bank & Jenson, 2015) or through studying children and adolescent participants directly (along the lines of Farr, Crain, Oakley, Krystal, & Garber, 2016).

It would also be worthwhile for future work to attempt to address the question: what is the effect on children of culturally competent K-12 teachers or children's television and movie characters who intervene when a microaggression has been committed? What happens when children who witness their parents committing a microaggression wish to talk to their parents about this? These and other similar scenarios would seem to be prime opportunities for children and adults alike to develop cultural knowledge, become more self-aware, and build culturally competent skill sets. Another research question might be at what age do children typically come to hold prejudice and when do they first commit microaggressions? In what way and to what degree does first-hand exposure to marginalized groups while young influence the formation of prejudice and microaggressive communication and behavior? (The topic of media will be addressed further in "Media Advocacy" below.) Such research will enable training professionals to effectively prepare those who work with children and adolescents in such a way that the formation of bias and stereotypes as well as the tendency to microaggress would be mitigated and the competency to identify, prevent, and intervene in microaggression incidents would be increased.

Intervention

Microaggressions training
Many successful training programs, workshops, Web sites, and courses (face-to-face and online) have been developed to address microaggressions across

a variety of contexts including schools (K-12 and higher education), corporations, health care, and law enforcement/emergency services. In this book, Young and Anderson discuss Metro State University (Denver) in depth as an example of an institute of higher learning that has embraced microaggressions training at the systemic level. This university employs education-based strategies to identify, address, and eradicate microaggressions across all levels of campus life (i.e., from the President's Office to dorms). Further, they've created an Office of Diversity and Inclusion that is housed in the Office of the President, signifying the prioritization and importance of diversity and cultural competence at the top of the academic hierarchy. This university is an excellent case study of how to meaningfully implement microaggression training in higher education settings. In the following section, we will discuss how future training protocols may be enhanced to maximize learning and minimize the harmful effects of microaggressions.

Train the trainers

In order for training on microaggressions to be successful, it is imperative that the trainers go through a formal training process that includes education about microaggression theory, manifestation, and impact, as well as interpersonal facilitation skills necessary for effective engagement with difficult dialogues and processes that are likely to arise in microaggression training sessions. This training can occur in a face-to-face classroom environment and can also be supplemented with online content. Expert trainers and academics that specialize in microaggressions research or those that possess the most up-to-date knowledge on research findings may be the most qualified to provide such training. Training manuals written by experts that incorporate the most recent research is sorely needed in the field. Peer-reviewed training manuals can then be widely disseminated to others in order to provide such training. Microaggression certification training may be offered through colleges and universities to ensure all trainers meet competencies that have been determined by experts in the field. Microaggression certification training would also benefit K-12 teachers and educators who often lack multicultural training in their programs, despite working closely with a diverse group of students—especially Students of color (Martin, in this book).

Training components

At the outset of any training, it is imperative for the trainer to define the term *microaggressions*, discuss the types of microaggressions (e.g., microassaults, microinvalidations), and provide common examples. In addition, providing participants with research findings on the impact and consequences of experiencing microaggressions (e.g., negative mental health outcomes) can assist participants with understanding the importance of the training. Moreover, having a common frame of knowledge can provide members with a solid foundation for ongoing discussion and analysis.

In addition, for any microaggressions training protocol to be effective, it should include a self-awareness or consciousness-raising component. In this book (see chapter on Workplace Interventions) Dr. Holder discusses the utilization of the IAT as a mechanism to raise awareness of one's biases. As discussed in this chapter, this computer-based tool asks participants to make quick judgments and associations about physical attributes (e.g., race) and favorable or unfavorable words (nice, angry, etc.). Results of this test can assist participants in understanding the extent to which they possess biases toward specific groups. Understanding oneself is a crucial step toward minimizing biases and thereby reducing microaggressions and the harm they can inflict on individuals.

In a longer-term training or in a classroom setting, further awareness of one's biases can develop through structured interviews or dialogues, journal writing, a personal autobiography, and modeling. A small group structured dialogue about one's personal understanding of one's own cultural groups (e.g., race, gender, and social class) can assist individuals with exploring their own racial-cultural development (Carter, 2003). Such dialogues can include prepared questions about such issues as stereotypes or personal development with regard to reference groups. In addition, participants can share their own personal experiences of perpetrating or experiencing microaggressions. Participants in the small groups can be asked to understand their various emotional and behavioral responses. Small group experiences can often lead to emotional and personal processing of didactic instruction (Yalom, 1995). This can help participants to develop understanding and knowledge from experiencing emotions such as fear and anger through group experiences such as confrontation.

Journal writing allows trainers to develop an understanding of individual participants to better adapt training strategies in ways that enhance learning (Garmon, 1998; Mio & Barker-Hackett, 2003). Journals are also effective at providing an opportunity for self-reflection as well as personal elaboration of the content presented in the session. Oftentimes, emotional reactions to experiential learning can be explored confidentially in the journals. Participants can also review earlier journal entries as a way of self-monitoring their progress and identifying challenges that warrant further exploration.

An approach that can be used in all microaggression training activities is that of modeling (Ponterotto, 1998). Instructors and other facilitators can provide an example in themselves of how to be open about their multicultural identities, attitudes, values, and beliefs. Instructors can talk about their own cultural identity development, including challenging and positive experiences and emotions. They can also talk about their experiences with committing microaggressions and share their own processes. As a multicultural mentor, the facilitator can be a role model to the participants. It is important to keep in mind the importance of the culture/race of both the mentor and the trainee in the effectiveness of multicultural mentoring/role modeling.

Addressing resistance

While the strategies outlined in this chapter are effective in increasing one's awareness of and ability to confront microaggressions (Arredondo & Arciniega, 2001; Arredondo & Perez, 2006; Arthur & Achenbach, 2002; Carter, 2003, 2005; Ibrahim, 2010; Mio & Barker-Hackett, 2003), participants often display resistance to such training. For example, dominant-group students may become defensive and resist fully exploring their own values, assumptions, and beliefs if they sense that the facilitators or others are blaming them for the historical oppression of other cultures (Mio & Barker-Hackett, 2003). In many instances, White individuals who are asked to explore what it means to be White may resist this task by denying that race is a salient factor in their life for fear of being labeled a racist and a perpetrator of microaggressions (Sue, 2003). As a way for participants to avoid critical reflection of personal beliefs, individual psychological resistances to training including intellectualization, projection, and denial have been noted specifically in classroom training experiences (Carter, 2003).

Moreover, strong emotions such as shame, guilt, anger, frustration, sadness, and confusion are demonstrated when students realize they hold racist or sexist assumptions, beliefs, and attitudes (Bergkamp, 2010; Mio & Barker-Hackett, 2003). Participants may also be afraid of how their peers will respond to their admission of socially undesirable characteristics, such as racism and sexism. They may not want to be judged negatively and to receive labels. It has been suggested that cultural competency training including microaggressions training would benefit from focusing on the utilization of "oppression mechanics," which contextualizes student experiences within a framework of systemic issues of power, privilege, prejudice, and discrimination (Bergkamp, 2010). Contextualizing one's experience of race, gender, and sexual orientation, for example, can assist individuals with understanding their own experiences of sexism within the larger framework of culturally institutionalized practices. For example, in the case of sexism, it might be helpful for men to understand that the oppression of women is communicated through various forms of institutional (e.g., criteria for promotion within an organization and communication styles) and cultural (e.g., sexually explicit media material) systems. By taking a more systemic focus, individual experiences can be better processed and understood within multicultural training experiences (Bergkamp, 2010).

Responding to microaggressions

In addition to increasing knowledge of microaggressions and increasing self-awareness, an essential component to microaggressions training protocols can include ways to respond to and to confront microaggressions. For example, training materials suggest that faculty can interrupt microaggressions in classroom settings and create dialogue that can facilitate learning (Kenney, 2014).

Examples of how to address microaggressions in the classroom include inquiry, reflection, reframing, redirecting, revisiting, and checking-in (Kenney, 2014). If a student states, "As a woman, I know what you go through as a Person of Color," the professor might intervene by saying, "So it sounds like you're equating gender and racial oppression. What are people's thoughts on that?" (Kenney, 2014). It is essential that individuals learn how to skillfully address microaggressions when they occur in order to open up rather than shut down dialogue.

Colleges and universities are taking microaggressions seriously and have initiated many outreach programs. For example, The New School recently launched a student health services Web site specifically addressing microaggressions. This site includes information on how to recognize a microaggression, suggestions for responding to microaggressions, witnessing microaggressions, and places to seek support if one is a recipient of a microaggression (see https://www.newschool.edu/student-health-services/anti-violence/microaggression/).

The authors of this book call for rigorous research to be conducted on the outcomes of all implemented training protocols. Outcome measures should be based on the specific learning outcomes of each training, and the effectiveness of training should be evaluated on this basis. The duration of the training should correspond to the context and to the intended learning outcomes of the training.

Media Advocacy

In an effort to reach a wide range of individuals, it might be advisable for culturally competent, microaggression-aware diversity consultants to approach major media production organizations, such as Hollywood movie and TV studios (including directors, actors, and scriptwriters) as well as advertising departments and agencies to discuss bias and microaggressions. The revised taxonomy's new categories of Environmental Spoken microaggressions and both categories of nonverbal environmental (i.e., Symbolic-Expressive and Behavioral) microaggressions would be especially helpful in this context (see Figure 19.2 and Table 19.1). Even limited increases in cultural diversity awareness on the part of these cultural producers are likely to have a wide-ranging effect by reducing subtly stereotypical depictions in entertainment media. Perhaps a more direct strategy would be to form a Microaggressions Speakers Council, members of which would have expertise in microaggressions theory and research and offer to appear on television and online news and information shows (e.g., *Tucker Carlson Tonight, The Rubin Report*). Such appearances would likely involve difficult dialogues about microaggressions, and resulting insights and perspectives would reach a much wider audience than, for example, the classroom setting.

Conclusion

The future of microaggression theory will be determined by continued progress in microaggressions theory, research, and practice. A systematic, transdisciplinary empirical research program as well as prevention and training initiatives informed by this research in a wide variety of settings will help to ensure that microaggressions are acknowledged and identified as a problem in our society as much as macroaggressions (e.g., structural and systemic mechanisms including laws, policies, and practices that reinforce oppression of marginalized group members). In such a context, solutions to the problem of microaggressions in our society, including the relationship between microaggressions and macroaggessions, can be constructively considered and implemented.

References

Arredondo, P., & Arciniega, G. M. (2001). Strategies and techniques for counselor training based on the multicultural counseling competencies. *Journal of Multicultural Counseling and Development, 29,* 263–273.

Arredondo, P., & Perez, P. (2006). Historical perspectives on the multicultural guidelines and contemporary applications. *Professional Psychology: Research and Practice, 37*(1), 1–5.

Arthur, N., & Achenbach, K. (2002). Developing multicultural counseling competencies through experiential learning. *Counselor Education & Supervision, 42*(1), 2–14.

Balsam, K. F., Molina, Y., Beadnell, B., Simoni, J., & Walters, K. (2011). Measuring multiple minority stress: The LGBT people of color microaggressions scale. *Cultural Diversity and Ethnic Minority Psychology, 17*(2), 163.

Bergkamp, J. (2010). *Research on multicultural training using grounded theory.* Presented at the American Psychological Convention, San Diego, CA.

Capodilupo, C. M., & Torino, G. C. (2017). Gender microaggressions scale (GMAS) for women: Exploratory and confirmatory factor analyses. *Advances in Psychology Research, 122,* 81–110.

Carter, R. T. (2003). Becoming racially and culturally competent: The racial-cultural counseling laboratory. *Journal of Multicultural Counseling and Development, 31,* 20–30.

Carter, R. T. (2005). Teaching racial-cultural counseling competence: A racially inclusive model. In R. T. Carter (Ed.), *Handbook of racial-cultural psychology and counseling: Training and practice* (Vol. 2, pp. 36–56). Hoboken, NJ: Wiley.

Collins, P. H. (2000). *Black feminist thought: Knowledge, consciousness and the politics of empowerment.* London: Routledge.

Donovan, R. A., Galban, D. J., Grace, R. K., Bennett, J. K., & Felicié, S. Z. (2013). Impact of racial macro-and microaggressions in Black Women's lives a preliminary analysis. *Journal of Black Psychology, 39*(2), 185–196.

Farr, R. H., Crain, E. E., Oakley, M. K., Krystal, K., & Garber, K. J. (2016). Microaggressions, feelings of difference, and resilience among adopted children with sexual minority parents. *Journal of Youth and Adolescence, 45,* 85. doi:10.1007/s10964-015-0353-6.

Forrest-Bank, S. S., & Jenson, J. M. (2015). The relationship among childhood risk and protective factors, racial microaggression and ethnic identity, and academic self-efficacy and antisocial behavior in young adulthood. *Children and Youth Services Review, 50,* 64–74.

Garmon, M. A. (1998). Using dialogue journals to promote student learning in a multicultural teacher education course. *Remedial and Special Education, 19*(1), 32–45.

Google Scholar. (2018, April 27). Scholar.google.com.

Greenwald, A. G., McGhee, D. E., & Schwartz, J. L. (1998). Measuring individual differences in implicit cognition: The implicit association test. *Journal of Personality and Social Psychology, 74*(6), 1464.

Grier-Reed, T. L. (2010). The African American student network: Creating sanctuaries and counterspaces for coping with racial microaggressions in higher education settings. *The Journal of Humanistic Counseling, 49*(2), 181–188.

Huynh, V. W. (2012). Ethnic microaggressions and the depressive and somatic symptoms of Latino and Asian American adolescents. *Journal of Youth and Adolescence, 41,* 831–846. doi:10.1007/s10964-012-9756-9.

Ibrahim, F. A. (2010). Social justice and cultural responsiveness: Innovative teaching strategies for group work. *Journal for Specialists in Group Work, 35*(3), 271–280.

Keith, V. M., Nguyen, A. W., Taylor, R. J., Mouzon, D. M., & Chatters, L. M. (2017). Microaggressions, discrimination, and phenotype among African Americans: A latent class analysis of the impact of skin tone and BMI. *Sociological Inquiry, 87*(2), 233–255.

Kenney, G. (2014). *Interrupting microaggressions.* College of the Holy Cross https://www.holycross.edu/sites/default/files/files/centerforteaching/interrupting_microaggressions_january2014.pdf.

Lakoff, G. (2002). *Moral politics: How liberals and conservatives think* (2nd ed.). Chicago, IL: University of Chicago Press.

Lewis, J. A., & Neville, H. A. (2015). Construction and initial validation of the gendered racial microaggressions scale for black women. *Journal of Counseling Psychology, 62*(2), 289.

Lilienfeld, S. O. (2017). Microaggressions: strong claims, inadequate evidence. *Perspectives on Psychological Science, 12*(1), 138–169.

Mio, J. S., & Barker-Hackett, L. (2003). Reaction papers and journal writing as techniques for assessing resistance in multicultural courses. *Journal of Multicultural Counseling and Development, 31,* 12–19.

Nadal, K. L. (2011). The Racial and Ethnic Microaggressions Scale (REMS): Construction, reliability, and validity. *Journal of Counseling Psychology, 58,* 470–480.

Nadal, K. L. (2013). *That's so gay! Microaggressions and the lesbian, gay, bisexual, and transgender community.* Washington DC: American Psychological Association.

Nadal, K. L. (2018). *Microaggressions and traumatic stress: Theory, research, and clinical practice.* Washington DC: American Psychological Association.

Nadal, K. L., Davidoff, K. C., Davis, L. S., & Wong, Y. (2014). Emotional, behavioral, and cognitive reactions to microaggressions: Transgender perspectives. *Psychology of Sexual Orientation and Gender Diversity, 1,* 72–81.

Nadal, K. L., Davidoff, K. C., Davis, L. S., Wong, Y., Marshall, D., & McKenzie, V. (2015). Intersectional identities and microaggressions: Influences of race, ethnicity, gender, sexuality, and religion. *Qualitative Psychology, 2,* 147–163.

Nadal, K. L., Griffin, K. E., Hamit, S., Leon, J., Tobio, M., & Rivera, D. P. (2012). Subtle and overt forms of Islamophobia: Microaggressions toward Muslim Americans. *Journal of Muslim Mental Health, 6,* 16–37.

Ong, A. D., Burrow, A. L., Fuller-Rowell, T. E., Ja, N. M., & Sue, D. W. (2013). Racial microaggressions and daily well-being among Asian Americans. *Journal of Counseling Psychology, 60*(2), 188–199. doi:10.1037/a0031736.

Pérez Huber, L., & Solórzano, D. G. (2015). Racial microaggressions as a tool for critical race research. *Race Ethnicity and Education, 18*(3), 297–320.

Pierce, C. M. (1970). Offensive mechanisms. In F. B. Barbour (Ed.), *The black '70's* (pp. 265–282). Boston: Porter Sargent.

Ponterotto, J. G. (1998). Charting a course for research in multicultural counseling training. *The Counseling Psychologist, 26*(1), 43–68.

Popper, K. (1959). *The logic of Scientific Discovery.* London: Hutchinson, 1959.

Rivera, D. P., Mazzula, S., & Campon, R. (2017). Psychological perspectives on ethnic minority physical health disparities. In A. Blume (Ed.), *Social Issues in Living Color: Challenges and solutions from the perspective of ethnic minority psychology* (pp. 53–76).

Ronquillo, J., Denson, T. F., Lickel, B., Lu, Z. L., Nandy, A., & Maddox, K. B. (2007). The effects of skin tone on race-related amygdala activity: An fMRI investigation. *Social Cognitive and Affective Neuroscience, 2*(1), 39–44.

Schacht, T. E. (2008). A broader view of racial microaggression in psychotherapy. *American Psychologist, 63*(4), 273. doi:10.1037/0003-066X.63.4.

Solórzano, D., Ceja, M., & Yosso, T. (2000). Critical race theory, racial microaggressions, and campus racial climate: The experiences of African American college students. *Journal of Negro Education,* 60–73.

Sue, D. W. (2003). *Overcoming our racism: The journey to liberation.* San Francisco, CA: Jossey-Bass.

Sue, D. W., Bucceri, J., Lin, A. I., Nadal, K. L., & Torino, G. C. (2007). Racial microaggressions and the Asian American experience. *Cultural Diversity and Ethnic Minority Psychology, 13*(1), 72.

Sue, D. W., Capodilupo, C. M., Torino, G. C., Bucceri, J. M., Holder, A., Nadal, K. L., & Esquilin, M. (2007). Racial microaggressions in everyday life: Implications for clinical practice. *American Psychologist, 62*(4), 271.

Sue, D. W., Lin, A. I., Torino, G. C., Capodilupo, C. M., & Rivera, D. P. (2009). Racial microaggressions and difficult dialogues on race in the classroom. *Cultural Diversity and Ethnic Minority Psychology, 15*(2), 183–190.

Thomas, K. R. (2008). Macrononsense in multiculturalism. *American Psychologist, 63*(4), 274–275. doi:10.1037/0003-066X.63.4.274.

Wilson, P. A., & Yoshikawa, H. (2007). Improving access to health care among African American, Asian and Pacific Islander, and Latino lesbian, gay, and bisexual populations. *The Health of Sexual Minorities,* 607–637.

Wright, A. J., & Wegner, R. T. (2012). Homonegative microaggressions and their impact on LGB individuals: A measure validity study. *Journal of LGBT Issues in Counseling, 6*(1), 34–54. doi:10.1080/15538605.2012.648578.

Yalom, I. D. (1995). *The theory and practice of group psychotherapy.* New York, NY: Basic Books (AZ).

Author Index

Microaggression Theory: Influence and Implications, First Edition. Edited by Gina C. Torino,
David P. Rivera, Christina M. Capodilupo, Kevin L. Nadal, and Derald Wing Sue.
© 2019 John Wiley & Sons, Inc. Published 2019 by John Wiley & Sons, Inc.

Subject Index

Microaggression Theory: Influence and Implications, First Edition. Edited by Gina C. Torino, David P. Rivera, Christina M. Capodilupo, Kevin L. Nadal, and Derald Wing Sue.
© 2019 John Wiley & Sons, Inc. Published 2019 by John Wiley & Sons, Inc.